BLACKSTONE'S (

The Extradition

BLACKSTONE'S GUIDE TO

The Extradition Act 2003

Julian B. Knowles (BA) (Oxon)

of the Inner Temple, Barrister

OXFORD
UNIVERSITY PRESS

This book has been printed digitally and produced in a standard specification
in order to ensure its continuing availability

OXFORD
UNIVERSITY PRESS

Great Clarendon Street, Oxford OX2 6DP

Oxford University Press is a department of the University of Oxford.
It furthers the University's objective of excellence in research, scholarship,
and education by publishing worldwide in

Oxford New York

Auckland Cape Town Dar es Salaam Hong Kong Karachi
Kuala Lumpur Madrid Melbourne Mexico City Nairobi
New Delhi Shanghai Taipei Toronto
With offices in
Argentina Austria Brazil Chile Czech Republic France Greece
Guatemala Hungary Italy Japan South Korea Poland Portugal
Singapore Switzerland Thailand Turkey Ukraine Vietnam

Oxford is a registered trade mark of Oxford University Press
in the UK and in certain other countries

Published in the United States
by Oxford University Press Inc., New York

ISBN 978-0-19-927266-2

Printed and bound in Great Britain by CPI Antony Rowe, Chippenham and Eastbourne

Contents—Summary

Contents

Contents

Contents

This book is dedicated to my mother
Patricia Knowles (1935–2003)

and to my father
Leo Knowles

with grateful love and thanks

Preface

Tempting though it is in this preface to embark upon a detailed critique of the Extradition Act 2003 I will refrain from doing so, not least because little purpose would be served. The Act is now in force and is here to stay, at least until some future time when political expediency will dictate that the few remaining safeguards it contains for extradition defendants are no longer 'necessary' and individual liberty will be sacrificed further in the interests of speedy (and cheap) justice.

Two fallacies in particular led to the passing of the Act. The first was that proceedings under the Extradition Act 1989 were unnecessarily protracted in comparison with those in other countries. (The *Pinochet* case was often cited as an example, in particular by the Home Office. However, that case was unique and cannot sensibly be regarded as representing the norm. No other case in recent memory required three appeals to the House of Lords.) More resources could have solved any delays in the system.

The second fallacy is that EU countries should have unquestioning deference for each other's legal systems. This is reflected by the introduction of the European arrest warrant scheme in Part 1 of the Act. However, it only takes a cursory examination of the legal systems of some of our EU partners to fill one with foreboding about how the European arrest warrant (the EAW) is going to work in practice and about the injustices that will result. For example, in *R (Ramda) v Secretary of State for the Home Department* [2002] EWHC 1278 Admin, the Administrative Court quashed the Secretary of State's decision to return Mr Ramda to France because of real (and unanswered) questions on whether evidence against him had been procured by police violence.

Also worrying is the prospect that the EAW will one day apply to countries whose commitment to human rights is even shallower. As recently as November 2003 the Government of Russia was found to have tortured a witness into providing evidence against a defendant, and extradition was refused because the court found that the defendant himself would be at risk of torture or death were he to be returned to Russia (*Government of the Russian Federation v Zakaev*, 13 November 2003, Senior District Judge Workman, Bow Street Magistrates Court).

Although the Act preserves political persecution as grounds for refusing extradition, the speed with which cases are to be heard means that mistakes will inevitably be made. Mr Zakaev was only able to unearth the evidence of torture through months of painstaking work. Future defendants may not be so lucky.

The UK Government's desire (on the back of *Pinochet*) to speed up extradition by removing protections for defendants was given added impetus by the events of 11 September 2001. But terrorism is the witchcraft of the twenty-first century—an easy accusation to make but a difficult one to refute, especially if the accused person is of the 'wrong' race or religion. This was evident in the early part of 2003, when certain groups in the UK (in particular North Africans) were accused of harbouring terrorists in article after article in the tabloid newspapers. At such a time, the right thing to do would have been to strengthen protections for the vulnerable rather than to reduce them.

Be that as it may, as practitioners we have to make the best of what the Act provides. I hope that this book will provide at least a little assistance in doing so. Extradition is a subtle and difficult area of the law that brings into play a number of different legal disciplines. Whilst attempting to remain faithful to the accessible spirit of the 'Blackstone's Guides' series, I have tried to deal with the underlying principles of extradition, as well as providing a guide to the Act.

I have been very fortunate throughout my career to have had the help and support of a large number of hugely talented practitioners. I am especially indebted to Clare Montgomery QC; Edward Fitzgerald QC; Clive Nicholls QC; James Lewis QC; Ben Emmerson QC; Ken Macdonald QC; Nicholas Blake QC; Alun Jones QC; Colin Nicholls QC; Chris Sallon QC; Michael Grieve QC; Keir Starmer QC; Tim Owen QC; Frank Panford QC; Geoffrey Robertson QC; Michael Caplan QC; John Hardy; James Hines; Helen Malcolm; David H Christie; Gareth Peirce; Philip 'Brave' Davis; Roger Minnis; Saul Lehrfreund; Parvais Jabbar; Peter Binning; Girish Thanki; Patricia Sheehan; Bernard O'Sullivan; Nicky Boulton; and District Judge John Zani.

I am also very grateful to the staff of OUP for producing such a striking volume in such a short space of time.

Finally, I am grateful to my family and to Nicky for all their love and support, especially through the difficult days of 2003.

I have attempted to state the law as at 6 January 2004.

Julian B Knowles
Hook Norton
Oxfordshire

14 January 2004

Table of Cases

Table of Statutes

Table of Secondary Legislation

Table of International Legislation

Glossary

This section sets out the definitions of some of the more important expressions used in this book together with the place in the EA 2003 where they are defined.

Appropriate judge

Under Parts 1 and 2 of the Act, the appropriate judge in England and Wales is a District Judge (Magistrates' Courts) (ss 67 and 139).

In Part 3, in England and Wales the appropriate judge is a District Judge (Magistrates' Courts), a justice of the peace or a judge entitled to exercise the jurisdiction of the Crown Court (s 149).

Asylum claim

This expression has the meaning given by s 113(1) of the Nationality, Immigration and Asylum Act 2002 (s 216(7)).

British overseas territories

These are the territories listed in Schedule 6 to the British Nationality Act 1981 (s 1(1), (3), British Overseas Territories Act 2002).

Category 1 territory

A country designated by an order of the Secretary of State, with whom the UK operates extradition procedures in accordance with Part 1 of the Act (s 1(2)). The relevant order is the Extradition Act 2003 (Designation of Part 1 Territories) Order 2003 (SI 2003/3333). As at January 2004, Category 1 territories were:

Belgium, Denmark, Finland, Ireland, Portugal, Spain, Sweden.

This list is liable to change, however, and the most up-to-date version of the order should always be consulted.

Category 2 territory

A country designated by an order of the Secretary of State, with whom the UK operates extradition procedures in accordance with Part 2 of the Act (s 69(2)). The relevant order is the Extradition Act 2003 (Designation of Part 2 Territories) Order

2003 (SI 2003/3334). As at January 2004, Category 2 territories were:

Albania, Andorra, Antigua and Barbuda, Argentina, Armenia, Australia, Austria, Azerbaijan, The Bahamas, Bangladesh, Barbados, Belize, Bolivia, Bosnia and Herzegovina, Botswana, Brazil, Brunei, Bulgaria, Canada, Chile, Colombia, Cook Islands, Croatia, Cuba, Cyprus, Czech Republic, Dominica, Ecuador, El Salvador, Estonia, Fiji, France, The Gambia, Georgia, Germany, Ghana, Greece, Grenada, Guatemala, Guyana, Hong Kong Special Administrative Region, Haiti, Hungary, Iceland, India, Iraq, Israel, Italy, Jamaica, Kenya, Kiribati, Latvia, Lesotho, Liberia, Liechtenstein, Lithuania, Luxembourg, Macedonia FYR, Malawi, Malaysia, Maldives, Malta, Mauritius, Mexico, Moldova, Monaco, Nauru, The Netherlands, New Zealand, Nicaragua, Nigeria, Norway, Panama, Papua New Guinea, Paraguay, Peru, Poland, Romania, Russian Federation, Saint Christopher and Nevis, Saint Lucia, Saint Vincent and the Grenadines, San Marino, Serbia and Montenegro, Seychelles, Sierra Leone, Singapore, Slovakia, Slovenia, Solomon Islands, South Africa, Sri Lanka, Swaziland, Switzerland, Tanzania, Thailand, Tonga, Trinidad and Tobago, Turkey, Tuvalu, Uganda, Ukraine, Uruguay, The United States of America, Vanuatu, Western Samoa, Zambia, Zimbabwe.

This list is liable to change, however, and the most up-to-date version of the order should always be consulted.

Certification — The process by which either a Part 1 warrant is checked by the designated authority under s 2, or an extradition request is checked by the Secretary of State under s 70.

Customs officer — A person commissioned by the Commissioners of Customs and Excise under s 6(3) of the Customs and Excise Management Act 1979 (s 216(8)).

Designated authority — The organization designated by order with the function of certifying Part 1 warrants received from Category 1 territories prior to the person's arrest (s 2(9)). Under the Extradition Act 2003 (Part 1 Designated Authorities)

Order 2003 (SI 2003/3190) the designated central authorities for the UK are the National Criminal Intelligence Service (NCIS) and the Crown Agent of the Scottish Crown Office.

European framework list — The list of conduct set out in Sch 2 to the Act (s 215). These are the offences for which dual criminality is not required under Part 1.

Excluded material — Material, records, or substances held in confidence (see Police and Criminal Evidence Act 1984, s 11).

Extradition hearing — The main part of the extradition process where the appropriate judge considers the request for extradition of the person against criteria laid out in the Act (ss 68 and 140).

Extradition offence — An offence over which another country has jurisdiction, for which the person has been requested to stand trial, be sentenced or serve a sentence abroad and for which the UK will consider extradition (ss 64–66, ss 137–8). Alternatively, an offence for which the UK seeks a person's extradition from another country (s 148).

Extradition request — The documentation transmitted on a government-to-government basis from a Category 2 territory which requests a person's arrest and extradition (s 70) To be valid, the extradition request must meet the criteria in s 70(3).

Initial hearing — The stage in the extradition process under Part 1 at which where the defendant is first brought before a district judge (ss 7–8).

Items subject to legal privilege — Communications between a professional legal adviser and the client that is concerned with the proceedings. Anything held with the intention of furthering a criminal cause is not covered (s 174(4); Police and Criminal Evidence Act 1984, s 10).

Judicial authority — The authority in a Category 1 territory which has the function of issuing a Part 1 warrant in that country.

Part 1 warrant — An arrest warrant issued by a judicial authority in a Category 1 territory containing the information required by s 2(2) (s 2(2)).

Part 3 warrant	A warrant obtained for the purposes of requesting extradition from a Category 1 territory under Part 3 (s 142(3)).
Production order	An order made under s 157 for the production of the documents referred to in s 158(2)(e).
Provisional arrest	(1) Arrest under Part 1 pending receipt of a certified Part 1 warrant or certified European arrest warrant; or (2) arrest under Part 2 under a provisional arrest warrant issued by a UK magistrate, pending receipt of the necessary documents required under s 70 of the Act (ss 5 and 73).
Search and seizure warrant	A warrant issued under s 156 authorizing the search of premises for material specified in s 156(6).
Service policeman	A member of the Royal Navy Regulating Branch, the Royal Marines Police, the Royal Military Police, or the Royal Air Force Police (s 216(13)).
Special procedure material	Journalistic material or material held in confidence by someone in a professional or official capacity, other than excluded material or items subject to legal privilege (s 174(6); Police and Criminal Evidence Act 1984, s 14).

Abbreviations

The following abbreviations are used in this book:

CPS — Crown Prosecution Service

Commencement Order — Extradition Act 2003 (Commencement and Savings) Order 2003 (SI 2003/3103)

EA 1870 — Extradition Act 1870

EA 1989 — Extradition Act 1989

EA 2003 — Extradition Act 2003

EAW — Council Framework Decision of 13 June 2002 on the European arrest warrant and the surrender procedures between Member States (2002/584/JHA) (ie the European arrest warrant)

EAW case — A EAW case specifying one or more of the offences in the European framework list, as defined in s 215.

ECHR — European Convention on Human Rights

Hong Kong SAR — Hong Kong Special Administrative Region of the People's Republic of China

HRA 1998 — Human Rights Act 1998

ICC — International Criminal Court

ICTY — The Tribunal for the Prosecution of Persons Responsible for Serious Violations of International Humanitarian Law Committed in the Territory of the Former Yugoslavia since 1991

PACE — Police and Criminal Evidence Act 1984

Refugee Convention — By s 40(4), this is the Convention relating to the Status of Refugees done at Geneva on 28 July 1951 and the Protocol to the Convention

1

INTRODUCTION AND OVERVIEW

1.1 INTRODUCTION

1.1.1 Definition of Extradition

Extradition is the formal name given to the process whereby one sovereign state (the requesting state) asks another sovereign state (the requested state) to return to the requesting state someone present in the requested state (the defendant) in order that he may be brought to trial on criminal charges in the requesting state. The process also applies where the defendant has escaped from lawful custody following conviction in the requesting state—or is otherwise unlawfully at large—and is found in the requested state (see *R v Evans ex p Pinochet Ugarte*, The Times, 3 November 1998).

Extradition should be distinguished from deportation, which involves the country in which the person is present initiating the removal process, and which is not necessarily connected to criminal proceedings (*R v Governor of Brixton Prison ex p Soblen* [1963] QB 243; *R v Staines Magistrates Court ex p Westfallen* [1998] 1 WLR 652).

1.1.2 History of Extradition Legislation in the UK

Extradition in the UK has a history stretching back into the early part of the second millennium when, in 1174, Henry II and William of Scotland agreed to deliver up fugitive offenders. Similar agreements were reached in 1303 between Edward I and Philip of France, and in 1496 between Henry VII and the Duke of Burgundy (Booth, *British Extradition Law and Procedure* (1980), Vol I, LVII).

The modern law of extradition started to develop in earnest in the nineteenth century when Great Britain began to negotiate extradition treaties with foreign states. A treaty was concluded with France in 1842, and the Webster-Ashburton treaty with the United States of America was signed in 1843 (Stephen, *History of the Criminal Law of England* (1883), Vol 2, 66). These treaties were incorporated into law in 1843 by Act of Parliament (6 & 7 Vict, c 75 and c 76).

These Acts only covered a limited number of serious crimes (*Ex p Windsor* (1865) 10 Cox CC 118; *Re Tivnan* (1864) 9 Cox CC 522), but were notable in that they contained the requirement for dual criminality, ie the requirement that the offence charged should be a crime in both countries. This remained a feature of extradition legislation until the incorporation of the European arrest warrant in Part 1 of the Extradition Act 2003 (EA 2003). This is discussed further in Chapter 2.

In 1868 a Select Committee inquired into the state of treaty relationships concerning extradition, and its recommendations were the model for what became the Extradition Act 1870 (EA 1870). The purpose of this Act was to provide the procedural machinery for the surrender of defendants under any treaty then in force and any that might be concluded after its enactment. Each extradition treaty set out the arrangements for extradition with the foreign state and the conditions under which extradition would be granted. Section 2 of the EA 1870 provided that, where such an arrangement had been made, Her Majesty might by Order in Council direct that the 1870 Act apply in the case of that foreign state, subject to the limitations contained in the Order in Council. Once an extradition treaty was concluded with a foreign state, an Order in Council under s 2 was made applying the 1870 Act and extradition to that foreign state became possible.

The EA 1870 made fugitive criminals liable to surrender for 'extradition crimes'. These were defined in s 26 to be crimes which, if they had been committed in England or within English jurisdiction, would be one of the crimes described in the First Schedule to the Act. The First Schedule (in its original form) contained a generic list of 19 offences for which extradition would be granted. Extradition could not be granted for offences not falling within the list (*Re Counhaye* (1873) LR 8 QB 410; *R v Secretary of State for the Home Department ex p Gilmore* [1999] QB 611). As new crimes were created, the list had to be amended to enable extradition to take place for these crimes.

In 1881 Parliament enacted separate legislation to regulate extradition within the Empire. The Fugitive Offenders Act 1881 governed the return of defendants between the various parts of the British Empire and continued in force until the 1960s, when the development of the Commonwealth necessitated fresh legislation.

In 1966 the Commonwealth Law Ministers drew up a new scheme, the 'Scheme relating to the Rendition of Fugitive Offenders within the Commonwealth' (Cmnd 3008). The scheme was based on reciprocity and substantially uniform legislation rather than on treaty arrangements. The Fugitive Offenders Act 1967 was passed to give effect to the scheme in the UK. The 1967 Act permitted extradition for offences against the law of the requesting Commonwealth country punishable with more than 12 months' imprisonment which fell within the general descriptions in Sch 1 to the Act.

In 1974 and 1982 Home Office working parties considered the operation of the EA 1870. Whilst the 1974 Report did not result in any changes to the law, by 1982 the need for reform had been recognized, in particular because of problems of compatibility between the English common law system and continental civil law jurisdictions. The 1982 Report (Inter-Department Working Party Report on Extradition (Home Office, 1982)) was followed in 1985 by a Green Paper on Extradition (Cmnd 9421) and a White Paper (Cmnd 9658).

The Criminal Justice Bill 1986 contained provisions relating to extradition, however these were removed when the Bill had to be passed in shortened form because of the 1987 general election. Part I of the Criminal Justice Act 1988 contained provisions relating to extradition which were never brought into force.

The Extradition Act 1989 (EA 1989), which came into force on 27 September 1989, was essentially a consolidation of three earlier pieces of legislation: Part 1 of the Criminal Justice Act 1988, the Fugitive Offenders Act 1967, and the EA 1870 (as amended). The earlier Acts were repealed.

Part III of the EA 1989 contained the machinery for processing requests for extradition from foreign states with whom the UK had general extradition arrangements (in practice, signatories to the European Convention on Extradition 1957 designated in an Order in Council under s 4; designated Commonwealth countries; and colonies). Schedule 1, whose provisions were largely derived from the EA 1870, governed the processing of requests from foreign states with whom there was an extant treaty embodied in an Order in Council made under s 2 of the EA 1870 (principally the United States of America). One of the principal features of the EA 1989 was the removal of the need in all cases for the requesting state to prove a *prima facie* case by admissible evidence. Whilst this requirement was retained in some cases, it was removed in respect of requests from the UK's European treaty partners.

1.1.3 Background to the Enactment of the EA 2003

In 1997 a review commenced to consider the legislative requirements of two European Union Conventions on Extradition signed in 1995 and 1996. However, it developed into a much more extensive inquiry following the Tampere Special European Council in October 1999. The Treaty of Amsterdam, signed on 2 October 1997, aimed to establish the European Union as an area of freedom, security, and justice. The implementation of the treaty was discussed at the Cardiff European Council in June 1998, and again at Tampere. The conclusion at Tampere was that mutual recognition of judicial decisions should become the cornerstone of judicial cooperation in both criminal and civil matters within the EU.

Spain's attempt between 1998 and 2000 to extradite General Augusto Pinochet from the UK for crimes against humanity focused world attention on the UK's extradition arrangements. It also caused the Government a significant degree of political embarrassment. On 2 March 2000, the day General Pinochet returned to Chile, the then Home Secretary announced in the House of Commons that a more wide-ranging review of the UK's extradition legislation was to be carried out.

The Government set out its proposals to reform the law in a consultation document 'The Law on Extradition: A Review' in March 2001 (www.homeoffice. gov.uk/docs/extradbody.pdf). Its proposals, which were aimed at modernizing arrangements between the UK and its extradition partners, included:

(a) creating a four-level framework with countries being designated for each tier by way of an Order in Council;

(b) a simple fast-track extradition procedure for member states of the European Union;

(c) retention of current arrangements for non-European Union states with modifications to reduce the duplication and complexity of extradition procedures;

(d) a single avenue of appeal for all extradition cases; and

(e) accession to the 1995 and 1996 European Union Conventions on Extradition.

In the event the proposals in the Review were overtaken by the events of 11 September 2001 and the onset of the 'war against terror' in Western Europe and the United States of America. This provided added political impetus for speeding up the extradition of criminal suspects. The Review was also overtaken by progress in respect of extradition to other EU member states, in particular the Council Framework Decision (following Tampere) of 13 June 2002 on the European arrest warrant and the surrender procedures between member states (2002/584/JHA—the European arrest warrant (EAW)). In essence, the EAW (considered below) creates a system of mutually enforceable arrest warrants within the EU.

The Extradition Bill was published in draft form on 27 June 2002 and was open to public consultation until 30 September 2002. The Bill was introduced in Parliament on 14 November 2002 and received Royal Assent on 20 November 2003.

1.2 OUTLINE OF THE EA 2003

The EA 2003 makes provision for new extradition procedures, the main features of which are as follows:

(a) A system where each of the UK's extradition partners is in one of two categories. Each country is designated by order for a particular category. It will therefore be possible for a country to move from one category to the other when appropriate, depending on the extradition procedures that the UK negotiates with each extradition partner.

(b) The adoption of the EAW creating a fast-track extradition arrangement within the EU and Gibraltar.

(c) Retention of the current arrangements for extradition with non-EU countries with modifications to reduce duplication and complexity.

(d) Significant reduction of the Secretary of State's role.

(e) A simplification of the rules governing the authentication of foreign documents.

(f) The abolition of the requirement to provide *prima facie* evidence in certain cases.

(g) A simplified single avenue of appeal for all cases.

The EA 2003 is divided into five Parts and four schedules:

Part 1: contains the fast-track extradition arrangements for Category 1 territories. These have been transposed into UK law from the EAW. Part 1 provides the legislative framework for incoming warrants from Category 1 territories.

Part 2: contains the procedure for extradition for countries with which the UK has bilateral treaty arrangements (Category 2 territories). Part 2 provides the legislative framework for incoming requests from such territories.

Part 3: covers the procedure for applying for a warrant for extradition to the UK from Category 1 territories. Part 3 provides the legislative framework for outgoing warrants to Category 1 territories. Requests to Category 2 territories continue to be made under the Royal Prerogative.

Part 4: outlines the powers supplementary to the Police and Criminal Evidence Act 1984 available to the police in extradition cases. Part 4 was placed in the Act following the decision of the House of Lords in the case of *R v Commissioner of Police for the Metropolis ex p Rottman* [2002] 2 WLR 1315, which held that the powers contained in Part II of the Police and Criminal Evidence Act 1984 did not apply in relation to offences committed abroad. Part 4 sets out which powers are available in extradition cases.

Part 5: contains miscellaneous provisions such as those that will apply for British overseas territories and the power to repeal the existing legislation. It also confers order-making powers on the Secretary of State.

Schedule 1: contains provisions relating to re-extradition (see ss 186–189).

Schedule 2: contains the list of conduct which to which a EAW can apply (see ss 64(2)(b) and 215(1)).

Schedule 3: contains amendments to other statutes.

Schedule 4: contains repeals.

1.3 COMMENCEMENT PROVISIONS

The EA 2003 came into force on 1 January 2004 in accordance with the Extradition Act 2003 (Commencement and Savings) Order 2003 (SI 2003/3103), as amended (the Commencement Order).

Article 3 of the Commencement Order (as substituted by the Extradition Act 2003 (Commencement and Savings) (Amendment No 2) Order 2003 (SI 2003/3312)) provides that the coming into force of the Act shall not apply for the purposes of any request for extradition, whether made under any of the provisions of the EA 1989 or of the Backing of Warrants (Republic of Ireland) Act 1965 or otherwise, which is received by the relevant authority in the UK on or before 31 December 2003. Article 4 provides that the coming into force of the Act shall not apply for the purposes of an extradition made from or to the UK on or before 31 December 2003. Hence, the EA 2003 applies to all extradition requests received on or after 1 January 2004, and persons extradited to or from the UK prior that date will be dealt with under the EA 1989.

1.4 THE EUROPEAN ARREST WARRANT

The EAW deserves special attention because it makes a number of significant changes to the way in which extradition requests have been processed under former legislation, and because the largest number of requests are likely to be made using the EAW.

The EAW is implemented in Part 1 of the EA 2003, which is considered in detail in later chapters. In essence, the EAW envisages a common form of arrest warrant which, after issue in one state, can be executed in any other member state of the EU (subject to local certification procedures) in order to secure the defendant's rapid return to the requesting state.

The European Council Framework decision of 13 June 2002 creating the EAW is available at www.homeoffice.gov.uk/docs/eaw.pdf, and a draft form of warrant is set out in the Annex to the decision.

The key features of the EAW as implemented in Part 1 are as follows:

(a) Removal of the dual criminality requirement for 32 types of offence for which, in pre-conviction cases, a maximum sentence of three years' imprisonment or more can be incurred and, in conviction cases, a sentence of twelve months or more has been imposed. The list of offences is contained in Sch 2 to the EA 2003.

(b) Removal of the role of the executive in the extradition process so that it becomes exclusively a judicial procedure.

(c) Abolition of the political offence exception to extradition.

(d) Imposition of time limits to ensure rapid surrender.

For a detailed discussion of the EAW, see Allegre and Leaf, *European Arrest Warrant* (2003).

2

LIABILITY TO EXTRADITION. EXTRADITION OFFENCES

2.1 INTRODUCTION

The first part of this chapter examines the circumstances in which a person becomes liable to extradition under the EA 2003 as either an accused person or a person who has been convicted and is unlawfully at large following his conviction.

The second part of this chapter considers the important topic of extradition offences. These are the offences for which extradition from the UK can be granted. Whilst there are some similarities with the way in which extradition offences were defined in Part III of the EA 1989, the scheme established by the EA 2003 contains a number of significant differences.

2.2 LIABILITY TO EXTRADITION

2.2.1 Introduction

The purpose of extradition is to secure the return for trial or punishment of those accused or convicted of crimes. Extradition should not be granted merely to secure the return for questioning of those who are suspected of committing crimes (*Re Ismail* [1999] AC 320, 326; *Kainhofer v Director of Public Prosecutions* 124 ALR 665). Accordingly, only a person who is accused of the commission of an extradition offence or who has been convicted of such an offence and who is unlawfully at large is properly liable to extradition under the EA 2003.

Under the EA 1989 the classification of defendants as either accused or convicted was not entirely straightforward. One difficulty was that neither term was defined in the Act. It remained a question of fact whether, in a given case, a defendant was properly regarded as being accused of an offence rather than merely suspected of it (*Re Ismail* [1999] AC 320). In many civil law jurisdictions trials *in absentia* are commonplace. Extradition requests are frequently made for the return of defendants who are unaware of their convictions and who, if returned, have a right to be re-tried. Under the EA 1989 this category of defendant had to be treated as an accused person even though they had already been convicted and sentenced (see eg, EA 1989, s 35(2); *Lodhi v Governor of HMP Brixton* [2001] EWHC Admin 178, para 54). The position was further complicated by the Secretary of State's duty to specify whether a defendant was accused or convicted. If he placed the defendant into the wrong category then the district judge was required to order discharge (*R (Guisto) v Governor of HM Brixton Prison* [2003] UKHL 19).

Liability to extradition under the EA 2003 remains dependent on the defendant being accused or convicted in the requesting state. However, the Act removes some of the difficulties which beset the previous legislative regime by relieving the Secretary of State of the duty of specifying the defendant's status in the requesting state, and by specifying with greater precision than the EA 1989 did how a defendant who has been convicted in his absence is to be dealt with (cf ss 20 and 86).

It is most convenient to consider Category 1 and 2 territories separately.

2.2.2 Liability to Return to a Category 1 Territory

Section 2 of the EA 2003 requires the judicial authority of the Category 1 territory to supply an arrest warrant containing either the information specified in s 2(2)(a) or the information specified in s 2(2)(b). These paragraphs deal respectively with accused and convicted persons.

2.2.2.1 *Accused Persons*

In *Re Ismail* [1999] AC 320 the House of Lords rejected the appellant's submission that he was not an accused person—and so not liable to extradition—because he had not been formally charged with an offence in Germany. Lord Steyn said at pp 325–326:

> It is common ground that mere suspicion that an individual has committed offences is insufficient to place him in the category of 'accused' persons. It is also common ground that it is not enough that he is in the traditional phrase 'wanted by the police to help them with their inquiries'. Something more is required . . . For my part I am satisfied that the Divisional Court in this case posed the right test by addressing the broad question whether the competent authorities in the foreign jurisdiction had taken a step which can fairly be described as the commencement of a prosecution.

Section 2(2)(a) requires the warrant to contain the statement referred to in s 2(3) and the information referred to in s 2(4). For present purposes s 2(3) is the relevant sub-section. The statement referred to in s 2(3) concerns the defendant's status in the requesting state and is intended to make clear that the defendant is properly to be regarded as an accused person. The warrant must specify:

(a) that the person in respect of whom the warrant is issued is accused in the Category 1 territory of the offence specified in the warrant; and

(b) that the Part 1 warrant is issued with a view to his arrest and extradition to the Category 1 territory for the purposes of being prosecuted for the offence.

2.2.2.2 Convicted Persons

Section 2(2)(b) requires the warrant to contain the statement referred to in s 2(5) and the information in s 2(6). This statement is:

(a) that the person in respect of whom the warrant is issued is alleged to be unlawfully at large after conviction of an offence specified in the warrant by a court in the Category 1 territory; and

(b) that the warrant has been issued with a view to his arrest and extradition to the requesting state for the purpose of being sentenced for the offence or of serving a sentence of imprisonment or another form of detention imposed in respect of the offence.

Accordingly, in relation to convicted defendants, there are two requirements. First, the defendant must have been convicted (but not necessarily sentenced). Secondly, he must be 'unlawfully at large'. This expression is not defined in the EA 2003, but the same expression was used in the EA 1989. In many civil law jurisdictions convicted defendants may not become liable to detention until, for example, their appeals have been exhausted. A defendant is not unlawfully at large until he is liable to be immediately detained for the purposes of being sentenced or serving his sentence (*Re Urru*, Unreported, 22 May 2000, CO/4009/99; *Re Barone*, Unreported, 7 November 1997, CO/2745/96; *Re Anderson* [1993] Crim LR 954).

If the defendant is specified as having been convicted and unlawfully at large, the judge at the extradition hearing has to determine whether the defendant was convicted in his presence (s 20(1)). If not, the person must be discharged unless the conditions in s 20 are made out. These are designed to ensure that the defendant will be treated fairly in the requesting state. They are considered in more detail at 5.8.8 and 6.11 below.

2.2.3 Liability to Return to a Category 2 Territory

Return to Category 2 territories is also based upon the defendant's status as an accused or convicted person.

An extradition request made by a Category 2 territory must be made to the Secretary of State and must be 'valid' as defined by s 70(3). In order to be valid the request must contain the statement referred to in s 70(4) and must be made in the approved way, as defined by s 70(7).

The statement in s 70(4) is that the person is accused in the Category 2 territory of the commission of an offence specified in the request, or that he is alleged to be unlawfully at large after conviction by a court in the Category 2 territory of an offence specified in the request.

If the request is valid the Secretary of State must issue his certificate under s 70. This must certify that the request is made in the approved way (s 70(8)). There is no requirement for the Secretary of State to specify whether the defendant is accused or convicted, or to specify the English offence constituted by equivalent conduct, and therefore the sorts of problems which arose in *Re Farinha* [1992] Imm 174 and *R (Guisto) v Governor of HM Brixton Prison* [2003] UKHL 19 are unlikely to arise under the EA 2003.

Where the defendant is specified as having been convicted and unlawfully at large the judge at the extradition hearing has to determine whether the defendant was convicted in his presence (s 85(1)). If not, the person must be discharged unless the conditions in s 85 are made out. These are designed to ensure that the defendant will be treated fairly in the requesting state. They are considered in more detail at 5.8.8 and 6.11 below.

2.3 EXTRADITION OFFENCES

2.3.1 Introduction

The concept of an 'extradition offence' (under the EA 1989 the term 'extradition crime' was used) is fundamental to extradition law. This is because only those accused or convicted of such offences in the requesting state can be extradited. One of the principal questions to be decided by the judge at the extradition hearing is whether the defendant is accused or has been convicted of an extradition offence in the requesting state (see ss 10(2) and 78(4)(b)).

Under the EA 1989 the expression 'extradition crime' bore different meanings in Part III and Sch 1 cases (cf s 2 (Part III cases) and para 20, Sch 1 (Sch 1 cases)). In cases dealt with under EA 1989, Sch 1, it was necessary to consult the Order in Council made under the EA 1870 in order to determine whether or not the alleged offence was an extradition crime. This was sometimes a difficult issue to resolve (see eg, *R v Secretary of State for the Home Department ex p Gilmore* [1999] QB 611).

To some extent the EA 2003 simplifies the definition of extradition offence, establishes the same basic definition in relation to Category 1 and Category 2 territories, and is analogous to the definition in s 2 of the EA 1989. However, some important differences remain.

One important change from the EA 1989 regime should be noted at the outset. Under the old law dual criminality had to be satisfied in all cases; that is, the alleged conduct had to be both an offence under the law of the requesting state and, had it been committed there, an offence in the UK (see EA 1989, s 2(1)). The EA 2003 removes dual criminality in relation to Category 1 territories which are part of the EAW scheme in relation to the offences specified in the EAW and listed in Sch 2. Accordingly, for the first time, defendants can be extradited for conduct that is not criminal under UK domestic law.

2.3.2 Extradition Offences in Relation to Category 1 Territories

The EA 2003 provides separate definitions of 'extradition offence' in ss 64 and 65 for persons not sentenced for their offence and those who have been sentenced, respectively.

2.3.2.1 *Expressions used in Sections 64 and 65*

Some of the basic terms used in ss 64 and 65 are defined in s 66.

An appropriate authority of a Category 1 territory is a judicial authority of the territory which the appropriate judge believes has the function of issuing arrest warrants in that territory (s 66(2)).

The law of a territory is the general criminal law of the territory (s 66(3)).

The relevant part of the UK is the part of the UK in which the relevant proceedings are taking place (s 66(4)). The relevant proceedings are the proceedings in which it is necessary to decide whether conduct constitutes an extradition offence (s 66(5)).

2.3.2.2 *Extradition Offence: Persons not Sentenced for Offence*

The definition of extradition offence in s 64 applies in relation to conduct of a person where:

(a) he is accused in a Category 1 territory of the commission of an offence constituted by the conduct; or

(b) he is alleged to be unlawfully at large after conviction by a court in a Category 1 territory of an offence constituted by the conduct and he has not been sentenced for the offence.

Section 64(2) defines extradition offences in EAW cases. The following conditions must each be satisfied:

(a) the conduct occurs in the Category 1 territory and no part of it occurs in the UK;

(b) a certificate issued by an appropriate authority of the Category 1 territory shows that the conduct falls within the European framework list;

(c) the certificate shows that the conduct is punishable under the law of the Category 1 territory with imprisonment or another form of detention for a term of three years or a greater punishment.

The European framework list is defined by s 215(1) to be the list of conduct contained in Sch 2 to the Act. The Secretary of State may, by order, amend Sch 2 for the purpose of ensuring that the list of conduct set out in the Schedule corresponds to the list of conduct set out in Article 2(2) of the European Framework Decision, namely, the framework decision of the Council of the European Union made on 13 June 2002 on the EAW and the surrender procedures between member states (2002/584/JHA) (s 216(3)). The text of the decision is available at www.homeoffice.gov.uk/docs/eaw.pdf).

The list of conduct in Schedule 2 is as follows:

1. Participation in a criminal organization.

2. Terrorism.

3. Trafficking in human beings.

4. Sexual exploitation of children and child pornography.

5. Illicit trafficking in narcotic drugs and psychotropic substances.

6. Illicit trafficking in weapons, munitions, and explosives.

7. Corruption.

8. Fraud, including that affecting the financial interests of the European Communities within the meaning of the Convention of 26 July 1995 on the protection of the European Communities' financial interests.

9. Laundering of the proceeds of crime.

10. Counterfeiting currency, including of the euro.

11. Computer-related crime.

12. Environmental crime, including illicit trafficking in endangered animal species and in endangered plant species and varieties.

13. Facilitation of unauthorized entry and residence.

14. Murder, grievous bodily injury.

15. Illicit trade in human organs and tissue.

16. Kidnapping, illegal restraint, and hostage-taking.

17. Racism and xenophobia.

18. Organized or armed robbery.

19. Illicit trafficking in cultural goods, including antiques and works of art.

20. Swindling.

21. Racketeering and extortion.

22. Counterfeiting and piracy of products.

23. Forgery of administrative documents and trafficking therein.

24. Forgery of means of payment.

25. Illicit trafficking in hormonal substances and other growth promoters.

26. Illicit trafficking in nuclear or radioactive materials.

27. Trafficking in stolen vehicles.

28. Rape.

29. Arson.

30. Crimes within the jurisdiction of the International Criminal Court.

31. Unlawful seizure of aircraft/ships.

32. Sabotage.

As mentioned above, the definition in s 64(2) does not require the conduct to be a criminal offence in the UK. It is sufficient if it is criminal in the requesting state and the conditions in sub-paragraphs (a), (b), and (c) of s 64(2) are satisfied.

It is apparent that these 32 offences are defined in generic terms and are probably better described as 'categories of offence'. The broad and ill-defined nature of these categories has led to concerns about how the EAW will operate in practice (see House of Commons Home Affairs Committee, Extradition Bill, First Report of Session 2002–2003, HC 138, paras 20–32).

Section 64(3) defines extradition offences where the conduct occurs in the territory of the requesting state. Conduct also constitutes an extradition offence in relation to a Category 1 territory if:

(a) the conduct occurs in the Category 1 territory;

(b) the conduct would constitute an offence under the law of the relevant part of the UK if it occurred in that part of the UK;

(c) the conduct is punishable under the law of the Category 1 territory with imprisonment or another form of detention for a term of 12 months or a greater punishment (however it is described in the law).

Sections 64(4), 64(5), and 64(6) deal with the situation where the alleged conduct constitutes an extra-territorial offence against the law of the requesting state. These are offences which take place wholly outside the territory of the state concerned rather than those which merely have some extra-territorial aspect on the evidence (*Re Inderjit Singh Reyat*, Unreported, 22 March 1989, CO/1157/88; *R v Governor of Brixton Prison ex p Rush* [1969] 1 WLR 165).

Under s 64(4) the conduct is an extradition offence if:

(a) the conduct occurs outside the Category 1 territory;

(b) the conduct is punishable under the law of the Category 1 territory with imprisonment or another form of detention for a term of 12 months or a greater punishment (however it is described in that law);

(c) in corresponding circumstances equivalent conduct would constitute an extra-territorial offence under the law of the relevant part of the UK punishable with imprisonment or another form of detention for a term of 12 months or a greater punishment.

Section 64(5) provides that conduct also constitutes an extradition offence in relation to the Category 1 territory if:

(a) the conduct occurs outside the Category 1 territory and no part of it occurs in the UK;

(b) the conduct would constitute an offence under the law of the relevant part of the UK punishable with imprisonment or another form of detention for a term of 12 months or a greater punishment if it occurred in that part of the UK;

(c) the conduct is so punishable under the law of the Category 1 territory (however it is described in that law).

Special provision is made in the EA 2003 for war crimes, genocide, etc. Section 64(6) provides that the conduct also constitutes an extradition offence in relation to the Category 1 territory if:

(a) the conduct occurs outside the Category 1 territory and no part of it occurs in the UK;

(b) the conduct is punishable under the law of the Category 1 territory with imprisonment or another form of detention for a term of 12 months or a greater punishment (however it is described in that law);

(c) the conduct constitutes or, if committed in the UK, would constitute an offence mentioned in s 64(7).

The offences mentioned in s 64(7) (in relation to England and Wales) are an offence under ss 51 or 58 of the International Criminal Court Act 2001 (genocide, crimes against humanity, and war crimes); an offence under ss 52 or 59 of that Act (conduct ancillary to genocide etc committed outside the jurisdiction); an ancillary offence, as defined in ss 55 or 62 of that Act, in relation to an offence falling within paragraph (a) or (b) of s 64(7).

Section 64(8) deals with fiscal offences. It provides that in relation to s 64(3)(b), (4)(c) and (5)(b) if the conduct relates to a tax or duty, it is immaterial that the law of the relevant part of the UK does not impose the same kind of tax or duty or does not contain rules of the same kind as those of the law of the Category 1 territory. Also, if the conduct relates to customs or exchange, it is immaterial that the law of the relevant part of the UK does not contain rules of the same kind as those of the law of the Category 1 territory.

2.3.2.3 *Extradition Offences: Person Sentenced for the Offence*
Section 65 defines the different types of conduct that constitute an extradition offence in respect of Category 1 territories in cases where the defendant has

been convicted and sentenced for the offence and is alleged to be unlawfully at large (s 65(1)).

In EAW cases, s 65(2) provides that the conduct constitutes an extradition offence in relation to the Category 1 territory if:

(a) the conduct occurs in the Category 1 territory and no part of it occurs in the UK;

(b) a certificate issued by an appropriate authority of the Category 1 territory shows that the conduct falls within the European framework list in Sch 2;

(c) the certificate shows that a sentence of imprisonment or another form of detention for a term of 12 months or a greater punishment has been imposed in the Category 1 territory in respect of the conduct.

Section 65(3) defines extradition offences that are territorial offences in the requesting state. In relation to offences committed within the requesting state, the conduct also constitutes an extradition offence if:

(a) the conduct occurs in the Category 1 territory;

(b) the conduct would constitute an offence under the law of the relevant part of the UK if it occurred in that part of the UK;

(c) a sentence of imprisonment or another form of detention for a term of four months or a greater punishment has been imposed in the Category 1 territory in respect of the conduct.

For offences committed outside of the requesting state, s 65(4), (5), and (6) apply. Section 65(4) states that conduct also constitutes an extradition offence in relation to the Category 1 territory if:

(a) the conduct occurs outside the Category 1 territory;

(b) a sentence of imprisonment or another form of detention for a term of four months or a greater punishment has been imposed in the Category 1 territory in respect of the conduct;

(c) in corresponding circumstances equivalent conduct would constitute an extra-territorial offence under the law of the relevant part of the UK punishable with imprisonment or another form of detention for a term of 12 months or a greater punishment.

Section 65(5) provides that the conduct also constitutes an extradition offence in relation to the Category 1 territory if:

(a) the conduct occurs outside the Category 1 territory and no part of it occurs in the UK;

(b) the conduct would constitute an offence under the law of the relevant part of the UK punishable with imprisonment or another form of detention for a term of 12 months or a greater punishment if it occurred in that part of the UK;

(c) a sentence of imprisonment or another form of detention for a term of four months or a greater punishment has been imposed in the Category 1 territory in respect of the conduct.

Special provision for war crimes, etc, is made in s 66(6) and (7). These are in *pari materia* with s 65(6) and (7) in relation to persons not sentenced for their offence.

Section 65(8) contains provisions in relation to fiscal offences which are also in *pari materia* with those in section 65(8) in relation to accused persons.

2.3.3 Extradition Offences in Relation to Category 2 Territories

Sections 137 and 138 define 'extradition offence' in relation to Category 2 territories for persons not sentenced for their offence and persons so sentenced, respectively.

The references in these two sections to 'relevant part of the UK' is to the part of the UK in which the extradition hearing took place, if the question of whether conduct constitutes an extradition offence is to be decided by the Secretary of State (for example, where he has to decide whether to give consent under s 129(4)), and in any other case, to the part of the UK where the proceedings in which it is necessary to decide that question are taking place (ss 137(8) and 138(8)).

2.3.3.1 Extradition Offences: Person not Sentenced for Offence
The definition of extradition offence in s 137 applies in relation to conduct of a person if:

(a) he is accused in a Category 2 territory of the commission of an offence constituted by the conduct, or

(b) he is alleged to be unlawfully at large after conviction by a court in a Category 2 territory of an offence constituted by the conduct and he has not been sentenced for the offence.

Section 137(2) applies to conduct committed within the territory of the requesting state. Such conduct is an extradition offence if:

(a) the conduct occurs in the Category 2 territory;

(b) the conduct would constitute an offence under the law of the relevant part of the UK punishable with imprisonment or another form of detention for a term of 12 months or a greater punishment if it occurred in that part of the UK;

(c) the conduct is so punishable under the law of the Category 2 territory (however it is described in that law).

Section 137(3), (4), and (5) define extradition offences where the conduct alleged is extra-territorial.

Section 137(3) provides that conduct also constitutes an extradition offence in relation to the Category 2 territory if:

(a) the conduct occurs outside the Category 2 territory;

(b) the conduct is punishable under the law of the Category 2 territory with imprisonment or another form of detention for a term of 12 months or a greater punishment (however it is described in that law);

(c) in corresponding circumstances equivalent conduct would constitute an extra-territorial offence under the law of the relevant part of the UK punishable with imprisonment or another form of detention for a term of 12 months or a greater punishment.

Section 137(4) provides that conduct also constitutes an extradition offence in relation to the Category 2 territory if:

(a) the conduct occurs outside the Category 2 territory and no part of it occurs in the UK;

(b) the conduct would constitute an offence under the law of the relevant part of the UK punishable with imprisonment or another form of detention for a term of 12 months or a greater punishment if it occurred in that part of the UK;

(c) the conduct is so punishable under the law of the Category 2 territory (however it is described in that law).

Section 137(5) makes provision for war crimes, etc. It provides that conduct also constitutes an extradition offence in relation to the Category 2 territory if these conditions are satisfied:

(a) the conduct occurs outside the Category 2 territory and no part of it occurs in the UK;

(b) the conduct is punishable under the law of the Category 2 territory with imprisonment for a term of 12 months or another form of detention or a greater punishment (however it is described in that law);

(c) the conduct constitutes or, if committed in the UK, would constitute an offence mentioned in s 137(6).

The offences mentioned in s 137(6) in relation to England and Wales are: an offence under ss 51 or 58 of the International Criminal Court Act 2001 (genocide, crimes against humanity, and war crimes); an offence under ss 52 or 59 of that Act (conduct ancillary to genocide etc committed outside the jurisdiction); an ancillary offence, as defined in ss 55 or 62 of that Act, in relation to an offence falling within s 137(6)(a) or (b) of the EA 2003.

Section 137(7) provides an important exclusion for military offences under the law of the requesting state. If the conduct constitutes an offence under the military law of the requesting Category 2 territory but does not constitute an offence under the general criminal law of the relevant part of the UK, it does not constitute an extradition crime.

2.3.3.2 Extradition Offences: Person Sentenced for the Offence

The definitions in s 138 apply in relation to conduct of a person if:

(a) he is alleged to be unlawfully at large after conviction by a court in a Category 2 territory of an offence constituted by the conduct, and

(b) he has been sentenced for the offence.

Section 138(2) relates to territorial offences and provides that the conduct constitutes an extradition offence in relation to the Category 2 if:

(a) the conduct occurs in the Category 2 territory;

(b) the conduct would constitute an offence under the law of the relevant part of the UK punishable with imprisonment or another form of detention for a term of 12 months or a greater punishment if it occurred in that part of the UK;

(c) a sentence of imprisonment or another form of detention for a term of four months or a greater punishment has been imposed in the Category 2 territory in respect of the conduct.

Extra-territorial offences are dealt with in s 138(3), (4), and (5). The conduct constitutes an extradition offence in relation to the Category 2 territory if:

(a) the conduct occurs outside the Category 2 territory;

(b) a sentence of imprisonment or another form of detention for a term of four months or a greater punishment has been imposed in the Category 2 territory in respect of the conduct;

(c) in corresponding circumstances equivalent conduct would constitute an extra-territorial offence under the law of the relevant part of the UK punishable with imprisonment or another form of detention for a term of 12 months or a greater punishment.

Section 138(4) provides that conduct also constitutes an extradition offence in relation to the Category 2 territory if:

(a) the conduct occurs outside the Category 2 territory and no part of it occurs in the UK;

(b) the conduct would constitute an offence under the law of the relevant part of the UK punishable with imprisonment or another form of detention for a term of 12 months or a greater punishment if it occurred in that part of the UK;

(c) a sentence of imprisonment or another form of detention for a term of four months or a greater punishment has been imposed in the Category 2 territory in respect of the conduct.

Section 138(5) and (6) contain provisions relating to war crimes in similar terms to s 138(5) and (6).

Section 138(7) excludes military offences in the same terms as s 137(7).

2.3.4 Temporal Issues

The concept of extradition offences in the EA 2003 raises two important issues in relation to the time when the conduct was committed:

(a) Is a defendant liable to be extradited for an offence committed before the EA 2003 came into force?

(b) Except in EAW cases, is he liable to be extradited for conduct which was not an offence in the UK at the time it was committed, but which has become an offence by the date of the extradition request?

The first issue was considered in *R v Secretary of State for the Home Department ex p Hill* [1999] QB 886 in relation to the EA 1989. The applicant argued that the Act only applied to offences committed after 27 September 1989, the date of its commencement. The Divisional Court rejected this submission. Hooper J held that as a matter of statutory construction, the definition of extradition crime in s 2(1) included conduct committed before the Act came into force, and that it was not necessary to consider the Government's submissions that because the 1989 Act was a procedural Act, the presumption against non-retroactive application did not apply.

The same reasoning is applicable to the EA 2003. It follows that extradition will not be prohibited under the EA 2003 merely because the alleged offence took place before the Act came into force.

The second question was one of the many issues considered by the House of Lords in *R v Metropolitan Stipendiary Magistrate ex p Pinochet Ugarte (No 3)* [2000] 1 AC 147. A number of the allegations of torture made against General Pinochet were not criminal in the UK at the time they were committed because s 134 of the Criminal Justice Act 1988 had not yet come into force. The House of Lords held that the conduct to be considered under Part III must have been a crime in the UK at the time it was committed and that it was not sufficient that it be a crime at the time the request for extradition is made.

The EA 2003 uses the same tense structure in its definitions of extradition offence as s 2(1) of the EA 1989—'. . . if it occurred . . . ' and '. . . if committed . . . '—and so the reasoning of the House of Lords would seem to be equally applicable to the EA 2003. Therefore, where dual criminality is required, in order to constitute an extradition offence, the alleged conduct must have been criminal in the UK at the time it was committed.

Section 196 contains special provisions in relation to genocide, war crimes, and the other crimes against humanity specified in s 196(2). Section 196(3) provides that the defendant cannot object to extradition under the EA 2003 on the grounds that he could not have been punished for the offence under the law in force at the time when and in the place where he is alleged to have committed the act of which he is accused or has been convicted.

3

CATEGORIZATION OF TERRITORIES. TERRITORIAL SCOPE OF THE EA 2003

3.1 CATEGORIZATION OF TERRITORIES

3.1.1 Introduction

Historically English extradition law provided different schemes of extradition for different categories of requesting country. In broad terms, these categories were foreign states (see the EA 1870 and s 3 of the EA 1989); colonies; and designated Commonwealth countries (see Fugitive Offenders Act 1967, s 5 of the EA 1989, and *R v Governor of Brixton Prison ex p Kahan* [1989] QB 716).

Under the EA 1989 requests for extradition by European countries (for these purposes, signatories to the European Convention on Extradition 1957 designated in an Order in Council made under s 4 of the EA 1989), designated Commonwealth countries, and colonies were dealt with under Part III of the 1989 Act. Requests made by countries in relation to whom an Order in Council made under the EA 1870 was in force (principally the United States of America) were dealt with under Sch 1 to the 1989 Act.

In addition to the differing evidential requirements in Part III and Sch 1 cases, there were also differences between European Part III cases, where no evidence was required (see eg, *R v Metropolitan Stipendiary Magistrate ex p Pinochet Ugarte (No 3)* [2000] 1 AC 147; *In re Evans* [1994] 1 WLR 1006) and Commonwealth Part III cases, where admissible evidence sufficient to amount to a *prima facie* case was required (see eg, *R (Saifi) v Governor of HMP Brixton* [2001] 1 WLR 1134).

The EA 2003 largely removes these complexities by designating extradition partners as either Category 1 or Category 2 territories. Claims for extradition by Category 1 territories are dealt with under Part 1, whilst requests for extradition by Category 2 territories are dealt with under Part 2.

3.1.2 Category 1 Territories

Category 1 territories are territories designated for the purposes of Part 1 by order (s 1(1)). In the Act, references to Category 1 territories are to the territories designated for the purposes of Part 1 (s 1(2)).

The EA 2003 does not provide any guidance as to which countries may be designated as Category 1 territories. The only restriction is contained in s 1(3), which provides that a territory may not be designated for the purposes of Part 1 if a person found guilty in the territory of a criminal offence may be sentenced to death for the offence under the general criminal law of the territory.

The Extradition Act 2003 (Designation of Part 1 Territories) Order 2003 (SI 2003/3333) designates the following territories as Category 1 territories:

Belgium; Denmark; Finland; Ireland; Portugal; Spain; Sweden.

However, it is unlikely that this list will remain unchanged for long. In time all EU member states will be designated as Category 1 territories as they implement the EAW. Moreover, the explanatory notes to the Extradition Bill suggest that the Secretary of State envisages at some stage designating non-EU states as Category 1 territories. The notes state that the fact that the designation as Category 1 and 2 territories will be carried out by order means that:

it will therefore be possible for a country to move from one category to the other when appropriate, depending on the extradition procedures that the UK negotiates with each extradition partner.

3.1.3 Category 2 Territories

Category 2 territories are those designated for the purposes of Part 2 of the EA 2003 by order (s 69(1)). In the Act, references to Category 2 territories are to those so designated (s 69(2)).

The Extradition Act 2003 (Designation of Part 2 Territories) Order 2003 (SI 2003/3334) designates the following as Category 2 territories:

Albania; Andorra; Antigua and Barbuda; Argentina; Armenia; Australia; Austria; Azerbaijan; The Bahamas; Bangladesh; Barbados; Belize; Bolivia; Bosnia and Herzegovina; Botswana; Brazil; Brunei; Bulgaria; Canada; Chile; Colombia; Cook Islands; Croatia; Cuba; Cyprus; Czech Republic; Dominica; Ecuador; El Salvador; Estonia; Fiji; France; The Gambia; Georgia; Germany; Ghana; Greece; Grenada; Guatemala; Guyana; Hong Kong Special Administrative Region; Haiti; Hungary; Iceland;

India; Iraq; Israel; Italy; Jamaica; Kenya; Kiribati; Latvia; Lesotho; Liberia; Liechtenstein; Lithuania; Luxembourg; Macedonia FYR; Malawi; Malaysia; Maldives; Malta; Mauritius; Mexico; Moldova; Monaco; Nauru; The Netherlands; New Zealand; Nicaragua; Nigeria; Norway; Panama; Papua New Guinea; Paraguay; Peru; Poland; Romania; Russian Federation; Saint Christopher and Nevis; Saint Lucia; Saint Vincent and the Grenadines; San Marino; Serbia and Montenegro; Seychelles; Sierra Leone; Singapore; Slovakia; Slovenia; Solomon Islands; South Africa; Sri Lanka; Swaziland; Switzerland; Tanzania; Thailand; Tonga; Trinidad and Tobago; Turkey; Tuvalu; Uganda; Ukraine; Uruguay; The United States of America; Vanuatu; Western Samoa; Zambia; Zimbabwe.

3.1.4 Parties to International Conventions

The UK is a signatory to a number of international conventions which place it under an obligation to criminalize certain types of conduct which have come to be known as 'international crimes' (see generally, *R v Metropolitan Stipendiary Magistrate ex p Pinochet Ugarte (No 3)* [2000] 1 AC 147; *Lodhi v Governor of Brixton Prison* [2001] EWHC Admin 178). Specifically, the UK is required by these conventions either to prosecute or extradite those accused of such offences who are found within its jurisdiction.

Where a request for extradition for such an offence is made by a Category 1 or 2 territory then, obviously, no difficulty arises in giving effect to the obligation to extradite. However, in order to fulfil this obligation in respect of states which have not been designated under the EA 2003 but which are parties to international criminal conventions, s 193 allows for them to be designated by order for the purposes of that section.

The effect of designation is that the territory is regarded as Category 2 territory, the Act applies to it subject to the amendments in s 193(3)(a) and as if the conduct that constituted an extradition offence for the purposes of Part 2 were the conduct specified in the designating order.

3.1.5 Special Extradition Arrangements

The EA 2003 contains provisions in s 194 which allow a suspect to be extradited even if the requesting state is not a Category 1 or Category 2 territory. Section 194 applies if the Secretary of State believes that arrangements have been made between the UK and another territory (which is not a Category 1 or 2 territory) for the extradition of a person to that territory (s 194(1)).

Where it applies, under s 194(2) the Secretary of State can issue a certificate to that effect. If he does so, the EA 2003 applies with the modifications in s 194(4) as if the requesting state were a Category 2 territory.

A certificate issued under s 194(2) is conclusive as to the existence of the conditions in s 194(1) (s 194(5)).

3.2 JURISDICTIONAL SCOPE OF THE EA 2003. BRITISH OVERSEAS TERRITORIES. THE REPUBLIC OF IRELAND

3.2.1 Introduction

Extradition law in the UK is complicated by the fact that the UK is responsible for the extradition arrangements of British possessions including the Channel Islands, the Isle of Man, and British overseas territories. This section considers the application of the EA 2003 in this context.

Before the EA 2003 came into force, extradition from colonies to other countries and colonies was governed by a mixture of pre-EA 1989 legislation and provisions in the EA 1989 itself. The applicable law depended upon the identity of the colony and of the requesting state, and this resulted in an unwieldy tangle of legislation.

Although the EA 2003 simplifies the law considerably, it is nevertheless important to have a proper understanding of the UK's constitutional structure in order to understand its provisions.

3.2.2 The United Kingdom, the Channel Islands, and the Isle of Man

The UK consists of England, Scotland, Wales, and Northern Ireland (Royal and Parliamentary Titles Act 1927, s 2(2); Interpretation Act 1978, Sch 1). Section 226 limits the operation of parts of the EA 2003 to certain parts of the UK. Sections 157–160, 166–168, 171, 173, and 205 do not extend to Scotland (s 226(1)). Sections 154, 198, 200, and 201 extend to England and Wales only. Sections 183 and 199 extend to Scotland only. Sections 184 and 185 extend to Northern Ireland only.

The Channel Islands consist of Jersey, Guernsey, Alderney, and Sark. They are not part of the UK (*Calvin's* Case 7 Co Rep 1, 21) although the UK has responsibility for their external affairs.

Similarly, the Isle of Man is not part of the UK although it became vested in the Crown in 1765 (Isle of Man Purchase Act 1765). The UK, the Isle of Man, and the Channel Islands together make up the British Islands (Interpretation Act 1978, Sch 1).

Section 222 states that an Order in Council may provide that the EA 2003 extend to the Channel Islands or the Isle of Man with such modifications, if any, as are specified in the Order.

Article 2 of the Extradition Act 2003 (Commencement and Savings) (Amendment) Order 2003 (SI 2003/3258) provides that the coming into force of the repeal of the EA 1989 by s 218(b) of, and Sch 4 to, the EA 2003 shall not apply for the purposes of the Bailiwick of Jersey, the Bailiwick of Guernsey, the Isle of Man, or any of the British overseas territories with the exception of

Gibraltar, until such time as any provision which is made for (or by) the dependency or territory in question (whether under ss 177, 178, or 222 of the Act or otherwise), and which has the effect of replacing the provisions of the EA 1989, comes into force. Accordingly, the EA 1989 will continue to apply to these territories until such time as fresh legislation is made by or for them to replace the EA 1989.

3.2.3 British Overseas Territories

Sections 177 and 178 of the EA 2003 deal with extradition to and from 'British overseas territories'. These territories, formerly known as dependent territories or colonies, are those specified in Sch 6 to the British Nationality Act 1981, as amended (see British Overseas Territories Act 2002, s 1(1) and (3)), namely:

Anguilla; Bermuda; British Antarctic Territory; British Indian Ocean Territory; Cayman Islands; Falkland Islands; Gibraltar; Montserrat; Pitcairn; Henderson; Ducie and Oeno Islands; St. Helena and Dependencies; South Georgia and the South Sandwich Islands; The Sovereign Base Areas of Akrotiri and Dhekelia (ie the areas mentioned in s 2(1) of the Cyprus Act 1960); Turks and Caicos Islands; and the Virgin Islands.

3.2.4 Extradition from British Overseas Territories

Section 177 applies in relation to extradition from British overseas territories to Category 1 and 2 territories (s 177(1)(a) and (c)), and to extradition from British overseas territories to the UK (s 177(1)(b)), and the Channel Islands and the Isle of Man (s 177(1)(d)).

Section 177(2) states that an Order in Council may provide for any provision of the EA 2003 applicable to extradition from the UK to apply to extradition from British overseas territories to Category 1 territories and the UK.

Section 177(3) states that an Order in Council may provide for any provision of the EA 2003 applicable to extradition from the UK to a Category 2 territory to apply to extradition from British overseas territories to a Category 2 territory, the Channel Islands, and the Isle of Man.

3.2.5 Extradition to British Overseas Territories

Section 178 deals with extradition to British overseas territories from Category 1 and Category 2 territories (s 178(1)(a) and (c)), and to extradition to British overseas territories from the UK (s 178(1)(b)), and the Channel Islands and the Isle of Man (s 178(1)(d)).

Section 178(2) states that an Order in Council may provide for any provision of the EA 2003 applicable to extradition to the UK to apply to extradition to British overseas territories from Category 1 territories and the UK.

Section 178(3) states that an Order in Council may provide for any provision of the EA 2003 applicable to extradition to the UK from a Category 2 territory to apply to extradition to British overseas territories from Category 2 territories, the Channel Islands, and the Isle of Man.

3.2.6 The Republic of Ireland

The UK and the Republic of Ireland are neighbours with close ties. Thus there are no immigration controls between Ireland and the UK. Also, the provisions for extradition between the UK and the Republic of Ireland have historically been much more simple and domesticated than the extradition procedures which applied to other foreign states. Ireland was almost treated as part of the UK, and *vice versa*, for the purposes of extradition.

Ireland was excluded from the EA 1989 by virtue of s 3(2)(iv) of that Act, and extradition between the UK and the Republic was governed instead by the Backing of Warrants (Republic of Ireland) Act 1965 (see *R v Governor of Belmarsh Prison ex p Gilligan* [2001] 1 AC 84). This Act allowed for the rendition of persons in accordance with a reciprocal system for backing and enforcing warrants between the two countries.

Ireland is a member of the EU and has been designated as a Category 1 territory. Accordingly, return to Ireland is now governed by Part 1 of the EA 2003. The Backing of Warrants (Republic of Ireland) Act 1965 is repealed by s 218(a) and Sch 3 of the EA 2003.

3.3 RETURN WITHIN THE BRITISH ISLANDS

3.3.1 Return to Scotland and Northern Ireland from England and Wales

Whilst England and Scotland form part of the UK, legally they are distinct countries (*Stuart v Stuart and Moore* (1861) 4 Macq 1, 49). Equally, it is obvious that the public interest requires that the authorities on either side of the border within the UK should co-operate with each other with the minimum of formality in the investigation and prosecution of crime.

Return from England and Wales to Scotland (and *vice versa*) is governed by a system of mutually enforceable arrest warrants. A warrant issued in England, Wales, or Northern Ireland for the arrest of a person charged with an offence may (without any endorsement) be executed in Scotland by any constable of any police force of the country of issue or of the country of execution as well as by any other persons within the directions in the warrant (Criminal Justice and Public Order Act 1994, s 136(1)).

Similarly, a warrant issued in Scotland or Northern Ireland for the arrest of a person charged with an offence may (without any endorsement) be executed in

England or Wales by any constable of any police force of the country of issue or of the country of execution as well as by any other persons within the directions in the warrant (ibid, s 136(2)).

A warrant issued in England or Wales or Scotland, for the arrest of a person charged with an offence may (without any endorsement) be executed in Northern Ireland by any constable of any police force of the country of issue or of the country of execution as well as by any other persons within the directions in the warrant (ibid, s 136(3)).

A person arrested in pursuance of a warrant must be taken, as soon as reasonably practicable, to any place to which he is committed by, or may be conveyed under, the warrant.

3.3.2 Return from England to the Isle of Man, Guernsey, Jersey, Alderney, and Sark

As explained above, these islands are not part of the UK and they have a distinct legal system. A backing of warrants system operates to secure the return of criminal defendants. Section 13 of the Indictable Offences Act 1848 allows warrants issued in England to be endorsed and executed in the Isle of Man, Guernsey, Jersey, Alderney, and Sark, and *vice versa* (*Richards v States of Jersey Police* [2003] All ER (D) 381 (Dec)).

3.4 RETURN TO INTERNATIONAL CRIMINAL TRIBUNALS

The conflict in the former Yugoslavia and the genocide in Rwanda in the 1990s led the United Nations to set up International Criminal Tribunals to try those accused of committing serious offences in the conflicts.

United Nations Security Council Resolution 827 of 1993 established the Tribunal for the Prosecution of Persons Responsible for Serious Violations of International Humanitarian Law Committed in the Territory of the Former Yugoslavia since 1991 (ICTY). In 1994 the Security Council passed a similar Resolution, No 955 of 1994, which established the International Criminal Tribunal for the Prosecution of Persons Responsible for Genocide and Other Serious Violations of International Humanitarian Law Committed in the Territory of Rwanda and Rwandan citizens responsible for genocide and other such violations committed in the territory of neighbouring states, between 1 January 1994 and 31 December 1994. Since the Tribunals were established they have tried and convicted a large number of defendants of extremely serious crimes including genocide, murder, rape, and torture.

Between 1953 and 1989 the question of the establishment of an international criminal court was considered periodically. Further impetus was given in the

1990s by the conflict in Yugoslavia and the genocide in Rwanda which led to the establishment of the two *ad hoc* tribunals referred to above. Shortly afterwards, the International Law Commission completed its work on the draft statute for an international criminal court and in 1994 submitted the draft statute to the General Assembly. The statute was finalized at a conference in Rome in 1998 and the Statute of the International Criminal Court (ICC) was opened for signature later that year. Part 9 of the Statute of the ICC contains provisions relating to extradition and mutual assistance.

Extradition from the UK to the jurisdiction of these tribunals is dealt with under legislation which was independent of the EA 1989. This legislation remains largely unaffected by the EA 2003.

Extradition to the ICTY is governed by the United Nations (International Tribunal) (Former Yugoslavia) Order 1996 (SI 1996/716), as amended.

Extradition to the Rwanda Tribunal is governed by the United Nations (International Tribunal)(Rwanda) Order 1996 (SI 1996/1296).

Part 2 of the International Criminal Court Act 2001 governs extradition to the jurisdiction of the ICC: see generally, Nicholls, Montgomery, and Knowles, *The Law of Extradition and Mutual Assistance* (2002), Chapter 13.

4

INITIAL STAGES OF THE EXTRADITION PROCESS

4.1 INTRODUCTION

This chapter examines the provisions of the EA 2003 which deal with arrest, legal aid, bail, and the initial hearing in the Magistrates' Court. The Act makes a number of important changes to the procedures under the EA 1989. In particular, the role of the Secretary of State is greatly reduced. He is no longer required to issue his authority to proceed and has a limited role in Category 2 cases only.

This chapter also examines relevant parts of the Codes of Practice relating to Part 4 issued by the Secretary of State under s 173. The Codes contain provisions relating to the detention and treatment of suspects arrested under the EA 2003.

4.2 ARREST FOR THE PURPOSES OF EXTRADITION

4.2.1 Introduction

In the case of Category 1 territories there are two methods of effecting arrest. These are dealt with in ss 3–6. The first method is arrest under a certified Part 1 warrant (defined in s 2(1)) which has been certified by a designated authority under s 2(7). The second method is arrest without a warrant under s 5. This is known as provisional arrest.

The powers to arrest for the purposes of extradition to Category 2 territories are contained in ss 71–75. There are two methods, both of which require a warrant. The first requires the Secretary of State to have received a valid request for extradition to a Category 2 territory under s 71. Once this has been sent to an appropriate judge under s 72(1) the judge may then issue an arrest warrant under s 72(2). The second method, provisional arrest, takes place where a judge issues a warrant under s 74. This method is utilized where there are reasons to believe that the defendant would flee from the UK if he were to be alerted to the possibility of proceedings.

Code B, issued under s 173, contains detailed guidance about the procedures which should be followed upon and after arrest and should be read alongside this chapter.

4.2.2 Arrest in Category 1 Cases

4.2.2.1 *Arrest under Part 1 Warrant*

The process of arrest under a Part 1 warrant commences when the authority designated for the purpose under s 2(9) receives a Part 1 warrant in respect of a person. Sections 203 and 204 permit the warrant to be sent by fax or other electronic means (eg as an e-mail document).

The Extradition Act 2003 (Part 1 Designated Authorities) Order 2003 (SI 2003/ 3190) designates both the National Criminal Intelligence Service and the Crown Agent of the Crown Office in Scotland as designated authorities, which allows both those bodies to certify Part 1 warrants in the UK.

A Part 1 warrant is defined by s 2(2) to be an arrest warrant which is issued by an authority of a Category 1 territory and which contains either the statement referred to in s 2(3) and the information referred to in s 2(4) (persons accused of offences), or the statement referred to in s 2(5) and the information referred to in s 2(6) (persons convicted of offences).

The statement referred to in s 2(3) is one that the person in respect of whom the Part 1 warrant is issued is accused in the Category 1 territory of the commission of an offence specified in the warrant, and the Part 1 warrant is issued with a view to his arrest and extradition to the Category 1 territory for the purpose of being prosecuted for the offence.

The information referred to in s 2(4) is:

(a) particulars of the person's identity;

(b) particulars of any other warrant issued in the Category 1 territory for the person's arrest in respect of the offence;

(c) particulars of the circumstances in which the person is alleged to have committed the offence, including the conduct alleged to constitute the offence and the time and place at which he is alleged to have committed the offence;

(d) particulars of the sentence which may be imposed under the law of the Category 1 territory in respect of the offence if the person is convicted of it.

The statement in s 2(5) is one that the person in respect of whom the Part 1 warrant is issued is alleged to be unlawfully at large after conviction of an offence specified in the warrant by a court in the Category 1 territory, and the Part 1 warrant is issued with a view to his arrest and extradition to the Category 1 territory for the purpose of being sentenced for the offence or of serving a sentence of imprisonment or another form of detention imposed in respect of the offence.

The information contained in s 2(6) is:

(a) particulars of the person's identity;

(b) particulars of the conviction;

(c) particulars of any other warrant issued in the Category 1 territory for the person's arrest in respect of the offence;

(d) particulars of the sentence which may be imposed under the law of the Category 1 territory in respect of the offence, if the person has not been sentenced for the offence;

(e) particulars of the sentence which has been imposed under the law of the Category 1 territory in respect of the offence, if the person has been sentenced for the offence.

The designated authority may issue a certificate under s 2 if it believes that the authority which issued the Part 1 warrant is a judicial authority of the Category 1 territory, and that it has the function of issuing arrest warrants in the territory. In many civil law jurisdictions Public Prosecutors and other non-judicial officers have the power to issue arrest warrants (see *R v Bow Street Magistrates' Court ex p van der Holst* (1986) 83 Cr App R 114). It follows that a certificate may not be issued under s 2(7) unless the warrant has been issued by a judicial authority as opposed to, for example, a prosecutor. Where the designated authority issues a certificate it must certify that the authority which issued the Part 1 warrant is a judicial authority of the Category 1 territory, and that it has the function of issuing arrest warrants in the territory.

Where a certificate has been issued under s 2(7), the person in respect of whom it has been issued can be arrested under s 3. The authority for the arrest is the Part 1 warrant and not the certificate. The warrant may be executed by a constable or a customs officer in any part of the UK (s 3(2)). The warrant may also be executed by a service policeman, subject to the conditions in s 3(3) and (4).

Section 4 contains certain procedural safeguards for a person arrested under a Part 1 warrant. If neither the warrant nor a copy of it was shown to the person at the time of his arrest, and he asks to be shown the warrant, the warrant or a copy of it must be shown to him as soon as practicable after his request (s 4(2)). The person must be brought as soon as practicable before the 'appropriate judge' (s 4(3)). In England and Wales the appropriate judge is a District Judge (Magistrates' Courts) designated for the purposes of Part 1 by the Lord Chancellor (s 67(1)).

Section 4(4) provides that if either s 4(2) or (3) is not complied with the person must be taken to be discharged. A person arrested under the warrant must be treated as continuing in legal custody until he is brought before the appropriate judge under s 4(3) or he is taken to be discharged under s 4(4).

4.2.2.2 *Provisional Arrest*

The provisional arrest powers in Part 1 of the EA 2003 permit, for the first time, arrest without a warrant in extradition cases.

Section 3(1) provides that a constable, a customs officer, or a service policeman may arrest a person without a warrant if he has reason to believe that a Part 1 warrant has been or will be issued in respect of the person by an authority of a Category 1 territory, and that the authority is a judicial authority of the Category 1 territory and has the function of issuing arrest warrants in the territory.

A constable or a customs officer can arrest the person under s 5(1) in any part of the UK (s 5(2)). A service policeman may also carry out an arrest under s 5(1) subject to the conditions in s 5(3) and (4).

A person arrested under s 5 must be dealt with speedily. Within 48 hours of arrest he must be brought before the appropriate judge (s 6(2)(a)) and the documents specified in s 6(4) must also be produced to the judge within the same period (s 6(2)(b)). These documents are a Part 1 warrant in respect of the person and a certificate under s 2 in respect of the warrant.

If s 6(2) is not complied with the person must be taken to be discharged. The person must be treated as continuing in legal custody until he is brought before the appropriate judge under s 6(2) or he is taken to be discharged under s 6(5).

4.2.3 Arrest in Category 2 Cases

The powers of arrest in Category 2 cases are contained in ss 71–75. There are two methods, which will be considered separately.

4.2.3.1 *Arrest following Receipt of Secretary of State's Certificate*

This method is analogous to arrest following receipt of an authority to proceed under s 8(1)(a) of the EA 1989.

Where under s 70 the Secretary of State receives a valid request for extradition from a Category 2 territory (as defined by s 70(3)) then he must issue a certificate under s 70(1). This must be sent to the appropriate judge together with the documents specified in s 70(9).

Section 203 permits faxed documents to be used as if they were original documents.

Once the appropriate judge has received these documents he may issue an arrest warrant if the conditions in s 71(2) are satisfied, namely, if it appears to him that:

(a) the offence in respect of which extradition is requested is an extradition offence, and

(b) there is evidence falling within s 71(3).

Section 71(3) specifies the evidence required to justify a warrant being issued:

(a) in accusation cases, evidence that would justify the issue of a warrant for the arrest of a person accused of the offence within the judge's jurisdiction, if the person whose extradition is requested is accused of the commission of the offence;

(b) in conviction cases, evidence that would justify the issue of a warrant for the arrest of a person unlawfully at large after conviction of the offence within the judge's jurisdiction, if the person whose extradition is requested is alleged to be unlawfully at large after conviction of the offence.

The evidentiary threshold for the grant of an arrest warrant is low. In *R v Weil* (1882) 9 QB 701, 705 it was said that 'very little evidence will do'. Nonetheless, evidence in the proper sense is required.

However, s 71(4) introduces an important modification of s 71(2) and (3) in the case of Category 2 territories which have been designated for the purposes of s 71 by order made by the Secretary of State. In such cases, s 72(2) and (3) have effect as if 'evidence' reads 'information'. This sub-section mirrors s 8(3) and (3A) of the EA 1989, which removed the requirement for 'evidence' in certain cases, and reversed the decision in *Re Dokleja*, Unreported, 31 January 1994, CO/523/93, in which it had been held that 'allegations, assertions, and hints' were insufficient to justify the grant of an arrest warrant.

The following countries have been designated for the purposes of s 71 by the Extradition Act 2003 (Designation of Part 2 Territories) Order 2003 (SI 2003/3334), Article 3:

Albania; Andorra; Armenia; Australia; Austria; Azerbaijan; Bulgaria; Canada; Croatia; Cyprus; Czech Republic; Estonia; France; Georgia; Germany; Greece; Hungary; Iceland; Israel; Italy; Latvia; Liechtenstein; Lithuania; Luxembourg; Macedonia FYR; Malta; Moldova; The Netherlands; New Zealand; Norway; Poland; Romania; Russian Federation; Serbia and Montenegro; Slovakia; Slovenia; South Africa; Switzerland; Turkey; Ukraine; The United States of America.

Once the warrant has been issued it may be executed in the manner provided for in s 71(5), (6), and (7). The warrant issued under this section may be executed in any part of the UK (s 71(7)). The warrant may be executed by any person to whom it is directed or by any constable or customs officer (s 71(5)(a)). It may also be executed even if neither the warrant nor a copy of it is in the possession of the person executing it at the time of the arrest (s 71(5)(b)).

If a warrant issued under this section in respect of a person is directed to a service policeman, it may only be executed in any place where the service police-man would have power to arrest the person under the appropriate service law (defined in s 71(8)) if the person had committed an offence under that law.

4.2.3.2 *Proceedings after Arrest*

Section 72 provides safeguards for the arrested person following his arrest. If neither the warrant nor a copy of it was shown to the person at the time of his arrest, the warrant or a copy of it must be shown to him as soon as practicable after his arrest (s 72(2)).

After his arrest the person must be brought as soon as practicable before the appropriate judge (s 72(3)). In England and Wales the appropriate judge is a District Judge (Magistrates' Courts) designated for the purposes of Part 1 by the Lord Chancellor (s 139(1)). However, this requirement does not apply if the person is granted bail by a constable following his arrest, or the Secretary of State decides under s 126 that the request for the person's extradition is not to be proceeded with (s 72(4)).

If either s 72(2) or (3) is not complied with and the person applies to the judge to be discharged, then the judge must order his discharge (s 72(5)).

When the person first appears or is brought before the appropriate judge, the judge must (s 72(7)):

(a) inform him of the contents of the request for his extradition;

(b) give him the required information about consent;

(c) remand him in custody or on bail. If the judge remands the person in custody he may later grant bail (s 72(9)).

The required information about consent is defined by s 72(8) as information that:

(a) the person may consent to his extradition to the Category 2 territory to which his extradition is requested;

(b) an explanation of the effect of consent and the procedure that will apply if he gives consent;

(c) that consent must be given in writing and is irrevocable.

Consent is dealt with in detail in Chapter 11.

4.2.3.3 *Provisional Arrest under Section 74*

A provisional warrant is essentially an emergency procedure for taking a person into custody. Hence, the issue of a provisional warrant is a relatively informal process. Although it is a preliminary step in the extradition process, at that stage the defendant is not strictly subject to extradition at all, and may never become so (*R v Governor of Pentonville ex p Osman (No 3)* [1990] 1 WLR 878, 887; *Government of the Federal Republic of Germany v Sotiriadis* [1975] AC 1, 25).

An application for a provisional warrant is generally made *ex parte* and those applying for the warrant are therefore under a duty to make full and frank disclosure to the court of all matters that are material to his decision (cf *R v Lewes Crown Court ex p Hill* (1991) 93 Cr App R 60). More than one provisional warrant can be issued and be in force at the same time if new material comes to light to justify additional warrants (*R v Evans ex p Pinochet Ugarte*, The Times, 3 November 1998). The court has a discretion to hear representations from the defendant before issuing a warrant (*R v West London Stipendiary Magistrate ex p Klahn* [1979] 1 WLR 933).

Section 73 empowers a justice of the peace to issue a provisional warrant if the conditions in the section are satisfied. Section 73 applies if the justice is satisfied on information in writing and on oath that a person who is within s 73(2) is (or is believed to be) either in or on his way to the UK. A person is within s 73(2) if he is accused in a Category 2 territory of the commission of an offence or he is alleged to be unlawfully at large after conviction of an offence by a court in a Category 2 territory.

The justice of the peace may issue a warrant for the arrest of the person under s 73(3) if it appears to him that the offence of which the person is accused or has been convicted is an extradition offence, and there is written evidence falling within s 73(4). This is evidence that:

(a) would justify the issue of a warrant for the arrest of a person accused of the offence within the justice's jurisdiction, if the person in respect of whom the warrant is sought is accused of the commission of the offence;

(b) would justify the issue of a warrant for the arrest of a person unlawfully at large after conviction of the offence within the justice's jurisdiction, if the person in respect of whom the warrant is sought is alleged to be unlawfully at large after conviction of the offence.

However, if the Category 2 territory is designated for the purposes of s 73 by order made by the Secretary of State, s 73(3) and (4) have effect as if 'evidence' reads 'information' (s 73(5)). The following countries have been designated by the Extradition Act 2003 (Designation of Part 2 Territories) Order 2003 (SI 2003/3334), Article 3:

Albania; Andorra; Armenia; Australia; Austria; Azerbaijan; Bulgaria; Canada; Croatia; Cyprus; Czech Republic; Estonia; France; Georgia; Germany; Greece; Hungary; Iceland; Israel; Italy; Latvia; Liechtenstein; Lithuania; Luxembourg; Macedonia FYR; Malta; Moldova; The Netherlands; New Zealand; Norway; Poland; Romania; Russian Federation; Serbia and Montenegro; Slovakia; Slovenia; South Africa; Switzerland; Turkey; Ukraine; The United States of America.

A provisional warrant can be executed in any part of the UK (s 73(8)) by any person to whom it is directed or by any constable or customs officer (s 73(6)(a)). It may be executed even if neither the warrant nor a copy of it is in the possession of the person executing it at the time of the arrest (s 73(6)(b)).

If the provisional warrant is directed to a service policeman, it may be executed in any place where the service policeman would have power to arrest the person under the appropriate service law if the person had committed an offence under that law (s 73(7)).

4.3 ARREST AND DETENTION OF EXTRADITION DEFENDANTS

4.3.1 Codes of Practice (Section 173)

There was a certain lack of clarity about the status of persons arrested under the EA 1989 regime. Although they were cautioned on arrest and taken to a police station like ordinary criminal suspects, their detention was not covered in terms by the Codes of Practice issued under the Police and Criminal Evidence Act 1984 and much was done on an *ad hoc* basis.

The EA 2003 aims to remove much of this ambiguity by putting a range of police powers on a statutory footing for the first time in Part 4. These are considered in detail in Chapter 13. The status of extradition detainees is also clarified, and their rights are defined both in the statute and in the Codes of Practice issued under s 173.

Section 171 applies in relation to cases where a person is arrested under an extradition arrest power at a police station, or is taken to a police station after being arrested elsewhere under an extradition arrest power, or is detained at a police station after being arrested under an extradition arrest power. The extradition arrest powers are defined in s 170(6).

In relation to these cases the Secretary of State may by order apply the provisions mentioned in s 172(3) with specified modifications, namely the following sections of the Police and Criminal Evidence Act 1984: s 54 (searches of detained persons); s 55 (intimate searches); s 56 (right to have someone informed when arrested); s 58 (access to legal advice).

Section 173 of the EA 2003 requires the Secretary of State to issue Codes of Practice in connection with the exercise of the powers conferred by Part 4, including the seizure and retention of evidence. The Codes are designed to provide guidance for officers in the handling of extradition cases and the operation of police powers under the EA 2003. A failure by a constable to comply with a provision of the Codes does not of itself make him liable to criminal or civil proceedings (s 173(6)). The Codes are admissible in evidence in proceedings under the

EA 2003 and must be taken into account by a judge or court in determining any question to which it appears to the judge or the court to be relevant (s 173(7)).

The Codes of Practice were laid before Parliament on 2 December 2003 and came into force on 1 January 2004 (Extradition Act 2003 (Police Powers: Codes of Practice) Order 2003 (SI 2003/3336)). They are available on the Home Office website at www.homeoffice.gov.uk/docs2/extradition.html. The Codes are:

Code B—Searches, seizure, retention, use and delivery of property

Code C—Arrest and detention and treatment of detained persons

Code D—Identification of persons

The Codes, which apply to police officers operating in England, Wales, and Northern Ireland, and to customs officers operating throughout the UK (para 1.12) must be readily available at all police stations for consultation by police officers, detained persons, and members of the public, and each police station in England, Wales, and Northern Ireland will be provided with a copy of them (paras 1.9 and 1.10).

4.3.1.1 *Caution on Arrest*
Code C, para 2.1 provides that an officer arresting a person under any of the powers in the EA 2003 must administer a caution in the following terms:

You do not have to say anything, but anything you do say may be given in evidence.

The arresting officer must take all reasonable steps to ensure that the person understands that they are being arrested and why they are being arrested. If necessary, the procedure should be repeated at the police station in the presence of an interpreter if there are language difficulties (para 2.6). Copies of relevant documents should also be served on the arrested person (para 2.4).

4.3.1.2 *Rights of Detainee*
Code C specifies the rights which the detainee has whilst in police custody. These include the right to have someone informed of his arrest, the right to consult privately with a solicitor, and to be told that free independent legal advice is available.

Annex B to Code C contains a checklist of duties for the custody officer in extradition cases. These include ensuring that the detainee understands why he has been arrested, explaining the extradition process to him, and ensuring that he is aware of his right to legal advice and to advice from his consulate or Embassy.

4.3.1.3 *Custody Records*
Code C, para 3 requires a custody record be opened and maintained as in a domestic criminal case.

4.3.1.4 *Treatment Generally*

Code C, paras 7–11 apply the relevant provisions of Code C issued under s 66 of the Police and Criminal Evidence Act 1984 relating to the right not to be held incommunicado, the right to legal advice, etc.

4.4 LEGAL AID

Legal aid is available for those arrested for the purposes of extradition proceedings.

Section 182 of the EA 2003 amends s 12 of the Access to Justice Act 1999 to include proceedings under the EA 2003 within the definition of 'criminal proceedings' in s 12(2). This means that extradition proceedings qualify for criminal legal aid funding in accordance with the Criminal Defence Service (General) (No 2) Regulations 2001 (SI 2001/1437). The application is made on the forms set out in Sch 2 to the Regulations.

Legal aid for counsel in the Magistrates' Court can be obtained under reg 12(1) where the court is of the opinion that, because of circumstances which make the proceedings unusually grave or difficult, representation by both a solicitor and an advocate would be desirable.

By virtue of reg 14(14) there is no power to grant legal aid for Queen's counsel in extradition proceedings.

4.5 BAIL

The effect of ss 7(9), 8(1)(d), 8(2), 9(1), 9(4), 9(5), 72(9), 74(7)(c), 74(9), and 77(1) is that the defendant can be granted bail at any stage of the extradition proceedings in the Magistrates' Court.

Section 198 of the EA 2003 makes important amendments to the Bail Act 1976 in respect of extradition proceedings. The effect of these is as follows.

4.5.1 Right to Bail for Extradition Defendants

The most important change is that defendants arrested for the purposes of extradition now have the right to bail under s 4 of the Bail Act 1976 accorded to all criminal defendants, except in one situation. The Bail Act 1976 is amended as follows:

(a) the exclusion of extradition proceedings in s 4(2) is deleted by s 198(4) of the EA 2003;

(b) section 4(2A), inserted by s 198(5), provides that the right to bail in s 4 applies when a defendant appears or is brought before a court in the course of or in connection with extradition proceedings in respect of the offence, or he applies to a court for bail or for a variation of the conditions of bail in connection with the proceedings;

(c) however, s 4(2B), also inserted by s 198(5) of the EA 2003, provides that s 4(2A) does not apply if the person is alleged to be unlawfully at large after conviction of the offence.

4.5.2 Powers of Arrest of Absent Defendants

Section 199(8) and (9) amend s 7 of the Bail Act 1976 to confer the power to issue an arrest warrant and the power to arrest without warrant where an extradition defendant absconds.

4.5.3 Reasons for Refusing Bail in Extradition Cases

Section 198(10) amends para 1, Sch 1 of the Bail Act 1976 so that the exceptions to the right to bail in Sch 1 apply when the judge is considering whether to grant bail in extradition proceedings. The most common exceptions are those in para 2, namely that there are substantial grounds for believing that the defendant, if released on bail, would:

(a) fail to surrender to custody; or
(b) commit an offence on bail; or
(c) interfere with witnesses.

Section 198(13) inserts an additional ground for refusing bail in extradition proceedings. Paragraph 2B of Sch 1 provides that the defendant need not be granted bail in extradition proceedings if:

(a) the conduct constituting the offence would, if carried out by the defendant in England and Wales, constitute an indictable offence or an offence triable either way; and

(b) it appears to the court that the defendant was on bail on the date of the offence.

4.5.4 Appeal against Grant of Bail

Section 20 of the EA 2003 amends the Bail (Amendment) Act 1993 and provides for a right of appeal by the prosecution (ie the person acting on behalf of the territory to which extradition is sought (s 201(9))) to the Crown Court against a grant of bail.

4.5.5 Bail in the High Court

The changes to the bail regime made by the EA 2003 do not affect the defendant's right to apply for bail to the High Court in accordance with RSC Ord 79 r 9, contained in Sch 1 to the Civil Procedure Rules 1998 (SI 1998/3132) (see generally, *Onen v Secretary of State for the Home Department*, Unreported, 28 December 2000, CO/4188/00).

4.6 ROLE OF THE CROWN PROSECUTION SERVICE IN EXTRADITION PROCEEDINGS

On 5 July 1996 the Attorney-General formally assigned responsibility for extradition to the Director of Public Prosecutions under s 3(2)(g) of the Prosecution of Offences Act 1985. The Crown Prosecution Service (CPS) represents the requesting state in nearly all extradition cases. In *R v Director of Public Prosecutions ex p Thom* [1995] COD 194 the Divisional Court held that the role of the CPS under the EA 1989 was that of a private solicitor to the requesting state and consequently that many of its powers, for example the power to discontinue proceedings under s 23(3) of the 1985 Act, did not apply in extradition cases.

The EA 2003 amends the Prosecution of Offences Act 1985 to put the CPS's conduct of extradition proceedings onto a statutory footing for the first time.

Section 190(2) inserts s 3(2)(ea) and (eb) into the 1985 Act. These provide that it shall be the duty of the Director to have the conduct of any extradition proceedings and to give, to such extent as he considers appropriate, and to such persons as he considers appropriate, advice on any matters relating to extradition proceedings or proposed extradition proceedings.

Section 3(2A) of the 1985 Act, inserted by s 191(3), makes clear that s 3(2)(ea) does not require the Director to have the conduct of proceedings where the requesting state asks him not to do so. This preserves the right of requesting states to retain private solicitors.

4.7 INITIAL HEARINGS

The EA 2003 introduces a system of initial hearings at which the judge is required to dispose of preliminary issues relating to the defendant's identity and to set a date for the extradition hearing at which the substantive issues arising in the case are to be determined in accordance with the Act.

4.7.1 Initial Hearings in Category 1 Cases

Sections 7 and 8 specify the judge's duties in Category 1 initial hearings.

4.7.1.1 *Identity*

Where the defendant has been arrested under a Part 1 warrant and brought before the judge under s 4(3), or the defendant has been provisionally arrested under s 5 and the documents received from the requesting state and produced to the judge, then the judge must hold a hearing to determine the questions arising under s 7 (s 7(1)).

The judge is required to decide on a balance of probabilities (s 7(3)) whether the person before him is the person in respect of whom the Part 1 warrant was issued (s 7(2)). If he answers this question negatively then the defendant must be discharged (s 7(4)). If he answers the question affirmatively then he must proceed to decide the issues arising under s 8.

Proving the defendant's identity in extradition matters is generally relatively straightforward. If a photograph has been supplied the judge is entitled to compare this with the person in the dock in order to determine whether they are the same person. Admissions or statements by the person on arrest may also be sufficient evidence of identity (*Re Bradshar*, Unreported, 28 February 1984, CO/301/83; *Re Rodriguez*, Unreported, 15 November 1984, CO/952/84; *Re Mullin*, Unreported, 31 July 1992, CO/341/92).

4.7.1.2 *Power to Adjourn*

Section 7(6) provides that in England and Wales the judge has the same powers (as nearly as may be) as a Magistrates' Court would have if the proceedings were the summary trial of an information against the person. One of these powers is the power to adjourn proceedings (Magistrates' Courts Act 1980, s 10(1)). It follows that the judge has the power to adjourn the initial inquiry until such time as the parties are in a position to adduce evidence about the defendant's identity. Generally there will no issue as to identity; however it is a matter which goes to the court's jurisdiction and, where it is in issue, the defendant is entitled to adduce evidence about it (*Re Anthony*, Unreported, 27 June 1995, CO/1657/94).

4.7.1.3 *Matters arising under Section 8*

If the judge decides that it is more likely than not that the person in the dock is the person to whom the Part 1 warrant relates, then he is required by s 7(5) to proceed under s 8.

Section 8(1) requires the judge to do the following:

(a) fix a date on which the extradition hearing is to begin;
(b) inform the defendant of the contents of the Part 1 warrant;
(c) give the defendant the required information about consent;
(d) remand the defendant in custody or on bail.

One of the purposes of the EA 2003 is to speed up the extradition process and to return defendants as quickly as possible. To this end, the Act imposes time limits in a number of places. Section 8(4) provides that the date for the extradition hearing which the judge is required to set by s 8(1)(a) must not be later than the end of the permitted period, which is 21 days starting with the date of the arrest referred to in s 7(1)(a) or (b). However, s 8(5) provides that if, before the date fixed under s 8(1)(a) for the start of the hearing, a party to the proceedings applies to the judge for a later date to be fixed, and the judge believes it is in the interests of justice to do so, he may fix a later date. More than one extension can be granted.

In considering whether to grant an extension under these provisions the judge should keep in mind the requirements of Article 5(4) of the European Convention on Human Rights as he is required to act compatibly with it (Human Rights Act 1998, s 6(1)). Article 5(4) guarantees detained persons the right to adequate time and facilities for the preparation of a challenge to the legality of their detention (*Farmakopoulos v Belgium* (1992) 16 EHRR 187). It follows that the judge must interpret s 8(5) so as not to infringe the defendant's right under the Convention to have sufficient time to gather evidence in support of his defence.

The required information about consent referred to in s 8(1) is defined by s 8(3) to be:

(a) the information that the defendant may consent to his extradition to the Category 1 territory in which the Part 1 warrant was issued;

(b) an explanation of the effect of consent and the procedure that will apply if he gives consent;

(c) that consent must be given before the judge and is irrevocable.

4.7.2 Initial Hearings in Category 2 Cases

4.7.2.1 *Hearing following Arrest under Provisional Warrant*
Where a defendant has been arrested under a provisional warrant then s 74 applies. If neither the warrant nor a copy of it was shown to him at the time of his arrest, the warrant or a copy of it must be shown to him as soon as practicable after his arrest (s 74(2)). The defendant must be brought before the appropriate judge as soon as practicable (s 74(3)). If either of these requirements is not complied with and the person applies to the judge to be discharged, the judge must order his discharge (s 74(5)). However, if the defendant is granted bail by the police, or the Secretary of State decides under s 126 that the request is not to be proceeded with, then there is no requirement to produce the defendant before a judge (s 74(4)(a)).

When the defendant first appears or is brought before the appropriate judge, the judge must, in accordance with s 74(7):

(a) inform him that he is accused of the commission of an offence in a Category 2 territory or that he is alleged to be unlawfully at large after conviction of an offence by a court in a Category 2 territory;

(b) give him the required information about consent;

(c) remand him in custody or on bail.

The required information about consent is defined by s 74(7) to be information:

(a) that the person may consent to his extradition to the Category 2 territory in which he is accused of the commission of an offence or is alleged to have been convicted of an offence;

(b) an explanation of the effect of consent and the procedure that will apply if he gives consent;

(c) that consent must be given in writing and is irrevocable.

If the judge remands the defendant in custody he may later grant bail (s 74(8)).

Under the EA 1989 the period during which a defendant could be detained under a provisional warrant was limited (*Quentin v Governor of Brixton Prison* [1998] COD 193; *Re Abdullah*, Unreported, 2 May 1997, CO/1440/97). The EA 2003 provides a similar restriction. Section 74(10) provides that the judge must order the person's discharge if the documents referred to in s 70(9) (request, etc) are not received by him within the 'required period'. This is defined in s 74(11) as:

(a) 45 days starting with the day on which the person was arrested; or

(b) if the Category 2 territory is designated by order made by the Secretary of State for the purposes of s 74, any longer period permitted by the order.

The Extradition Act 2003 (Designation of Part 2 Territories) Order 2003 (SI 2003/3334), Article 4, designates the following territories for the purposes of s 74(11)(b) with the relevant longer period for each territory following in brackets:

Bolivia (65 days); Bosnia and Herzegovina (65 days); Chile (90 days); Cuba (65 days); Haiti (65 days); Iraq (65 days); Liberia (95 days); Monaco (65 days); Nicaragua (65 days); Panama (65 days); Paraguay (65 days); Peru (95 days); San Marino (65 days); Thailand (65 days); The United States of America (65 days).

Once the documents specified in s 70(9) have been received, the judge must fix a date on which the extradition hearing is to begin, in accordance with s 76(1) and (2). The date fixed must not be later than the end of the permitted period, which is two months starting with the date on which the judge receives the documents (s 76(3)). However, if before the date fixed under s 76(2) a party to the proceedings applies to the judge for a later date to be fixed and the judge believes there are exceptional circumstances, he may fix a later date (s 76(4)). If the extradition hearing does not begin on or before the date fixed under this section and the person applies to the judge to be discharged, the judge must order his discharge (s 76(5)).

For the reasons given above, these provisions must be interpreted so as to be compatible with Article 5(4) of the European Convention on Human Rights.

4.8 THE SECRETARY OF STATE'S ROLE AT THE BEGINNING OF THE EXTRADITION PROCESS

Under the EA 1989 extradition from the UK was an executive act. As well as deciding whether to order extradition at the end of judicial proceedings, the Secretary of State was also required to decide whether to allow proceedings to commence at all. The mechanism by which he signified his consent was by issuing an authority to proceed/order to proceed under s 7 or para 4(2) of Sch 1. He had a discretion whether or not to issue an authority to proceed, and in taking the decision he was required to consider a variety of factors including whether the offence was a political offence, whether interests of the UK would be harmed if the request was allowed to proceed, and whether he would in fact order extradition in due course (*R v Chief Metropolitan Stipendiary Magistrate ex p Government of Denmark* (1983) 79 Cr App R 1, 11).

The authority to proceed was the foundation of the district judge's jurisdiction at committal. The Secretary of State was required to specify the English offences which it appeared to him were constituted by the foreign conduct, and the district judge had no jurisdiction to commit for any offence not included on the authority to proceed (*In re Nielsen* [1984] AC 606, 619). Any defect in the authority to proceed rendered the committal unlawful (*Re Farinha* [1992] Imm LR 174).

In practice, the Secretary of State very seldom refused to issue an authority to proceed and the courts discouraged challenges by the applicant to his decision to issue an authority (*Government of United States of America v Bowe* [1990] 1 AC 500; *R v Governor of Brixton Prison ex p Kahan* [1989] QB 716; *R v Secretary of State for the Home Department ex p Pinochet Ugarte*, Unreported, 27 May 1999, CO/1786/99).

The Home Office Consultation Paper of March 2001 made the case for reducing the Secretary of State's role in extradition proceedings, and for removing it altogether in some cases (see paras 80 and 81). These proposals are largely reflected in the EA 2003. In the following paragraphs the Secretary of State's role at the start of the extradition process is examined.

4.8.1 Category 1 Cases

The EA 2003 removes the Secretary of State entirely from the process in Category 1 cases. As has been seen, the Part 1 warrant is received by the designated authority under s 2(1), and forwarded directly to the appropriate judge if the formalities required by s 2 are complied with. As explained above, the Extradition Act 2003 (Part 1 Designated Authorities) Order 2003 (SI 2003/3190) designates both the National Criminal Intelligence Service and the Crown Agent of the Crown Office in Scotland as designated authorities.

The Secretary of State is only likely to become involved in a Category 1 case if he is required to exercise his powers under s 179 to regulate competing claims to extradition under Part 1 and Part 2. These are considered in Chapter 8. He may also intervene on national security grounds as specified in s 208.

4.8.2 Category 2 Cases

The Secretary of State has a limited role in Category 2 cases.

4.8.2.1 *Section 70 Certificate*
Where the Secretary of State receives a valid request from a Category 2 territory, then he must (subject to s 126) issue a certificate under s 70(1) containing the statement required by s 70(8). He then must send the request, the certificate, and a copy of any relevant Order in Council to the appropriate judge (s 70(9)).

4.8.2.2 *Competing Extradition Requests*
Section 126 deals with competing extradition requests. It applies if:

(a) the Secretary of State receives a valid request for a person's extradition to a Category 2 territory;

(b) the person is in the UK;

(c) before the person is extradited in pursuance of the request or discharged, the Secretary of State receives another valid request for the person's extradition.

Where these conditions are satisfied the Secretary of State may do one of two things. If neither of the requests has been disposed of, he can order proceedings (or further proceedings) on one of the requests to be deferred until the other one has been disposed of. Alternatively, if an order for extradition in pursuance of the request under consideration has been made, he can order the person's extradition to be deferred until the other request has been disposed of. In taking these decisions, s 126(3) requires the Secretary of State to take into account the relative seriousness of the offences concerned; the place where each offence was committed (or was alleged to have been committed); the date when each request was received; and whether, in the case of each offence, the person is accused of its commission (but not alleged to have been convicted) or is alleged to be unlawfully at large after conviction.

These powers are considered further in Chapter 8.

4.8.2.3 *National Security*
The Secretary of State can also intervene in Part 2 cases on national security grounds under s 208.

5

THE EXTRADITION HEARING
IN CATEGORY 1 CASES

5.1 INTRODUCTION

In this chapter the appropriate judge's duties and functions in an extradition hearing under Part 1 of the EA 2003 are considered. This is the hearing at which the appropriate judge must decide whether a person in respect of whom a Part 1 warrant has been issued is to be extradited to the Category 1 territory in which it was issued (s 68(1)). The equivalent hearings under the EA 1989 were known as 'committal hearings'.

In England and Wales the appropriate judge is a District Judge (Magistrates' Courts) designated for the purposes of Part 1 by the Lord Chancellor (s 67(1)(a)).

Under the EA 1989 the district judge's functions at committal were relatively circumscribed. His task was principally to assess the evidence (where a *prima facie* case had to be proved under Part III or Sch 1), or decide whether the conduct alleged was an extradition crime in cases where no evidence was required, and also to determine whether any of the restrictions in s 6 were applicable. Issues relating to delay and whether extradition would breach the defendant's human rights were matters for the High Court on an application for *habeas corpus* under s 11, or for the Secretary of State when he came to decide whether to make an order for return under s 12. The classic exposition of the judge's powers in European Convention cases dealt with under Part III of the EA 1989 is the speech of Lord Templeman in *In re Evans* [1994] 1 WLR 1006, 1010–1111:

> There are thus six steps in the extradition of a suspect from the United Kingdom. First, the foreign court must consider that a charge of serious crime has been properly laid against the suspect on the basis of information which justifies the issue of a warrant for his arrest. Secondly, the administration of the foreign country must consider that the charge, the law of the foreign country and the circumstances justify a request for extradition in accordance with the provisions of the Convention. Thirdly, the foreign state must identify the suspect, authenticate the foreign warrant for his arrest, give particulars of the alleged conduct which constitutes the offence and produce a translation of the relevant foreign law which establishes the offence and makes it punishable by 12 months' imprisonment or more. Fourthly, the Secretary of State must satisfy himself that the request is in order. The Secretary of State must then satisfy himself that equivalent conduct in the United Kingdom would constitute an offence under the law of the United Kingdom punishable by 12 months' imprisonment or more. The Secretary of State may then issue an authority to proceed and must identify and specify the relevant law of the United Kingdom. Fifthly, the metropolitan magistrate sitting as a court of committal must be satisfied, after he has heard representations, that the alleged conduct would constitute a serious offence in the foreign state and in the United Kingdom. In other words the magistrate must be satisfied that a charge of serious crime offensive in the foreign country and offensive in the United Kingdom has been properly laid against the accused. The suspect can then be committed and the magistrate must certify the offence against the law of the United Kingdom which would be constituted by his conduct. Sixthly, subject to any habeas corpus proceedings, the Secretary of State may enforce extradition.

The scheme contained in the EA 2003 represents a fundamentally different approach. Virtually all issues now have to be decided by the appropriate judge at the extradition hearing. There is a right of appeal to the High Court against the judge's decision, however the original jurisdiction that the High Court enjoyed under ss 6 and 11(3) of the EA 1989 has been removed and its function now is essentially to act as a court of appeal from the appropriate judge. Appeals are considered in Chapter 9.

5.2 EXTRADITION HEARINGS UNDER PART 1: A SUMMARY

The extradition hearing in a Category 1 case can be summarized as follows:

(a) The judge must first decide whether the offence specified in the Part 1 warrant is an extradition offence (s 10(2)).

(b) If it is not, then the defendant has to be discharged.

(c) If it is, the judge must go on to consider whether any of the bars to extradition specified in s 11 are applicable.

(d) If none of them are, and the defendant is alleged to be unlawfully at large after conviction, the judge must then consider whether the defendant falls to be discharged under s 20 (convictions in absence).

(e) If s 20 does not apply, or the restrictions in it are not made out, the judge must then consider whether extradition would violate the defendant's rights under the Human Rights Act 1998 (s 21).

(f) If it would not, he must order the defendant's extradition to the requesting Category 1 territory.

(g) The extradition hearing is then at an end. Subject to any appeal by the defendant to the High Court or House of Lords, he is liable to be extradited.

5.3 THE JUDGE'S POWERS AT THE EXTRADITION HEARING

Section 9(1) provides that in England and Wales at the extradition hearing the appropriate judge has the same powers (as nearly as may be) as a Magistrates' Court would have if the proceedings were the summary trial of an information against the person in respect of whom the Part 1 warrant was issued. This provision applies the general powers of a Magistrates' Court in Part I of the Magistrates' Courts Act 1980. Where the judge adjourns the extradition hearing he must remand the person in custody or on bail (s 9(4)). If the defendant is remanded in custody he may later be granted bail (s 9(5)).

5.4 BURDEN AND STANDARD OF PROOF

Section 206 contains provisions relating to the burden and standard of proof. Section 206(1) applies if, in proceedings under this Act, a question arises as to burden or standard of proof. By s 206(2), the question must be decided by applying any enactment or rule of law that would apply if the proceedings were proceedings for an offence. Any enactment or rule of law so applied must be applied as if the person whose extradition is sought (or who has been extradited) were accused of an offence and the Category 1 or Category 2 territory concerned were the prosecution.

5.5 AUTHENTICATION OF DOCUMENTS

Section 202(1) provides that a Part 1 warrant may be received in evidence in proceedings under the EA 2003. Sections 203 and 204 permit faxed or electronic copies to be used also.

By s 202(2) and (3), any other document issued in a Category 1 or Category 2 territory may be received in evidence if it is duly authenticated. A document issued in a Category 1 or Category 2 territory is duly authenticated if (and only if) one of these applies:

(a) it purports to be signed by a judge, magistrate, or other judicial authority of the territory;

(b) it purports to be authenticated by the oath or affirmation of a witness.

The oath must be given in court in the UK and not the requesting state: *Re Majeed Ahmed*, Unreported, 14 July 1983, CO/85/1983.

In *Re De Canha*, Unreported, 7 July 1997, CO/0769/97, the Divisional Court held that a court clerk was a proper officer of the foreign state for the purposes of s 26 of the EA 1989, which is in similar terms to s 202. Other cases in which the status of foreign officials has been considered are *R v Bow Street Magistrates' Court ex p Van Der Holst* (1986) 83 Cr App R 114 (public prosecutor in the Netherlands is a judicial officer); *Re Espinosa* [1986] Crim LR 684 (notary public is a proper officer); and *Re Kern*, Unreported, 25 March 1987, CO/502/96 (deputy court clerk is a proper officer).

In *Schtraks v Government of Israel* [1964] AC 556, 582 the House of Lords held that material submitted by the defendant in support of his religious persecution submissions did not have to be authenticated as required by the EA 1870. Section 202(5) of the EA 2003 provides that the authentication requirements in s 202(2) and (3) do not prevent a document that is not duly authenticated from being received in evidence in proceedings under the EA 2003. This preserves the right of the defendant to rely on unauthenticated material in support, for example, of an extraneous considerations argument under s 13 or s 81 (see 5.8.2 and 6.9.2 below).

5.6 CHARGES AND MULTIPLE OFFENCES

5.6.1 English Charges

The almost invariable practice under the EA 1989 was for the requesting state to supply a list of the English offences which it alleged were constituted by equivalent conduct, and the same practice will no doubt be followed in extradition hearings under the EA 2003 where dual criminality is required. In *R v Bow Street Magistrates' Court ex p Kline*, Unreported, 30 June 1999, CO/813/99, the Court explained:

Although there is nothing in the statute or any subordinate legislation which requires it, it is the practice for the Government to set out in the form of what are described as charges the offences which would have been committed in England and Wales as a result of the allegations in an accusation case or the conviction in a conviction case.

In *R v Governor of Pentonville Prison ex p Osman* [1990] 1 WLR 277, 302 Lloyd LJ observed:

The practice in extradition cases has been that the English 'offences' are stated in the authority to proceed in very general terms. The magistrate is not, of course, concerned with whether the offence is made out in foreign law. He is concerned solely with whether the evidence would support committal for trial in England, if the conduct complained of had taken place in England: see *In re Nielsen* [1984] AC 606. So the magistrate is furnished at the commencement of the hearing with a schedule of charges based on the alleged conduct and formulated in accordance with English law. The schedule of charges is frequently amended in the course of the hearing.

In *Charron v Government of the United States* [2000] 1 WLR 1793 the Privy Council held in a case involving the Bahamas Extradition Act 1994 (in similar form to the EA 1989) that a failure to supply a list of charges would only invalidate the committal if the defendant could demonstrate that he had been prejudiced by a lack of particulars.

The charges are prepared by the Crown Prosecution Service for the use of the court and the defendant as an aid to identifying the precise conduct of which the defendant is accused or has been convicted in the requesting state. It is important to recognize, however, that the charges have no formal status as such in the extradition process. The appropriate judge is not limited to determining whether the conduct in the Part 1 warrant (or extradition request in Part 2 cases) amounts to the extradition offences in the list of charges. His task is to determine whether the conduct amounts to an extradition offence as defined in the Act irrespective of whether it is one of the offences specified on the list of English charges (*R v Bow Street Magistrates' Court ex p Kline*, Unreported, 30 June 1999, CO/813/99).

5.6.2 Multiple Offences

In an extradition hearing the appropriate judge must apply the relevant statutory provisions in respect of each of the offences contained in the Part 1 warrant (or extradition request in Part 2 cases). Section 207 provides that the Secretary of State may by order provide for the Act to have effect with specified modifications in relation to a case where a Part 1 warrant is issued in respect of more than one offence or a request for extradition is made in respect of more than one offence.

The Extradition Act 2003 (Multiple Offences) Order 2003 (SI 2003/3150) has been made under s 207. Article 2(2) provides that the Act is to have effect with the modifications specified in the Schedule to the Order in relation to a case where the Part 1 warrant or extradition request contains more than one offence.

Accordingly, the following chapters should be read subject to the modifications contained in the Schedule to the Order where the extradition hearing is concerned with multiple offences.

5.7 IS THE OFFENCE SPECIFIED IN THE PART 1 WARRANT AN EXTRADITION OFFENCE?

Extradition offences were considered at 2.3 above. The district judge is required to consider the particulars of conduct on the warrant and to determine whether it amounts to an extradition offence within the definitions set out in ss 64–66.

In determining this question the judge must carry out a transposition exercise on the conduct contained in the Part 1 warrant. This process was explained in *R v Governor of Pentonville Prison ex p Tarling* (1980) 70 Cr App R 77, 136:

> In considering the jurisdiction aspect it is necessary to suppose that England is substituted for Singapore as regards all the circumstances of the case connected with the latter country, and to examine the question whether upon that hypothesis and upon the evidence adduced the English courts would have jurisdiction to try the offences charged.

The speech of Lord Hope of Craighead in *R v Metropolitan Stipendiary Magistrate ex p Pinochet Ugarte (No 3)* [2000] 1 AC 147, 229–240 is a useful example of how the question of whether the alleged conduct amounts to an extradition offence is to be carried out.

5.8 BARS TO EXTRADITION

The bars to extradition are specified in s 11(1)(a) to (f) and defined in ss 12–21. Each will be considered in turn.

5.8.1 The Rule against Double Jeopardy (Section 12)

Section 12 provides a bar to return where extradition would violate the rule against double jeopardy, also known as *non bis in idem*. It is similar, but not identical, to s 6(3) of the EA 1989.

The defendant's return to a Category 1 country is barred by reason of the rule against double jeopardy if and only if it appears that he would be entitled to be discharged under any rule of law relating to previous acquittal or conviction on the assumption:

(a) that the conduct constituting the extradition offence constituted an offence in the part of the UK where the judge exercises jurisdiction;

(b) that the person were charged with the extradition offence in that part of the UK.

The purpose of this provision is to stop a defendant from being prosecuted twice for the same offence in different jurisdictions.

A defendant can rely on s 12 in circumstances where, if he were charged in the UK with the conduct for which his extradition is being sought, he could plead *autrefois acquit* or *autrefois convict* in the narrow sense in which the pleas were stated by the House of Lords in *Connelly v Director of Public Prosecutions* [1964] AC 125 and *Director of Public Prosecutions v Humphreys* [1977] AC 1.

In *Re Oncel* [2001] EWHC Admin 1142 the applicant had been tried and acquitted by a military court in Turkey. The Court of Appeal set aside the acquittal and ordered a retrial and an arrest warrant was issued. The applicant's extradition was requested from the UK. He sought to rely on s 6(3), arguing that as he had been acquitted, if charged with the offence in the UK, he would be able to plead *autrefois acquit*. His argument was rejected. Lord Woolf CJ said (paras 14–15):

Although the position has to be governed on the basis that the person is being charged with the offence in the United Kingdom, it does not necessarily follow that the United Kingdom will treat what has happened in another country such as Turkey in exactly the same way as we would treat what occurred in Turkey if the same facts had occurred in the United Kingdom . . . What is critical is whether there is more than one prosecution involved.

Because the second trial resulted from the same prosecution, the applicant was not in 'double' jeopardy and he could not rely on s 6(3) even though in analogous circumstances in England (acquittal by a jury) the acquittal would have been final.

The defendant may also be entitled to rely on s 12 in circumstances where he could rely on the doctrine of abuse of process as it applies where a defendant is re-prosecuted for a different offence arising out of the same facts as an offence of which he has already been acquitted or convicted.

In *Connelly v Director of Public Prosecutions* [1964] AC 125 and *Director of Public Prosecutions v Humphreys* [1977] AC 1 the majority held that outside the narrow confines of the pleas of *autrefois acquit* and *autrefois convict* there was a wider discretionary power, not within the scope of either plea, to stay proceedings where a situation of double jeopardy was recognized as occurring. This power was exercised in *Beedie* [1998] QB 356 where a landlord pleaded guilty to various offences under the Health and Safety at Work etc Act 1974. One of the victims died and he was charged with manslaughter. The trial judge refused a plea of *autrefois convict*. The Court of Appeal held that the plea of *autrefois* is applicable only where the same offence is charged in the second indictment, but that the judge had discretion to stay the proceedings where the second offence arises out of the same or substantially the same set of facts as the first, and that discretion should be exercised in favour of the defendant unless the prosecution establishes that there are special circumstances for not doing so.

5.8.2 Extraneous Considerations (Section 13)

The jurisdiction to decline to extradite a defendant because he is accused or has been convicted of a political offence is a long standing principle of extradition law (*Re Castioni* [1891] 1 QB 149; *In re Meunier* [1894] 2 QB 415). From the nineteenth century onwards, when much of Europe was in a state of political upheaval, Parliament and the courts were anxious to ensure that extradition was not used as a tool of political repression. In *R v Governor of Pentonville Prison ex p Cheng* [1973] AC 931, 944, Lord Diplock said that s 3(1) of the EA 1870 (no extradition for political offences):

... contemplated that a foreign government in its eagerness to revenge itself upon a political opponent might attempt to misuse an extradition treaty for this purpose.

During the twentieth century, extradition treaties came to include bars to extradition where there was a risk that the defendant would suffer discrimination in the requesting state on the grounds of his race, religion, nationality, or political opinions (see eg, Article 3 of the European Convention on Extradition 1957). The growth of international terrorism in the latter part of the twentieth century was reflected in legislation which reduced the scope of the political offence exception and in the attitude of the courts to those who sought refugee status after committing acts of violence (see *T v Secretary of State for the Home Department* [1996] AC 742). The Suppression of Terrorism Act 1978 deemed a range of violent offences (murder, kidnapping, etc) not to be political offences for the purposes of extradition, and they were therefore excluded from the scope of the protection given by s 6(1)(a) of the EA 1989.

The EA 2003 has taken this trend to its conclusion by removing entirely the political offence exception to extradition for both Category 1 and Category 2 countries. However, extradition remains barred where there is a risk of persecution on one or more of the grounds specified in the Act.

Section 13 provides that a person's extradition to a Category 1 territory is barred by reason of extraneous considerations if and only if it appears that:

(a) the Part 1 warrant issued in respect of him (though purporting to be issued on account of the extradition offence) is in fact issued for the purpose of prosecuting or punishing him on account of his race, religion, nationality, gender, sexual orientation, or political opinions;

(b) if extradited he might be prejudiced at his trial or punished, detained, or restricted in his personal liberty by reason of his race, religion, nationality, gender, sexual orientation, or political opinions.

These provisions are derived from s 6(1)(c) and (d) of the EA 1989, which in turn were derived from provisions in the Fugitive Offenders Act 1967, and so much of the earlier case law remains relevant.

It is important to note that both s 13(a) and (b) require there to be a causal link between the issue of the warrant, or the likely prejudice, and one of the stated grounds (*Lodhi v Governor of HMP Brixton* [2001] EWHC 178, para 89 *et seq*).

The defendant bears the burden of showing that one of these defences is made out on the evidence. In relation to s 13(b), which is concerned with what may happen in the future, he does not need to show that it is more likely than not that he will be prejudiced. It is sufficient if he can establish that there is a 'reasonable chance' or 'serious possibility' of prejudice. In *Fernandez v Government of Singapore* [1981] 1 WLR 987 the House of Lords considered the provisions of s 4(1)(c) of the Fugitive Offenders Act 1967, from which s 6(1)(d) of the EA 1989 was derived (now s 13(b) of the EA 2003). It was suggested that the defendant had to establish the defence on a balance of probabilities. This contention was rejected by Lord Diplock (p 994):

My Lords, bearing in mind the relative gravity of the consequences of the court's expectation being falsified either in one way or in the other, I do not think that the test of the applicability of paragraph (c) is that the court must be satisfied that it is more likely than not that the fugitive will be detained or restricted if he is returned. A lesser degree of likelihood is, in my view, sufficient; and I would not quarrel with the way in which the test was stated by the magistrate or with the alternative way in which it was expressed by the Divisional Court. 'A reasonable chance,' 'substantial grounds for thinking,' 'a serious possibility'. I see no significant difference between these various ways of describing the degree of likelihood of the detention or restriction of the fugitive on his return which justifies the court in giving effect to the provisions of section 4 (1) (c).

Section 13 reflects the grounds for claiming refugee status under Article 1A(2) of the Convention and Protocol relating to the Status of Refugees (1951) (Cmd 9171) and (1967) (Cmd 3906). This provides that persecution on the grounds of 'race, religion, nationality, membership of a particular social group or political opinion' is grounds for claiming refugee status. It follows that much of the asylum case law under the Convention will be relevant to s 13:

(a) for persecution on grounds of gender, see *R v Immigration Appeal Tribunal ex p Shah* [1999] 2 AC 629;

(b) for persecution on grounds of sexual orientation, see *Z v Secretary of State for the Home Department* [2002] EWCA Civ 952; *Egan v Canada* (1995) 29 CRR (2d) 79; *NAGL v Minister for Home Affairs* (2000) (2) SA 1.

The defendant is able to rely on any relevant material in support of a submission under s 13, whether or not it is admissible as a matter of strict evidence (*Schtraks v Government of Israel* [1964] AC 556).

5.8.3 Passage of Time (Section 14)

A person's extradition to a Category 1 territory is barred by reason of the passage of time if (and only if) it appears that it would be unjust or oppressive to extradite him by reason of the passage of time

(a) since he is alleged to have committed the extradition offence; or

(b) since he is alleged to have become unlawfully at large (as the case may be).

This provision is similar but not identical to s 11(3)(b) of the EA 1989, which was derived from s 8(3) of the Fugitive Offenders Act 1967 (see *Union of India v Narang* [1978] AC 278). These provisions gave rise to a considerable amount of case law. The principles are as follows (*R v Secretary of State for the Home Department ex p Patel* (1992) 7 Admin LR 56, 65–66):

(a) 'Unjust' and 'oppressive' were construed in the context of the 1967 Act by Lord Diplock in the House of Lords in *Kakis v Government of the Republic of Cyprus* [1978] 1 WLR 779, 782:

'Unjust' I regard as directed primarily to the risk of prejudice to the accused in the conduct of the trial itself, 'oppressive' as directed to hardship to the accused resulting from changes in his circumstances that have occurred during the period to be taken into consideration; but there is room for overlapping, and between them they would cover all cases where to return him would not be fair.

(b) The relevant period runs from the date of the alleged offence to the date of the challenge (*Kakis v Government of Cyprus* [1978] 1 WLR 779, 782; *R v Governor of Pentonville Prison ex p Tarling* [1979] 1 WLR 1417, 1425; *Re Davies* [1998] COD 30).

(c) The court is required to ascertain the facts relied upon by the defendant as giving rise to injustice or oppression. The relevant standard of proof is the balance of probabilities (*Union of India v Narang* [1978] AC 278, 293–4).

(d) A refusal to return the defendant must be based on injustice or oppression caused by the passage of time as it operated in the circumstances of the particular case to give to that particular passage of time a quality or significance which leads to the conclusion that return would be unjust or oppressive (*Kakis v Government of Cyprus* [1978] 1 WLR 779, 785; *Union of India v Narang* [1978] AC 278, 290). In other words, delay must have operated as the 'cradle of events' giving rise to injustice or oppression (*Kakis v Government of Cyprus* [1978] 1 WLR 779, 790).

(e) The defendant cannot rely on the passage of time caused by him fleeing the country, or concealing his crime or whereabouts, or evading arrest. However, if the requesting government can be shown to have been inexcusably dilatory in taking steps to bring the defendant to justice, then this may serve to establish the necessary injustice and oppressiveness, whereas the issue may be left in some doubt if the only known fact relates to the passage of time (*Kakis v Government of Cyprus* [1978] 1 WLR 779, 785 *per* Lord Fraser). The conflict between these *dicta* of Lord Fraser and Lord Diplock in *Kakis* at p 783—where he appeared to suggest that dilatoriness on the part of the requesting state was not a relevant factor—was explained by Woolf LJ in *R v Governor of·Brixton Prison ex p Osman (No 4)* [1992] 1 All ER 579, 587.

(f) A sense of false security engendered in the defendant is also a relevant consideration. If the actions of the government have led him to believe that he will not be extradited then it may be oppressive if the government then proceeds to try to do so (*Kakis v Government of Cyprus* [1978] 1 WLR 779, 790 *per* Lord Scarman).

The jurisdiction to discharge under s 14 has similarities with the common law domestic abuse of process jurisdiction in so far as both may require consideration of the effect of delay on the fairness of the trial (*Attorney-General's Reference (No 2 of 2001)* [2003] UKHL 68; *Attorney-General's Reference (No 1 of 1990)* [1992] QB 630; cf *Re Anwar*, Unreported, 2 November 1993, CO/216/93). If the defendant can show he will be prejudiced at his trial by reason of the passage of time because evidence has been lost, memories have faded, or for any other reason, then the statutory bar to extradition is engaged.

It is important to recognize, however, that the judge's powers under s 14 are broader than the court's power in domestic criminal cases. This is because discharge can be granted in extradition cases where no question as to the fairness of the trial arises but it would nevertheless be oppressive to return the defendant.

The oppression limb of s 14 allows the court to consider a wide variety of factors. Whilst no exhaustive list can be given, factors which have been held to give rise to oppression include the effect of return on the defendant's own life and that of his family (*Cookeson v Government of Australia* [2001] EWHC Admin 149 (serious psychiatric illness of defendant's adult son of whom he was principal carer); *Re Ashley-Riddle*, Unreported, 22 November 1993, CO/216/93 (oppression to school age son)), and health issues.

Where the defendant's health has deteriorated since the alleged offence then if the deterioration is severe enough it may be oppressive to return him (*Re Davies* [1998] COD 30; *R v Secretary of State for the Home Department ex p Kingdom of Belgium*, Unreported, 15 February 2000, CO/236/00). In particular, where the defendant's health is such that he is unfit to stand trial, and the evidence shows that he is unlikely ever to be fit to be tried then, given that the purpose of extradition proceedings is to return for trial, return in such circumstances would *per se* be unjust and/or oppressive. Extradition of a seriously ill person may also raise issues under Articles 2 and/or 3 of the European Convention on Human Rights (*Bulus v Sweden* (1984) 35 DR 57; *D v United Kingdom* (1997) 24 EHRR 423). Extradition and the European Convention on Human Rights is considered in Chapter 7.

Delay may be so protracted that it is oppressive to return the defendant for that reason alone, irrespective of whether the defendant can point to specific harm arising from it. In *R v Secretary of State ex p Patel* (1995) 7 Admin LR 56 there had been a delay of three and a half years in making the extradition request from the start of inquiries into offences occurring several years previously.

The High Court held that the Home Secretary had erred in his approach to this delay and that the delay was such that the only reasonable conclusion was that it would be unjust or oppressive to return the defendant. Henry LJ said at pp 51–52:

Wherever law is practised, justice is reproached by delay. There is a real danger that those of us who have spent a lifetime in the law become inured to delay. So too laymen associate the law with delay, and their expectation of it may harden them to the fact of it. So the years trip off the tongue, and so we reach a position where a citizen may be surrendered to face a trial in another state for matters at least 9 years stale without examination of the reasons for the length of the delay or consequences of it . . . So it is we are left with a delay period . . . of 9 to nearly 12 years, with yet some time to pass before trial. It is salutary to look back over one's own life to evaluate the real length of that period, so as not to regard it just as a figure on a piece of paper. And when, in all the circumstances of this case, we additionally consider that the 6 years of false security included in that period, and then set that against the bland few lines dealing with lapse of time in the affidavit in support of the Minister's decision . . . we conclude that the Minister's decision cannot stand. We judge the irresistible inference to be drawn from the facts in this case is that it would be unjust and oppressive to surrender the applicant, and that the Minister could not properly have reached any other conclusion.

In *Sagman v Government of Turkey* [2001] EWHC Admin 474 the Turkish Government submitted insufficient papers to the UK which were repeatedly returned for amendment. This pattern continued for a number of years. Rose LJ allowed the defendant's application for *habeas corpus* under s 11(3)(b) of the 1989 Act on the grounds that the delay by itself made return unjust and oppressive (para 27):

The history of this matter, as I have set it out, in my judgment demonstrates both oppression and injustice if the applicant were to be returned to Turkey. The length of delay in this case is not only enormous in itself, in that 15 years or thereabouts has elapsed since the criminal conduct is said to have taken place, but there have been many, many years during which the Turkish government has made no significant attempt to obtain the applicant's extradition . . . the whole history of this matter is such as to demonstrate oppression resulting from delay in his case.

Re Oncel [2001] EWHC Admin 1142 also involved a Turkish request, for offences committed in 1980. Extradition was requested in 2000. Lord Woolf CJ ordered the applicant's discharge under s 11(3)(b) on the basis of the delay alone without identifying any specific feature as giving rise to oppression.

5.8.4 Age (Section 15)

Section 15 introduces a new bar to extradition based on the defendant's age. Extradition of a person who would have been under the age of criminal responsibility at the time the alleged offence was committed is now prohibited.

The defendant's extradition to a Category 1 territory is barred by reason of his age if (and only if) it would be conclusively presumed because of his age that he could not be guilty of the extradition offence on the assumption:

(a) that the conduct constituting the extradition offence constituted an offence in the part of the UK where the judge exercises jurisdiction;

(b) that the person carried out the conduct when the extradition offence was committed (or alleged to be committed);

(c) that the person carried out the conduct in the part of the UK where the judge exercises jurisdiction.

These assumptions require the court to assume that the offence was committed by the defendant in the UK and that the conduct amounts to an offence in the UK. The question then is whether the defendant would be conclusively presumed not to be guilty on the grounds of his age.

In England and Wales it is conclusively presumed that no child under the age of ten years can be guilty of any offence (Children and Young Persons Act 1933, s 50).

5.8.5 Hostage-taking Considerations (Section 16)

Section 16 provides a new bar to extradition, derived from Article 9 of the International Convention against the Taking of Hostages, which opened for signature at New York on 18 December 1979 (available at www.unodc.org/unodc/terrorism_convention_hostages.html). Article 9(1)(b)(ii) of the Convention provides:

A request for the extradition of an alleged offender, pursuant to this Convention, shall not be granted if the requested State Party has substantial grounds for believing . . . that the person's position may be prejudiced . . . for the reason that communication with him by the appropriate authorities of the State entitled to exercise rights of protection cannot be effected.

A person's extradition to a Category 1 territory is barred by reason of hostage-taking considerations if (and only if) the territory is a party to the Hostage-taking Convention and it appears that:

(a) if extradited he might be prejudiced at his trial because communication between him and the 'appropriate authorities' would not be possible;

(b) the act or omission constituting the extradition offence also constitutes an offence under s 1 of the Taking of Hostages Act 1982 or an attempt to commit such an offence.

The appropriate authorities are the authorities of the territory which are entitled to exercise rights of protection in relation to him (ie, the relevant consular authorities).

5.8.6 Speciality (Section 17)

Speciality (also called 'specialty') is a rule of extradition law that is intended to ensure that a person extradited is not dealt with in the requesting state for any offence other than that for which he was extradited. The term derives from the French *specialité* which means 'particularity' (Feller, 'Reflections on the nature of the speciality principle in extradition relations' (1977) 12 Israel Law Rev 466).

The rule as stated has been widely relaxed in modern extradition legislation, including the EA 2003. That relaxation is generally expressed in one or both of two ways:

(a) First, the requesting state may be permitted to deal with the defendant for offences other than those for which he was returned which are disclosed by the facts upon which his surrender was based. This may be expressed to include in some cases greater as well as lesser offences.

(b) Secondly, the requesting state may be permitted to seek from the requested state its consent to try the defendant for another offence not covered by its original request, provided that the offence is extraditable.

Section 17(1) of the EA 2003 incorporates speciality protection for defendants whose return is sought by a Category 1 territory. A person's extradition to a Category 1 territory is barred by reason of speciality if (and only if) there are no 'speciality arrangements' with the Category 1 territory. This provision is analogous to, but not identical to, s 6(4) of the EA 1989.

Section 17(2) states that there are speciality arrangements with a Category 1 territory if, under the law of that territory, or arrangements made between it and the UK, a person who is extradited to the territory from the UK may be dealt with in the territory for an offence committed before his extradition only if either:

(a) the offence is:

(i) the offence in respect of which the person is extradited;

(ii) an extradition offence disclosed by the same facts as that offence;

(iii) an extradition offence in respect of which the appropriate judge gives his consent under s 54;

(iv) an offence which is not punishable with imprisonment or another form of detention;

(v) an offence in respect of which the person will not be detained in connection with his trial, sentence, or appeal;

(vi) an offence in respect of which the person waives the right that he would have (but for s 17(3)(f)) not to be dealt with for the offence, or

(b) the person is given the opportunity to leave the Category 1 territory and he does not do so before the end of 45 days starting with the day he arrives in the Category 1 territory, or he does leave before the end of the permitted period and returns there.

These protections may be found in the requesting state's domestic law (*Ex p Bouvier* (1872) 12 Cox CC 303 (circular instruction issued to the law officers in France sufficient legal provision guaranteeing speciality protection)); or the treaty governing extradition (see eg, Article 14 of the European Convention on Extradition 1957; United States of America (Extradition) Order 1976 (SI 1976/2144), Sch 1, Article 12); or in an arrangement with the requesting state of general application or made for the particular case.

Section 17(6) provides that arrangements may be made with Commonwealth countries or British overseas territories for a particular case or more generally. Section 17(7) provides that a certificate issued by the Secretary of State confirming the existence of such arrangements with a Commonwealth country or British overseas territory and stating the terms of the arrangement is conclusive.

A conclusive certificate may only be issued by the Secretary of State in relation to Commonwealth countries and British overseas territories. Although arrangements may be made with other territories, any certificate will not be conclusive, and the court therefore has jurisdiction to inquire into the effectiveness of the arrangements and whether they provide the protections required by s 17(3) and (4) (*R v Secretary of State for the Home Department, ex p Launder (No 2)* [1998] QB 944).

5.8.7 Extradition Barred by Reason of Earlier Extradition to the UK (Sections 18 and 19)

Sections 18 and 19 prohibit the defendant's extradition under certain circumstances where he has already been extradited to the UK from a Category 1 territory (s 18) or non-Category 1 territory (s 19). The prohibition on re-extradition is closely related to the rule on speciality (*R v Secretary of State for the Home Department ex p Johnson* [1999] QB 1174).

A person's extradition to a Category 1 territory is barred by reason of his earlier extradition to the UK from another Category 1 territory if and only if (s 18):

(a) the person was extradited to the UK from another Category 1 territory (the extraditing territory);

(b) under arrangements between the UK and the extraditing territory, that territory's consent is required to the person's extradition from the UK to the Category 1 territory in respect of the extradition offence under consideration;

(c) that consent has not been given on behalf of the extraditing territory and the arrangements do not treat it as having been given.

Article 15 of the European Convention on Extradition 1957 is an example of the arrangements referred to in s 18(b). It provides:

Except as provided for in Article 14, paragraph 1(b), the requesting Party shall not, without the consent of the requested Party, surrender to another Party or to a third State a person surrendered to the requesting party and sought by the said other Party or third State in respect of offences committed before his surrender.

A person's extradition to a Category 1 territory is barred by reason of his earlier extradition to the UK from a non-Category 1 territory if and only if (s 19):

(a) the person was extradited to the UK from a territory that is not a Category 1 territory (the extraditing territory);

(b) under arrangements between the UK and the extraditing territory, that territory's consent is required to the person's being dealt with in the UK in respect of the extradition offence under consideration;

(c) consent has not been given on behalf of the extraditing territory to the person's extradition from the UK to the Category 1 territory in respect of the extradition offence under consideration.

5.8.8 Convictions in Absence (Section 20)

Trials *in absentia* are a common feature of civil law jurisdictions (*R v Governor of Brixton Prison ex p Caborn-Waterfield* [1960] 2 QB 498; *R v Governor of Pentonville Prison ex p Zezza* [1983] 1 AC 46; *Lodhi v Governor of HMP Brixton* [2001] EWHC 178; *Re Foy*, Unreported, 14 April 2000, CO/3969/99). Section 20 is intended to ensure that defendants who were convicted *in absentia* but who did not have an opportunity to appear at their trial (eg, because they were unaware of it) are not extradited unless they are guaranteed a fair trial in their presence in the Category 1 requesting state.

Section 6(2) of the EA 1989 provided a bar to return where a defendant had been convicted in his absence and it was not in the interests of justice to return him. Section 20 removes this generalized test and replaces it with an inquiry into whether the defendant deliberately absented himself from his trial. If he did so then he is not able to rely on this fact to avoid extradition.

The judge is required to proceed under s 20 if the defendant is alleged to be unlawfully at large after conviction of an extradition offence (s 11(4)).

The first question to be decided under s 20 is whether the defendant was convicted in his presence (s 20(1)). If he was, the inquiry under s 20 is at an end, and the judge must proceed under s 21 (s 20(2)).

If the judge decides that the defendant was convicted in his absence he must then decide whether the defendant deliberately absented himself from his trial (s 20(3)). If the judge decides that he did, he must proceed under s 21 (s 20(4)).

If the judge decides that the person did not deliberately absent himself he must decide whether he would be entitled to a retrial or (on appeal) to a review amounting to a retrial (s 20(5)). This may require the judge to hear expert evidence of foreign law. Although s 20(5) uses the word 'entitled', an undertaking by the requesting state that the defendant will be given a retrial may be sufficient, even if he is not guaranteed a retrial as a matter of law (*Lodhi v Governor of HM Prison Brixton* [2001] EWHC 178; *Re Peci*, Unreported, 5 November 1999, CO/1368/99).

If the judge decides that the defendant would be entitled to a retrial then he must proceed under s 21. If the judge decides that question in the negative he must order the person's discharge.

Section 20(8) specifies the ingredients of a retrial sufficient for the purposes of s 20(5). The judge should not regard as a retrial or (on appeal) a review amounting to a retrial, any proceedings that do not include provision for:

(a) the suspect to be present at the retrial;

(b) the suspect to have like rights to hear and examine witnesses as he would have done at the original trial;

(c) the suspect to have the same right to publicly funded legal services as any suspect or defendant.

5.8.9 Human Rights (Section 20)

Section 21 prohibits the judge from ordering extradition where to do so would be incompatible with the defendant's Convention rights within the meaning of the Human Rights Act 1998. This topic is dealt with separately in Chapter 7.

5.9 OTHER BARS TO EXTRADITION

5.9.1 Physical or Mental Condition (Section 25)

Section 25 gives the judge power to discharge the defendant on the grounds of his physical or mental condition at any stage of the proceedings.

Section 25 applies if at any time in the extradition hearing it appears to the judge that the condition in s 25(2) is satisfied (s 25(1)). This condition is that the physical or mental condition of the person in respect of whom the Part 1 warrant is issued is such that it would be unjust or oppressive to extradite him.

If the condition is satisfied the judge must either order the person's discharge, or adjourn the extradition hearing until it appears to him that the condition in s 25(2) is no longer satisfied.

Extradition of a defendant who is unfit to stand trial is *per se* oppressive (*Re Davies* [1998] COD 30). For the approach of the Secretary of State under the

EA 1989, see *R v Secretary of State for the Home Department ex p Kingdom of Belgium*, Unreported, 15 February 2000, CO/236/00.

Extradition of a person who is physically or mentally ill may also violate Article 3 of the ECHR if the illness is sufficiently severe (*Bulus v Sweden* (1984) 35 DR 57): see Chapter 7, at 7.3.3.

5.9.2 Abuse of Process and Bad Faith

Prior to the enactment of the Human Rights Act 1998 it was established that neither the court of committal nor the High Court had jurisdiction to discharge a defendant in extradition proceedings on the grounds of abuse of process (*Atkinson v Government of the United States of America* [1971] AC 197; *R v Governor of Pentonville Prison ex p Sinclair* [1991] 2 AC 64; *R v Governor of Pentonville Prison ex p Alves* [1993] AC 284, 294; *In re Schmidt* [1995] 1 AC 399).

Under the EA 1989 the High Court had a statutory jurisdiction under s 11(3)(c) in Part III cases to discharge a defendant where it concluded that the accusation against him was not made in good faith in the interests of justice (*R (Saifi) v Governor of HMP Brixton* [2001] 1 WLR 1134; *Re Sutej* [2003] EWHC 1940 (Admin)) but, other than that, abuse of process or bad faith on the part of the requesting state were matters for the Secretary of State to consider at the order for return stage.

In *R (Kashamu) v Governor of Brixton Prison* [2002] QB 887 the applicants contended that, following the incorporation of Article 5(4) of the ECHR, as scheduled to the Human Rights Act 1998, the Magistrates' Court had jurisdiction to determine whether extradition proceedings against them amounted to an abuse of process. They argued that the absence of any judicial abuse of process jurisdiction was inconsistent with Article 5(4) of the Convention, which requires the 'lawfulness' of detention (*inter alia* for the purposes of extradition under Article 5(1)(f)) to be 'speedily' decided by a 'court'. In this context, 'lawfulness' does not just mean domestic lawfulness, but also means lawfulness in the Convention sense, ie non-arbitrary detention (*R v Governor of Brockhill Prison ex p Evans* [2001] AC 19, 38). Detention arising from bad faith or abuse of power, in particular, renders detention arbitrary and unlawful under the Convention. Consequently, the applicants contended that the effect of incorporation of Article 5(4) into domestic law was to confer such a jurisdiction on the court of committal.

The Administrative Court upheld the applicants' arguments, holding that the jurisprudence of the European Court of Human Rights meant that, in order to comply with the requirements in Article 5(4), the Magistrates' Court hearing the committal proceedings had jurisdiction to determine the question of whether a fugitive's detention was lawful. The Court said that the district judge's obligation under s 6(1) of the Human Rights Act 1998 Act to act compatibly with the

Convention required him to make a determination under Article 5(4) as to whether the detention was lawful by English domestic law, complied with the general requirements of the Convention and was not arbitrary. Rose LJ said at paras 32–34:

What is in issue in the present case is whether, when lawful extradition procedures are being used, a resultant detention may be unlawful by virtue of abuse of the court's process. The magistrates' court, rather than the High Court, is, in my judgment, the appropriate tribunal for hearing evidence and submissions, finding facts relevant to abuse and doing so speedily. Furthermore, as it seems to me, the district judge's obligation under section 6(1) of the Human Rights Act 1998 to act compatibly with Convention rights requires him to make a determination under article 5(4). It seems to me that . . . he must consider whether the detention is lawful by English domestic law, complies with the general requirements of the Convention and is not open to criticism for arbitrariness . . . What is pertinent here in the present cases is solely whether the detention is unlawful by English domestic law and/or arbitrary, because of bad faith or deliberate abuse of the English courts' procedure.

Although the issue has yet to be decided under the EA 2003, it is submitted that the reasoning in *R (Kashamu) v Governor of Brixton Prison* [2002] QB 887 is equally applicable to the new Act, including persons detained under a EAW. Hence, it is submitted that persons arrested under the EA 2003 can challenge their extradition on the grounds that the request is made in bad faith, or amounts to an abuse of process, either directly or through the human rights provision in s 21. Although the EA 2003 is intended to speed up the extradition process, nevertheless, persons are detained under it for the purposes of extradition, and it follows that they have the right to challenge the legality of their detention in accordance with Article 5(4).

There are good reasons why there should be jurisdiction to refuse extradition on the grounds of bad faith or abuse of process. To say that an extradition request is made in bad faith is not necessarily to impugn the good faith of the high sovereign authorities who make the request on behalf of the state (*R (Saifi) v Governor of HMP Brixton* [2001] 1 WLR 1134, para 63). Extradition requests are the product of criminal investigations and so can become infected with the corruption or dishonesty of witnesses, police, or prosecutors. In *Atkinson v Government of the United States of America* [1971] AC 197, 232 Lord Reid said:

There can be cases where it would clearly be contrary to natural justice to surrender a man although there is sufficient evidence to justify committal. Extradition may be either because the man is accused of an extradition crime or because he has been convicted in the foreign country of an extradition crime. It is not unknown for convictions to be obtained in a few foreign countries by improper means, and it would be intolerable if a man so convicted had to be surrendered. Parliament can never have so intended when the 1870 Act was passed.

There have been numerous cases where even close extradition partners have sought extradition in circumstances where it would be an affront to justice to return the defendant. For example:

(a) In *R (Saifi) v Governor of HMP Brixton* [2001] 1 WLR 1134, an Indian request for conspiracy to murder, there was serious non-disclosure by the Government and improper pressure was brought to bear on the only witness against the defendant. The High Court discharged the defendant under s 11(3)(c) of the EA 1989.

(b) In *Re Asliturk* [2002] EWHC 2326 Admin, the Government of Turkey sought the defendant's extradition for political reasons, because of jealousy, enhanced by media references to her being seen as a future Prime Minister, and because it disapproved of her as a divorced westernized woman. The High Court discharged her under s 11(3)(c).

(c) *Re Murat Calis*, Unreported, 19 November 1993, CO/2757/92, the defendant's principal accuser changed his story repeatedly and was motivated by a desire to claim a reward rather than because he believed the defendant to be guilty. Sedley LJ held this amounted to bad faith and discharged the defendant.

(d) In *R (Ramda) v Secretary of State for the Home Department* [2002] EWHC 1278 (Admin), the Administrative Court quashed the Secretary of State's decision to return the applicant to France because he had failed properly to investigate serious allegations that the principal witness had been tortured by the French police to provide evidence incriminating the applicant. Significantly, Sedley LJ said at para 27 that it was no answer to rely on France's status as a signatory to the European Convention on Human Rights as sufficient protection for the applicant if he were to be returned to France.

(e) *Re Sutej* [2003] EWHC 1940 was a case where the court found that some of the allegations made against the defendant by one of the complainants were demonstrably untrue and made for the purposes of bolstering a parallel civil action for damages and ordered the defendant's partial discharge under s 11(3)(c).

(f) In *Gale v Governor of HMP Holloway* [2001] EWHC Admin 430, the Administrative Court discharged the applicant (a young woman with a small child) whose extradition was sought by Portugal, even though, as a matter of law, the Government accepted she was bound to be acquitted at trial but nonetheless declined to withdraw its extradition request. The Court was narrowly persuaded not to hold the Portuguese Government guilty of bad faith, and discharged the defendant under s 11(3)(b).

(g) In *Government of Russian Federation v Zakaev*, Unreported, 13 November 2003, the Senior District Judge at Bow Street Magistrates' Court found as a fact that the Russian Government had tortured a witness to give evidence incriminating the defendant, a leading Chechen politician, and that it had alleged that the defendant had murdered a priest whom it knew to be alive.

On the other hand, it can be argued that to allow an abuse of process jurisdiction—at least in EAW cases—would undermine its undeniable purpose, namely, to provide quick return within the EU. In *R v Governor of Belmarsh Prison ex p Gilligan* [2001] 1 AC 84, the House of Lords held that there was no abuse of process jurisdiction under the Backing of Warrants (Republic of Ireland) Act 1965, on the grounds that to discharge a fugitive for abuse of process would undermine the Act's legislative purpose of a single and expeditious procedure between neighbouring countries. However, this case pre-dates the incorporation of Article 5(4) into domestic law, and in *Re Darren Hayes*, Unreported, 9 October 2000, CO/1339/2000, the Administrative Court declined to follow it. The Court held that Article 5(4) meant that there had to be such a jurisdiction even under the simple 1965 Act procedure (paras 45–47):

45. Those cases, including *Gilligan*, were decided before the Human Rights Act came into effect on 2 October 2000, but in my view it is clear from decisions of the European Court of Human Rights, and from the consideration of such decisions by Lord Hope in *R v Governor of Brockhill Prison ex p Evans* (No 2) [2000] 4 AER 15, at 29J to 30C, that there are three requirements of Article 5(1) as it applies to the arrest or detention of a person against whom action is being taken with a view to extradition, including rendition to Ireland.

46. Firstly, the detention must be lawful under domestic law, for these purposes English law; secondly, the domestic law must comply with Convention law in the sense of being sufficiently precise and accessible to the individual; thirdly, domestic law must comply with Convention law in the sense that the detention must not be arbitrary because, for instance, it was resorted to in bad faith or was not 'proportionate'.

47. In addition, the decision leading to arrest and detention should be susceptible to speedy review by a superior court with a view to the fugitive's release if the detention does not accord with domestic law, including the Convention rights which are now part of the domestic law of England and Wales: see Article 5(4).

5.9.3 Sovereign, Diplomatic, and Consular Immunity

The defendant may in an appropriate case claim sovereign or diplomatic immunity from arrest or detention for the purposes of extradition proceedings.

Section 1 of the Diplomatic Privileges Act 1964 incorporates the provisions of the Vienna Convention on Diplomatic Relations 1961 contained in Sch 1 into UK law. The Convention confers absolute immunity from arrest for diplomats, members of their families, and their immediate households.

Section 20(1)(a) of the State Immunity Act 1978 confers the same immunity *mutatis mutandis* on visiting heads of state. Section 4 of the 1964 Act provides that where any question arises whether or not any person is entitled to any privilege or immunity under the Act a certificate issued by the Secretary of State under the

Act stating any fact relating to that question is conclusive evidence of that fact. The burden is on the defendant to produce the certificate.

The immunity of former heads of state in respect of offences committed whilst they were head of state was one of the issues considered at length by the House of Lords in *R v Metropolitan Stipendiary Magistrate ex p Pinochet Ugarte (No 3)* [2000] 1 AC 147. All seven of the Law Lords gave speeches. The majority held that a former head of state had immunity from the criminal jurisdiction of the UK for acts done in his official capacity as head of state pursuant to s 20 of the State Immunity Act 1978 when read with Article 39(2) of Sch 1 to the Diplomatic Privileges Act 1964. However, because torture was an international crime against humanity, after the coming into effect of the United Nations International Convention against Torture and other Cruel, Inhuman or Degrading Treatment or Punishment 1984, there had been a universal jurisdiction in all the Convention state parties to either extradite or punish a public official who committed torture. Therefore, in the light of that universal jurisdiction, state parties could not have intended that an immunity for ex-heads of state for official acts of torture would survive their ratification of the Convention. The UK, Spain, and Chile had ratified the Convention by 8 December 1998 and so Senator Pinochet had no immunity from extradition for offences of torture or conspiracy to torture alleged to have occurred after 8 December 1988 and that the extradition could proceed on those charges.

The *Pinochet* case raised a number of moral, political, cultural, historical, and social issues. As discussed in Chapter 1, the controversy it generated gave added impetus to the UK Government's ongoing review of extradition law which led directly to the EA 2003. A full discussion of all these issues is outside the scope of this book. For a thorough discussion of the case see Woodhouse (ed), *The Pinochet Case: A Legal and Constitutional Analysis* (2000). Among the many law review articles on the case are: Byers, 'The law and politics of the *Pinochet* case', (2000) 10 Duke Jour Comp Int'l Law 415; Nicholls, 'Reflections on Pinochet', (2000) 41 Va J Int'l Law 140; Turns, 'Pinochet's fallout: jurisdiction and immunity for criminal violations of international law' (2000) 20 LS 566; Perera, '*Ex parte Pinochet* and the concept of state immunity: some reflections' (1999) 25 CLB 647; Boister and Burchill, 'The implications of the *Pinochet* decisions for the extradition or prosecution of former South African heads of state for crimes committed under apartheid' (1999) 11 RADIC 619; Caplan, 'The *Pinochet* case—a personal view' (2000) 144 SJ 372; Malleson, 'Judicial bias and disqualification after *Pinochet (No 2)* (2000) 63 MLR 119; Tierney, 'The extradition case against Pinochet Ugarte' (1999) 5 EPL 500; Warbrick, 'Extradition law aspects of *Pinochet No 3*' (1999) 48 ICLQ 958; Bianchi, 'Immunity versus human rights: the *Pinochet* case' (1999) 10 EJIL 237; Wedgewood, 'International criminal law and Augusto Pinochet' (2000) 40 Va J Int'l Law 829.

The persuasiveness of the House of Lords' reasoning on immunity was called into question by the International Court of Justice in its decision in *Democratic Republic of Congo v Belgium*, Unreported, 14 February 2002, www.icj-cij.org. In its application to the Court the Congo requested the Court to declare that the Kingdom of Belgium should annul the international arrest warrant issued on 11 April 2000 by a Belgian investigating judge against the Minister for Foreign Affairs in office of the Democratic Republic of the Congo seeking his provisional detention pending a request for extradition to Belgium for alleged crimes constituting 'serious violations of international humanitarian law', including grave breaches of the Geneva Conventions of 1949 and its Additional Protocols, and crimes against humanity. The Congo argued that as a Foreign Minister he was immune from criminal jurisdiction. One of Belgium's arguments in opposition was that immunities accorded to incumbent Ministers for Foreign Affairs cannot protect them where they are suspected of having committed war crimes or crimes against humanity.

In support of this position, Belgium relied on the decision in *R v Metropolitan Stipendiary Magistrate ex p Pinochet Ugarte (No 3)* [2000] 1 AC 147, which it contended established an exception to the immunity rule in the case of serious crimes under international law. According to Belgium the *Pinochet* decision recognized an exception to the immunity rule when Lord Millett stated that '[i]nternational law cannot be supposed to have established a crime having the character of a *jus cogens* and at the same time to have provided an immunity which is co-extensive with the obligation it seeks to impose', or when Lord Phillips of Worth Matravers said that 'no established rule of international law requires state immunity *rationae materiae* to be accorded in respect of prosecution for an international crime'.

At para 58 of its judgment the Court said that it had carefully examined state practice, including national legislation and those few decisions of national higher courts, such as the House of Lords. It said it was unable to deduce that there exists under customary international law any form of exception to the rule according immunity from criminal jurisdiction and inviolability to incumbent Ministers for Foreign Affairs, where they are suspected of having committed war crimes or crimes against humanity. The Court also examined the rules concerning the immunity or criminal responsibility of persons having an official capacity contained in the legal instruments creating international criminal tribunals, and found that these rules likewise did not enable it to conclude that any such exception exists in customary international law in regard to national courts. The Court concluded that serving ministers have immunity from arrest, and former ministers have immunity for all official acts committed in office.

5.10 COMPETING PART 1 WARRANTS

Where two Part 1 warrants have been issued in respect of a defendant then the appropriate judge must decide which of them is to take precedence in accordance with s 44.

If a Part 1 warrant and an extradition request under Part 2 have been sent to the UK for execution then it is for the Secretary of State to decide which of them should be dealt with first under s 179. This power is considered in Chapter 8.

Section 44 applies if at any time in the relevant period the conditions in s 44(3) are satisfied in relation to a person in respect of whom a Part 1 warrant has been issued. These conditions are that:

(a) the judge is informed that another Part 1 warrant has been issued in respect of the person;

(b) the other warrant falls to be dealt with by the judge or by a judge who is the appropriate judge in another part of the UK;

(c) the other warrant has not been disposed of.

For these purposes the relevant period is the period starting when the person is first brought before the appropriate judge following his arrest under Part 1 and ending when the person is extradited in pursuance of the warrant or discharged (s 44(2)).

Where s 44 applies the judge may do one of two things. He may:

(a) order further proceedings on the warrant under consideration to be deferred until the other warrant has been disposed of, if the warrant under consideration has not been disposed of;

(b) order the person's extradition in pursuance of the warrant under consideration to be deferred until the other warrant has been disposed of, if an order for his extradition in pursuance of the warrant under consideration has been made.

If the judge makes an order under s 44(4) and the person is not already remanded in custody or on bail, the judge must remand the person in custody or on bail (s 44(5)). If the judge remands the person in custody he may later grant bail (s 44(6)).

In considering what order to make under s 44(4) the judge must take account of the following matters in particular:

(a) the relative seriousness of the offences concerned;

(b) the place where each offence was committed (or was alleged to have been committed);

(c) the date on which each warrant was issued;

(d) whether, in the case of each offence, the person is accused of its commission (but not alleged to have been convicted) or is alleged to be unlawfully at large after conviction.

5.11 DEFERRAL OF EXTRADITION HEARING
FOR DOMESTIC PROCEEDINGS

Section 22 applies if at any time during a Part 1 extradition hearing the judge is informed that the defendant has been charged with an offence in the UK. The judge must adjourn the extradition hearing until one of the following occurs (s 22(2)):

(a) the charge is disposed of;
(b) the charge is withdrawn;
(c) proceedings in respect of the charge are discontinued;
(d) an order is made for the charge to lie on the file (or its Scottish equivalent).

If the defendant is sentenced to imprisonment or another form of detention then the judge may adjourn the extradition hearing until the sentence has been served (s 22(3)).

In some cases the domestic proceedings may relate to the offence for which extradition has been requested. This may raise double jeopardy issues. Accordingly, s 22(4) provides that if the extradition hearing is adjourned under s 22(2) and the judge has already decided the double jeopardy question under s 11, the judge must decide that question again after the resumption of the hearing.

Section 23 applies if during the extradition hearing the judge is informed that the defendant has been sentenced to imprisonment or another form of detention in the UK. The judge may then adjourn the extradition hearing until the sentence has been served (s 23(2)).

5.12 COSTS

The EA 2003 introduces, for the first time, a power to award costs against a person whose extradition is ordered.

Section 60(2) provides that where an order for extradition is made under Part 1 the appropriate judge may make such order as he considers just and reasonable with regard to the costs to be paid by the person. The order for costs must specify their amount, and may name the person to whom they are to be paid (s 60(4)).

Where the defendant is discharged then an order for costs in his favour can be made under s 61(5). An order under s 61(5) is an order for a payment of the appropriate amount to be made to the person out of money provided by Parliament. Section 61(6) provides that the appropriate amount is such amount as the judge or court making the order considers reasonably sufficient to compensate the person in whose favour the order is made for any expenses properly incurred by him in the proceedings under this Part. Section 61(7) confers a power to reduce this amount in appropriate circumstances.

The practice under the EA 1989 was to award a successful defendant the whole of his costs out of central funds under s 16 of the Prosecution of Offences Act 1985.

6

THE EXTRADITION HEARING IN CATEGORY 2 CASES

6.1 INTRODUCTION

In this chapter the appropriate judge's duties and functions in an extradition hearing under Part 2 of the EA 2003 are considered. This is the hearing at which the appropriate judge is to deal with a request for extradition to a Category 2 territory (s 140(1)).

As in Category 1 cases, in England and Wales the appropriate judge is a District Judge (Magistrates' Courts) designated for the purposes of Part 2 by the Lord Chancellor (s 140(1)(a)).

The judge's functions in a Part 2 extradition hearing are, or may be, more elaborate than in a Part 1 hearing. This is because s 84 preserves the requirement for *prima facie* evidence except where the requesting Category 2 territory has been designated by the Secretary of State under s 84(7).

Many of the provisions of Part 2 are in similar form to those in Part 1. Therefore in this chapter cross-reference will be made to the relevant parts of Chapter 5 (Category 1 cases) where appropriate.

6.2 EXTRADITION HEARINGS UNDER PART 2: A SUMMARY

The extradition hearing in a Category 2 case can be summarized as follows:

(a) Within the period specified in ss 75 and 76 the judge must first decide whether the documents sent to him by the Secretary of State include the documents and information specified in s 78(2). If they do not, then the defendant must be discharged (s 78(3)).

(b) If the documents are in order the judge must decide the following questions (s 78(4)):

(i) whether, on a balance of probabilities, the person appearing or brought before him is the person whose extradition is requested;

(ii) whether the offence specified in the request is an extradition offence;

(iii) whether copies of the documents sent to the judge by the Secretary of State have been served on the defendant.

(c) If the judge decides these questions affirmatively he must then go on to decide whether any of the bars to extradition in s 79 are applicable. If one or more of them is applicable then the defendant must be discharged (s 79(3)).

(d) If there are no applicable bars to extradition under s 79:

(i) and the person is accused of the commission of the extradition offence but is not alleged to be unlawfully at large after conviction of it, the judge must proceed under s 84 (s 79(4)). This requires the judge to decide whether there is a *prima facie* case, unless the requesting state has been designated by the Secretary of State under s 84(7). In that case, the judge is required to proceed under s 87.

(ii) and the person is alleged to be unlawfully at large after conviction of the extradition offence, the judge must proceed under s 85 (s 79(5)). This requires the judge to decide if the defendant was convicted in his absence and, if so, whether he will receive a retrial. If he will, the judge must proceed under s 86. This is in similar terms to s 84.

(e) If the issues arising under the sections mentioned above are decided adversely to the defendant, the judge must then decide under s 87 whether extradition would be compatible with the defendant's Convention rights within the meaning of the Human Rights Act 1998.

(f) If it would not, the defendant must be discharged (s 87(2)). If it would, the judge must send the case to the Secretary of State for his decision whether the defendant is to be extradited (s 87(3)). The judge must inform the defendant of his right to appeal in accordance with s 92.

The extradition hearing is then at an end. The Secretary of State's role in Category 2 cases is considered in Chapter 8.

6.3 JUDGE'S POWERS AT EXTRADITION HEARING

In England and Wales, at the extradition hearing the appropriate judge has the same powers (as nearly as may be) as a Magistrates' Court would have if the proceedings were the summary trial of an information against the person whose extradition is requested. This provision applies the general powers of a Magistrates' Court in Part I of the Magistrates' Courts Act 1980. Where the judge adjourns the extradition hearing he must remand the person in custody or on bail (s 77(4)). If the defendant is remanded in custody he may later be granted bail (s 77(5)).

6.4 BURDEN AND STANDARD OF PROOF

This is dealt with in s 206: see 5.4 above.

6.5 AUTHENTICATION

This is dealt with in s 202: see 5.5 above.

6.6 INITIAL STAGES OF EXTRADITION HEARING

6.6.1 Sufficiency of Documents

Section 70 requires the Secretary of State to issue his certificate where he receives a valid extradition request which has been made in the approved way. He is then required by s 70(9) to send the following documents to the appropriate judge:

(a) the request;
(b) the certificate;
(c) a copy of any relevant Order in Council.

By s 78(2) the first task for the appropriate judge at the extradition hearing is to determine that the documents sent to him by the Secretary of State include the documents and information required by s 78(2), namely:

(a) the documents referred to in s 70(9);

(b) particulars of the person whose extradition is requested;

(c) particulars of the offence specified in the request;

(d) in the case of a person accused of an offence, a warrant for his arrest issued in the Category 2 territory;

(e) in the case of a person alleged to be unlawfully at large after conviction of an offence, a certificate issued in the Category 2 territory of the conviction and (if he has been sentenced) of the sentence.

If the documents are deficient then the defendant must be discharged.

6.6.2 The Section 78(4) Questions

Assuming that the paperwork is in order, the judge must go on to decide the three questions specified in s 78(4).

The first question is whether, on a balance of probabilities (s 78(5)), the person appearing or brought before the judge is the person whose extradition is requested. Proving identity in extradition cases is a relatively straightforward matter: see 4.7.1.1 above.

The second question is whether the offence specified in the request is an extradition offence. This is dealt with at 5.7 above.

The third question is whether copies of the documents sent to the judge by the Secretary of State have been served on the person. This should have happened well before the extradition hearing commences.

6.7 ENGLISH CHARGES AND MULTIPLE OFFENCES

See 5.5 above, and the Extradition Act 2003 (Multiple Offences) Order 2003 (SI 2003/3150).

6.8 IS THE OFFENCE IN THE REQUEST AN EXTRADITION OFFENCE?

Extradition offences in Category 2 cases were considered at 2.3.3 above. The district judge is required to consider the particulars of conduct in the request and to determine whether they amount to an extradition offence within the definitions set out in ss 137–138.

See further 5.6 above.

6.9 BARS TO EXTRADITION
(SECTION 79)

The judge's next task is to determine whether any of the bars to extradition in s 79 are applicable. These are:

(a) the rule against double jeopardy;
(b) extraneous considerations;
(c) the passage of time;
(d) hostage-taking considerations.

6.9.1 Rule against Double Jeopardy (Section 80)

A person's extradition to a Category 2 territory is barred by reason of the rule against double jeopardy if (and only if) it appears that he would be entitled to be discharged under any rule of law relating to previous acquittal or conviction if he were charged with the extradition offence in the part of the UK where the judge exercises his jurisdiction.

This is virtually identical to s 6(3) of the EA 1989 but in a different form from s 12, the equivalent provision in Part 1: see 5.8.1 above.

6.9.2 Extraneous Considerations (Section 81)

A person's extradition to a Category 2 territory is barred by reason of extraneous considerations if (and only if) it appears that:

(a) the request for his extradition (though purporting to be made on account of the extradition offence) is in fact made for the purpose of prosecuting or punishing him on account of his race, religion, nationality, gender, sexual orientation, or political opinions, or

(b) if extradited he might be prejudiced at his trial or punished, detained, or restricted in his personal liberty by reason of his race, religion, nationality, gender, sexual orientation, or political opinions.

This section is similar to s 13, considered at 5.8.2 above.

6.9.3 Passage of Time (Section 82)

A person's extradition to a Category 2 territory is barred by reason of the passage of time if (and only if) it appears that it would be unjust or oppressive to extradite him by reason of the passage of time since he is alleged to have committed the extradition offence or since he is alleged to have become unlawfully at large (as the case may be).

This provision is identical to s 14 in Category 1 cases: see 5.8.3 above.

6.9.4 Hostage-taking Considerations (Section 83)

A person's extradition to a Category 2 territory is barred by reason of hostage-taking considerations if (and only if) the territory is a party to the International Convention against the Taking of Hostages opened for signature at New York on 18 December 1979 and it appears that:

(a) if extradited, he might be prejudiced at his trial because communication between him and the appropriate authorities would not be possible; and

(b) the act or omission constituting the extradition offence also constitutes an offence under s 1 of the Taking of Hostages Act 1982 or an attempt to commit such an offence.

This provision is identical to s 16 in Category 1 cases: see 5.8.5 above.

6.10 *PRIMA FACIE* EVIDENCE

Under the EA 1989 evidence sufficient to amount to a *prima facie* case was required in Sch 1 cases (principally requests from the United States of America), and in cases under Part III, unless the requesting state was designated in an Order in Council under s 9(4) and (8). In practice, this meant that designated Commonwealth countries, colonies, and the Hong Kong Special Administrative Region were required to adduce *prima facie* evidence, whereas signatories to the European Convention on Extradition 1957 were not so required.

Although the policy of the EA 2003 is to simplify and remove evidential requirements where possible, *prima facie* evidence is required in Category 2 cases unless the requesting Category 2 territory has been designated by the Secretary of State in an order under s 84(7) or s 86(7). The following countries have been designated for these purposes by the Extradition Act 2003 (Designation of Part 2 Territories) Order 2003 (SI 2003/3334), Article 3:

Albania; Andorra; Armenia; Australia; Austria; Azerbaijan; Bulgaria; Canada; Croatia; Cyprus; Czech Republic; Estonia; France; Georgia; Germany; Greece; Hungary; Iceland; Israel; Italy; Latvia; Liechtenstein; Lithuania; Luxembourg; Macedonia FYR; Malta; Moldova; The Netherlands; New Zealand; Norway; Poland; Romania; Russian Federation; Serbia and Montenegro; Slovakia; Slovenia; South Africa; Switzerland; Turkey; Ukraine; The United States of America.

Accordingly, it is not necessary for these territories to prove a *prima facie* case against the defendant.

However, where evidence is required, the rules of evidence are simplified by ss 84(2) and 86(2), which give the judge a discretion to admit hearsay evidence.

6.10.1 The Test for a *Prima Facie* Case

Sections 84(1) and 86(1) provide that if the judge is required to proceed under s 84 or s 86 he must decide whether there is evidence which would be sufficient to make a case requiring an answer by the defendant if the proceedings were the summary trial of an information against him.

The reference to 'the summary trial of an information' makes clear that the evidence has to be admissible under ordinary criminal rules of evidence, subject to the provisions of ss 84(2)–(4) and 86(2)–(4).

The test the judge has to apply is the test in *Galbraith* [1981] 1 WLR 1039, 1042, namely whether the prosecution evidence, taken at its highest, is such that no jury properly directed could properly convict upon it. This was held to be the correct test for extradition cases by the House of Lords in *R v Governor of Pentonville Prison ex p Alves* [1993] AC 284, 290, 292.

Lord Goff of Chieveley observed in *R v Governor of Pentonville Prison ex p Alves* [1993] AC 284, 290 that it became the practice during the twentieth century after the case of *Zossenheim* (1903) 20 TLR 121 for the magistrate to take into account evidence tendered on behalf of the defendant in extradition proceedings when deciding whether there was a case to answer. Even though the judge is required to behave as if he were conducting a summary trial, in deciding whether there is a *prima facie* case, he is required to have regard to evidence called on behalf of the defendant (*R v Governor of Brixton Prison ex p Gross* [1999] QB 538). In that case, the Divisional Court held that the amendments made to the EA 1989 by the Criminal Justice and Public Order Act 1994 (which introduced the language of summary trials) had not altered this practice. It follows that the defendant is entitled to give evidence and call witnesses in extradition hearings where evidence is required (cf *R v Governor of Pentonville Prison ex p Alves* [1993] AC 284, 292; *Re Tomlins*, Unreported, 18 November 1994, CO/1257/94; *R (Saifi) v Governor of Brixton Prison* [2001] 1 WLR 1134).

The mechanics of the process the judge has to go through in reaching his conclusion were explained by Lloyd LJ in *R v Governor of Pentonville Prison ex p Osman* [1990] 1 WLR 277, 299:

. . . it was the magistrate's duty to consider the evidence as a whole, and to reject any evidence which he considered worthless. In that sense it was his duty to weigh up the evidence. But it was not his duty to weigh the evidence. He was neither entitled nor obliged to determine the amount of weight to be attached to any evidence, or to compare one witness with another. That would be for the jury at the trial.

6.10.2 Form of Evidence and Issues as to Admissibility

The evidence in extradition cases will generally consist of a combination of one or more of the following forms of evidence:

(a) Evidence from the requesting state properly translated (*R v Governor of Brixton Prison ex p Saifi* [2001] 1 WLR 1134; *Lodhi v Governor of HMP Brixton* [2001] EWHC Admin 178; *R v Governor of Brixton Prison ex p Lennon* [1963] Crim LR 41; *Kruger v Governor of Northward Prison* [1996] CILR 157) and duly authenticated in accordance with s 202 of the EA 2003.

Duly authenticated evidence from the requesting state is not necessarily admissible in evidence: it is receivable in evidence and only admissible to the extent that it complies with English rules of evidence (and any express statutory provision) (*R v Governor of Pentonville Prison ex p Kirby* [1979] 2 All ER 1094, 1099).

(b) Live evidence (*R v Governor of Pentonville Prison ex p Herbage (No 3)* (1987) 84 Cr App R 149). Witnesses who appear in person can be cross-examined, and the old practice of recording their evidence in the form of a deposition under the Magistrates' Courts Act 1980 has continued even though the procedure now is that of a summary trial. Where properly authenticated evidence is presented; however, there is no duty on the requesting state to make the witness available for cross-examination (*R v Governor of Brixton Prison ex p Caldough* [1961] 1 WLR 464; *R v Secretary of State for India ex p Ezekiel* [1941] 2 KB 169).

(c) Written evidence in the form required by s 9 of the Criminal Justice Act 1967, read by consent.

(d) Formal admissions under s 10 of the Criminal Justice Act 1967.

Section 205(1) of the EA 2003 provides that ss 9 and 10 of the Criminal Justice Act 1967 apply in relation to proceedings under the Act as they apply in relation to proceedings for an offence.

6.10.2.1 *The Discretionary Exclusion of Evidence*
Whilst the evidence tendered by the requesting state must in general comply with English evidential rules, failure to observe English procedural rules relating to evidence does not necessarily render the evidence inadmissible (*R v Governor of Pentonville Prison ex p Schneider* (1981) 73 Cr App R 200, 211–212).

The following have been characterized as rules of practice whose breach does not render evidence inadmissible in extradition proceedings:

(a) rules relating to the identification of witnesses (*R v Governor of Pentonville Prison ex p Voets* [1986] 1 WLR 470);

(b) rules relating to anonymous witnesses (*R (Al-Fawwaz) v Governor of HMP Brixton* [2002] 1 AC 556);

(c) rules relating to the interviewing of witnesses (*Beese v Governor of Ashford Remand Centre* [1973] 1 WLR 1426);

(d) rules relating to memory-refreshing documents (*R v Governor of Gloucester Prison ex p Miller* [1979] 2 All ER 1103).

Section 78 of the Police and Criminal Evidence Act 1984 applies to extradition proceedings (*R (Saifi) v Governor of HMP Brixton* [2001] 1 WLR 1134; *Re Proulx* [2000] 1 All ER 57). However, evidence should only be excluded where it has been obtained in a way which outrages civilized values (*R v Governor of Brixton Prison ex p Levin* [1997] AC 741, 748).

In *R (Saifi) v Governor of Brixton Prison* [2001] 1 WLR 1134 the Divisional Court gave guidance on the application of s 78:

Section 78 confers a power in terms wide enough for its exercise on the court's own motion. The power is to be exercised whenever an issue appears as to whether the court could conclude that the evidence should not be admitted. The concept of a burden of proof has no part to play in such circumstances. No doubt it is for that reason that there is no express provision as to the burden of proof, and we see no basis for implying such a burden. The prosecution desiring to adduce and the defence seeking to exclude evidence will each seek to persuade the court about impact on fairness. We regard the position as neutral and see no reason why section 78 should be understood as requiring the court to consider upon whom the burden of proof rests . . .

Under section 78 any circumstance which can reasonably have a bearing on fairness should be considered. The weight to be attached to an individual circumstance may increase or decrease because of the presence of other related or unrelated circumstances. The preponderance of all the circumstances may show that the admission of the evidence would have such an adverse effect on fairness as to require its exclusion.

The absence from section 78 of words suggesting that facts are to be established or proved to any particular standard is, in our judgment, deliberate. It leaves the matter open and untrammelled by rigid evidential considerations.

6.10.2.2 *Disclosure*

The developing case law in the 1980s on the prosecution's duty of disclosure in criminal cases (*Ward* [1993] 1 WLR 619; *Keane* [1994] 1 WLR 746) left open the question of the extent to which there is a similar duty in extradition proceedings. That there should be such a duty of disclosure is consistent with the need for a fair hearing: if the requesting state is in possession of exculpatory or potentially exculpatory material then fairness should require that it be disclosed to the defence. However, the fact that in domestic proceedings disclosure does not normally take place until after committal (and in summary proceedings, may not take place at all) would appear to point away from any duty of disclosure in extradition proceedings.

In *R v Governor of Pentonville Prison ex p Lee* [1993] 1 WLR 1294 the Divisional Court held that it was for the requesting state alone to decide what material should be placed before the magistrate and that it was not under a duty to comply with any request for other material, including unused material, which might be requested by the defence.

The impact of the Human Rights Act 1998 on extradition disclosure was considered in *R v Governor of Brixton Prison ex p Kashamu*, Unreported, 6 October 2000, CO/2141/2000, where the committal was quashed because of serious non-disclosure by the Government of the United States of America. However, the Court did not take the opportunity to state authoritatively the extent of the Government's duty of disclosure in extradition cases.

In *Lodhi v Governor of HMP Brixton* [2001] EWHC Admin 178 the approach to disclosure in *R v Governor of Pentonville Prison ex p Lee* [1993] 1 WLR 1294 was approved.

One difficulty with the decisions in *ex p Lee* and *Lodhi* is that they are inconsistent with the underlying duty of fairness which undoubtedly applies to extradition hearings. Moreover, Article 5(4) of the European Convention on Human Rights, which applies to extradition hearings, places a limited duty of disclosure on the prosecution (*Sanchez-Reisse v Switzerland* (1987) 9 EHRR 71; *Lamy v Belgium* (1989) 11 EHRR 529). Therefore the extent of the requesting state's duty of disclosure in extradition cases remains to be satisfactorily determined.

6.10.2.3 *Hearsay Evidence*

Sections 84(2) and 86(2) relax the rule against hearsay in extradition hearings. They give the judge a discretion to treat a statement made by a person in a document as admissible evidence of a fact if:

(a) the statement is made by the person to a police officer or another person charged with the duty of investigating offences or charging offenders, and

(b) direct oral evidence by the person of the fact would be admissible.

Thus, if the evidence in the request includes a police report in which the police officer records the witness, W, as telling him that D committed the crime, then the judge has a discretion to admit the statement as evidence that D committed the crime because the statement was made to a police officer and direct oral evidence at trial from W that D committed the crime would be admissible.

However, if the report recorded W as telling the officer that A told him that D committed the crime then this would not be even potentially admissible. This is because, although the statement was made to a police officer, evidence from W at trial about what A told him would not be admissible to show D committed the offence.

Sections 84(3) and 86(3) require the judge to have regard to certain matters before admitting a statement under s 84(2) or s 86(2). The judge must have regard:

(a) to the nature and source of the document;

(b) to whether or not, having regard to the nature and source of the document and to any other circumstances that appear to the judge to be relevant, it is likely that the document is authentic;

(c) to the extent to which the statement appears to supply evidence which would not be readily available if the statement were not treated as being admissible evidence of the fact;

(d) to the relevance of the evidence that the statement appears to supply to any issue likely to have to be determined by the judge in deciding the question in ss 84(1) and 86(1);

(e) to any risk that the admission or exclusion of the statement will result in unfairness to the person whose extradition is sought, having regard in particular to whether it is likely to be possible to controvert the statement if the person making it does not attend to give oral evidence.

6.11 CONVICTIONS IN ABSENCE

Where the defendant is alleged to be unlawfully at large after conviction of the extradition offence, the judge must proceed under s 85. This is intended to ensure that a defendant who has been convicted *in absentia* will be treated fairly in the requesting state by being retried in his presence.

Section 85 is in similar terms to s 20. For further details, see 5.8.8 above.

6.12 HUMAN RIGHTS

Section 87 prohibits the judge from ordering extradition where to do so would be incompatible with the defendant's Convention rights within the meaning of the Human Rights Act 1998. This topic is dealt with separately in Chapter 7.

6.13 OTHER BARS TO EXTRADITION

6.13.1 Physical or Mental Condition

Section 91 provides a bar to extradition where the judge is satisfied it would be unjust or oppressive to return the defendant because of his physical or mental condition. It is in similar terms to s 26 in Part 1 cases: see 5.9.1 above.

6.13.2 Bad Faith/Abuse of Process

See 5.9.2 above.

6.13.3 Sovereign and Diplomatic Immunity

See 5.9.3 above.

6.14 DEFERRAL OF PROCEEDINGS UNDER PART 2

Sections 88–90 deal with the situation where the defendant becomes subject to other extradition proceedings or criminal proceedings in the UK. The appropriate judge has power to adjourn the hearing until the other proceedings are disposed of.

6.14.1 Person Charged with Offence in the UK (Section 88)

If the judge is informed during the extradition hearing that the defendant has been charged with an offence in the UK he must adjourn the extradition hearing until one of these occurs (s 88(1) and (2)):

(a) the charge is disposed of;
(b) the charge is withdrawn;
(c) proceedings in respect of the charge are discontinued;
(d) an order is made for the charge to lie on the file.

If a sentence of imprisonment or another form of detention is imposed in respect of the offence charged, the judge may adjourn the extradition hearing until the sentence has been served.

If before he adjourns the extradition hearing under s 88(2) the judge has decided under s 79 whether the defendant's extradition is barred by reason of the rule against double jeopardy, the judge must decide that question again after the resumption of the hearing (s 88(4)).

6.14.2 Person Serving Sentence in the UK (Section 89)

If the judge is informed at any time in the extradition hearing that the person is serving a sentence of imprisonment or another form of detention in the UK then he may adjourn the extradition hearing until the sentence has been served (s 89).

6.14.3 Competing Extradition Claims (Section 90)

The Secretary of State has power under ss 126 and 179 to regulate competing requests by ordering that one set of proceedings be deferred until the conclusion of the other. These powers are considered in Chapter 8.

Section 90 prescribes the appropriate judge's function where the Secretary of State has exercised his powers. Section 90 applies if at any time in the extradition hearing the judge is informed that the conditions in s 90(2) or 90(3) are met. The conditions in s 90(2) are that:

(a) the Secretary of State has received another valid request for the person's extradition to a Category 2 territory;

(b) the other request has not been disposed of;

(c) the Secretary of State has made an order under s 126(2) for further proceedings on the request under consideration to be deferred until the other request has been disposed of.

The conditions in s 90(3) are that:

(a) a certificate has been issued under s 2 in respect of a Part 1 warrant issued in respect of the person;

(b) the warrant has not been disposed of;

(c) the Secretary of State has made an order under s 179(2) for further proceedings on the request to be deferred until the warrant has been disposed of.

Where the judge orders a deferral he must remand the defendant in custody or on bail. If the remand is in custody the judge may later grant bail.

6.15 COSTS

Section 135 provides for costs to be awarded against a person whose extradition is ordered under Part 2. Section 136 allows for an award of costs in favour of a person who is discharged. They are in *pari materia* to ss 61 and 62 in Part 1 cases: see 5.12 above.

7

EXTRADITION AND HUMAN RIGHTS

7.1 INTRODUCTION

UK extradition law has given rise to a number of important decisions under the European Convention on Human Rights. For example, in *Soering v United Kingdom* (1989) 11 EHRR 439, the European Court held that it would be a breach of Article 3 to return the applicant to the United States on charges of capital murder because of the lengthy detention on death row which he would have faced prior to execution.

This chapter examines the inter-relationship between the UK's extradition process and the ECHR. It also considers the substantive content of the Convention rights most relevant to extradition.

Since 2 October 2000, when the Human Rights Act 1998 (HRA 1998) came into force, district judges hearing extradition cases have been under a duty to act compatibly with the defendant's Convention rights, as defined in s 1 of the HRA 1998 (see s 6(1) and *R (Kashamu) v Governor of Brixton Prison* [2002] QB 887, para 32). However, under the EA 1989 they were not required to consider whether extradition itself would breach the ECHR. This was because an order for committal did not amount to an order for extradition. The compatibility of extradition with the ECHR was for the Secretary of State to determine. In *R (St John) v Governor of Brixton Prison* [2002] QB 613, 624, Harrison J said:

... the committal order does not, on its own, violate the applicant's Convention rights. I accept the submission that the potential issue of violation of the applicant's Convention rights arises at the time when the Secretary of State decides whether to extradite the applicant.

The position is fundamentally different under the EA 2003. The ECHR now impacts on the extradition process in two ways:

(a) In carrying out his functions under the EA 2003 the district judge must act compatibly with the defendant's Convention rights (HRA 1998, s 6(1)).

(b) In addition, ss 21 and 88 require him to determine whether the defendant's extradition would be compatible with his Convention rights within the meaning of the HRA 1998.

The House of Commons and House of Lords Joint Committee on Human Rights examined the human rights implications of the Draft Extradition Bill in the Twentieth Report of its 2001–2002 session (26 July 2002, HC 1140).

To begin with, it is necessary to examine some of the key provisions of the HRA 1998.

7.2 OUTLINE OF THE HRA 1998

Prior to the coming into force of the HRA 1998 the ECHR had a limited, although important, effect in domestic law. This could be summarized as follows:

(a) Courts sought to interpret ambiguous legislation consistently with the ECHR (*JH Rayner (Mincing Lane) Ltd v Department of Trade and Industry* [1990] AC 418).

(b) Courts sought to exercise judicial discretions consistently with the ECHR and to develop the common law in a manner not inconsistent with the Convention (*Sultan Khan* [1997] AC 558).

(c) Although ministers and other public authorities had no duty to exercise discretionary powers in a manner consistent with the Convention (*R v Secretary of State for the Home Department ex p Brind* [1991] 1 AC 696) the human rights involved were relevant to the question of whether the authority had acted reasonably and/or taken all relevant matters into account (*R v Ministry of Defence ex p Smith* [1996] QB 517; *R v Lord Saville of Newdigate ex p B* [2000] 1 WLR 1855).

The HRA 1998 imposes a number of duties on courts and public authorities so as to give effect to certain Convention rights in domestic law. A detailed discussion of the history and effect of the HRA 1998 is outside the scope of this work (for a detailed account see Clayton and Tomlinson, *The Law of Human Rights* (2000); Starmer, *European Human Rights Law* (1999); Lester and Pannick, *Human Rights Law and Practice* (1999)). The following is a summary of its more important provisions.

(a) Section 1 provides which Convention rights are to be given further effect in domestic law. These are Articles 2–12 and 14 of the Convention, Articles 1–3 of the First Protocol, and Articles 1 and 2 of the Sixth Protocol, in each case read with Articles 16–18 of the Convention. These are referred to in the HRA 1998 as 'Convention rights' and the judge's task under ss 21 and 88 of the EA 2003 is to determine whether extradition is compatible with these rights.

(b) Section 2 provides that a court or tribunal determining a question which has arisen in connection with a Convention right must take into account any:

(i) judgment or decision of the European Court of Human Rights;

(ii) opinion of the Commission given in a report adopted under Article 31 of the Convention;

(iii) decision of the Commission in connection with Article 26 or 27(2) of the Convention; or

(iv) decision of the Committee of Ministers taken under Article 46 of the Convention;

so far as, in the opinion of the court or tribunal, it is relevant to the proceedings in which that question has arisen.

It is important to be clear about what s 2 does and does not do. It does *not* make the decisions of the European Court binding on domestic courts. They merely have to be taken into account. During the debate on the Human Rights Bill in Parliament the Lord Chancellor said that domestic courts may 'depart from existing Strasbourg decisions and upon occasion it might well be appropriate to do so, and it is possible they might give a successful lead to Strasbourg'. However, he added that 'where it is relevant we would of course expect our courts to apply Convention jurisprudence and its principles to the cases before them (583 HL Official Reports (5th Series), cols 514–515 (18 November 1997)).

In practice, domestic courts are reluctant to depart from relevant decisions of the European Court of Human Rights. In *R (Anderson) v Secretary of State for the Home Department* [2003] 1 AC 837, para 18, the House of Lords said:

While the duty of the House under section 2(1)(a) of the Human Rights Act 1998 is to take into account any judgment of the European Court, whose judgments are not strictly binding, the House will not without good reason depart from the principles laid down in a carefully considered judgment of the court sitting as a Grand Chamber.

Stare decisis itself does not apply to decisions of the Court or Commission because of the interpretative approach adopted by the Convention organs. They interpret the Convention as a 'living instrument' in the light of modern standards. Its meaning is therefore capable of evolving over time. In *Tyrer v United Kingdom* (1978) 2 EHRR 1 the Court said that:

The Convention is a living instrument which, as the Commission rightly stressed, must be interpreted in the light of present day conditions.

(c) Section 3 requires legislation, whenever enacted (s 3(2)(a)), to be read and given effect to in a way which is compatible with, that is, 'consistent with' Convention rights. This interpretative obligation goes far beyond the previous rule which permitted courts to take the Convention into account when resolving an ambiguity in a statutory provision (see above). Section 3(1) requires courts to strive for compatibility, if necessary by reading down over-broad legislation or reading necessary safeguards into an Act (cf *Attorney-General of Gambia v Momodou Jobe* [1984] AC 689, 702). It may involve giving a meaning to a statutory provision which it would not ordinarily bear (*Webb v EMO Air Cargo (UK) Ltd (No 2)* [1995] 1 WLR 1454), if necessary by jettisoning particular words in a section (cf *O'Brien v Sim-Chem Ltd* [1980] 1 WLR 1011, 1017), or by implying words into a section (*Vasquez and O'Neil v R* [1994] 1 WLR 1304, 1314).

In *R v A (No 2)* [2002] 1 AC 45, para 44, Lord Steyn described the interpretative obligation in section 3 as a 'strong one':

In accordance with the will of Parliament as reflected in section 3 it will sometimes be necessary to adopt an interpretation which linguistically may appear strained. The techniques to be used will not only involve the reading down of express language in a statute but also the implication of provisions. A declaration of incompatibility is a measure of last resort. It must be avoided unless it is plainly impossible to do so.

The obligation in s 3(1) applies to all courts and tribunals. Lower courts are thus no longer bound by a previous construction which has been given to existing legislation by a higher court if, in the opinion of the inferior court, this construction would lead to a result which would be incompatible with the Convention rights. For examples, see *R v Offen* [2001] 1 WLR 253; *R v A (No 2)* [2002] 1 AC 45; *Lambert* [2001] 3 WLR 206.

(d) Section 6(1) makes it unlawful for a public authority to act in a way which is incompatible with a Convention right. Acting incompatibly with Convention rights is hence a fourth head of judicial review alongside the classical three-fold categorization of domestic illegality, irrationality, and procedural impropriety (*Council of Civil Service Unions v Minister for the Civil Service* [1985] AC 374).

Section 6(3) defines 'public authority' as including a court or tribunal, and any person certain of whose functions are functions of a public nature. An appropriate judge under the EA 2003 is therefore a public authority.

(e) Section 7 allows a person who claims that a public authority acts (or proposes to act) in a way which is made unlawful by s 6(1) can bring proceedings against the authority in respect of the act and can rely on the Convention. Section 9 provides that in respect of judicial acts the proceedings in s 7 can only be brought by way of appeal.

7.3 EXTRADITION AND CONVENTION RIGHTS

7.3.1 Introduction

The ECHR specifically allows for extradition and detention pending extradition. It does not prevent cooperation between states, within the framework of extradition treaties or in matters of deportation, for the purpose of bringing fugitive offenders to justice, provided that it does not interfere with any specific rights recognized in the Convention (*Ocalan v Turkey* (2003) 37 EHRR 10).

Article 5(1)(f), which defines the circumstances in which the state can lawfully detain an individual, provides:

5(1) Everyone has the right to liberty and security of person. No-one shall be deprived of his liberty save in the following cases and in accordance with a procedure prescribed by law . . .

. . .

(f) the lawful arrest or detention of a person to prevent his effecting an unauthorized entry into the country or of a person against whom action is being taken with a view to deportation or extradition.

In *Altun v Germany* (1983) 36 DR 209, 231 the European Commission held that extradition does not *per se* breach Article 3 even if it takes place in breach of national or international law.

Extradition proceedings may raise issues under the ECHR where:

(a) there is a real risk that extradition itself will breach the defendant's Convention rights (see eg, *Soering v United Kingdom* (1989) 11 EHRR 439, para 85); or

(b) where the domestic extradition procedure results in a violation of the Convention (*R (Al-Fawwaz) v Governor of Brixton Prison* [2001] 1 WLR 1234, paras 58–62; *R v Governor of Pentonville Prison ex p Chinoy* [1992] 1 All ER 317).

7.3.2 Article 2: Right to Life

Article 2 provides:

2(1) Everyone's right to life shall be protected by law. No one shall be deprived of his life intentionally save in the execution of a sentence of a court following his conviction of a crime for which this penalty is provided by law.

(2) Deprivation of life shall not be regarded as inflicted in contravention of this Article when it results from the use of force which is no more than absolutely necessary:

(a) in defence of any person from unlawful violence;
(b) in order to effect a lawful arrest or to prevent the escape of a person lawfully detained;
(c) in action lawfully taken for the purpose of quelling a riot or insurrection.

Article 2 protects the individual's right to life. It places a positive duty on the state to safeguard the lives of those within its jurisdiction and a negative duty to refrain from the unlawful taking of life (*Osman v United Kingdom* (1988) 29 EHRR 245). Extradition in circumstances which put the defendant's life in jeopardy may therefore violate Article 2 and/or Article 3 (*Lynas v Switzerland* (1976) 6 DR 141).

In assessing claims under Article 2, the Commission has held that there needs to be an 'almost certainty' of the applicant being killed before a violation of Article 2 is established. Allegations of the existence of a risk fall to be examined under Article 3.

In *Launder v United Kingdom*, Application 27279/95 (see also *R v Secretary of State for the Home Department ex p Launder* [1997] 1 WLR 839; *R v Secretary of State for the Home Department ex p Launder (No 2)* [1998] QB 994), the defendant was sought by Hong Kong for various offences of bribery and corruption. He argued that because Hong Kong had been returned to China as the Hong Kong SAR, and there was evidence to show that the Chinese had executed those convicted of financial crimes in the past (in breach of undertakings given to the requested state), his extradition would breach Article 2. The Commission rejected his claim, holding that the evidence presented did not demonstrate the 'near certainty' required under Article 2:

As regards intentional deprivation of life the Commission further recalls its case-law according to which it is not excluded that an issue might be raised under Article 2 in circumstances in which an expelling State knowingly puts the person concerned at such high risk of losing his life as for the outcome to be a near-certainty. However, there must be a 'near-certainty' of loss of life to make expulsion an 'intentional deprivation of life' prohibited by Article 2. Allegations of the existence of a 'real risk' only fall to be examined under the prohibition of inhuman treatment as enshrined in Article 3.

The Commission considers that a similar approach is justified not only in cases of expulsion, but also of extradition.

The defendant's allegation that he would be tortured in Hong Kong if returned was also rejected under the less stringent 'real risk' standard.

The exception for the death penalty in Article 2(1) is discussed below under the Sixth Protocol.

7.3.3 Article 3: Prohibition of Torture and Inhuman Treatment

Article 3 provides:

No-one shall be subjected to torture or inhuman and degrading treatment or punishment.

The Court has repeatedly stressed that the protection afforded by Article 3 ranks among the most important guaranteed by the Convention. The fact that the defendant is accused of serious crimes or that there are national security reasons for seeking his removal are irrelevant. The protection provided by Article 3 is absolute (*Chahal v United Kingdom* (1996) 23 EHRR 413, para 80).

'Torture' encompasses deliberate inhuman treatment causing very severe and cruel suffering, whether physical or mental (*Ireland v United Kingdom* (1978) 2 EHRR 25).

Mistreatment falling short of torture must reach a minimum level of severity to breach Article 3 (*Tyrer v United Kingdom* (1978) 2 EHRR 1, paras 29, 80). In the context of expulsion or extradition cases the ill-treatment must be such that 'it is an affront to fundamental humanitarian principles to remove an individual to a country where there is a real risk of serious ill-treatment' (*R (Razgar) v Secretary of State for the Home Department* [2003] EWCA Civ 840, para 10).

In determining whether the threshold has been crossed all the circumstances must be taken into account, including the nature and context of the treatment or punishment, the manner and method of its execution, its duration, its physical and mental effects, and the sex, age, and state of health of the victim.

Article 3 makes it unlawful for the UK to extradite an individual to a country where he or she is foreseeably at real risk of being seriously ill-treated in a manner sufficiently severe to engage Article 3 (see *Soering v United Kingdom* (1989) 11 EHRR 439; *R (Ullah) v Special Adjudicator* [2003] 1 WLR 770, para 47).

The burden of establishing an Article 3 claim lies on the appellant (*Aziz v Secretary of State for the Home Department* [2003] EWCA Civ 118, para 19). The material point in time for the assessment of risk is the date of the Court's consideration of the case (*Chahal v United Kingdom*, (1996) 23 EHRR 413, para 97). The Court is able to take into account all the material placed before it as well as information obtained of its own motion.

The appellant has to establish that there are 'substantial grounds for believing that there is a real risk of ill-treatment' of the requisite degree of severity in the receiving state (*R (Razgar) v Secretary of State for the Home Department* [2003] EWCA Civ 840, para 11, referring to *Soering v United Kingdom* (1989) 11 EHRR 439, para 91, and *Chahal v United Kingdom* (1996) 23 EHRR 413, para 74).

An applicant may be able to establish a breach of Article 3 either by referring to evidence specific to his own circumstances or by reference to evidence applicable to a class of which he is a member. In the second category of case the applicant will only be able to demonstrate substantial grounds for believing that there is such a real risk if he can point to a consistent pattern of gross and systematic violation of rights under Article 3 (*Batayav v Secretary of State for the Home Department* [2003] EWCA Civ 1489, para 7; *Hariri v Secretary of State for the Home Department* [2003] EWCA Civ 807, para 8).

The question in *Soering v United Kingdom* (1989) 11 EHRR 439 was whether the extradition of the defendant to Virginia on charges of capital murder would violate Article 3 of the Convention in view of the fact that the evidence showed he would spend between six and eight years on death row before being executed.

A preliminary issue was whether the UK could be held responsible for inhuman and degrading treatment inflicted by a foreign state. The Court said at para 88:

The question remains whether the extradition of a fugitive to another state where he would be subjected to or likely to be subjected to torture or to inhuman and degrading treatment or punishment would itself engage the responsibility of a Contracting State under Article 3 ... It would hardly be compatible with the underlying values of the Convention, that 'common heritage of political traditions, ideals, freedom and the rule of law' to which the Preamble refers, were a Contracting State knowingly to surrender a fugitive to another State where there were substantial grounds for believing that he would be in danger of being subjected to torture, however heinous the crime allegedly committed. Extradition in such circumstances, while not explicitly referred to in the brief and general wording of Article 3, would plainly be contrary to the spirit and intendment of the Article, and in the Court's view this inherent obligation not to extradite also extends to cases in which the fugitive would be faced in the receiving state by a real risk of exposure to inhuman and degrading treatment or punishment prescribed by that Article.

The Court concluded at para 111:

... having regard to the very long period of time spent on death row in such extreme conditions, with the ever present and mounting anguish of awaiting execution of the death penalty, and to the personal circumstances of the applicant, especially his age and mental state at the time of the offence, the applicant's extradition to the United States would expose him to a real risk of treatment going beyond the threshold set by Article 3. A further consideration of relevance is that in the particular instance the legitimate purpose of extradition could be achieved by another means which would not involve suffering of such exceptional intensity or duration.

To establish a breach of Article 3 it is not necessary to show an intention on the part of the state to humiliate or debase the victim (*Peers v Greece* (2001) 33 EHRR 1192, para 74; *Batayav v Secretary of State for the Home Department* [2003] EWCA Civ 1489, para 11). In *D v United Kingdom* (1997) 24 EHRR 423, D was a serving prisoner who was due to be deported to St Kitts at the conclusion of his sentence. Whilst in prison he developed AIDS. He argued that his deportation would violate Article 3 because of the lack of health-care in St Kitts for AIDS patients. The Court agreed, holding that Article 3 was not violated only by intentionally inflicted acts, but that it could also be infringed as a result of factors which did not engage the responsibility of public authorities and which did not, in themselves, infringe Article 3.

Where there is a risk of the defendant being detained in poor prison conditions in the requesting state then extradition may violate Article 3 if it can be shown that the minimum threshold of severity is passed (*Kalashnikov v Russia* (2002) 36 EHRR 587).

The extradition of a person who is physically or mentally ill may violate Article 3 if the illness is sufficiently severe (*Bulus v Sweden* (1984) 35 DR 57).

Article 3 may also be violated if there is a significant risk that speciality provisions will not be observed or that the defendant will be subjected to a totally disproportionate sentence (*Altun v Germany* (1983) 36 DR 209).

Article 3 will be violated not only where there is a real risk of ill-treatment by state officials. Extradition or deportation where there is a risk of ill-treatment by private individuals in the requesting state may violate Article 3 provided that it can be shown that the risk is significant and the requesting state cannot or will not obviate the risks (*Osman v United Kingdom* (1988) 29 EHRR 245; *HLR v France* (1997) 26 EHRR 29; *Horvath v Secretary of State for the Home Department* [2001] 1 AC 489; *R (Bagdanavicius) v Secretary of State for the Home Department*, The Times, 21 November 2003).

In *R (Ramda) v Secretary of State for the Home Department* [2002] EWHC 1278 (Admin) the Administrative Court quashed the Secretary of State's decision to return the applicant to France because he had failed properly to investigate serious allegations that the principal witness had been tortured by the French police to provide evidence incriminating the applicant. Significantly, Sedley LJ said at para 27 that it was no answer to rely on France's status as a signatory to the European Convention on Human Rights as sufficient protection for the applicant if he were to be returned to France.

7.3.4 Article 5: Right to Liberty and Security

7.3.4.1 *Article 5(1)(f)*
Article 5(1)(f) permits the detention of a person 'against whom action is being taken with a view to deportation or extradition'. This provision is subject to implied limitations. In *R v Governor of Brockhill Prison ex p Evans* [2001] 2 AC 19, 38, Lord Hope of Craighead summarized the relevant principles as follows:

The jurisprudence of the European Court of Human Rights indicates that there are various aspects to Article 5(1) which must be satisfied in order to show that the detention is lawful for the purposes of that article. The first question is whether the detention is lawful under domestic law. Any detention which is unlawful in domestic law will automatically be unlawful under Article 5(1). It will thus give rise to an enforceable right to compensation under Article 5(5), the provisions of which are not discretionary but mandatory. The second question is whether, assuming that the detention is lawful under domestic law, it nevertheless complies with the general requirements of the Convention. These are based upon the principle that any restriction on human rights and fundamental freedoms must be prescribed by law: see Articles 8 to 11 of the Convention. They include the requirements that the domestic law must be sufficiently accessible to the individual and that it must be sufficiently precise to enable the individual to foresee the consequences of the restriction: *Sunday Times v United Kingdom* (1979) 2 EHRR 245 and *Zamir v United Kingdom* (1983) 40 DR 42, paras 90–91. The third question is whether, again assuming that the detention is lawful under domestic law, it is nevertheless open to criticism on the ground that it is arbitrary because, for example, it was resorted to in bad faith or was not proportionate: *Engel v The Netherlands (No 1)* (1976) 1 EHRR 647, para 58 and *Tsirlis and Kouloumpas v Greece* (1997) 25 EHRR 198, para 56.

It follows that, for detention to be lawful, the state must act in good faith (*Bozano v Italy* (1987) 9 EHRR 297; *Quinn v France* (1995) 21 EHRR 529). Detention for the purposes of disguised extradition will violate Article 5(1)(f) (*Ocalan v Turkey* (2003) 37 EHRR 10). See Liu, 'European Court of Human Rights rules that the continued detention after a judicial decision directing release and the subsequent detention with a view to extradition constituted violations of Article 5(1) of the European Convention on Human Rights' (1997) 10 New York Int'l Law Rev 137.

Detention for the purposes of extradition is justified only so long as the deportation or extradition proceedings remain in progress; it will cease to be justified if such proceedings are not prosecuted with due diligence. In *Lynas v Switzerland* (1976) 6 DR 141 the Commission stated:

Article 5(1)(f) clearly permits the Commission to decide on the lawfulness of the detention of a person against whom action is being taken with a view to extradition . . . The wording of both the French and English texts makes it clear that only the existence of extradition proceedings justifies deprivation of liberty in such a case. It follows that if for example the proceedings are not conducted with the requisite diligence or if the detention results from some misuse of authority it ceases to be justifiable under Article 5(1)(f). Within these limits the Commission might therefore have cause to consider the length of time spent in detention pending extradition from the point of view of the above cited provision.

However, delays caused by a defendant's utilization of all available avenues of appeal will not violate Article 5(1)(f) provided the authorities have not demonstrated a lack of diligence (*Osman v United Kingdom*, Application 15933/89 (second application)).

Article 5(1)(f) refers to 'lawful arrest or detention' pursuant to a procedure 'prescribed by law'. The meaning of these terms was examined in *Day v Italy*, Application 34573/97. The applicant was an American citizen arrested and detained in Italy pursuant to a request from the United States. He alleged that his arrest and detention were neither 'lawful' within the meaning of the Convention nor governed by a procedure 'prescribed by law'. The Commission stated:

The Commission recalls that when requiring that a detention be 'lawful' and in compliance with a 'procedure prescribed by law' the Convention essentially refers back to national law and states the obligation to conform to the substantive and procedural rules thereof. It further requires that any deprivation of liberty should be consistent with the overall purpose of Article 5, namely to protect individuals from arbitrariness . . . If detention is to be 'lawful', including the observance of a procedure prescribed by law, it must essentially comply with national law and the substantive and procedural rules thereof . . . Article 5(1)(f) does not require the Commission to provide its own interpretation on questions of national law concerning the legality of the detention or extradition. The scope of the Commission's review is limited to examining whether there was a legal basis for the detention and whether the decision of the courts on the question of lawfulness could be described as arbitrary in the light of the facts of the case . . .

The use of unlawfully obtained evidence in extradition proceedings may in exceptional circumstances result in a violation of Article 5(1)(f). In *Chinoy v United Kingdom*, Application 15199/89, the applicant was sought by the United States for conspiring to possess cocaine with intent to distribute, conspiring to launder drugs money, and knowingly laundering drugs money. Much of the evidence against him had been obtained by United States' investigators in France, possibly in breach of French law. He argued that the requirements of Article 5 excluded the possibility of detention for extradition solely on the basis of evidence which, although not unlawful in domestic terms, is considered unlawful under the domestic law of a third state and which may have been obtained in violation of that state's sovereignty, and which is considered to be in violation of the Convention. The Commission analysed the problem as follows:

The question therefore arises as to what extent the alleged unlawfulness of evidence falls to be considered under Article 5(1)(f) of the Convention. The European Court of Human Rights has held, in the context of Article 5(1)(e) of the Convention: 'On the question whether the detention is "lawful" including whether it complies with "a procedure prescribed by law", the Convention refers back essentially to national law and lays down the obligation to conform to the substantive and procedural rules thereof. However, it requires in addition that any deprivation of liberty should be consistent with the purpose of Article 5, namely to protect individuals from arbitrariness . . . There is no indication in the present case that the procedural or substantive rules of domestic law were infringed. Moreover, although the domestic courts appear, in the absence of evidence to the contrary, to have accepted as admitted that the recording of the evidence was in fact in violation of French law and/or of the Convention, the Commission has already found that this cannot be accepted as the final conclusion, either as to French law or as to the Convention. Moreover, the domestic courts considered that breaches of French law and/or the Convention "could carry no more weight than breaches of English law". The Commission finds no indication of arbitrariness in the decision of the United Kingdom courts to admit evidence which may have been obtained, and appears to have been accepted by the domestic courts as having been obtained, in breach of French law and/or the Convention. It follows that at all relevant times the applicant's detention was covered by Article 5(1)(f) of the Convention and this part of the application is therefore manifestly ill-founded.'

Therefore the Commission, whilst rejecting the complaint on the facts, left open the possibility that an extradition based on illegally obtained evidence could breach Article 5(1)(f). This is of particular importance because, as discussed below, the Commission has held that Article 6 does not apply to extradition proceedings.

7.3.4.2 *Article 5(3)*
Article 5(3) requires all persons to be eligible for bail where they are detained under Article 5(1)(c). Whilst on its face this excludes extradition proceedings

(the ground for detention in such cases being Article 5(1)(f)), in *Osman v United Kingdom*, Application 15933/89, the Commission stated:

> ... given the primordial importance of the right to liberty ensured by Article 5(1) of the Convention, the Commission may examine whether the refusal of bail to an individual, even if his detention falls within Article 5(1)(f) of the Convention, could be said to be unreasonable or arbitrary, thus affecting the general notion of lawfulness, which is a common thread throughout the provisions of Article 5(1) of the Convention.

The European Court has recognized a number of grounds which can, in principle, justify a refusal of bail. Pre-trial detention may be compatible with the defendant's right to release under Article 5(3) if, were the defendant released, he or she would fail to attend trial (*Wemhoff v Germany* (1987) 1 EHRR 55, para 14; *Matznetter v Austria* (1969) 1 EHRR 198, para 8; *Stögmüller v Austria* (1969) 1 EHRR 155, para 15; *B v Austria* (1990) 13 EHRR 20, para 41; *Letellier v France* (1991) 14 EHRR 83, paras 40–43; *Kemmache v France (No 3)* (1994) 19 EHRR 349, para 52), interfere with evidence or witnesses, or otherwise obstruct the course of justice (*Clooth v Belgium* (1991) 14 EHRR 717, paras 43–44), or commit a serious offence (*Matznetter v Austria* (1969) 1 EHRR 198, para 9).

Detention may also be justified if it is necessary for the purposes of the investigation into the defendant's case (*Clooth v Belgium* (1991) 14 EHRR 717), if his or her release would result in a disturbance to public order (*Tomasi v France* (1992) 15 EHRR 1, para 91), or if it is necessary for the defendant's own protection.

These grounds are merely *capable* of justifying pre-trial detention. Whether any of them will *in fact* justify such detention in a particular case will depend (i) on the circumstances of the individual case, (ii) the strength of the evidence that the risk to be averted by the detention is a real risk, (iii) the length of the detention, and the persuasiveness of the arguments put forward to justify it.

The European Court attaches particular importance to the standard of reasoning in bail decisions (*Letellier v France* (1991) 14 EHRR 83, paras 40–43):

> It falls in the first place to the national judicial authorities to ensure that, in a given case, the pre-trial detention of an accused person does not exceed a reasonable time. To this end they must examine all the circumstances arguing for or against the existence of a genuine requirement of public interest justifying, with due regard to the principle of the presumption of innocence, a departure from the rule of respect for individual liberty and set them out in their decisions on the application for release. It is essentially on the basis of the reasons given in these decisions and of the true facts mentioned by the applicant in his applications for release and his appeals that the Court is called upon to decide whether or not there has been a violation of Article 5(3) of the Convention.

The European Court requires a high standard of reasoning to justify the refusal of bail. The reasons must be concrete and focused on the facts of the case rather than be abstract or stereotyped; be consistent with, and sustained by, the facts as assessed by the court; and must take into account the defendant's arguments.

In *Ringeisen v Austria* (1971) 1 EHRR 455 the Court stated that the length of the applicant's detention exceeded a reasonable time and violated Article 5(3) since the reasons that the national courts had given for detaining him could not sustain their conclusions as to the existence of the grounds upon which they sought to rely in order to justify their decisions on his applications for release. In *Letellier v France* (1991) 14 EHRR 83 the Court moved directly from a critical summary of the reasoning of the French courts to the conclusion that 'therefore' the detention of the applicant, after a certain point in time, 'ceased to be based on relevant and sufficient grounds'. *Yagci and Sargin v Turkey* (1995) 20 EHRR 505 concerned the detention of the leaders of two left-wing parties charged with attacks on the constitution and the Turkish state. The national courts based their decision to refuse bail on the 'nature of the offences', the 'state of the evidence', and the 'date of [the] arrest'. The Court found that the applicants' rights under Article 5(3) had been violated by the refusal of the domestic courts to release them, and based this finding on the fact that, in its view, the reasons which the national courts had given for their decisions did not 'stand up to scrutiny'. The Court said:

... the danger of an accused's absconding cannot be gauged solely on the basis of the severity of the sentence risked. It must be assessed with reference to a number of other relevant factors which may either confirm the existence of a danger of absconding or make it appear so slight that it cannot justify detention pending trial.

The significance of these decisions for domestic bail decisions is that, usually, where bail is refused, the district judge does no more than recite that the statutory conditions in Sch 1 of the Bail Act 1976 are satisfied, and boxes are ticked on the bail form reflecting that this is because of the nature and seriousness of the offence, etc. These reasons do not record the defence's submissions. This method of adjudicating upon bail applications risks falling foul of the European Court's case law that reasons must not be abstract or stereotyped. The court should be required to provide detailed reasons which, while they need not be elaborate, should show that the court has identified the main factual submissions made to it, and what conclusions it reached upon them.

Bail under the EA 2003 is dealt with at 4.5 above.

7.3.4.3 *Article 5(4)*

Article 5(4) provides that:

... everyone who is deprived of his liberty by arrest or detention shall be entitled to take proceedings by which the lawfulness of his detention shall be decided speedily by a court and his release ordered if his detention is not lawful.

In *R (Kashamu) v Governor of Brixton Prison* [2002] QB 887, a case under the EA 1989, the Administrative Court held that in order to comply with Article 5(4) the Magistrates' Court holding committal proceedings was required to have jurisdiction to determine the question of whether a fugitive's detention was lawful in the Convention sense, ie, non-arbitrary detention (*R v Governor of Brockhill Prison ex p Evans* [2001] AC 19, 38). It held that detention arising from bad faith or an abuse of power, in particular, would render detention arbitrary and unlawful under the Convention. See also *Re Darren Hayes*, Unreported, 9 October 2000, CO/1339/2000.

The *Kashamu* abuse jurisdiction applies equally to those who are on bail in extradition proceedings. This is because for fundamental extradition purposes, including the right to apply for *habeas corpus*, they are effectively in, and have to be treated as in, custody (*R v Secretary of State ex p Launder (No 2)* [1998] QB 994, 1011).

Abuse of process under the EA 2003 is discussed at 5.9.2 above.

The European Court has held that the reference to a 'court' in Article 5(4) guarantees certain procedural rights for the defendant (*De Wilde v Belgium (No 1)* (1971) 1 EHRR 373 paras 76–79). The form of procedural guarantees which are required to ensure compliance with Article 5(4) vary according to the facts of the case. Where the conduct relied on as justifying detention is criminal in nature (in that it could give rise to criminal charges) the procedural guarantees should not be markedly inferior to those under Article 6.

Article 5(4) requires there to be 'equality of arms' between the parties of the type contained in Article 6 (*Toth v Austria* (1991) 14 EHRR 551, para 84). This means that the defendant in extradition proceedings must have 'a reasonable opportunity of presenting his case to the court under conditions which do not place him at a substantial disadvantage vis-à-vis his opponent' (*Neumeister v Austria* 1 EHRR 91, para 22; *Delcourt v Belgium* 1 EHRR 355; *Borgers v Belgium* 15 EHRR 92, paras 26–28; *Jespers v Belgium* 27 DR 61, paras 51–56; *Bendenoun v France* (1994) 18 EHRR 54, para 52). The procedure adopted must ensure equal treatment and it must be 'truly adversarial' which requires, where necessary, adequate disclosure (*Lamy v Belgium* (1989) 11 EHRR 529, para 29; *Sanchez-Reisse v Switzerland* (1986) 9 EHRR 71; *R v Governor of Brixton Prison ex p Kashamu*, Unreported, 6 October 2000, CO/2141/2000). The defendant must have legal advice prior to the hearing and representation at it where this is necessary to make the hearing effective (*Zamir v United Kingdom* (1983) 40 DR 42). The defendant must be given time and facilities for the preparation of his case and the time must not be so short as to restrict the tangibility and availability of the remedy (*Farmakopoulous v Belgium* (1992) 16 EHRR 187 at para 51 (Commission Report)).

7.3.5 Article 6: Right to Fair Trial

Article 6(1) provides:

In the determination of his civil rights and obligations or of any criminal charges against him, everyone is entitled to a fair and public hearing within a reasonable time by an independent and impartial tribunal established by law. Judgment shall be pronounced publicly but the press and public may be excluded from all or part of the trial in the interests of morals, public order or national security in a democratic society, where the interests of juveniles or the protection of the private life of the parties so require, or to the extent strictly necessary in the opinion of the court in special circumstances where publicity would prejudice the interests of justice.

Article 6(2) provides that everyone charged with a criminal offence shall be presumed innocent until proved guilty according to law, and Article 6(3) sets out a number of specific guarantees applicable in criminal cases.

Article 6 does not apply in terms to extradition proceedings. In other words, the domestic extradition process does not have to offer all the guarantees in Article 6(3), eg, the right to cross-examine witnesses (*R (Al-Fawwaz) v Governor of HMP Brixton* [2001] 1 WLR 1234, para 59; *Lodhi v Governor of HMP Brixton* [2001] EWHC Admin 178). This is because Article 6 only applies to the full process of the examination of an individual's guilt or innocence of an offence and not the mere process of determining whether a person can be extradited to another country (*Kirkwood v United Kingdom* (1984) 37 DR 158; *H v Spain* (1983) 37 DR 93). The fact that in domestic law extradition proceedings are classified as criminal proceedings (*R v Governor of Brixton Prison ex p Levin* [1997] AC 741) is not determinative of the issue because the Court adopts an autonomous approach to the interpretation of terms such as 'civil' and 'criminal' in the Convention. However, Article 6 still has relevance in extradition because, as explained above, Article 5(4) imports into extradition hearings many, although not all, of the procedural protections in Article 6.

Extradition will be incompatible with Article 6 if there is a real risk that the defendant will suffer a flagrant denial of justice in the requesting state (*R (Ramda) v Secretary of State for the Home Department* [2002] EWHC 1278 (Admin), para 10; *Soering v United Kingdom* (1989) 11 EHRR 439, para 113; *Drozd and Janousek v France* (1992) 14 EHRR 745, para 110; *R (Eliott) v Secretary of State for the Home Department* [2001] EWHC Admin 559; *R v Secretary of State ex p Johnson* [1999] QB 1174, 1190; *Launder v United Kingdom*, Application 27279/95). It follows that the proceedings in the requesting state may need to be closely scrutinized in order to see whether they meet the requirements of Article 6, although other legal systems should not be judged necessarily by reference to the UK's system (*R (Abdullah) v Secretary of State* [2001] EWHC Admin 263, paras 42–43).

Where an extradition defendant faces a trial based upon evidence obtained by torture then his extradition is likely to breach Article 6. This is because an accused who is convicted on evidence obtained from him (or someone else) by torture has not had a fair trial (*R (Ramda) v Secretary of State for the Home Department* [2002] EWHC 1278 (Admin), para 9). The breach of Article 6(1) lies not in the use of torture (which is, separately, a breach of Article 3) but in the reception of the evidence by the court for the purposes of determining the charge (*Montgomery v HM Advocate* [2001] 2 WLR 779, 785).

7.3.6 Article 8 (Respect for Private and Family Life)

Article 8 provides:

8(1) Everyone has the right to respect for his private and family life, his home and his correspondence.

(2) There shall be no interference by a public authority with the exercise of this right except such as is in accordance with the law and is necessary in a democratic society in the interests of national security, public safety or the economic well-being of the country, for the prevention of disorder or crime, for the protection of health or morals, or for the protection of the rights and freedoms of others.

The concept of private life in Article 8 is broadly defined (*Niemietz v Germany* 16 EHRR 97, para 29). It includes not only personal information, but an individual's relationships with others, including (in certain circumstances) business relationships (ibid). Family life extends beyond the formal relationships created by marriage, and includes, for example, relationships between a parent and an illegitimate child (*Marckx v Belgium* 2 EHRR 330).

The right to privacy under Article 8 may be violated by intrusive surveillance, for example, telephone intercepts or the use of listening and tracking devices (*Klass v Germany* (1978) 2 EHRR 214; *Malone v United Kingdom* (1984) 7 EHRR 14).

Article 8 imposes strict standards on the regulation and supervision of such evidence-gathering techniques. Where the requesting state seeks to rely on evidence obtained in breach of Article 8 it does not, however, automatically fall to be excluded under s 78 of the Police and Criminal Evidence Act 1984 (*R v Governor of Brixton Prison ex p Levin* [1997] AC 741; *Khan* [1997] AC 558). Nor does the use of such evidence at trial automatically lead to such unfairness that Article 6 is breached (*Khan v United Kingdom* (2000) 8 BHRC 310).

A criminal prosecution constitutes an 'interference by a public authority' for the purposes of Article 8(2) (*Laskey v United Kingdom* (1997) 24 EHRR 39; *Dudgeon v United Kingdom* (1981) 4 EHRR 149). The mere threat of a prosecution may be sufficient if it directly interferes with private life (*Norris v Ireland* 13 EHRR 186).

Extradition also constitutes an interference with the right to respect for family life in Article 8(1). Such an interference will be in breach of Article 8 unless it is justified under Article 8(2) as being 'in accordance with the law' and 'necessary in a democratic society' for one of the aims set out (*Launder v United Kingdom*, Application 27279/95). Given that extradition can in general only be ordered in respect of offences of a minimum level of seriousness, it is likely that striking facts will be required before a violation of Article 8 would be established. In *Launder v United Kingdom*, Application 27279/95, the Commission indicated its general approach:

The Commission finds that the applicant's extradition would amount to an interference with his family life, it being common ground that his wife currently lives in the

United Kingdom. However, it appears undisputed that the decision to extradite the applicant complied with the formal requirements of United Kingdom law. As regards the applicant's claim that his extradition some 19 years after the alleged offences would be contrary to legal certainty and that the courts' approach to the issue of the passage of time was not reasonably foreseeable the Commission has already found that when examining whether extradition should be allowed the decisions of the domestic courts were neither arbitrary nor unreasonable. Furthermore, the Commission finds that the decision to extradite the applicant has a legitimate aim, namely the prevention of disorder or crime. As regards the question whether the interference was necessary, the Commission recalls that the notion of necessity implies a pressing social need and requires that the interference at issue be proportionate to the legitimate aim pursued . . . The Commission considers that it is only in exceptional circumstances that the extradition of a person to face trial on charges of serious offences committed in the requesting State would be held to be an unjustified or disproportionate interference with the right to respect for family life. The Commission finds that in the present case no such circumstances have been shown to exist. The Commission notes that the applicant and, apparently, his family lived in Hong Kong for about ten years. Also for several years prior to the applicant's arrest they were living outside the United Kingdom and were changing their domicile. Furthermore, the applicant has not shown that his wife or children would not be able to travel with him to the HKSAR or visit him there.

7.3.7 Sixth Protocol to the Convention (Death Penalty)

As drafted, Article 2 of the Convention specifically preserves the death penalty. However, in *Ocalan v Turkey* (2003) 37 EHRR 10 the European Court said that it could not exclude, in the light of the developments in state practice on capital punishment during the 1990s, that state parties to the Convention had agreed through their practice to modify the second sentence in Article 2(1) in so far as it permits capital punishment in peacetime. The Court said it could also be argued that the implementation of the death penalty can be regarded as inhuman and degrading treatment contrary to Article 3. However the Court did not reach a final conclusion on this point.

The Sixth Protocol to the Convention is the instrument which prohibits the death penalty. The UK ratified the Sixth Protocol in 1999 and it forms one of the Convention rights in Sch 1 to the HRA 1998. Article 1 provides:

1. The death penalty shall be abolished. No-one shall be condemned to such penalty or executed.

The UK's ratification of the Sixth Protocol had two principal consequences. First, it required the UK to abolish the death penalty entirely for peacetime offences. In fact, the Government commendably went further and abolished capital punishment for offences committed in time of war also (Crime and Disorder Act 1998, s 36; HRA 1998, s 21(5)). Second, ratification resulted in the UK acquiring a new international obligation not to subject those under its control to a risk of either being sentenced to death or being executed (*Soering v United Kingdom* (1989) 11 EHRR 439).

Extradition from the UK is no longer permissible for offences where there is a real risk of the defendant being sentenced to death, irrespective of whether the sentence is likely to be carried out. This follows from the wording of Article 1 of the Sixth Protocol, which prohibits *both* the sentencing of prisoners to death *and* the carrying out of the execution.

However, there is a tension between this prohibition and the provisions of the EA 2003. Section 95 provides:

95(1) The Secretary of State must not order a person's extradition to a category 2 territory if he could be, will be or has been sentenced to death for the offence concerned in the category 2 territory.

(2) Subsection (1) does not apply if the Secretary of State receives a written assurance which he considers adequate that a sentence of death:

(a) will not be imposed, or
(b) will not be carried out (if imposed).

Given that Article 1 of the Sixth Protocol prohibits the sentencing of any person to death irrespective of whether or not the sentence will be carried out it is difficult to see how the Secretary of State would be acting compatibly with Article 1 if he were to accept an undertaking that a person would be sentenced to death but not executed.

It is therefore submitted that, in order for extradition to be compatible with Article 1 of the Sixth Protocol, the Secretary of State must receive a written assurance that the death penalty will not be imposed in the requesting state (*R (St John) v Governor of Brixton Prison* [2002] QB 613; *Minister of Justice v Burns* [2001] SCC 7). The effectiveness of any such undertaking must be critically scrutinized by the Secretary of State, and ideally there should be evidence of the undertaking's effectiveness in the domestic law of the requesting state (*R v Secretary of State for the Home Department ex p Launder (No 2)* [1998] QB 994). English courts have jurisdiction to scrutinize the effectiveness of undertakings concerning the death penalty (*R (St John) v Governor of Brixton Prison* [2002] QB 613, para 64). Only where it is clear that the undertaking provides adequate protection for the defendant should the Secretary of State accept it under s 95(2).

In the United States, undertakings are given by the Department of Justice on behalf of the Federal Government. However, capital punishment is nearly always imposed by individual states at the instance of the local district attorney. There have been cases where, despite the fact that the Federal Government has requested a state not to carry out an execution, the execution has proceeded regardless (see *Paraguay v United States* (The *Breard* Case), Unreported, 9 April 1998 (ICJ); Koh, 'Paying "decent respect" to world opinion on the death penalty' 35(5) UC Davis Law Review, 1085–1131; Rieter, 'Interim measures by the World Court to suspend the execution of an individual: the *Breard* case', NQHR 1998, 16(4), 475–494; *Germany v United States of America* [1999] ICJ Rep 9 (ICJ); Feria Tinta, 'Due process and the right to life in the context of the Vienna Convention on Consular Relations: arguing the *LaGrand* case' (2001) 12 EJIL 363). It follows that the effectiveness of undertakings given by the United States Government must be scrutinized carefully to ensure that they will be effective at the state level (see House of Commons and House of Lords Joint Committee on Human Rights, 20th Report, 26 July 2002, para 28).

There is considerable literature on the tensions between, in particular, the United States' use of the death penalty and extradition; see especially Nanda, 'Bases for refusing international extradition requests—capital punishment and torture' (2000) 23 Fordham Int'l Law Jour 1369; Williams, 'Extradition to a state that imposes the death penalty' (1990) 28 Can YBIL 117; Pinkard, 'The death penalty for drug kingpins' (1999) 24 Vermont Law Rev 1; Schabas, 'International law and the abolition of the death penalty: recent developments' (1998) 4 ILSA Jour Int'l Law 535; De Witt, 'Extradition enigma: Italy and human rights v. America and the death penalty' (1998) 47 Cath Uni Law Rev 535; McGarvey, 'Missed opportunity? The affirmation of the death penalty in the AEDPA: extradition scenarios' (1998) 24 Jour of Legislation 99.

8

THE ROLE OF THE SECRETARY OF STATE. DEFERRAL OF EXTRADITION

8.1 INTRODUCTION

In Chapters 4 and 5 the Secretary of State's limited role at the beginning of the extradition process in Category 2 cases was considered. This chapter examines his role in Category 2 cases after the extradition hearing has taken place, when he has to decide whether to order extradition. One of the major changes to the extradition regime effected by the EA 2003 is the substantially reduced role of the Secretary of State. He is no longer required to consider whether extradition would be wrong, unjust, or oppressive before ordering return (cf EA 1989, s 12; *Atkinson v Government of the United States of America* [1971] AC 197, 232). His principal task under the EA 2003 is to consider whether any of the restrictions in ss 94–96 are made out. The main part of this chapter analyses these provisions.

This chapter also considers the Secretary of State's and appropriate judge's duty to regulate competing extradition claims; their obligations where an extradition defendant is the subject of domestic criminal proceedings; and their powers where the defendant has claimed asylum in the UK.

8.2 THE SECRETARY OF STATE'S DECISION AFTER THE EXTRADITION HEARING UNDER PART 2

As explained in Chapter 5, in Part 1 cases the Secretary of State has virtually no role. If no national security issue under s 208 arises, once the extradition order has been made by the appropriate judge under s 21(3) then, subject to any appeal, the defendant is liable to be extradited.

In Part 2 cases, if the appropriate judge decides that there are no bars to extradition then he is required to send the case to the Secretary of State for his decision whether the defendant is to be extradited (s 87(3)). Section 93 then applies. Section 93(2) provides that the Secretary of State must decide whether he is prohibited from ordering the defendant's extradition under:

(a) section 94 (death penalty);
(b) section 95 (speciality);
(c) section 96 (earlier extradition to the UK from other territory).

If the Secretary of State decides that any of these restrictions is applicable then he must order the defendant's discharge (s 93(3)). Otherwise, he must order the defendant to be extradited unless:

(a) he is informed the request has been withdrawn;

(b) he makes an order under s 126(2) or s 179(2) for further proceedings on the request to be deferred and the person is discharged under s 180;

(c) he orders discharge under s 208.

8.2.1 Representations

Under s 13 of the EA 1989 the defendant had the right to make written representations to the Secretary of State setting out why an order for return should not be made in his case. The process of making representations could be a complex one. The Secretary of State was under a duty to consider representations fairly and, where necessary, to provide adequate disclosure to interested parties to enable them to make further representations (*R v Secretary of State for the Home Department ex p Ramda* [2002] EWHC 1272 Admin; *R v Secretary of State for the Home Department ex p Kingdom of Belgium*, Unreported, 15 February 2000, CO/236/00). He was also under a duty to keep his order for return under continuous review and to revisit it if further relevant information came to light (*R v Secretary of State for the Home Department ex p Launder* [1997] 1 WLR 839, 852).

The EA 2003 reduces the Secretary of State's burden by simplifying the questions he has to address following the appropriate judge's decision. Also, s 93(5) provides that he is not required to consider any representations received by him after the end of the 'permitted period'. By s 93(6), this is the period of six weeks starting with the 'appropriate day'. The 'appropriate day' is defined in s 102. In most cases, it is the day on which the appropriate judge makes his decision (s 102(7)).

8.2.2 Death Penalty (Section 94)

Section 94 provides that the Secretary of State must not order a person's extradition to a Category 2 territory if he could be, will be, or has been sentenced to death for the offence concerned in the Category 2 territory (s 94(1)). However, s 94(1) does not apply if the Secretary of State receives a written assurance which he considers adequate that a sentence of death:

(a) will not be imposed, or
(b) will not be carried out (if imposed).

This section is considered in detail at 7.3.7 above.

8.2.3 Speciality (Section 95)

Section 95(1) provides that the Secretary of State must not order the defendant's extradition to a Category 2 territory if there are no speciality arrangements with the Category 2 territory, unless the defendant consented to his extradition under s 27 before his case was sent to the Secretary of State (s 95(2)).

Section 95(3) defines when there are speciality arrangements. There are speciality arrangements with a Category 2 territory if (and only if) under the law of that territory or arrangements made between it and the UK a person who is extradited to the territory from the UK may be dealt with in the territory for an offence committed before his extradition only if:

(a) the offence is one falling within s 95(4), or
(b) he is first given an opportunity to leave the territory.

The offences in s 95(4) are the offence in respect of which the person is extradited; an extradition offence disclosed by the same facts as that offence, other than one in respect of which a sentence of death could be imposed; an extradition offence in respect of which the Secretary of State consents to the person being dealt with; and an offence in respect of which the person waives the right that he would have (but for s 95(4)(d)) not to be dealt with for the offence.

Section 95 requires the protection of the defendant in the law of the requesting state against re-surrender to another jurisdiction. This is a form of 'dealing with' prohibited by s 95 (*R v Secretary of State for the Home Department ex p Launder (No 2)* [1998] QB 994, 1001).

Arrangements made with a Category 2 territory which is a Commonwealth country or a British overseas territory may be made for a particular case, or more generally (s 95(5)). A certificate issued by or under the authority of the Secretary of State confirming the existence of arrangements with a Category 2 territory which is a Commonwealth country or a British overseas territory and stating the terms of the arrangements is conclusive evidence of those matters (s 95(6)) (cf EA 1989, s 6(4) and (7)).

Hence, although arrangements may be made with other territories, a certificate will not be conclusive, and a court therefore has jurisdiction to inquire into the effectiveness of the arrangements and whether they provide the protections required by s 95(3) and (4) (*R v Secretary of State for the Home Department, ex p Launder (No 2)* [1998] QB 994, 1003–1004.)

8.2.4 Earlier Extradition to UK from other Territory

Section 96(1) provides that the Secretary of State must not order a person's extradition to a Category 2 territory if:

(a) the person was extradited to the UK from another territory (the extraditing territory);

(b) under arrangements between the UK and the extraditing territory, that territory's consent is required to the person's extradition from the UK to the Category 2 territory in respect of the extradition offence under consideration;

(c) that consent has not been given on behalf of the extraditing territory.

A problem relating to re-extradition arose in *R v Secretary of State for the Home Department ex p Akbar*, Unreported, 31 July 1996, CO/1707/96. The defendant had been extradited to the UK from France in respect of certain offences. The United States requested his extradition and the French Government was asked to consent to re-extradition under Article 15 of the European Convention on Extradition 1957. Consent was not immediately forthcoming, and the Secretary of State proposed to extradite the defendant without waiting for consent. It was argued for the Secretary of State that Article 15 of the European Convention on Extradition 1957 had no application because the request for extradition was being made under Sch 1 to the EA 1989, which had no relevant provision, and nor did the extradition treaty between the UK and the United States. This argument was rejected by the Divisional Court:

It seems to me that, having regard to principles of international comity, firstly the Secretary of State would not wish that the applicant should be returned to the United States against the wishes of the French government; equally the United States government would not wish to cause the Secretary of State the embarrassment of acting against the wishes of the French government; and the French government for its part would not wish, except for sound reasons, to refuse consent to re-extradition for a serious offence committed by the applicant in the United States which has come to light since it originally returned the applicant to the United Kingdom in 1993.

8.3 THE SECRETARY OF STATE'S DECISION

8.3.1 Procedure

Where the Secretary of State orders the defendant's extradition under Part 2 he must inform the defendant of the order, inform him in ordinary language that he has a right of appeal to the High Court (unless the defendant has consented to his extradition under s 127), and inform a person acting on behalf of the Category 2 territory of the order (s 100(1)).

If the Secretary of State has received an assurance concerning the death penalty, as mentioned in s 94(2), he must give the defendant a copy of the assurance when he informs him under s 100(1) of the order (s 100(3)).

If the Secretary of State orders the defendant's discharge he must inform him of the order and inform a person acting on behalf of the Category 2 territory of the order (s 100(4)).

Orders for extradition or discharge under s 93, and an order for discharge under s 123, must be made under the hand of the Secretary of State, a Minister of State, a Parliamentary Under-Secretary of State, or a senior official (s 101(1) and (3)). 'Senior officials' are members of the Senior Civil Service and members of the Senior Management Structure of Her Majesty's Diplomatic Service.

8.3.2 Time Limits

In keeping with the EA 2003's underlying policy of speeding up extradition, Part 2 imposes a timetable within which the Secretary of State must take his decision on return.

Section 99 applies if the appropriate judge sends a case to the Secretary of State under Part 2 for his decision whether the defendant is to be extradited, and within the 'required period' the Secretary of State does not make an order for his extradition or discharge. Then, if the defendant applies to the High Court to be discharged, the court must order his discharge (s 99(2)).

However if, before the required period ends, the Secretary of State applies to the High Court for it to be extended, the High Court may make an order accordingly; and this may happen on more than one occasion (s 99(4)).

The required period is the period of two months starting with the appropriate day (s 99(3)). The appropriate day is defined in detail in s 102.

8.4 COMPETING EXTRADITION CLAIMS AND DEFERRAL OF EXTRADITION

Where a defendant is being dealt with under Part 1, and a second Category 1 territory sends a Part 1 warrant to the UK for execution, then it is for the appropriate judge to decide which of the warrants is to take priority, in accordance with s 44. This provision is considered at 5.10 above.

However, where there are competing proceedings under Part 1 and Part 2, or two or more sets of proceedings under Part 2, the Secretary of State has power under the EA 2003 to regulate the proceedings to ensure their orderly processing and disposal.

Also, where an extradition defendant is charged with a domestic offence then the appropriate judge (in Category 1 cases) or the Secretary of State (in Category 2 cases) has power to defer processing of the extradition case until after the domestic offence has been disposed of.

These powers will be now be examined.

8.4.1 Competing Part 1 Warrant and Request under Part 2

Section 179 applies if at the same time:

(a) there is a Part 1 warrant in respect of a person, a certificate has been issued under s 2 in respect of the warrant, and the person has not been extradited in pursuance of the warrant or discharged, and

(b) there is a request for the same person's extradition, a certificate has been issued under s 70 in respect of the request, and the person has not been extradited in pursuance of the request or discharged.

In this situation the Secretary of State may (s 179(2)):

(a) order proceedings (or further proceedings) on one of them (the warrant or the request) to be deferred until the other one has been disposed of, if neither the warrant nor the request has been disposed of;

(b) order the defendant's extradition in pursuance of the warrant to be deferred until the request has been disposed of, if an order for his extradition in pursuance of the warrant has been made;

(c) order the defendant's extradition in pursuance of the request to be deferred until the warrant has been disposed of, if an order for his extradition in pursuance of the request has been made.

Section 179(3) prescribes the matters that the Secretary of State must take into account in taking his decision under s 179(2):

(a) the relative seriousness of the offences concerned;

(b) the place where each offence was committed (or was alleged to have been committed);

(c) the date when the warrant was issued and the date when the request was received;

(d) whether, in the case of each offence, the person is accused of its commission (but not alleged to have been convicted) or is alleged to be unlawfully at large after conviction.

8.4.2 Competing Extradition Requests under Part 2

Section 126 regulates competing requests for extradition under Part 2. It applies if:

(a) the Secretary of State receives a valid request for the defendant's extradition to a Category 2 territory;

(b) the person is in the UK;

(c) before the person is extradited in pursuance of the request or discharged, the Secretary of State receives another valid request for the defendant's extradition.

The Secretary of State may then do one of two things (s 126(2)). He may:

(a) order proceedings (or further proceedings) on one of the requests to be deferred until the other one has been disposed of, if neither of the requests has been disposed of;

(b) order the defendant's extradition in pursuance of the request under consideration to be deferred until the other request has been disposed of, if an order for his extradition in pursuance of the request under consideration has been made.

In taking this decision the Secretary of State must take into account in particular the following (s 126(3)):

(a) the relative seriousness of the offences concerned;

(b) the place where each offence was committed (or was alleged to have been committed);

(c) the date when each request was received;

(d) whether, in the case of each offence, the defendant is accused of its commission (but not alleged to have been convicted) or is alleged to be unlawfully at large after conviction.

8.4.3 Resumption of Deferred Proceedings

Section 180 governs what is to happen where proceedings have been deferred under the EA 2003 because of a competing extradition claim. Section 180 applies if:

(a) an order is made under the EA 2003 deferring proceedings on an extradition claim in respect of the defendant (the deferred claim) until another extradition claim in respect of the person has been disposed of, and

(b) the other extradition claim is disposed of.

In this context, an extradition claim is made in respect of a defendant if a Part 1 warrant is issued in respect of him or a request for his extradition is made (s 180(9)).

Section 180(2) provides that the judge may make an order for proceedings on the deferred claim to be resumed but, by s 180(3), no such order may be made after the end of the required period. The 'required period' is 21 days starting with the day on which the other extradition claim is disposed of (s 180(6)).

By s 180(4), the judge has a general discretion to order the defendant's discharge. However, s 180(5) provides that if the defendant applies to the appropriate judge to be discharged, the judge *must* order his discharge if:

(a) the required period has ended, and

(b) the judge has not made an order under s 180(2) or already ordered the person's discharge.

If the proceedings on the deferred claim were under Part 1, s 67 applies for determining the appropriate judge (s 180(7)). If the proceedings on the deferred claim were under Part 2, s 139 applies for determining the appropriate judge (s 180(8)).

8.4.4 Proceedings where Extradition has been Deferred

Section 181 applies where a direction has been given deferring the defendant's extradition, rather than proceedings in respect of the extradition request. Section 181 applies if:

(a) an order is made under the EA 2003 deferring the defendant's extradition in pursuance of an extradition claim (the deferred claim) until another extradition claim in respect of him has been disposed of;

(b) the other extradition claim is disposed of.

An extradition claim is made in respect of the defendant if a Part 1 warrant is issued in respect of him or a request for his extradition is made (s 181(9)).

By s 181(2), the judge may make an order for the defendant's extradition in pursuance of the deferred claim to cease to be deferred, however no order under subsection (2) may be made after the end of the required period (s 181(3)). The required period is 21 days starting with the day on which the other extradition claim is disposed of.

Section 181(4) provides that if the defendant applies to the appropriate judge to be discharged, the judge may order his discharge. By s 181(5), if the defendant applies to the appropriate judge to be discharged, the judge *must* order his discharge if:

(a) the required period has ended, and

(b) the judge has not made an order under subsection (2) or already ordered the defendant's discharge.

If the defendant's extradition in pursuance of the deferred claim was ordered under Part 1, s 67 applies for determining the appropriate judge (s 181(7)). If the defendant's extradition in pursuance of the deferred claim was ordered under Part 2, s 139 applies for determining the appropriate judge (s 181(8)).

8.4.5 Deferral of Part 2 Extradition Hearing because of Domestic Proceedings

The EA 2003 contains provisions governing how conflicting extradition and domestic criminal proceedings are to be dealt with. In Part 1 cases the power to defer is given to the appropriate judge rather than the Secretary of State in ss 22 and 23: see 5.11 above.

In Part 2 cases ss 97 and 98 are the relevant provisions. Section 97 applies if the appropriate judge has sent a case to the Secretary of State under Part 2 for his decision whether the defendant is to be extradited, and the defendant is then charged with an offence in the UK (s 97(1)). In this case the Secretary of State must not make his decision until (s 97(2)):

(a) the charge is disposed of;
(b) the charge is withdrawn;
(c) proceedings in respect of the charge are discontinued;
(d) an order is made for the charge to lie on the file (or its Scottish equivalent).

If a sentence of imprisonment or detention is imposed in respect of the offence the Secretary of State may defer making a decision on the extradition request until the sentence has been served.

Where the appropriate judge sends a case to the Secretary of State for his decision whether the defendant is to be extradited, and the defendant is serving a sentence of imprisonment or another form of detention in the UK, then the Secretary of State may defer making a decision with regard to the defendant's extradition until after he has served his sentence (s 98(2)).

8.5 ASYLUM CLAIMS

States which carry out persecution of minority social groups frequently resort to the criminal law as a method of persecution, and the grounds for claiming asylum under the Refugee Convention and the extraneous considerations referred to in ss 13 and 81 of the EA 2003 are similar in many respects. It is not uncommon for an extradition defendant also to claim asylum in the UK either prior to arrest or following the commencement of extradition proceedings.

The general practice under the EA 1989 was for extradition proceedings to continue until the order for return stage under ss 12 and 13, and for the Secretary of State then to determine the issues of whether to order return and whether to grant asylum at the same time. The courts were generally reluctant to adjourn extradition proceedings pending the outcome of asylum proceedings (*R (Karpichkov) v Latvia and the Republic of South Africa*, Unreported, 26 April 2001, CO/2553/2000).

The EA 2003 contains provisions to regulate the determination of an extradition defendant's asylum claim. These are ss 39 and 40 in Part 1 cases, and s 121 in Part 2 cases.

8.5.1 Asylum Claims in Part 1 Cases

Section 39 applies if a defendant in respect of whom a Part 1 warrant is issued makes an asylum claim at any time in the 'relevant period', or an order is made under Part 1 for the person to be extradited in pursuance of the warrant.

For the purposes of s 39, the 'relevant period' is the period starting when a certificate is issued under s 2 in respect of the warrant and ending when the defendant is extradited in pursuance of the warrant (s 39(2)).

Section 39(3) provides that the defendant must not be extradited in pursuance of the warrant before the asylum claim is finally determined, and ss 35, 36, 47, and 49 of the Act, which govern the time for extradition, have effect subject to this stipulation. These are considered in Chapter 10.

However, the right not to be extradited in s 39(3) is subject to s 40 (s 39(4)). Section 40(1) provides that s 39(3) does not apply in relation to a person if the Secretary of State has certified that the conditions in s 40(2) or the conditions in s 40(3) are satisfied in relation to him.

The conditions in s 40(2) are that:

(a) the Category 1 territory to which the person's extradition has been ordered has accepted that, under standing arrangements, it is the responsible state in relation to the person's asylum claim;

(b) in the opinion of the Secretary of State, the person is not a national or citizen of the territory.

The conditions in s 40(3) are that, in the opinion of the Secretary of State:

(a) the person is not a national or citizen of the Category 1 territory to which his extradition has been ordered;

(b) the person's life and liberty would not be threatened in that territory by reason of his race, religion, nationality, political opinion, or membership of a particular social group;

(c) the government of the territory would not send the person to another country otherwise than in accordance with the Refugee Convention.

Section 40(4) provides that in s 40 the term 'Refugee Convention' has the meaning given by s 167(1) of the Immigration and Asylum Act 1999, and 'standing arrangements' means arrangements in force between the UK and the Category 1 territory for determining which state is responsible for considering applications for asylum.

Section 39(5) and (6) define when an asylum claim is finally determined for the purposes of s 39(3). If the Secretary of State allows the asylum claim, the claim is finally determined when he makes his decision on the claim (s 39(5)).

However, if the Secretary of State rejects the asylum claim, the claim is finally determined (s 39(6)):

(a) when the Secretary of State makes his decision on the claim, if there is no right to appeal against the Secretary of State's decision on the claim;

(b) when the period permitted for appealing against the Secretary of State's decision on the claim ends, if there is such a right but there is no such appeal;

(c) when the appeal against that decision is finally determined or is withdrawn or abandoned, if there is such an appeal.

An appeal against the Secretary of State's decision on an asylum claim is not finally determined for the purposes of s 39(6) at any time when a further appeal or an application for leave to bring a further appeal has been instituted and has not been finally determined or withdrawn or abandoned, or may be brought. By s 39(8), the remittal of an appeal is not a final determination for the purposes of s 39(7), and the possibility of an appeal out of time with leave must be ignored for the purposes of s 39(6) and (7).

8.5.2 Asylum Claims in Part 2 Cases

Section 121 applies where the defendant whose extradition has been requested under Part 2 makes an asylum claim at any time in the 'relevant period' and an order is made under Part 2 for him to be extradited in pursuance of the request (s 121(1)).

The relevant period is the period starting when a certificate is issued under s 70 in respect of the request and ending when the person is extradited in pursuance of the request (s 121(2)).

By s 121(3), the defendant must not be extradited in pursuance of the request before the asylum claim is finally determined; and ss 117 and 118 have effect subject to this right.

Section 121(4) provides that if the Secretary of State allows the asylum claim, the claim is finally determined when he makes his decision on the claim.

If the Secretary of State rejects the asylum claim, the claim is finally determined (s 121(5)):

(a) when the Secretary of State makes his decision on the claim, if there is no right to appeal against his decision on the claim;

(b) when the period permitted for appealing against the Secretary of State's decision on the claim ends, if there is such a right but there is no such appeal;

(c) when the appeal against that decision is finally determined or is withdrawn or abandoned, if there is such an appeal.

An appeal against the Secretary of State's decision on an asylum claim is not finally determined for the purposes of s 121(5) at any time when a further appeal or an application for leave to bring a further appeal has been instituted and has not been finally determined or withdrawn or abandoned, or may be brought.

By s 121(7) the remittal of an appeal is not a final determination for the purposes of s 121(6), and the possibility of an appeal out of time with leave must be ignored for the purposes of s 121(5) and (6).

9

APPEALS

9.1 INTRODUCTION

Since the nineteenth century the traditional form of appeal by an extradition defendant following his committal was by way of an application for a writ of *habeas corpus ad subjiciendum* (*Re Tivnan* (1864) 5 B & S 645; *Re Windsor* (1865) 6 B & S 522). Section 11 of the EA 1870 and s 11(1) of the EA 1989 required the committing magistrate to inform the defendant of his right to apply for a writ of *habeas corpus*, and the defendant was protected from return for a period of 15 days to allow him to apply to the High Court and, thereafter, until his application was disposed of.

Although the original purpose of a writ of *habeas corpus* was to bring the body of a detained person before the court so that the legality of the gaoler's justification for his detention (known as the return to the writ) could be examined, over time the scope of review in extradition cases expanded so that the court could review not just the return but the case as it appeared before the magistrate, not only to look at the evidence which was before him, but to consider whether any magistrate, properly applying his mind to the question, could reasonably have come to the conclusion that there was a *prima facie* case (*Armah v Government of Ghana* [1968] AC 1982).

Section 10 of the Fugitive Offenders Act 1881, s 8(3) of the Fugitive Offenders Act 1967, and s 11(3) of the EA 1989 provided additional, statutory, grounds for applying for a writ of *habeas corpus*.

Also, although the original purpose of the writ was to enable the legality of detention to be determined, its compass expanded to include those who had been released on bail but were subject to an extradition request, who for all purposes were treated as if they were in custody (EA 1989, s 11; *R v Secretary of State for the Home Department ex p Launder* [1998] QB 994, 1011).

In Part III cases the defendant also had a statutory right to seek judicial review of the Secretary of State's decision to return him (EA 1989, s 13).

So far as the requesting state was concerned, in cases dealt with under Part III of the EA 1989, it had the right to appeal to the High Court by way of case stated under s 10 if the district judge refused to make an order of committal. In Sch 1 cases its remedy was to seek a judicial review of the judge's decision to discharge the defendant (*Atkinson v Government of the United States of America* [1971] AC 197, 235).

The EA 2003 removes these complexities by creating a statutory right of appeal to the High Court against the appropriate judge's decision following the extradition hearing and (in Category 2 cases) against the Secretary of State's decision to order or refuse extradition. The right of appeal is granted to both the defendant and the requesting state, and the defendant cannot be returned whilst such an appeal is outstanding. The Act also introduces time limits for the hearing of such appeals in an effort to speed up the extradition process.

The Act also provides for a right of appeal to the House of Lords with leave where the case involves a point of law of general public importance.

Rules of court (referred to in various places in this chapter) have been made governing extradition appeals. They are contained in para 22.6A of the Practice Direction to Part 52 (Appeals) (available at www.dca.gov.uk/civil/procrules_fin/contents/practice_directions/pd_part52.htm).

9.2 APPEALS IN CATEGORY 1 CASES

The relevant provisions are ss 26–34. Section 34 provides that a decision of the judge under Part 1 may be questioned in legal proceedings only by means of an appeal under Part 1.

9.2.1 Appeal by Defendant against an Order for Extradition

If the appropriate judge orders the defendant's extradition under Part 1, the defendant may appeal to the High Court against the order unless he consented to his extradition (s 26(1)). The appeal may be brought on a question of law or fact (s 26(3)).

Notice of an appeal under this section must be given in accordance with rules of court before the end of the permitted period, which is seven days starting with the day on which the order is made (s 27(6)).

Section 27(1) provides that on an appeal under s 26 the High Court may:

(a) allow the appeal; or
(b) dismiss the appeal.

The court may allow the appeal only if the conditions in s 26(3) or (4) are satisfied. The conditions in s 26(3) are that:

(a) the appropriate judge ought to have decided a question before him at the extradition hearing differently;

(b) if he had decided the question in the way he ought to have done, he would have been required to order the person's discharge.

The conditions in s 26(4) are that:

(a) an issue is raised that was not raised at the extradition hearing or evidence is available that was not available at the extradition hearing;

(b) the issue or evidence would have resulted in the appropriate judge deciding a question before him at the extradition hearing differently;

(c) if he had decided the question in that way, he would have been required to order the person's discharge.

If the High Court allows the appeal it must order the person's discharge and quash the order for his extradition (s 27(5)).

9.2.2 Appeal by the Requesting State against an Order for Discharge

If the judge orders a person's discharge at the extradition hearing, the authority which issued the Part 1 warrant may appeal to the High Court against the relevant decision, ie, the decision which resulted in the order for the person's discharge (s 28(3)), unless the order for discharge was under s 41 (withdrawal of warrant) (s 28(1) and (2)).

An appeal under s 28 may be brought on a question of law or fact (s 28(4)). Notice of an appeal must be given in accordance with rules of court before the end of the permitted period, which is seven days starting with the day on which the order for the person's discharge is made (s 28(5)). The 34th update to the Civil Procedure Rules 1998 (SI 1998/3132) amends Practice Direction 52 with effect from 1 January 2004 to cover appeals under the EA 2003.

On an appeal under s 28 the High Court may (s 29(1)):

(a) allow the appeal;
(b) dismiss the appeal.

The court may allow the appeal only if the conditions in s 29(3) or (4) are satisfied. The conditions in s 29(3) are that:

(a) the judge ought to have decided the relevant question differently;

(b) if he had decided the question in the way he ought to have done, he would not have been required to order the person's discharge.

The conditions in s 29(4) are that:

(a) an issue is raised that was not raised at the extradition hearing or evidence is available that was not available at the extradition hearing;

(b) the issue or evidence would have resulted in the judge deciding the relevant question differently;

(c) if he had decided the question in that way, he would not have been required to order the person's discharge.

If the court allows the appeal it must (s 29(5)):

(a) quash the order discharging the person;

(b) remit the case to the judge;

(c) direct him to proceed as he would have been required to do if he had decided the relevant question differently at the extradition hearing.

By s 29(6), a question is the relevant question if the judge's decision on it resulted in the order for the person's discharge.

9.2.3 Detention of Defendant Pending Conclusion of Appeal by the Requesting State under Section 29

Where the judge orders the defendant's discharge then the requesting state has the right to have the defendant detained in custody or on bail pending an appeal to the High Court under s 29 provided that, *immediately* after the judge orders the defendant's discharge, the judge is informed by the authority which issued the Part 1 warrant that it intends to appeal under s 28 (s 30(1)). The judge must then remand the person in custody or on bail while the appeal is pending (s 30(2)) and if the judge remands the person in custody, he may later grant bail (s 30(3)).

An appeal under s 28 ceases to be pending at the earliest of these times (s 30(4)):

(a) when the proceedings on the appeal are discontinued;

(b) when the High Court dismisses the appeal, if the authority does not immediately inform the court that it intends to apply for leave to appeal to the House of Lords;

(c) at the end of the permitted period, which is 28 days starting with the day on which leave to appeal to the House of Lords against the decision of the High Court on the appeal is granted;

(d) when there is no further step that can be taken by the authority which issued the Part 1 warrant in relation to the appeal (ignoring any power of a court to grant leave to take a step out of time).

9.2.4 Time Limit for Start of Hearing of Appeal to High Court

In accordance with its overall purpose of speeding up the extradition process, the EA 2003 contains provisions requiring time limits to be set for the hearing of appeals against the appropriate judge's decision.

Section 31(1) and (2) contain provisions relating to the making of rules of court regarding time limits for appeals. The rules must prescribe the period (the relevant period) within which the High Court must begin to hear an appeal under s 26 or s 28. They must also provide for the relevant period to start with the date on which the person in respect of whom a Part 1 warrant is issued:

(a) was arrested under s 5, if he was arrested under that section;
(b) was arrested under the Part 1 warrant, if he was not arrested under s 5.

The High Court must begin to hear the appeal before the end of the relevant period (s 31(3)).

The High Court may extend the relevant period if it believes it to be in the interests of justice to do so (s 31(4)). The power in s 31(4) may be exercised even after the end of the relevant period.

If s 27(3) is not complied with, and the appeal is under s 26, the appeal must be taken to have been allowed by a decision of the High Court; the person whose extradition has been ordered must be taken to have been discharged by the High Court; and the order for the person's extradition must be taken to have been quashed by the High Court (s 31(6)).

If s 26(3) is not complied with and the appeal is under s 28 the appeal must be taken to have been dismissed by a decision of the High Court (s 31(7)).

9.2.5 Appeals to the House of Lords

Under the EA 1989 regime the defendant or requesting state could appeal, with leave, to the House of Lords from a decision of the High Court dismissing or allowing an application for a writ of *habeas corpus ad subjiciendum* (Administration of Justice Act 1960, s 1). By s 15(3), no certificate of a point of law of general public importance was required. The EA 2003 removes this indulgence and brings extradition appeals into line with other criminal appeals by requiring a certificate from the High Court.

Section 32(1) provides that an appeal lies to the House of Lords from a decision of the High Court on an appeal under s 26 or s 28. The appeal can be brought by:

(a) the person in respect of whom the Part 1 warrant was issued;
(b) the authority which issued the Part 1 warrant.

An appeal lies only with the leave of the High Court or the House of Lords (s 32(3)). Section 32(4) provides that leave to appeal must not be granted unless:

(a) the High Court has certified that there is a point of law of general public importance involved in the decision, and

(b) it appears to the court granting leave that the point is one which ought to be considered by the House of Lords.

An application to the High Court for leave to appeal must be made before the end of the permitted period, which is 14 days starting with the day on which the court makes its decision on the appeal (s 32(5)).

An application to the House of Lords for leave to appeal under s 33 must be made before the end of the permitted period, which is 14 days starting with the day on which the High Court refuses leave to appeal. It is to be observed that this time limit is absolute and, unlike s 2(3) of the Administration of Justice Act 1960, there is no power for the High Court or House of Lords to grant an extension. This inflexibility has the potential to cause serious difficulties for an extradition defendant, and may breach his right under Article 5(4) of the European Convention on Human Rights to have the legality of his detention reviewed by a court (cf *Perez de Rada Cavanilles v Spain* [1999] EHRLR 208, para 45). As Lord Bingham of Cornhill said in *R v Weir* [2001] 1 WLR 421, 426, explaining why defendants had been granted the right to seek an extension of time for appeals to the House of Lords but prosecutors had not:

A defendant unsuccessful in the Court of Appeal may well be in prison and experience difficulty in giving instructions, obtaining legal aid and perhaps instructing different solicitors and counsel for an appeal to the House. But none of these problems would prevent a professional prosecutor who had already appeared at the trial and in the Court of Appeal making application to the House of Lords within the period of 14 days.

If leave to appeal is granted, the appeal must be brought before the end of the permitted period, which is 28 days starting with the day on which leave is granted (s 32(7)). Section 32(8) provides that if s 32(7) is not complied with:

(a) the appeal must be taken to have been brought;

(b) the appeal must be taken to have been dismissed by the House of Lords immediately after the end of the period permitted under s 32(7).

The EA 2003 does not define when an appeal is 'brought' but it plainly cannot mean 'heard'. Under the House of Lords' procedures, an appeal is brought when the Petition of Appeal is lodged.

By s 32(9), the following must be ignored for the purposes of s 32(8)(b):

(a) any power of a court to extend the period permitted for bringing the appeal;

(b) any power of a court to grant leave to take a step out of time.

The High Court may grant bail to a person appealing under s 32 or applying for leave to appeal under this section (s 32(10)).

Section 32(11) and (12) contain provisions relating to the composition of the House of Lords for the hearing and determination of appeals.

9.2.6 Powers of House of Lords on Appeal under Section 32

Section 33 sets out the powers of the House of Lords on an appeal under s 32. The House of Lords may:

(a) allow the appeal;
(b) dismiss the appeal.

Where the appeal is brought by the defendant and the appeal is allowed, the House of Lords must order the person's discharge and quash the order for his extradition, if the appeal was against a decision of the High Court to dismiss an appeal under s 26 (s 33(3)).

Where the High Court allows an appeal under s 26 by the defendant and the authority which issued the warrant brings an appeal under s 32 against the decision of the High Court, and the House of Lords allows the appeal it must (s 33(5)):

(a) quash the order of the High Court under s 27(5) discharging the person;

(b) order the person to be extradited to the Category 1 territory in which the warrant was issued.

Section 33(7) and (8) apply if:

(a) the High Court dismisses an appeal under s 28 against a decision made by the judge at the extradition hearing;

(b) the authority which issued the Part 1 warrant brings an appeal under s 32 against the decision of the High Court; and

(c) the House of Lords allows the appeal.

Section 33(7) provides that if the judge would have been required to order the person in respect of whom the warrant was issued to be extradited had he decided the relevant question differently, the House of Lords must:

(a) quash the order of the judge discharging the person;

(b) order the person to be extradited to the Category 1 territory in which the warrant was issued.

Section 33(8) provides that in any other case, the House of Lords must:

(a) quash the order of the judge discharging the person in respect of whom the warrant was issued;

(b) remit the case to the judge;

(c) direct him to proceed as he would have been required to do if he had decided the relevant question differently at the extradition hearing.

By s 33(9), a question is the relevant question if the judge's decision on it resulted in the order for the person's discharge.

9.3 APPEALS IN CATEGORY 2 CASES

The relevant provisions are ss 103–116. They provide for appeals against decisions made by the appropriate judge under Part 2 and also decisions made by the Secretary of State.

By s 116, a decision under Part 2 of the judge or the Secretary of State may be questioned in legal proceedings only by means of an appeal under Part 2.

9.3.1 Appeal by the Defendant against Appropriate Judge's Decision

If the appropriate judge sends a case to the Secretary of State under Part 2 for his decision whether the defendant is to be extradited, the defendant may appeal to the High Court against the relevant decision (s 103(1)), unless he consented to his extradition under s 127 (s 103(2)). The relevant decision is the decision that resulted in the case being sent to the Secretary of State (s 103(3)). The appeal may be brought on a question of law or fact (s 103(4)). No appeal can be brought under this section if the Secretary of State has ordered the person's discharge (s 103(7)).

Notice of the appeal must be given in accordance with rules of court before the end of the permitted period, which is 14 days starting with the day on which the Secretary of State informs the defendant under s 100(1) or (4) of the order he has made in respect of him.

Importantly, s 103(5) provides that if the appeal is brought before the Secretary of State has decided whether the person is to be extradited, the appeal must not be heard until after the Secretary of State has made his decision. If the Secretary of State then orders the person's discharge the appeal must not be proceeded with (s 103(6)).

Where the Secretary of State discharges the defendant, and notice of an appeal under s 110 is given, s 103(6) and (7) do not apply and no appeal may be brought under s 103 if the High Court has made its decision on the appeal (s 103(9)).

On an appeal under s 103 the High Court may:

(a) allow the appeal;

(b) direct the judge to decide again a question (or questions) which he decided at the extradition hearing;

(c) dismiss the appeal.

However, the court may only allow the appeal if the conditions in s 104(3) or (4) are satisfied.

The conditions in s 104(3) are that:

(a) the judge ought to have decided a question before him at the extradition hearing differently;

(b) if he had decided the question in the way he ought to have done, he would have been required to order the person's discharge.

The conditions in s 104(4) are that:

(a) an issue is raised that was not raised at the extradition hearing or evidence is available that was not available at the extradition hearing;

(b) the issue or evidence would have resulted in the judge deciding a question before him at the extradition hearing differently;

(c) if he had decided the question in that way, he would have been required to order the person's discharge.

If the court allows the appeal it must order the person's discharge and quash the order for his extradition (s 104(5)).

Where the case is remitted to the appropriate judge for re-determination under s 104(1)(b), and the judge comes to a different decision on the question remitted, he must order the person's discharge (s 104(6)). If the judge comes to the same decision as he did at the extradition hearing on the question that is (or all the questions that are) the subject of a direction under s 104(1)(b) the appeal must be taken to have been dismissed by a decision of the High Court (s 104(7)).

9.3.2 Appeal by the Requesting State against Discharge at Extradition Hearing

If at the extradition hearing the judge orders a person's discharge, an appeal to the High Court may be brought on behalf of the Category 2 territory under s 105 against the relevant decision (s 105(1)), namely, the decision which resulted in the order for the person's discharge (s 105(3)). However, no appeal is possible if the discharge took place under s 122 (withdrawal of request).

The appeal may be brought on a question of law or fact.

Notice of an appeal under s 105 must be given in accordance with rules of court before the end of the permitted period, which is 14 days starting with the day on which the order for the defendant's discharge is made.

On an appeal under s 105(1) the High Court may:

(a) allow the appeal;
(b) direct the judge to decide the relevant question again;
(c) dismiss the appeal.

By s 106(2), a question is the relevant question if the judge's decision on it resulted in the order for the person's discharge.

The court may allow the appeal only if the conditions in s 106(4) or (5) are satisfied.

The conditions in s 106(4) are that:

(a) the judge ought to have decided the relevant question differently;

(b) if he had decided the question in the way he ought to have done, he would not have been required to order the person's discharge.

The conditions in s 106(5) are that:

(a) an issue is raised that was not raised at the extradition hearing or evidence is available that was not available at the extradition hearing;

(b) the issue or evidence would have resulted in the judge deciding the relevant question differently;

(c) if he had decided the question in that way, he would not have been required to order the person's discharge.

If the court allows the appeal it must quash the order discharging the defendant, remit the case to the judge, and direct him to proceed as he would have been required to do if he had decided the relevant question differently at the extradition hearing (s 106(6)).

If the court makes a direction under s 106(1)(b) and the judge decides the relevant question differently he must proceed as he would have been required to do if he had decided that question differently at the extradition hearing (s 106(7)).

If the court makes a direction under subsection (1)(b) and the judge does not decide the relevant question differently the appeal must be taken to have been dismissed by a decision of the High Court.

9.3.3 Detention Pending Conclusion of Appeal under Section 105

The requesting state has the right to ask the judge to remand the defendant in custody or on bail where it wishes to appeal under s 105 against an order for discharge.

Section 107 is in similar terms to s 30, discussed above at 9.2.3.

9.3.4 Appeal by the Defendant against Secretary of State's Extradition Order

Sections 108 and 109 provide for a right of appeal by the defendant where the Secretary of State orders his extradition under Part 2.

If the Secretary of State orders a person's extradition under Part 2, the person may appeal to the High Court against the order (s 108(1)), unless the defendant consented to his extradition under s 127.

The appeal under s 108 may be brought on a question of law or fact (s 108(3)).

Notice of an appeal under s 108 must be given in accordance with rules of court before the end of the permitted period, which is 14 days starting with the day on which the Secretary of State informs the person of the order under s 100(1).

On an appeal under s 108 the High Court may allow the appeal or dismiss the appeal (s 109(1)). However, the court may allow the appeal only if the conditions in s 109(3) or (4) are satisfied.

The conditions in s 109(3) are that:

(a) the Secretary of State ought to have decided a question before him differently;

(b) if he had decided the question in the way he ought to have done, he would not have ordered the person's extradition.

The conditions in s 109(4) are that:

(a) an issue is raised that was not raised when the case was being considered by the Secretary of State or information is available that was not available at that time;

(b) the issue or information would have resulted in the Secretary of State deciding a question before him differently;

(c) if he had decided the question in that way, he would not have ordered the person's extradition.

If the court allows the appeal it must order the defendant's discharge and quash the order for his extradition (s 109(5)).

9.3.5 Appeal by the Requesting State against Secretary of State's Order Discharging the Defendant

The requesting Category 2 territory can appeal to the High Court under ss 110 and 111 against a decision by the Secretary of State to discharge the defendant (s 110(1)), unless the discharge took place under s 123 (withdrawal of request) (s 110(2)).

An appeal under s 110 may be brought on a question of law or fact (s 110(4)).

Notice of an appeal under s 110 must be given in accordance with rules of court before the end of the permitted period, which is 14 days starting with the day on which (under s 100(4)) the Secretary of State informs a person acting on behalf of the Category 2 territory of the order.

On an appeal under s 110 the High Court may allow the appeal or dismiss the appeal (s 111(1)). However, the court may allow the appeal only if the conditions in s 111(3) or (4) are satisfied.

The conditions in s 111(3) are that:

(a) the Secretary of State ought to have decided a question before him differently;

(b) if he had decided the question in the way he ought to have done, he would have ordered the defendant's extradition.

The conditions in s 111(4) are that:

(a) an issue is raised that was not raised when the case was being considered by the Secretary of State or information is available that was not available at that time;

(b) the issue or information would have resulted in the Secretary of State deciding a question before him differently;

(c) if he had decided the question in that way, he would have ordered the defendant's extradition.

If the court allows the appeal it must quash the order discharging the defendant and order his extradition (s 111(5)).

9.3.6 Detention Pending Appeal by the Requesting State

Section 112 applies if, immediately after the Secretary of State orders the defendant's discharge, he is informed on behalf of the Category 2 territory of an intention to appeal under s 110.

The judge must remand the person in custody or on bail while the appeal is pending (s 112(2)).

9.3.7 Time Limits for Appeals to High Court

Section 113 contains provisions for the making of rules of court concerning the time within which appeals to the High Court must begin. It is in similar terms to s 31, described above at 9.2.4.

9.3.8 Appeals to the House of Lords

An appeal lies to the House of Lords under s 114 from a decision of the High Court on an appeal under ss 103, 105, 108, or 110 (s 114(1)) at the instance of the defendant or a person acting on behalf of the Category 2 territory (s 114(2)).

Section 114 is in similar terms to s 32, considered above at 9.2.5.

The powers of the High Court on appeal are contained in s 115, which is in terms similar to s 33, considered above at 9.2.6.

10

TIME FOR EXTRADITION

10.1 INTRODUCTION

The policy of extradition legislation from the EA 1870 onwards has been to require return to take place as quickly as possible after the Secretary of State orders the defendant's return. Section 16 and para 10 of Sch 1 to the EA 1989 gave the defendant the right to apply for discharge if he was not extradited within a certain period following the making of an order for his return, unless there was a good reason for the delay.

This policy is continued in the EA 2003. The Act lays down time limits within which extradition has to take place following the conclusion of proceedings, in default of which the defendant is entitled to be discharged unless there are reasonable grounds for the delay.

10.2 TIME FOR EXTRADITION IN PART 1 CASES

Sections 35 and 36 specify when extradition must take place in cases where there is no appeal, and where there has been an appeal, respectively.

10.2.1 Time for Extradition where there is No Appeal

Section 35 applies where the appropriate judge has ordered the defendant's extradition to a Category 1 territory and no notice of appeal has been given under s 26 before the end of period permitted under that section. For these purposes, any power of a court to extend the period permitted for giving notice of appeal and any power of a court to grant leave to take a step out of time has to be ignored (s 35(6)).

However, s 35 does not apply if the judge's order is made under s 46 or s 48 (consent to extradition).

Where s 35 applies, the defendant must be extradited before the end of the required period (s 35(3)). This period is:

(a) 10 days starting with the day on which the judge makes the order;

(b) if the judge and the authority which issued the Part 1 warrant agree a later date, 10 days starting with that later date.

If s 35(3) is not complied with and the person applies to the appropriate judge for discharge the judge must order discharge unless reasonable cause is shown for the delay (s 35(5)). For the principles applicable to the exercise of this power, see *In re Shuter* [1960] 1 QB 142; *R v Governor of Brixton Prison ex p Enahoro* [1963] 2 QB 455; *Re Oskar*, Unreported, 29 February 1988, CO/190/88; *Re Lindley*, Unreported, 29 October 1997, CO/1183/97.

10.2.2 Time for Extradition where the Defendant Appeals

Section 36 applies where the defendant has appealed to the High Court under s 26 and the effect of the High Court's decision (or that of the House of Lords) is that the person is to be extradited.

The defendant must be extradited to the Category 1 territory before the end of the required period (s 36(2)). By s 36(3), this period is:

(a) 10 days starting with the day on which the decision of the relevant court (ie the High Court or House of Lords) on the appeal becomes final or proceedings on the appeal are discontinued; or

(b) if the relevant court and the authority which issued the Part 1 warrant agree a later date, 10 days starting with that later date.

'Finality' is defined in s 36(5). The decision of the High Court on the appeal becomes final:

(a) when the period permitted for applying to the High Court for leave to appeal to the House of Lords ends, if there is no such application;

(b) when the period permitted for applying to the House of Lords for leave to appeal to it ends, if the High Court refuses leave to appeal and there is no application to the House of Lords for leave to appeal;

(c) when the House of Lords refuses leave to appeal to it;

(d) at the end of the permitted period, which is 28 days starting with the day on which leave to appeal to the House of Lords is granted, if no such appeal is brought before the end of that period.

For these purposes, any power of a court to extend the period permitted for giving notice of appeal and any power of a court to grant leave to take a step out of time has to be ignored (s 36(6)).

The decision of the House of Lords on the appeal becomes final when it is made (s 36(7)).

For these purposes, any power of a court to extend the period permitted for giving notice of appeal and any power of a court to grant leave to take a step out of time has to be ignored (s 35(6)).

If s 36(2) is not complied with and the person applies to the appropriate judge to be discharged the judge must order his discharge unless reasonable cause is shown for the delay (s 36(8)).

10.2.3 Undertaking from Part 1 Territory concerning Person Serving Sentence

As explained in Chapter 5, s 23 confers a discretion on the appropriate judge to postpone a Category 1 extradition hearing until after a defendant who is serving a sentence of imprisonment in the UK has completed his sentence. However, under s 37, the judge also has the power to order extradition provided that an appropriate undertaking is received from the Category 1 territory that the defendant will be returned to the UK at the conclusion of his sentence.

Section 37 applies if:

(a) the appropriate judge orders the defendant's extradition to a Category 1 territory (other than under s 46 or s 48 (consent));

(b) the defendant is serving a sentence of imprisonment or another form of detention in the UK.

Section 37(3) provides that the judge may make the order for extradition subject to the condition that extradition is not to take place before he receives an undertaking given on behalf of the Category 1 territory in terms specified by him. If the judge makes such an order then s 37(7) and (8) apply:

(a) Section 37(7) provides that if the judge does not receive the undertaking before the end of the period of 21 days starting with the day on which he makes the order and the defendant applies for discharge then the judge must order his discharge.

(b) Section 37(8)(a) provides that in a case where s 35 applies, the required period for the purpose of s 35(3) is 10 days starting with the day on which the judge receives the undertaking. Section 37(8)(b) states that where s 36 applies, the required period for the purposes of s 36(2) is 10 days starting with the day on which the decision of the relevant court on the appeal becomes final within the meaning of s 36 or (if later) the day on which the judge receives the undertaking.

Section 37(4) specifies the terms of the undertaking which the judge can seek from the requesting state. Where the person is accused of an offence they include:

(a) that the defendant be kept in custody until the conclusion of the proceedings against him for the offence and any offence in respect of which he is permitted to be dealt with in the Category 1 territory;

(b) that the defendant be returned to the UK to serve the remainder of his sentence on the conclusion of those proceedings.

If the defendant is alleged to be unlawfully at large after conviction the terms which the judge can seek in the form of an undertaking include that the defendant be returned to the UK to serve the remainder of his sentence after serving any sentence imposed on him in the Category 1 territory (s 37(5)).

10.2.4 Time for Extradition where Extradition has been Deferred

The power of the appropriate judge under s 44 to defer extradition under Part 1 until the conclusion of other Part 1 proceedings was considered at 5.11 above. The power of the Secretary of State to make such an order in the face of a competing extradition request under Part 2 was considered at 8.4 above.

Section 38 specifies the time within which the defendant must be extradited where the appropriate judge makes an order under s 181(2) that the defendant be extradited following disposal of the competing claim. Section 38 applies if:

(a) an order is made under Part 1 for the defendant to be extradited to a Category 1 territory in pursuance of a Part 1 warrant (except under ss 46 or 48 (consent));

(b) before the defendant is extradited, an order is made under s 44(4)(b) or s 179(2)(b) for his extradition in pursuance of the warrant to be deferred;

(c) the appropriate judge makes an order under s 181(2) for the defendant's extradition in pursuance of the warrant to cease to be deferred.

In a case where s 35 applies, the required period for the purposes of s 35(3) is 10 days starting with the day on which the order under s 181(2) is made.

In a case where s 36 applies, the required period for the purposes of s 36(2) is 10 days starting with the day on which the decision of the relevant court on the appeal becomes final (within the meaning of that section) or (if later) the day on which the order under s 181(2) is made.

10.3 TIME FOR EXTRADITION IN PART 2 CASES

10.3.1 Time for Extradition where there is No Appeal

Section 117 specifies the time within which the defendant must be extradited in a Part 2 case where he does not appeal against the Secretary of State's decision to order his extradition. Section 117 applies if:

(a) the Secretary of State orders the defendant's extradition to a Category 2 territory under this Part; and

(b) no notice of an appeal under s 103 or s 108 is given before the end of the permitted period, which is 14 days starting with the day on which the Secretary of State informs the defendant under s 100(1) that he has ordered his extradition. For this purpose, any power of a court to extend the period permitted for giving notice of appeal and any power of a court to grant leave to take a step out of time must be ignored.

By s 117(2), the defendant must be extradited to the Category 2 territory before the end of the required period, which is 28 days starting with the day on which the Secretary of State makes the order.

If s 117(2) is not complied with and the defendant applies to the appropriate judge to be discharged the judge must order his discharge, unless reasonable cause is shown for the delay.

10.3.2 Time for Extradition where there has been an Appeal

The time period for extradition where the defendant has appealed to the High Court/House of Lords is specified in s 118. The section applies if:

(a) there is an appeal to the High Court under ss 103, 108, or 110 against a decision or order relating to the defendant's extradition to a Category 2 territory; and

(b) the effect of the decision of the relevant court on the appeal is that the defendant is to be extradited there.

By s 118(2), the defendant must be extradited to the requesting Category 2 territory before the end of the required period, which is 28 days starting with:

(a) the day on which the decision of the relevant court on the appeal becomes final; or

(b) the day on which proceedings on the appeal are discontinued.

The relevant court is the High Court if there is no appeal to the House of Lords against the decision of the High Court on the appeal, or, if there is such an appeal, the House of Lords (s 118(3)).

137

The decision of the High Court on the appeal becomes final (s 118(4)):

(a) when the period permitted for applying to the High Court for leave to appeal to the House of Lords ends, if there is no such application;

(b) when the period permitted for applying to the House of Lords for leave to appeal to it ends, if the High Court refuses leave to appeal and there is no application to the House of Lords for leave to appeal;

(c) when the House of Lords refuses leave to appeal to it;

(d) at the end of the permitted period, which is 28 days starting with the day on which leave to appeal to the House of Lords is granted, if no such appeal is brought before the end of that period.

The decision of the House of Lords on the appeal becomes final when it is made (s 188(6)).

The power of a court to extend the period permitted for applying for leave to appeal and any power of a court to grant leave to take a step out of time must be ignored for the purposes of s 118(4).

If s 118(2) is not complied with and the defendant applies to the appropriate judge to be discharged the judge must order his discharge, unless reasonable cause is shown for the delay.

10.3.3 Time for Extradition where Undertakings Sought from Requesting State

Where the extradition is sought of a defendant serving a sentence of imprisonment in the UK, the Secretary of State has the power to order extradition prior to completion of the sentence on condition that the requesting state gives appropriate undertakings to ensure the defendant returns to the UK to complete his sentence. In such a case, s 119 of the EA 2003 specifies the time within which such undertakings must be given and the time within which the defendant must be extradited.

Section 119 applies if the Secretary of State orders the defendant's extradition to a Category 2 territory under Part 2 and the defendant is serving a sentence of imprisonment or another form of detention in the UK.

The Secretary of State may make the order for extradition subject to the condition that extradition is not to take place before he receives an undertaking given on behalf of the Category 2 territory in terms specified by him (s 119(2)).

The terms which may be specified by the Secretary of State in relation to a defendant accused in a Category 2 territory of the commission of an offence include terms:

(a) that the defendant be kept in custody until the conclusion of the proceedings against him for the offence and any other offence in respect of which he is permitted to be dealt with in the Category 2 territory;

(b) that the defendant be returned to the United Kingdom to serve the remainder of his sentence on the conclusion of those proceedings.

The terms which may be specified by the Secretary of State in relation to a defendant alleged to be unlawfully at large after conviction of an offence by a court in a Category 2 territory include terms that he be returned to the UK to serve the remainder of his sentence after serving any sentence imposed on him in the Category 2 territory for the offence, and any other offence in respect of which he is permitted to be dealt with in the Category 2 territory.

Section 119(6) and (7) apply if the Secretary of State makes an order for extradition subject to a condition under s 119(2):

(a) By s 119(6), if the Secretary of State does not receive the undertaking before the end of the period of 21 days starting with the day on which he makes the order and the person applies to the High Court to be discharged, the court must order his discharge.

(b) By s 119(7), if the Secretary of State receives the undertaking before the end of that period:

(i) in a case where s 117 applies, the required period for the purposes of s 117(2) is 28 days starting with the day on which the Secretary of State receives the undertaking;

(ii) in a case where s 118 applies, the required period for the purposes of s 118(2) is 28 days starting with the day on which the decision of the relevant court on the appeal becomes final (within the meaning of that section) or (if later) the day on which the Secretary of State receives the undertaking.

10.3.4 Time for Extradition following Deferral for Competing Claim

Section 120 specifies the time limit for extradition where the Secretary of State has deferred extradition under Part 2 because of a competing Part 1 warrant or Part 2 request and, for whatever reason, the order for deferral has been lifted under s 181.

Section 120 applies if:

(a) an order is made under Part 2 for the defendant to be extradited to a Category 2 territory in pursuance of a request for his extradition;

(b) before the defendant is extradited to the territory an order is made under s 126(2) or s 179(2) for his extradition in pursuance of the request to be deferred;

(c) the appropriate judge makes an order under s 181(2) for the defendant's extradition in pursuance of the request to cease to be deferred.

Section 120(2) provides that in a case where s 117 applies, the required period for the purposes of s 117(2) is 28 days starting with the day on which the order under s 181(2) is made.

In a case where s 118 applies, the required period for the purposes of s 118(2) is 28 days starting with the day on which the decision of the relevant court on the appeal becomes final (within the meaning of that section) or (if later) the day on which the order under s 181(2) is made.

11

CONSENT TO EXTRADITION. WITHDRAWAL OF CLAIMS FOR EXTRADITION

11.1 INTRODUCTION

Some defendants do not wish to contest the request for their extradition and want to return as quickly as possible to the state seeking their extradition. The EA 1870 did not, however, provide any mechanism for expedited return. This was recognized as undesirable in 1982 by the Home Office Working Party on Extradition, which made appropriate recommendations in its Report. In the EA 1989 Parliament introduced a simplified procedure in s 14 and para 9 of Sch 1 by which the defendant could waive his rights under the Act. Appropriate forms of consent were contained the Schedule to the Magistrates' Court (Extradition) Rules 1989 (SI 1989/1527). However, these provisions gave rise to some difficulties in their application (see *In the Matter of Akbar*, Unreported, 31 July 1996, CO/1797/96), and the European Union Extradition Regulations 2002 (SI 2002/419) introduced significant changes to the procedure for consenting to return in EU cases.

The EA 2003 introduces revised procedures by which the defendant can consent to extradition. These are considered in the first part of this chapter.

The Act also deals in detail with the withdrawal of Part 1 warrants and extradition requests by the requesting state. These sections are considered later in this chapter.

11.2 CONSENT TO EXTRADITION

11.2.1 Consent to Extradition in Part 1 Cases

Section 45(1) and (2) provide that a defendant arrested under a Part 1 warrant, or a person provisionally arrested under s 5, may consent to his extradition to the Category 1 territory in which the warrant was issued.

By s 45(3), if the defendant consents to his extradition under s 45 he must be taken to have waived any right he would have (apart from the consent) not to be dealt with in the Category 1 territory for an offence committed before his extradition. Accordingly, a defendant who consents to his return waives his speciality protection in the requesting state. Speciality has been considered at 5.8.6 above in the context of bars to extradition.

Section 45(4) is an important provision. It provides that consent under s 45:

(a) must be given before the appropriate judge;
(b) must be recorded in writing;
(c) is irrevocable.

Section 45(5) provides that the defendant may not give his consent under s 45 unless he is legally represented before the appropriate judge at the time he gives consent. However, by s 45(6), he need not be legally represented if he has been informed of his right to apply for legal aid and has had the opportunity to apply for legal aid, but he has refused or failed to apply; he has applied for legal aid but his application has been refused; or he was granted legal aid but the legal aid was withdrawn.

By s 45(8) a defendant is to be treated as legally represented before the appropriate judge if (and only if) he has the assistance of counsel or a solicitor to represent him in the proceedings before the appropriate judge.

Once the defendant has given his consent under s 45 then the procedure under s 46 applies. The judge must remand the defendant in custody or on bail (s 46(2)) although, if he remands in custody, he may later grant bail (s 46(3)).

Section 46(4) disapplies the duty under s 8 to fix a date for the start of the extradition hearing. Also, if the extradition hearing has begun, the judge is no longer required to proceed (or continue proceeding) under ss 10–25.

By s 46(6), the judge must order the defendant's extradition to the Category 1 territory within the period of 10 days starting with the day on which consent is given. This sub-section has effect subject to ss 48 and 51.

Importantly, if s 46(6) is not complied with and the person applies to the judge to be discharged the judge must order his discharge.

Once the order for extradition has been made by the appropriate judge under s 46(6) then s 47 applies. By s 47(2), the defendant must be extradited to the Category 1 territory before the end of the required period. This is 10 days starting with the day on which the order is made or, if the judge and the authority which issued the Part 1 warrant agree a later date, 10 days starting with the later date.

If s 47(2) is not complied with and the defendant applies to the judge to be discharged the judge must order his discharge, unless reasonable cause is shown for the delay.

If before the defendant is extradited the judge is informed by the designated authority that the Part 1 warrant has been withdrawn then s 47(2) does not apply and the judge must order the defendant's discharge.

11.2.1.1 *Other Part 1 Warrant Issued following Consent to Return to Category 1 Territory*

Where the defendant has consented to his extradition to a Category 1 territory and another Part 1 warrant is issued before he has been extradited then ss 48 and 49 apply. These require the judge to decide whether to order extradition pursuant to the consent or defer proceedings to allow the second warrant to be disposed of.

Section 48 applies if:

(a) the defendant consents under s 45 to his extradition to a Category 1 territory; and

(b) the conditions in s 48(2) are satisfied before the judge orders his extradition under s 46(6).

The conditions in s 48(2) are that:

(a) the judge is informed that another Part 1 warrant has been issued in respect of the defendant;

(b) the warrant falls to be dealt with by the judge or by a judge who is the appropriate judge in another part of the UK;

(c) the warrant has not been disposed of.

In such a case, the duty of the judge to order extradition under s 46(6) within 10 days of the defendant's consent does not apply, and the judge may either order the defendant's extradition pursuant to his consent, or order further proceedings on the warrant under consideration to be deferred until the other warrant has been disposed of (s 48(3)).

In deciding under s 48(3) what order to make, the judge must take account in particular (s 48(5)):

(a) the relative seriousness of the offences concerned;

(b) the place where each offence was committed (or was alleged to have been committed);

(c) the date on which each warrant was issued;

(d) whether, in the case of each offence, the defendant is accused of its commission (but not alleged to have been convicted) or is alleged to be unlawfully at large after conviction.

If the judge makes an order under s 48(3)(a) for the defendant's extradition to a Category 1 territory pursuant to his consent then s 49 applies (s 49(1)).

Section 49(2) requires that the defendant be extradited to the Category 1 territory before the end of the required period. The required period is 10 days starting with the day on which the order is made, or, if the judge and the authority which issued the Part 1 warrant agree a later date, 10 days starting with the later date (s 49(3)).

If s 49(2) is not complied with and the defendant applies to the judge to be discharged the judge must order his discharge, unless reasonable cause is shown for the delay (s 49(4)).

However, if before the defendant is extradited to the Category 1 territory the judge is informed by the designated authority (see s 2(9)) that the Part 1 warrant has been withdrawn then s 49(2) does not apply, and the judge must order the defendant's discharge (s 49(5)).

If, however, the judge makes an order under s 48(3)(b) for proceedings on the Part 1 warrant to be deferred until the other warrant has been disposed of then s 50 applies (s 50(1)). The judge must remand the person in respect of whom the warrant was issued in custody or on bail (s 50(2)), although if the judge remands the person in custody he may later grant bail (s 50(3)).

If an order is made under s 180 for proceedings on the warrant to be resumed, the period specified in s 46(6) within which extradition has to take place must be taken to be 10 days starting with the day on which the order under s 180 is made (s 50(4)).

11.2.1.2 *Extradition Request made under Part 2 following Consent to Return to Category 1 Territory*

Section 51 governs the procedure where an extradition request is made by a Category 2 territory in respect of a defendant who has consented to his return to a Category 1 territory.

Section 51 applies if:

(a) a defendant in respect of whom a Part 1 warrant is issued consents under s 45 to his extradition; and

(b) the condition in s 51(2) is satisfied before the judge orders his extradition under s 46(6) or s 48(3)(a). This condition is that a certificate has been issued by the Secretary of State under s 70 in respect of the extradition request, and the request has not been disposed of.

As explained in Chapter 10, s 179 allows the Secretary of State to regulate competing extradition claims by making appropriate orders for deferral. Where s 51 applies, the judge must not make an order under s 46(6) or s 48(3) until he has been informed what order has been made by the Secretary of State under s 179(2).

If the order under s 179(2) is for further proceedings on the warrant to be deferred until the request has been disposed of, the judge must remand the person in custody or on bail (s 51(4)). If the judge remands the person in custody he may later grant bail (s 51(5)).

If the order under s 179(2) is for further proceedings on the warrant to be deferred until the request has been disposed of, and an order is made under s 180 for proceedings on the warrant to be resumed, the period specified in s 46(6) must be taken to be 10 days starting with the day on which the order under s 180 is made.

If the order under s 179(2) is for further proceedings on the request to be deferred until the warrant has been disposed of, the period specified in s 46(6) must be taken to be 10 days starting with the day on which the judge is informed of the order.

11.2.1.3 *Undertaking in Relation to Defendant Serving Sentence who has Consented to Extradition*

Section 52 allows the appropriate judge to seek a suitable undertaking from the requesting territory that a defendant who is a serving prisoner in the UK who has consented to extradition will be returned to the UK at the conclusion of the foreign proceedings to serve the remainder of his sentence.

Section 52 applies if:

(a) the appropriate judge makes an order under s 46(6) or s 48(3)(a) for the defendant's extradition to a Category 1 territory;

(b) the defendant is serving a sentence of imprisonment or another form of detention in the UK.

The judge may make the order for extradition subject to the condition that extradition is not to take place before he receives an undertaking given on behalf of the Category 1 territory in terms specified by him (s 52(2)).

The terms which may be specified in relation to an accused person include terms (s 52(3)):

(a) that the defendant be kept in custody until the conclusion of the proceedings against him for the offence and any other offence in respect of which he is permitted to be dealt with in the Category 1 territory;

(b) that the defendant be returned to the UK to serve the remainder of his sentence on the conclusion of those proceedings.

The terms which may be specified by the judge in relation to a defendant alleged to be unlawfully at large after conviction of an offence include terms he be returned to the UK to serve the remainder of his sentence after serving any sentence imposed on him in the Category 1 territory for the offence and any other offence in respect of which he is permitted to be dealt with in the Category 1 territory (s 52(4)).

If the judge makes an order for extradition subject to a condition under s 52(2) then the required period for the purposes of ss 47(2) and 49(2) is 10 days starting with the day on which the judge receives the undertaking (s 52(5)).

11.2.2 Consent to Extradition in Part 2 Cases

The mode of giving consent to extradition in Part 2 cases is dealt with in ss 127 and 128.

Section 127(1) provides that a defendant who has been arrested under a warrant issued under s 71 may consent to his extradition to the Category 2 territory to which his extradition is requested. Also, a defendant who has been arrested under a provisional warrant issued under s 73 may consent to his extradition to the Category 2 territory in which he is accused of the commission of an offence or is alleged to have been convicted of an offence (s 127(2)). By s 127(3), consent under s 127 must be given in writing and is irrevocable.

Where consent is given under s 127 before the defendant's case is sent to the Secretary of State for his decision whether the defendant is to be extradited then the consent must be given before the appropriate judge (s 127(4)). In any other case, consent must be given to the Secretary of State (s 127(5)).

The defendant may not give his consent under s 127 before the appropriate judge unless he is legally represented before the appropriate judge at the time he gives consent, or he is a person to whom s 127(7) applies. This subsection applies to the defendant if he has been informed of his right to apply for legal aid and has had the opportunity to apply for legal aid, but he has refused or failed to apply; he has applied for legal aid but his application has been refused; or he was granted legal aid but the legal aid was withdrawn. Legal aid is defined in s 127(8).

For the purposes of s 127(6) the defendant is to be treated as legally represented before the appropriate judge if (and only if) he has the assistance of counsel or a solicitor to represent him in the proceedings before the appropriate judge.

Section 128 applies if a person gives his consent under s 127 to the appropriate judge. If the judge has not fixed a date under s 75 or s 76 on which the extradition hearing is to begin he is not required to do so (s 128(2)). If the extradition hearing has begun, the judge is no longer required to proceed or continue proceeding under ss 78–91 (s 128(3)). The judge must send the case to the Secretary of State for his decision whether the person is to be extradited.

By s 128(5), consent under Part 2 constitutes a waiver of the speciality protection to which the defendant would otherwise be entitled. The defendant must be taken to have waived any right he would have (apart from the consent) not to be dealt with in the Category 2 territory for an offence committed before his extradition. By s 95(2), the prohibition on return where there are no speciality arrangements with the requesting Category 2 territory does not apply where the defendant consented to return before his case was sent to the Secretary of State.

11.3 WITHDRAWAL OF THE CLAIM FOR EXTRADITION

For a variety of reasons the requesting state may decide not to pursue its claim for the defendant's extradition. For example, further investigation may reveal that there is insufficient evidence to secure a conviction, or circumstances may change so that continued prosecution is undesirable or even unlawful. Whereas the EA 1989 did not specify what was to happen in such circumstances, the EA 2003 contains provisions to deal with this eventuality. There are separate sections dealing with Part 1 and Part 2 cases.

11.3.1 Withdrawal of Part 1 Warrant

The operative provisions in relation to Part 1 cases are ss 41–43.

Section 41 applies if at any time in the relevant period the appropriate judge is informed by the designated authority that a Part 1 warrant issued in respect of the defendant has been withdrawn (s 41(1)). Section 41(3) provides that in such a case the judge must order the defendant's discharge. If the person is not before the judge at the time the judge orders his discharge, the judge must inform him of the order as soon as practicable.

By s 41(2), the relevant period is the period starting when the person is first brought before the appropriate judge following his arrest under Part 1 and ending when the person is extradited in pursuance of the warrant or discharged.

Section 42 deals with withdrawal of the warrant whilst an appeal to the High Court under ss 26 or 28 is pending. It applies if at any time in the relevant period the High Court is informed by the designated authority that a Part 1 warrant issued in respect of the defendant has been withdrawn (s 42(1)). In such a case, if the appeal is under s 26, the court must order the defendant's discharge and quash the order for his extradition; if the appeal is under s 28, the court must dismiss the appeal (s 42(3)).

If the defendant is not before the court at the time the court orders his discharge the court must inform him of the order as soon as practicable (s 42(4)).

In this case the relevant period is the period starting when notice of an appeal to the High Court is given by the person or the authority which issued the warrant and ending when proceedings on the appeal are discontinued or the High Court makes its decision on the appeal (s 42(2)).

Section 43 provides for the discharge of the defendant whilst an appeal to the House of Lords is pending. It applies if at any time in the 'relevant period' the House of Lords is informed by the designated authority that a Part 1 warrant issued in respect of the defendant has been withdrawn (s 43(1)). If the appeal is brought by the defendant the House of Lords must order the person's discharge and quash the order for his extradition, in a case where the appeal was against a decision of the High Court to dismiss an appeal under s 26 (s 43(3)). If the appeal is brought by the authority which issued the warrant the House of Lords must dismiss the appeal (s 43(4)).

In this case the relevant period is the period starting when leave to appeal to the House of Lords is granted to the defendant or the authority which issued the warrant and ending when proceedings on the appeal are discontinued or the House of Lords makes its decision on the appeal (s 43(2)).

If the defendant is not before the House of Lords at the time it orders his discharge, the House of Lords must inform him of the order as soon as practicable (s 43(5)).

11.3.2 Withdrawal of the Extradition Request

The relevant sections in Part 2 cases are ss 122–125.

Section 122 applies if at any time in the relevant period the appropriate judge is informed by the Secretary of State that a request for the defendant's extradition has been withdrawn (s 122(1)). The judge must then order the defendant's discharge (s 122(3)). If the defendant is not before the judge at the time the judge orders his discharge, the judge must inform him of the order as soon as practicable (s 122(4)).

By s 122(2) the relevant period is the period starting when the defendant first appears or is brought before the appropriate judge following his arrest under Part 2 and ending when the judge orders the defendant's discharge or sends the case to the Secretary of State for his decision whether the person is to be extradited.

Section 123 applies if during the relevant period the Secretary of State is informed that a request for a person's extradition has been withdrawn. In that case, the Secretary of State must order the person's discharge (s 123(3)).

By s 123(2) the relevant period is the period starting when the judge sends the case to the Secretary of State for his decision whether the defendant is to be extradited and ending when the person is extradited in pursuance of the request or discharged.

Section 124 deals with the situation where the extradition request is withdrawn whilst an appeal to the High Court by the defendant or the requesting state is pending. It applies if, during the relevant period, the High Court is informed by the Secretary of State that a request for the defendant's extradition has been withdrawn (s 124(1)). If the appeal is under s 103 or s 108, the court must order the defendant's discharge and quash the order for his extradition, if the Secretary of State has ordered his extradition (s 124(3)). If the appeal is under s 105 or s 110, the court must dismiss the appeal (s 124(4)). If the person is not before the court at the time the court orders his discharge, the court must inform him of the order as soon as practicable (s 124(5)).

The relevant period is the period starting when notice of an appeal to the court is given by the defendant or by a person acting on behalf of the Category 2 territory to which his extradition is requested, and ending when proceedings on the appeal are discontinued or the court makes its decision on the appeal.

Where the extradition request is withdrawn whilst an appeal to the House of Lords is pending then s 125 applies. It applies if at any time in the relevant period the House of Lords is informed by the Secretary of State that a request for a person's extradition has been withdrawn. In such a case, if the appeal is brought by the defendant, the House of Lords must order his discharge and quash the order for his extradition, in a case where the appeal was against a decision of the High Court to dismiss an appeal under ss 103 or 108 (s 125(3)).

If the appeal is brought by a person acting on behalf of the Category 2 territory the House of Lords must dismiss the appeal (s 125(4)). If the person whose extradition is requested is not before the House of Lords at the time it orders his discharge, the House of Lords must inform him of the order as soon as practicable (s 125(5)).

For these purposes, the relevant period is the period starting when leave to appeal to the House of Lords is granted to the defendant or a person acting on behalf of the requesting Category 2 territory, and ending when proceedings on the appeal are discontinued or the House of Lords makes its decision on the appeal (s 125(2)).

12

RETURN TO THE
UNITED KINGDOM

12.1 INTRODUCTION

The EA 1989 was primarily concerned with incoming extradition requests. The principal provisions applicable to defendants extradited to the UK were Part IV and para 17 of Sch 1, which provided the speciality protection required by nearly all extradition treaties (see *Corrigan* [1931] 1 KB 527; *R v Aubrey-Fletcher ex p Ross Munro* [1968] 1 QB 620; *Kerr and Smith* (1976) 62 Cr App R 210).

The EA 1989 did not provide statutory authority for the making of extradition requests by the UK (known as outgoing requests), which were made under the Royal Prerogative (*Barton v The Commonwealth of Australia* [1974] 131 CLR). The arrest warrant and necessary supporting evidence were forwarded to the Home Office for certification, and the request was forwarded to the Foreign and Commonwealth Office for service on the foreign state through diplomatic channels.

On occasion, rather than pursuing a legitimate extradition request, UK prosecuting authorities resorted to illegal methods to obtain the return of a defendant for trial (see eg, *R v Horseferry Road Magistrates' Court ex p Bennett* [1994] 2 AC 42; *R v Horseferry Road Magistrates' Court ex p Bennett (No 3)* [1995] 1 Cr App R 147; *Mullen* [2000] QB 520). This is known as disguised extradition.

The bulk of this chapter examines Part 3 of the EA 2003. Part 3 puts the making of outgoing requests on a statutory footing for the first time where the requested territory is a Category 1 territory. It specifies how the necessary arrest warrant is to be obtained, and it clarifies the offences for which extradition can be requested by the UK (cf *R v Secretary of State for the Home Department ex p Bagudu*, Unreported, 8 September 2002, CO/4208/2003; *R v Secretary of State for Trade and Industry ex p Levitt*, Unreported, 16 January 1998, CO/3811/97).

Requests for extradition to Category 2 territories continue to be dealt with under the Royal Prerogative.

The second part of this chapter considers the return of extradited persons to the UK to serve the remainder of their sentences.

12.2 EXTRADITION FROM CATEGORY 1 TERRITORIES

12.2.1 Offences for which Extradition may be Requested

The UK may seek the extradition of a defendant from a Category 1 territory in respect of the extradition offences specified in s 148. It is therefore convenient to consider this definition before examining the mechanism for seeking the defendant's extradition.

Conduct constitutes an extradition offence in relation to the UK if it occurs in the UK and is punishable under the law of the relevant part of the UK (as defined in s 142(6)) with imprisonment or another form of detention for a term of 12 months or a greater punishment (s 148(1)).

Conduct also constitutes an extradition offence in relation to the UK if the conduct occurs outside the UK and the conduct constitutes an extra-territorial offence punishable under the law of the relevant part of the UK with imprisonment or another form of detention for a term of 12 months or a greater punishment (s 148(2)).

However, s 148(1) and (2) do not apply in relation to the defendant's conduct if he is alleged to be unlawfully at large after conviction by a court in the UK and he has been sentenced for the offence. In such a case s 148(4) and (5) apply. By s 148(4), conduct also constitutes an extradition offence in relation to the UK if the conduct occurs in the UK and a sentence of imprisonment or another form of detention for a term of four months or a greater punishment has been imposed in the UK in respect of the conduct.

By s 148(5), conduct also constitutes an extradition offence in relation to the UK if the conduct occurs outside the UK; the conduct constitutes an extra-territorial offence; and a sentence of imprisonment or another form of detention for a term of four months or a greater punishment has been imposed in the UK in respect of the conduct.

The relevant part of the UK is the part of the UK in which the relevant proceedings are taking place (s 142(6)). The relevant proceedings are the proceedings in which it is necessary to decide whether conduct constitutes an extradition offence (s 142(7)).

The definitions in s 148(1)–(5) apply for the purposes of ss 142–147.

12.2.2 Part 3 Warrants

The first stage in seeking the extradition of a defendant from a Category 1 territory involves obtaining a Part 3 warrant from an appropriate judge (s 142(3)). A Part 3 warrant is defined by s 142(3) to be an arrest warrant which contains the statement referred to in s 142(4) or the statement referred to in s 142(5), and the certificate referred to in s 142(6).

By s 142(1), an appropriate judge (defined in s 149 to be, in England and Wales, a District Judge (Magistrates' Courts), a justice of the peace, or a judge entitled to exercise the jurisdiction of the Crown Court) may issue a Part 3 warrant in respect of a person if a constable or an 'appropriate person' applies to him for a Part 3 warrant, and the condition in s 142(2) is satisfied.

Section 142(9) defines an appropriate person to be a person of a description specified in an order made by the Secretary of State for the purposes of s 142. The Extradition Act 2003 (Part 3 Designation) Order 2003 (SI 2003/3335) has specified that the following are appropriate persons for these purposes:

... any Inland Revenue officer, of grade B1 or above, attached to the Inland Revenue Extradition Group; any member of the Serious Fraud Office designated by the Director of the Serious Fraud Office under section 1(7) of the Criminal Justice Act 1987; the Director of Public Prosecutions, any Crown Prosecutor and any counsel or solicitor instructed by the Crown Prosecution Service for the purposes of the case concerned; and the Commissioners of Customs and Excise.

The condition in s 142(2) is that a 'domestic warrant' has been issued in respect of the person and there are reasonable grounds for believing:

(a) that the person has committed an extradition offence, or

(b) that the person is unlawfully at large after conviction of an extradition offence by a court in the UK.

A domestic warrant is a warrant for the arrest or apprehension of a person which is issued under the provisions specified in s 142(8), namely, s 72 of the Criminal Justice Act 1967; s 7 of the Bail Act 1976; s 51 of the Judicature (Northern Ireland) Act 1978; s 1 of the Magistrates' Courts Act 1980; Articles 20 or 25 of the Magistrates' Courts (Northern Ireland) Order 1981 (SI 1981/1675 (NI 26)); the Criminal Procedure (Scotland) Act 1995.

The statement referred to in s 142(4) concerns defendants who are accused of offences. It is a statement that the person in respect of whom the warrant is issued is accused in the UK of the commission of an extradition offence specified in the warrant, and the warrant is issued with a view to his arrest and extradition to the UK for the purpose of being prosecuted for the offence.

The statement referred to in s 142(5) relates to persons convicted of extradition offences. It is a statement that the person in respect of whom the warrant is issued is alleged to be unlawfully at large after conviction of an extradition offence specified in the warrant by a court in the UK, and the warrant is issued with a view to his arrest and extradition to the UK for the purpose of being sentenced for the offence or of serving a sentence of imprisonment or another form of detention imposed in respect of the offence.

The certificate referred to in s 142(6) is one certifying:

(a) whether the conduct constituting the extradition offence specified in the warrant falls within the European framework list as defined in s 215;

(b) whether the offence is an extra-territorial offence;

(c) what is the maximum punishment that may be imposed on conviction of the offence or (if the person has been sentenced for the offence) what sentence has been imposed.

The conduct which falls within the European framework list includes conduct which constitutes an attempt, conspiracy, or incitement to carry out conduct falling within the list, or aiding, abetting, counselling, or procuring the carrying out of conduct falling within the list (s 142(7)).

12.2.3 Speciality Protection for Defendants Extradited to the UK

A defendant extradited to the UK from a Category 1 territory is entitled to the speciality protection contained in s 146. In other words, following his extradition, he may only be tried in respect of the offences specified in that section.

Section 146 applies if the defendant is extradited to the UK from a Category 1 territory in pursuance of a Part 3 warrant (s 146(1)). Section 146(2) provides that the defendant may be dealt with in the UK for an offence committed before his extradition only if the offence falls within s 146(3) or the condition in s 146(4) is satisfied.

The offences specified in s 146(3) are as follows:

(a) the offence in respect of which the defendant is extradited;

(b) an offence disclosed by the information provided to the Category 1 territory in respect of that offence;

(c) an extradition offence in respect of which consent to the defendant being dealt with is given on behalf of the territory;

(d) an offence which is not punishable with imprisonment or another form of detention;

(e) an offence in respect of which the person will not be detained in connection with his trial, sentence, or appeal;

(f) an offence in respect of which the person waives the right that he would have (but for s 146(6)(f)) not to be dealt with for the offence.

The condition in s 146(4) is that the defendant has been given an opportunity to leave the UK and either he has not done so before the end of the 'permitted period', or he has done so before the end of the permitted period and has returned to the UK. The permitted period is 45 days starting with the day on which the defendant arrives in the UK (s 146(5)).

The operation of the speciality principle in this context can be illustrated by an example, based on the facts of *Kerr and Smith* (1976) 62 Cr App R 210 (a case under the Extradition Act 1870). Suppose that a Part 3 warrant is submitted to Denmark for the return of D for an offence of robbery contrary to s 8(1) of the Theft Act 1968. The Part 3 warrant only specifies the offence of robbery; however the factual account of the offence provided to Denmark refers to D as having carried a sawn-off shotgun in the course of the robbery. This is an offence contrary to s 18 of the Firearms Act 1968. Extradition is granted. D could be tried for robbery and for the s 18 offence because it was disclosed in the information provided to Denmark and s 146(6)(b) would therefore apply. If, however, evidence came to light that prior to the robbery D had assaulted his wife, then he could not be tried for this offence until after he had been given an opportunity to leave the UK after serving his sentence for the robbery, unless Denmark consented or he waived his rights. This is because the offence of assault did not form part of the information supplied in support of the application for his extradition.

Where the defendant consents to his extradition in the Category 1 state then s 147 applies. This section clarifies the uncertainty in the law under the EA 1989 discussed in *R v Secretary of State for the Home Department ex p Johnson* [1999] QB 1174, namely whether a defendant who had waived his rights in the foreign state retained speciality protection in the UK.

Section 147 applies if the defendant is extradited to the UK from a Category 1 territory in pursuance of a Part 3 warrant and he consented to his extradition to the UK in accordance with the law of the Category 1 territory. By s 147(2), s 146(2) does not apply if the conditions in s 147(3) or (4) are satisfied.

The conditions in s 147(3) are that under the law of the Category 1 territory, the effect of the defendant's consent is to waive his right under s 146(2) and he has not revoked his consent in accordance with that law, if he is permitted to do so under that law.

The conditions in s 147(4) are that:

(a) under the law of the Category 1 territory, the effect of the defendant's consent is not to waive his right under s 146(2);

(b) he has expressly waived his right under s 146(2) in accordance with that law;

(c) he has not revoked his consent in accordance with that law, if he is permitted to do so under that law;

(d) he has not revoked the waiver of his right under s 146(2) in accordance with that law, if he is permitted to do so under that law.

12.2.4 Extradition of Serving Prisoners to the UK

Just as the UK is able to grant extradition to Category 1 territories of serving prisoners subject to suitable undertakings that they will be returned to the UK at the conclusion of foreign proceedings (see s 37), so the UK is able to request the extradition of defendants serving sentences of imprisonment in Category 1 territories in exchange for suitable undertakings by the Secretary of State.

Section 143 applies if:

(a) a Part 3 warrant is issued in respect of a defendant;

(b) the defendant is serving a sentence of imprisonment or another form of detention in a Category 1 territory;

(c) the defendant's extradition to the UK from the Category 1 territory in pursuance of the warrant is made subject to a condition that an undertaking is given on behalf of the UK with regard to his treatment in the UK or his return to the Category 1 territory (or both).

Section 143(2) provides that the Secretary of State may give an undertaking to a person acting on behalf of the Category 1 territory with regard to the treatment in the UK of the defendant and/or his return to the Category 1 territory.

The terms which may be included by the Secretary of State in an undertaking given under s 143(2) in relation to a defendant accused of an offence include terms:

(a) that the defendant be kept in custody until the conclusion of the proceedings against him for the offence and any other offence in respect of which he is permitted to be dealt with in the UK;

(b) that the person be returned to the Category 1 territory to serve the remainder of his sentence on the conclusion of those proceedings.

The terms which may be included by the Secretary of State in an undertaking given under s 143(2) in relation to a defendant alleged to be unlawfully at large after conviction of an offence by a court in the UK include terms that he will be returned to the Category 1 territory to serve the remainder of his sentence after serving any sentence imposed on him in the UK.

12.2.5 Return to Category 1 Territory to Serve Sentence Imposed in the UK

The EA 2003 contains powers allowing sentences imposed in the UK on extradited defendants to be served in the Category 1 territory from where they were extradited.

Section 144 applies where a Part 3 warrant is issued in respect of a defendant; the warrant states that it is issued with a view to his extradition to the UK for the purpose of being prosecuted for an offence; he is extradited to the UK from a Category 1 territory in pursuance of the warrant; he is extradited on the condition that, if he is convicted of the offence and a sentence of imprisonment or another form of detention is imposed in respect of it, he must be returned to the Category 1 territory to serve the sentence; and he is convicted of the offence and a sentence of imprisonment or another form of detention is imposed in respect of it.

Section 144(2) provides that the person must be returned to the Category 1 territory to serve the sentence as soon as is reasonably practicable after the sentence is imposed. If s 144(2) is complied with the punishment for the offence must be treated as remitted but the person's conviction for the offence must be treated as a conviction for all other purposes. If s 144(2) is not complied with and the person applies to the appropriate judge to be discharged the judge must order his discharge, unless reasonable cause is shown for the delay.

12.2.6 Service of Sentence in the Requested Category 1 Territory

The EA 2003 also allows sentences imposed in the UK prior to the service of the Part 3 warrant to be served in the requested Category 1 territory.

Section 145 applies if a Part 3 warrant is issued in respect of a defendant; the certificate contained in the warrant certifies that a sentence has been imposed; an undertaking is given on behalf of a Category 1 territory that the defendant will be required to serve the sentence in the territory; on the basis of the undertaking the person is not extradited to the United Kingdom from the Category 1 territory.

In such a case, so far as the UK is concerned, the punishment for the offence must be treated as remitted but the person's conviction for the offence must be treated as a conviction for all other purposes (s 145(2)).

12.3 EXTRADITION FROM CATEGORY 2 TERRITORIES

The provisions of the EA 2003 dealing with return to the UK from Category 2 territories are less elaborate than those governing return from Category 1 territories considered earlier in this chapter. In particular, there is no power to allow sentenced prisoners to be imprisoned in the requested state.

The content of the extradition request continues to be governed by relevant treaty provisions (see eg, Article 8 of the Extradition Treaty concluded in 2003 between the UK and the United States of America (Cm 5821)) and the request is made pursuant to the Royal Prerogative.

Sections 150 and 151 of the EA 2003 provide speciality protection for defendants returned from Category 2 territories.

12.3.1 Defendants Returned from Commonwealth Countries, British Overseas Territories, and the Hong Kong SAR

Section 150 applies where:

(a) a defendant is extradited to the UK from a Category 2 territory under the law of the territory corresponding to Part 2 of the EA 2003, and

(b) the territory is a Commonwealth country, a British overseas territory, or the Hong Kong SAR.

Section 150(2) provides that in such a case the defendant may be 'dealt with' in the UK for an offence committed before his extradition only if the offence is one falling within s 150(3) or the condition in s 150(6) is satisfied. By s 150(8), a person is dealt with in the UK for an offence if he is tried there for it or he is detained with a view to trial there for it.

The offences in s 150(3) are:

(a) the offence in respect of which the defendant is extradited;

(b) a 'lesser offence' disclosed by the information provided to the Category 2 territory in respect of that offence;

(c) an offence in respect of which consent to the defendant being dealt with is given by or on behalf of the 'relevant authority'.

Section 150(4) defines 'lesser offences'. An offence is a lesser offence in relation to another offence if the maximum punishment for it is less severe than the maximum punishment for the other offence.

By s 150(5), the relevant authority is:

(a) if the person has been extradited from a Commonwealth country, the government of the country;

(b) if the person has been extradited from a British overseas territory, the person administering the territory;

(c) if the person has been extradited from the Hong Kong SAR, the government of the Region.

The condition in s 150(6) referred to in s 150(2)(b) is that the protected period has ended. The protected period is 45 days starting with the first day after his extradition to the UK on which the defendant is given an opportunity to leave the UK.

12.3.2 Return from Other Category 2 Territories

Section 151 provides speciality protection for defendants extradited to the UK from Category 2 territories other than those specified by s 150. Section 151 applies where:

(a) a defendant is extradited to the UK from a Category 2 territory under the law of the territory corresponding to Part 2 of the EA 2003; and

(b) the territory is not one falling within s 150(1)(b).

Where s 151 applies the defendant may be dealt with in the UK for an offence committed before his extradition only if the offence is one falling within s 151(3) or the condition in s 151(4) is satisfied. By s 151(5), a person is dealt with in the UK for an offence if he is tried there for it or he is detained with a view to trial there for it.

The offences in s 151(3) are:

(a) the offence in respect of which the person is extradited;

(b) an offence disclosed by the information provided to the Category 2 territory in respect of that offence;

(c) an offence in respect of which consent to the person being dealt with is given on behalf of the territory.

The condition in s 151(4) is that the person has returned to the territory from which he was extradited, or the person has been given an opportunity to leave the UK.

12.4 CLAIMING SPECIALITY PROTECTION IN THE UK

English case law decided under the EA 1870 and the EA 1989 has developed a number of principles in the application of the speciality rule to those returned to the UK. First, the onus is on the defendant to show that his trial or sentence breaches the rule of speciality (*Corrigan* [1931] 1 KB 527). In making this determination the court of trial may examine the documents in the extradition proceedings to determine whether the offence charged satisfies the rule of speciality (*R v Aubrey-Fletcher ex p Ross-Munro* [1968] 1 QB 620).

Whilst the prosecution is prevented from trying a defendant for offences other than those which comply with the rule, there is no bar to their obtaining and adducing additional evidence to support charges which do so comply. In *R v Aubrey-Fletcher ex p Ross-Munro* [1968] 1 QB 620 the defendant was extradited from France on a warrant containing six charges. At committal the magistrate indicated that in his view the evidence was insufficient and he granted the prosecution an adjournment. At the next hearing the prosecution sought to adduce the evidence of a witness whose evidence had not been used in the extradition. Objection was taken, but it was held that the only restriction was that the crime should be based on the same allegation as the crime in the warrant.

Restrictions imposed by foreign courts on the offences for which the defendant can be tried in the UK do not override the terms of domestic legislation.

R v Davidson (1977) 64 Cr App R 209 concerned an extradition from West Germany. The German Court had entered a caveat that the fugitive should only be tried in relation to the management of companies named in the warrant. The Court of Appeal took the view that neither the decision of the German Court nor the UK treaty were appropriate matters for inquiry in this country. The English courts should be concerned only to ensure compliance with the domestic extradition legislation.

The rule of speciality does not extend to protect the defendant from civil proceedings. In *Pooley v Whitham* [1880] 15 Ch D 435, Pooley was arrested in France on a warrant in respect of bankruptcy offences. He was returned to the UK, tried, and acquitted of the bankruptcy charges, then detained in custody as a result of outstanding contempt proceedings as a result of his having disobeyed a court order in a civil action. The Court of Appeal held that Pooley was not entitled to be discharged until he had purged his contempt. It held that the word 'offence' in s 19 of the EA 1870 meant a criminal act triable in a criminal court. It did not cover the consequences of failing to comply with a court order.

12.5 GENERAL PROVISIONS RELATING TO RETURN TO THE UK

Sections 152–155 of Part 3 relate to return from both Category 1 and 2 territories.

12.5.1 Grant of Bail where Undertaking Given to Requested State

As has been seen, in some cases extradition to the UK may be made subject to undertakings given by the Secretary of State. Section 154 applies where the Secretary of State has given such an undertaking and it includes terms that the defendant be kept in custody until the conclusion of proceedings against him in the UK.

Section 154(2) provides that in such a case a court, judge, or justice of the peace may grant bail to the person in the proceedings only if the court, judge, or justice of the peace considers that there are exceptional circumstances which justify it.

This section must be applied in a manner which is compatible with Articles 5(3) and (4) of the ECHR (see Chapter 7).

12.5.2 Outstanding Convictions and Remission of Punishment

Section 152 applies if:

(a) a person is extradited to the UK from a Category 1 territory under law of the territory corresponding to Part 1 of the EA 2003, or a Category 2 territory under law of the territory corresponding to Part 2 of the Act;

(b) before his extradition he has been convicted of an offence in the UK;

(c) he has not been extradited in respect of that offence.

By s 152(2), the defendant's punishment for the offence must be treated as remitted but the person's conviction for the offence must be treated as a conviction for all other purposes.

12.5.3 Return of Persons who are Acquitted or Not Tried

Of course, not all defendants who are extradited to the UK will be convicted of the offence for which their extradition was sought. They may be acquitted, or they may not be proceeded against for any one of a number of reasons. Such defendants are entitled under the EA 2003 to be returned to the territory from where they were extradited free of charge as quickly as possible after the conclusion of the proceedings against them.

Section 153 applies where:

(a) the defendant is accused in the UK of the commission of an offence;

(b) he is extradited to the UK in respect of the offence from a Category 1 territory under law of the territory corresponding to Part 1 of the EA 2003, or a Category 2 territory under law of the territory corresponding to Part 2 of the Act; and

(c) the condition in s 153(2) or s 153(3) is satisfied.

The condition in s 153(2) is that proceedings against the defendant are not begun before the end of the required period, which is six months starting with the day on which the person arrives in the UK, and before the end of the period of three months starting immediately after the end of the required period the person asks the Secretary of State to return him to the territory from which he was extradited.

The condition in s 153(3) is that at his trial for the offence the person is acquitted or is discharged under any of the provisions specified in s 153(4), and before the end of the period of three months starting immediately after the date of his acquittal or discharge the person asks the Secretary of State to return him to the territory from which he was extradited.

The provisions mentioned in s 153(4) are s 12(1) of the Powers of Criminal Courts (Sentencing) Act 2000; s 246(1), (2) or (3) of the Criminal Procedure (Scotland) Act 1995; Article 4(1) of the Criminal Justice (Northern Ireland) Order 1996 (SI 1996/3160).

Where a defendant requests return, the Secretary of State must arrange for him to be sent back, free of charge and with as little delay as possible, to the territory from which he was extradited to the UK in respect of the offence.

12.5.4 Service Personnel

Section 155 confers power on the Secretary of State to make an order applying Part 3 to defendants whose extradition is sought under military law, air-force law or the Naval Discipline Act 1957.

12.6 RETURN OF PERSONS TO THE UK TO SERVE THE REMAINDER OF THEIR SENTENCES

12.6.1 Return from Category 1 Territory (Section 59)

Section 59 applies where a person who is serving a sentence of imprisonment or another form of detention in the UK is extradited to a Category 1 territory in accordance with Part 1 and he is returned to the UK to serve the remainder of his sentence.

A person who is returned in these circumstances is liable to be detained in pursuance of his sentence (s 59(2)) and, if he is at large, he must be treated as being unlawfully at large (s 59(3)).

Time during which the person was not in the UK as a result of his extradition does not count as time served by him as part of his sentence (s 59(4)). However s 59(4) does not apply if he was extradited for the purpose of being prosecuted for an offence, and the person has not been convicted of the offence or of any other offence in respect of which he was permitted to be dealt with in the Category 1 territory (s 59(5)).

In a case falling within s 59(5), time during which the person was not in the UK as a result of his extradition counts as time served by him as part of his sentence if (and only if) it was spent in custody in connection with the offence or any other offence in respect of which he was permitted to be dealt with in the territory.

12.6.2 Return from Category 2 Territory (Section 132)

Section 132 is in similar terms to s 59, considered at 12.6.1 above.

13

POLICE POWERS IN EXTRADITION CASES

13.1 INTRODUCTION

Part 4 of the EA 2003 is entitled 'Police Powers' and contains new powers of entry, search, and seizure for use in extradition cases. It also contains provisions for dealing with extradition detainees who are in police custody following arrest.

Before considering Part 4 in detail it is instructive to consider some of the difficulties created by the former law which Part 4 is intended to remedy.

13.1.1 History of Search and Seizure in Extradition Cases

Extradition treaties commonly include provisions requiring the requested state to hand over property which might be relevant to the offence for which extradition is requested. For example, Article 20 of the European Convention on Extradition 1957 requires the requested state ' . . . so far as its law permits and at the request of the requesting party, to seize and hand over property . . .'. It follows that the power of search and seizure in extradition cases is governed by the ordinary domestic law.

Between 1881 and 1989 Parliament enacted various provisions allowing magistrates to issue search warrants in relation to offences committed in Empire and Commonwealth countries. Section 24 of the Fugitive Offenders Act 1881, which, until its repeal by the Fugitive Offenders Act 1967, governed extradition within the Empire and Commonwealth, permitted a magistrate to issue a warrant to search for any property alleged to be stolen or to be otherwise unlawfully taken or obtained by the defendant, or otherwise to be the subject of the offence for which extradition was requested. These powers were the same as the court or magistrate would have if the property had been stolen or otherwise unlawfully taken or obtained, or the offence had been committed, within the jurisdiction of the magistrate.

In contrast, the EA 1870 did not contain any provisions relating to search and seizure for the purposes of extradition to foreign states.

Section 6(5) of the Fugitive Offenders Act 1967 also contained a special search provision where the defendant was accused of an offence of stealing or receiving stolen property. This provision was replicated in s 8(6) of the EA 1989 in relation to designated Commonwealth countries and colonies. Other than this section, the EA 1989 was silent as to search and seizure in extradition cases.

13.1.2 Part II of the Police and Criminal Evidence Act 1984

The principal legislation concerning entry, search, and seizure is Part II of the Police and Criminal Evidence Act 1984 (PACE). Sections 8–23 consolidate many but not all police powers of entry, search, and seizure. Part II contains new provisions on search warrants, various categories of sensitive or privileged material (ss 8–16), and powers of seizure (ss 19–22). In particular, s 8 creates a general power to obtain a search warrant in the case of a 'serious arrestable offence', as defined in s 116, whilst s 9 and Sch 1 enables search warrants and production orders to be obtained for special procedure material and excluded material. Common law powers of entry following arrest are also codified in Part II.

13.1.3 The Decision in *R (Rottman) v Commissioner of Police for the Metropolis*

In *R v Southwark Crown Court ex p Sorsky Defries* [1996] Crim LR 195 the Divisional Court held that the word 'offence' in Part II of PACE refers to domestic offences and not foreign offences (cf *Air-India v Wiggins* [1980] 1 WLR 815; *Cox v Army Council* [1963] AC 48).

In *R (Rottman) v Commissioner of Police for the Metropolis* [2002] 2 WLR 1315 the principal question before the House of Lords was whether the powers of entry and search in Part II of PACE are applicable in extradition cases. Despite the decision in *R v Southwark Crown Court ex p Sorsky Defries* [1996] Crim LR 195, some police forces continued to rely on their Part II powers when carrying out extradition arrests in the belief that the statutory powers of entry and search contained in Part II applied to foreign offences.

The facts of *Rottman* were as follows. An arrest warrant was issued in Germany for R's arrest in connection with alleged fraud offences. A provisional warrant for R's arrest was issued by the Bow Street Magistrates' Court under s 8(1)(b) of the EA 1989 whilst R was living in the UK. R was arrested in the driveway of his house by three police officers a few yards from his front door. The officers then entered and searched the house, and removed items belonging to R which they suspected might hold evidence of the alleged offences or proceeds of the offences, having acted in purported reliance on ss 18, 19, and 32 in Part II of PACE and in the belief that they had in any event power under the common law to search the premises of a suspect following his arrest on an extradition warrant.

Before the House of Lords the Commissioner argued that the powers in Part II of PACE applied in extradition cases. The House of Lords rejected this argument. Lord Hutton said at paras 66–67:

66. . . . [counsel] also submitted that . . . police had power under both section 18 and section 19 to search the respondent's house and to seize the articles. I would reject, as did the Divisional Court, the argument that the police had such a power under either section. Section 18 only applies to the premises of a person who is under arrest for an 'arrestable offence'. An 'arrestable offence' is defined in section 24(1) as an offence for which the sentence is fixed by law, an offence for which a person of 21 years or over (not previously convicted) may be sentenced to imprisonment for a term of five years (or might be so sentenced but for the restrictions imposed by section 33 of the Magistrates' Courts Act 1980) or a long list of domestic offences created by United Kingdom statutes. Therefore it is clear, in my opinion, that an 'arrestable offence' is a domestic offence and the extradition crime alleged to have been committed by the respondent in Germany cannot be regarded as an 'arrestable offence' within the meaning of section 24(1).

67. Nor, in my opinion, can the appellant rely on section 19(3)(a). That section only applies to the seizure of evidence in relation to 'an offence which [the police officer] is investigating or any other offence'. In *R v Southwark Crown Court ex p Sorsky Defries* [1996] Crim LR 195 the Divisional Court held that the words in section 19(3)(a) 'any other offence' were confined to domestic offences because . . . in the absence of an express provision to the contrary the word 'offence' in a statute meant a domestic offence.

In para 68 Lord Hutton also rejected the Commissioner's contention that power to enter and search was conferred by s 32.

However, by a 4:1 majority (Lord Hope of Craighead dissenting), the House of Lords held that the police had a limited power at common law to enter and search R's house following his arrest and that, contrary to what the Administrative Court had held, this power had survived the coming into force of PACE. The power relied upon was that identified by Lloyd LJ in *R v Governor of Pentonville Prison ex p Osman* [1990] 1 WLR 277, 311 where documents had been seized following O's arrest on a provisional warrant issued under s 6 of the Fugitive Offenders Act 1967. Objection was taken that there was no common law power to search and seize documents in relation to a crime alleged to have been committed abroad. Lloyd LJ held at p 311:

We do not accept Mr Ross-Munro's first objection. It is beyond dispute that, in relation to a domestic offence, a police officer entering a house in pursuance of a warrant of arrest, or otherwise lawfully arresting a defendant, is entitled to take any goods or documents which he reasonably believes to be material evidence in relation to the crime for which the defendant is being arrested: *Ghani v Jones* [1970] 1 QB 693, 706. Is there then any difference between a warrant of arrest in domestic proceedings and a provisional warrant under section 6 of the Fugitive Offenders Act 1967? We can see none. The police powers of search and seizure consequent on a lawful arrest ought to be, and in our judgment are, the same in both cases.

The narrowness of the *Osman/Rottman* common law power was demonstrated in *R (Hewitson) v Chief Constable of Dorset*, The Times, 6 January 2004, in which the Administrative Court held that the police had acted unlawfully in searching the house of man who had been arrested under a provisional warrant several hours earlier some distance away from the flat. The Court declined to extend the common law power of search further than the limits identified in *Rottman*, saying that do so would represent a substantial leap in—rather than an incremental development of—the common law.

13.1.4 Outline of Part 4 of the EA 2003

The decision in *Rottman* led Parliament to enact Part 4 of the EA 2003 so as to make available to the police entry, search, and seizure powers analogous to those contained in Part II of PACE.

Before considering these powers in detail it is useful to give an overview of its more important sections.

13.1.4.1 *Search and Seizure under Warrant*

Section 156 permits a justice of the peace to issue a search and seizure warrant where a person's extradition is sought under Part 1 or Part 2. A search and seizure warrant is a warrant authorizing a constable to enter and search the premises specified in the application for the warrant, and to seize and retain any material found there which falls within s 156(6) which is not legally privileged material, excluded material, or special procedure material (as defined in ss 10, 11, and 14 of PACE: see s 174 of the EA 2003).

Section 157 empowers a Circuit Judge to make a production order in respect of material which is not legally privileged material. A production order is an order either requiring the person in possession or control of special procedure material or excluded material to produce it to a constable for him to take away, or requiring that person to give a constable access to the special procedure material or excluded material within the period stated in the order.

Section 160 allows a Circuit Judge to issue a warrant in respect of excluded material and special procedure material if he is satisfied that the requirements for the making of a production order are fulfilled, and the further requirements for the issue of a warrant under s 160(8) are fulfilled.

13.1.4.2 *Search and Seizure without Warrant*

Section 161 applies if a constable has power to arrest a person under an 'extradition arrest power' as defined in s 174(2). By s 161(2), a constable may enter and search any premises for the purpose of exercising the power of arrest if he has reasonable grounds for believing that the person is on the premises.

By s 162, if a person has been arrested under an extradition arrest power at a place other than a police station a constable may enter and search any premises in which the person was at the time of his arrest or immediately before his arrest if he has reasonable grounds for believing the matters set out in s 162(2).

Section 163 governs the search of the defendant after his arrest. A constable may search the defendant as provided for in s 163(2) and (3).

Section 164 provides for entry and search of premises after arrest. It represents a codification of the *Osman/Rottman* common law power discussed above. Section 164 applies if a person has been arrested under an extradition arrest power. In such a case a constable may enter and search any premises occupied or controlled by the person if the constable has the reasonable grounds specified in s 164(2).

13.1.4.3 *Treatment after Arrest and Delivery up of Seized Property*

Sections 166–171 deal with treatment of the arrested person in the police station. Section 166 deals with fingerprints and samples; s 167 covers searches and examination for the purposes of establishing identity; and s 171 provides for application of other rights in PACE to be applied to extradition defendants by order.

Section 172 deals with the delivery up of property to the requesting state.

13.1.4.4 *Definitions*

Section 174 is the definitions section for Part 4.

13.2 CODES OF PRACTICE

These have already been referred to in the context of arrest in Chapter 4.

In the same way that Codes of Practice have been issued under s 66 of PACE in order to regulate the conduct of persons charged with the duty of investigating offences under PACE, so s 173 of the EA 2003 requires the Secretary of State to issue Codes of Practice in connection with the police's powers under the EA 2003.

Section 173(1) requires the Secretary of State to issue Codes of Practice in connection with the following matters: the exercise of the powers conferred by Part 4; the retention, use, and return of anything seized or produced under Part 4; access to and the taking of photographs and copies of anything so seized or produced; and the retention, use, disclosure, and destruction of fingerprints, a sample, or a photograph taken under Part 4.

The first edition of the Codes was published on 18 December 2003 and they came into force on 1 January 2004 (The Extradition Act 2003 (Police Powers: Codes of Practice) Order 2003 (SI 2003/3336)). The Codes can be obtained from the Home Office website at www.homeoffice.gov.uk/docs2/extradition.html.

At the time of writing three Codes have been published:

Code B, which deals with searches, seizure, retention, use, and delivery of property;

Code C, which governs arrest and detention and treatment of detained persons;

Code D, which deals with identification of persons.

The proper approach to the application of the Codes is set out in paras 1.5–1.6:

1.5 These Codes set out the police powers which may be relied upon in extradition cases, additional to the police's common law powers. The powers in the Act are modelled on those contained in PACE, but where necessary and appropriate, they supplement domestic provisions to enable officers to respond to extradition requests effectively.

1.6 Where these Codes are silent, officers should have regard to relevant domestic provisions set out in the revised edition of the PACE Codes of Practice (PACE Codes), effective from 1 April 2003. Where procedures in extradition cases are the same as those in domestic cases, these Codes refer officers to the relevant section in the PACE Codes.

Section 173(6) makes clear that a failure by a constable to comply with a provision of the Codes does not of itself make him liable to criminal or civil proceedings. Section 173(4) states that a Code issued under the section is admissible in evidence in proceedings under the Act and must be taken into account by a judge or court in determining any question to which it appears to the judge or the court to be relevant.

13.3 USE OF FORCE IN EXERCISE OF PART 4 POWERS

Section 209 provides that a person may use reasonable force, if necessary, in the exercise of a power conferred by the EA 2003 (cf s 117 of PACE).

13.4 APPLICATION OF PART 4 TO CUSTOMS OFFICERS

The powers in Part 4 are exercisable by constables. However, s 175 states that the Treasury may by order provide for any provision of Part 4 which applies in relation to police officers or persons arrested by police officers to apply with specified modifications in relation to customs officers or persons arrested by customs officers. By s 216(8) a customs officer is a person commissioned by the Commissioners of Customs and Excise under s 6(3) of the Customs and Excise Management Act 1979.

13.5 MEANING OF 'PREMISES'

The powers in Part 4 included the power to search 'premises'. By s 174(5)(a), in England and Wales, 'premises' has the meaning given by s 23 of PACE, namely:

... 'premises' includes any place and, in particular, includes—(a) any vehicle, vessel, aircraft or hovercraft; (b) any offshore installation; and (c) any tent or movable structure; and 'offshore installation' has the meaning given to it by section 1 of the Mineral Workings (Offshore Installations) Act 1971.

(See *Cowan v Condon* [2000] 1 WLR 254.)

13.6 SEARCH AND SEIZURE WARRANTS AND PRODUCTION ORDERS

The following paragraphs consider the powers of search and seizure conferred by ss 156–160. These create two principal methods of obtaining documents:

(a) under a search and seizure warrant issued under s 156 if the material sought does not consist of or include excluded material or special procedure material; or

(b) under a production order issued under s 157 or a search warrant issued under s 160 if the material sought does consist of or include such items.

The terms 'excluded material' and 'special procedure material' bear the same meanings as in ss 11 and 14 of PACE respectively (s 174(3) and (6)).

Documents subject to legal privilege can never lawfully be seized under Part 4. In the EA 2003 'legal privilege' bears the same meaning as in s 10 of PACE (s 174(4); *R v Central Criminal Court ex p Francis & Francis (a Firm)* [1989] AC 346; *R (Miller Gardner Solicitors (a firm)) v Minshull Street Crown Court* [2002] EWHC 3077 (Admin); *R (Rogers) v Manchester Crown Court* [1999] 1 WLR 832).

Code B makes clear that the police should not be drawn into investigating foreign offences when executing searches under Part 4. Paragraph 1.3 states:

Searches conducted under powers in the Extradition Act 2003 may only be undertaken for the purpose of obtaining evidence of the extradition offence for use in the prosecution of the person accused of the extradition offence. Officers may not investigate crimes on behalf of the requesting authority or territory, other than to speak to persons for the purpose of assisting establishing ownership or connection to the property.

13.6.1 Search and Seizure Warrants (Section 156)

The issue of a search warrant is a serious matter. In *Williams v Summerfield* [1972] QB 512 Lord Widgery CJ said:

> . . . generations of justices have, or I would hope have, been brought up to recognise that the issue of a search warrant is a very serious interference with the liberty of the subject, and a step which would only be taken after the most mature careful consideration of all the facts of the case.

Section 156 confers power on a justice of the peace to issue a search and seizure warrant on application by a constable provided the requirements in s 156(8) for the grant of such a warrant are met.

A search and seizure warrant is defined by s 156(5) to be a warrant authorizing a constable to enter and search the premises specified in the application for the warrant, and to seize and retain any material found there which falls within s 156(6).

Section 156 is the equivalent of s 8 of PACE in that it only permits a warrant to be issued in respect of material which does not consist of or include special procedure material, excluded material, or items subject to legal privilege.

For guidance on applying for a warrant under s 156, see Code B, para 3.

13.6.1.1 *Material which can be Sought under a Search and Seizure Warrant*
The material that can be sought under a search and seizure warrant is specified in s 156(6). Material may be seized if:

(a) it would be likely to be admissible evidence at a trial in the relevant part of the UK for the offence specified in the application for the warrant (on the assumption that conduct constituting that offence would constitute an offence in that part of the UK); and

(b) it does not consist of or include items subject to legal privilege, excluded material, or special procedure material.

Sections 50 and 51 of the Criminal Justice and Police Act 2001 confer additional powers of seizure to deal with the 'sifting' problem identified in *R v Chesterfield Justices ex p Bramley* [2000] QB 576. In that case the Administrative Court held that an officer executing a search warrant issued under s 8 of PACE is only empowered to seize material falling within the scope of the warrant or within s 19 of PACE. Therefore, the court held that there was no power for an officer to seize material for the purpose of sifting through it to determine whether it came within the scope of the warrant. Accordingly, if an officer seized items which when examined were found to be outside the scope of the warrant and not covered by s 19, even if the officer had acted in good faith, there was no defence in PACE to an action for trespass to goods based on the seizure.

Section 50 allows material to be seized from premises for the purpose of determining whether it is material which may be lawfully seized. Section 165(1) of the

EA 2003 extends Sch 1 of the Criminal Justice and Police Act 2001 to include the powers of seizure in ss 156(5), 160(5), 161(4), 162(6) and (7) of the EA 2003 among the powers to which s 50 applies.

Section 20 of PACE as amended by s 70 of the Criminal Justice and Police Act 2001 extends the powers of seizure in the EA 2003 to include information stored in an electronic form.

13.6.1.2 *Requirements for Grant of Search and Seizure Warrant*

Section 156(8) sets out the conditions which have to be met before a search and seizure warrant can be issued. There must be reasonable grounds for believing that:

(a) the offence specified in the application has been committed by the person so specified;

(b) the person is in the UK or is on his way to the UK;

(c) the offence is an extradition offence within the meaning given by s 64 (if the person's extradition is sought by a Category 1 territory) or s 137 (if extradition is sought by a Category 2 territory);

(d) there is material on premises specified in the application which falls within s 156(6);

(e) any of the conditions referred to in s 156(9) are satisfied.

The conditions in s 156(9) are:

(a) that it is not practicable to communicate with a person entitled to grant entry to the premises;

(b) that it is practicable to communicate with a person entitled to grant entry to the premises but it is not practicable to communicate with a person entitled to grant access to the material referred to in s 156(8)(d);

(c) that entry to the premises will not be granted unless a warrant is produced;

(d) that the purpose of a search may be frustrated or seriously prejudiced unless a constable arriving at the premises can secure immediate entry to them.

It is not a condition precedent to the grant of a warrant under s 156 that other methods of obtaining the material have been tried without success or have not been tried because they are bound to fail (cf *R v Billericay Justices ex p Frank Harris (Coaches) Ltd* [1991] Crim LR 472).

A justice to whom application is made under s 156 must be careful to ensure that the applicant is entitled to the warrant. In particular, he must be personally satisfied on the material before him that the conditions in s 156(8) are satisfied. He is not entitled simply to accept the applicant's assertions. In *R v Guildhall Magistrates Court ex p Primlaks Holdings (Panama) Limited* [1990] 1 QB 261, 272 Parker LJ said in relation to s 8 of PACE in words that are equally applicable to s 156 of the EA 2003:

Before concluding this judgment I find it necessary to make certain observations with regard to applications under section 8 of the Act. It confers a draconian power and it is of vital importance that it should be clearly understood by all concerned that it is for the justice to satisfy himself that there are reasonable grounds for believing the various matters set out. The fact that a police officer, who has been investigating the matter, states in the information that he considers that there are reasonable grounds is not enough. The justice must himself be satisfied. In the present case Detective Inspector Keating did not even so state. He merely stated that the matters set out led to the belief that there were reasonable grounds for suspecting that the first of the conditions was satisfied. This would not be completely fatal, for a justice would be entitled to consider that the facts went further. But if the applicant goes no further than to speak of reasonable grounds for suspicion, a justice would in my judgment need to be very cautious indeed before he went further. In the present case he clearly could not have done so.

13.6.1.3 *Contents of the Application for a Search and Seizure Warrant*

Section 156(2), (3), and (4) specify the information that an application for a search and seizure warrant must contain. It must state that:

(a) the extradition of a person specified in the application is sought under Part 1 or Part 2;

(b) the warrant is sought in relation to premises specified in the application;

(c) the warrant is sought in relation to material, or material of a description, specified in the application;

(d) that material, or material of that description, is believed to be on the premises.

If the application states that the extradition of the person is sought under Part 1, the application must also state that the person is accused in a Category 1 territory specified in the application of the commission of an offence which is specified in the application, and which is an extradition offence within the meaning given by s 64 (s 156(3)).

If the application states that the extradition of the person is sought under Part 2, the application must also state that the person is accused in a Category 2 territory specified in the application of the commission of an offence which is specified in the application, and which is an extradition offence within the meaning given by s 137 (s 156(4)).

Section 15 of PACE imposes additional requirements for the contents of the application for the warrant. These are considered in the next section.

The applicant is under a duty to make full disclosure when applying for a warrant or order under ss 156, 157, or 160 (*R v Lewes Crown Court ex p Hill* (1991) 93 Cr App R 60, 69; *R v Acton Crown Court ex p Layton* [1993] Crim LR 458). In particular, it is the duty of the applicant to set out, either in the notice itself or in further documentation, a description of all that is sought (*R v Central Criminal*

Court ex p Adegbesan 84 Cr App R 219; *R v Inner London Crown Court ex p Baines and Baines (a Firm)* [1988] QB 579).

13.6.1.4 *Safeguards in the Execution of Search and Seizure Warrants*
Warrants issued under s 156 are subject to the safeguards contained in ss 15 and 16 of PACE by virtue of s 15(1) of PACE which states:

> This section and section 16 below have effect in relation to the issue to constables under any enactment, including an enactment contained in an Act passed after this Act, of warrants to enter and search premises; and an entry on or search of premises under a warrant is unlawful unless it complies with this section and section 16 below.

The protections in ss 15 and 16 are designed to protect the person whose premises are being searched and are stringent in their effect (*R v Central Criminal Court ex p AJD Holdings Ltd* [1992] Crim LR 669). Failure to comply with any of the requirements of either section will render the entry, search, and seizure unlawful, and leave the relevant police force exposed to an action for damages (*R v Chief Constable of Warwickshire ex p Fitzpatrick* [1999] 1 WLR 564, 574; *R v Chief Constable of Lancashire ex p Parker* [1993] QB 577, 584).

Section 15 requires the warrant to contain essential information such as the name of the person who applies for it, the name of the enactment under which it is issued, the address of the premises to be searched, and the date on which it is issued (s 15(6)). The warrant must also authorize entry on one occasion only (s 15(5)).

Section 16 contains procedural requirements for the conduct of searches. Section 16(1) provides that a warrant to enter and search premises may be executed by any constable. Such a warrant may authorize persons to accompany any constable who is executing it (s 16(2)). If a person not named on the warrant accompanies the constable in the execution of the warrant then the entry, search, and seizure will be unlawful (*Gross v Southwark Crown Court*, Unreported, 24 July 1998, CO/1759/98). Therefore, if foreign investigators wish to be present then this must be made clear in the request, and they should be named on the warrant. They are not permitted to take part in the search itself, but merely to assist the officers in identifying relevant material (cf *R v Reading Justices ex p Southwest Meats Ltd* [1992] Crim LR 672).

The entry and search must take place within one month of the date of the warrant (s 16(3)), and must take place at a reasonable hour unless the constable executing it considers that this would frustrate the purpose of the search (s 16(4)). The constable must identify himself to the occupier (or other person present), produce the warrant, and supply him with a copy of it (s 16(5) and (6)). If no one is present then a copy of the warrant must be left at the premises (s 16(7)).

Section 16(8) provides that the search must be a search to the extent required for the purpose for which the warrant was issued. It follows that if items are seized which fall outside the terms of the warrant then their seizure will be unlawful unless the items seized can properly be described as *de minimis* (*R v Chief Constable of Warwickshire ex p Fitzpatrick*, [1999] 1 WLR 564, 575; *R v Southwark Crown Court ex p Sorsky Defries* [1996] Crim LR 195; cf *R v Chesterfield Justices ex p Bramley* [2000] QB 576, 588).

13.6.2 Production Orders (Section 157)

As s 156(6) makes clear, sensitive material relating to an extradition offence cannot be seized under a search and seizure warrant. In this context, sensitive material means excluded material as defined by s 11 of PACE, and special procedure material as defined by s 14 of PACE. These definitions apply in relation to the EA 2003 by virtue of s 174(3) and (6).

Where there are grounds for believing that the material to be sought includes such material, then a production order under s 157 or a warrant under s 160 must be obtained. These provisions contain powers analogous to those contained in s 9 and Sch 1 of PACE.

A production order is defined by s 157(5) to be an order either:

(a) requiring the person the application for the order specifies as appearing to be in possession or control of special procedure material or excluded material to produce it to a constable (within the period stated in the order) for him to take away; or

(b) requiring that person to give a constable access to the special procedure material or excluded material within the period stated in the order.

Production orders have effect as if they were orders of the court (s 157(7)). Hence it is a contempt of court to fail to comply with a production order.

The period stated in a production order must be a period of seven days starting with the day on which the order is made, unless it appears to the judge by whom the order is made that a longer period would be appropriate (s 157(6)).

Unlike a search and seizure warrant, which can be issued by a justice of the peace, a production order may only be issued by a Circuit Judge (in England and Wales) (s 157(1) and (8)).

For guidance on applying for a production order under s 157, see Code B, para 3.

13.6.2.1 *Requirements for Making a Production Order*

Because production orders provide access to material which by definition is sensitive and confidential the case law emphasizes the heavy responsibility borne by those who apply for them and by judges considering whether to grant them. In *R v Lewes Crown Court ex p Hill* (1991) 93 Cr App R 60, 65 Bingham LJ said:

The Police and Criminal Evidence Act governs a field in which there are two very obvious public interests. There is, first of all, a public interest in the effective investigation and prosecution of crime. Secondly, there is a public interest in protecting the personal and property rights of citizens against infringement and invasion. There is an obvious tension between these two public interests because crime could be most effectively investigated and prosecuted if the personal and property rights of citizens could be freely overridden and total protection of the personal and property rights of citizens would make investigation and prosecution of many crimes impossible or virtually so. The 1984 Act seeks to effect a carefully judged balance between these interests and that is why it is a detailed and complex Act. If the scheme intended by Parliament is to be implemented, it is important that the provisions laid down in the Act should be fully and fairly enforced. It would be quite wrong to approach the Act with any preconception as to how these provisions should be operated save in so far as such preconception is derived from the legislation itself. It is, in my judgment, clear that the courts must try to avoid any interpretation which would distort the parliamentary scheme and so upset the intended balance. In the present field, the primary duty to give effect to the parliamentary scheme rests on circuit judges. It seems plain that they are required to exercise those powers with great care and caution.

Sections 157(1) and 158(2) provide that a production order may be made if the judge has reasonable grounds for believing that:

(a) the offence specified in the application has been committed by the person so specified;

(b) the person is in the UK or is on his way to the UK;

(c) the offence is an extradition offence within the meaning given by s 64 (if extradition is sought by a Category 1 territory) or s 137 (if extradition is sought by a Category 2 territory);

(d) there is material which consists of or includes special procedure material or excluded material on premises specified in the application;

(e) the material would be likely to be admissible evidence at a trial in the relevant part of the UK for the offence specified in the application (on the assumption that conduct constituting that offence would constitute an offence in that part of the UK). By s 158(3), the relevant part of the UK is the part of the UK where the judge exercises jurisdiction.

Section 158(4) is an important provision. It provides that it must appear that other methods of obtaining the material either have been tried without success or have not been tried because they were bound to fail.

It is not sufficient for a constable simply to assert that the conditions in s 158 have been met. The judge should not make an order unless personally satisfied that the conditions are fulfilled (cf *R v Crown Court at Lewes ex p Hill* 93 Cr App R 60; *R v Guildhall Magistrates' Court ex p Primlaks Holdings (Panama) Inc* [1990] 1 QB 261, 272). In *R (Bright) v Central Criminal* Court [2000] 1 WLR 662, 677 Judge LJ said:

. . . it is clear that the judge personally must be satisfied that the statutory requirements have been established. He is not simply asking himself whether the decision of the constable making the application was reasonable, nor whether it would be susceptible to judicial review on *Wednesbury* grounds . . . This follows from the express wording of the statute,

175

'If . . . a circuit judge is satisfied that one . . . of the sets of access conditions is fulfilled'. The purpose of this provision is to interpose between the opinion of the police officer seeking the order and the consequences to the individual or organisation to whom the order is addressed the safeguard of a judgment and decision of a circuit judge.

Section 158(5) provides that it must be in the public interest that the material should be produced or that access to it should be given. This provision makes clear that the judge retains an overall discretion whether or not to grant a production order even if all the other conditions are fulfilled. However, if the offence to which the application relates is serious enough it is inconsistent to refuse an application for access to material by finding that it is not in the public interest that access should be given (*R v Crown Court at Northampton ex p Director of Public Prosecutions* 93 Cr App R 376).

In *R (Bright) v Central Criminal Court* [2000] 1 WLR 662 the Divisional Court held in a case under Sch 1 of PACE that the fact that compliance with the order by the person ordered to make production may involve him in incriminating himself is not *per se* a reason for not making an order.

The judge must give reasons for making an order under s 157 (cf *R v Central Criminal Court ex p Propend Finance Property Ltd* [1996] 2 Cr App R 26; *R v Lewes Crown Court ex p Nigel Weller & Co (a firm)*, Unreported, 12 May 1999, CO/2890/98).

13.6.2.2 *Contents of Application for a Production Order*

Section 157(2) requires an application for a production order to state that:

(a) the extradition of a person specified in the application is sought under Part 1 or Part 2;

(b) the order is sought in relation to premises specified in the application;

(c) the order is sought in relation to material, or material of a description, specified in the application;

(d) the material is special procedure material or excluded material;

(e) a person specified in the application appears to be in possession or control of the material.

If the application states that the extradition of the person is sought under Part 1, the application must also state that the person is accused in a Category 1 territory specified in the application of the commission of an offence which is specified in the application, and which is an extradition offence within the meaning given by s 64 (s 157(3)).

If the application states that the extradition of the person is sought under Part 2, the application must also state that the person is accused in a Category 2 territory specified in the application of the commission of an offence which is specified in the application, and which is an extradition offence within the meaning given by s 137 (s 157(4)).

As explained above, an applicant for a production order is under a duty to make full and frank disclosure of all relevant matters.

13.6.2.3 *Information Held Electronically*
Section 159 applies if any of the special procedure material or excluded material specified in an application for a production order consists of information stored in any electronic form (s 159(1)).

If the production order is an order requiring a person to produce the material to a constable for him to take away, it has effect as an order to produce the material in a form (s 159(2)):

(a) in which it can be taken away by him;

(b) in which it is visible and legible or from which it can readily be produced in a visible and legible form.

If the order is an order requiring a person to give a constable access to the material, it has effect as an order to give him access to the material in a form (s 159(3)):

(a) in which it is visible and legible, or

(b) from which it can readily be produced in a visible and legible form.

13.6.3 Search Warrants under Section 160 for Special Procedure Material and Excluded Material

A warrant under s 160 authorizes a constable to enter and search the premises specified in the application for the warrant and:

(a) to seize and retain any material found there which falls within s 160(6) and which is special procedure material, if the application for the warrant states that the warrant is sought in relation to special procedure material;

(b) to seize and retain any material found there which falls within s 160(6) and which is excluded material, if the application for the warrant states that the warrant is sought in relation to excluded material.

Material falls within s 160(6) if it would be likely to be admissible evidence at a trial in the relevant part of the UK for the offence specified in the application for the warrant (on the assumption that conduct constituting that offence would constitute an offence in that part of the UK).

The power to allow access to excluded and special procedure material under warrant is a draconian power which should only be used as a last resort where no other method of obtaining the material is available (cf *R v Southwark Crown Court ex p Bowles* [1998] AC 641, 649).

In *R v Central Criminal Court ex p AJD Holdings* [1992] Crim LR 669 the Court said in relation to the equivalent power in para 12 of Sch 1 of PACE that it was important before any search warrant was applied for that careful consideration was given to what material it is hoped a search might reveal, so as to be clear to anyone subsequently considering the lawfulness of the warrant. The application should make clear that the material sought related to the crime under investigation. A written note should be made of anything said in support of the application beyond what was set out in the written application. There should be careful briefing of the officers who were to execute the search, including how material to be searched for might be thought to relate to the crime under investigation.

For guidance on applying for a warrant under s 160, see Code B, para 3.

13.6.3.1 *Requirements for Issuing a Search Warrant under Section 160*
Section 160 provides that a judge may, on an application made to him by a constable, issue a warrant under s 160 if he is satisfied:

(a) that the requirements for the making of a production order contained in s 158 are fulfilled, and

(b) that the further requirement for the issue of a warrant under s 160, contained in s 160(8), is fulfilled.

The requirements for the making of a production order have been considered above. The further requirement for the issue of a warrant under s 160(8) is that any one of these conditions is satisfied:

(a) it is not practicable to communicate with a person entitled to grant entry to the premises;

(b) it is practicable to communicate with a person entitled to grant entry to the premises but it is not practicable to communicate with a person entitled to grant access to the material referred to in s 158(2)(d);

(c) the material contains information which is subject to a restriction on disclosure or an obligation of secrecy contained in an enactment (including one passed after the EA 2003) and is likely to be disclosed in breach of the restriction or obligation if a warrant is not issued.

13.6.3.2 *Contents of the Application for a Section 160 Warrant*
In addition to the information required by s 15 of PACE, an application for a warrant under s 160 must state that:

(a) the extradition of a person specified in the application is sought under Part 1 or Part 2 of the EA 2003;

(b) the warrant is sought in relation to premises specified in the application;

(c) the warrant is sought in relation to material, or material of a description, specified in the application;

(d) the material is special procedure material or excluded material.

If the application states that the extradition of the person is sought under Part 1, the application must also state that the person is accused in a Category 1 territory specified in the application of the commission of an offence which is specified in the application, and which is an extradition offence within the meaning given by s 64.

If the application states that the extradition of the person is sought under Part 2, the application must also state that the person is accused in a Category 2 territory specified in the application of the commission of an offence which is specified in the application, and which is an extradition offence within the meaning given by s 137.

As explained above, an applicant for a s 160 warrant is under a duty to make full and frank disclosure of all relevant matters.

13.6.3.3 *Safeguards in the Execution of Section 160 Warrants*
The safeguards contained in ss 15 and 16 of PACE apply in relation to s 160 warrants by virtue of s 15(1). Sections 15 and 16 are considered above at 13.6.1.4.

13.7 SEARCH AND SEIZURE WITHOUT WARRANT

This section considers the police's search powers under ss 161–164. There are four principal powers:

(a) the power to enter and search premises for the purposes of arrest (s 161);

(b) the power to enter and search premises in which the person was at time of arrest (s 162);

(c) the power to search a person on arrest (s 163); and

(d) the power to enter and search premises controlled by a person under arrest (s 164).

13.7.1 Entry and Search of Premises for Purposes of Making an Arrest (Section 161)

Section 161 applies if a constable has power to arrest a person under an extradition arrest power. Each of the following is an extradition arrest power:

(a) a Part 1 warrant in respect of which a certificate under s 2 has been issued;
(b) s 5;
(c) a warrant issued under s 71; and
(d) a provisional warrant issued under s 73 (s 174(2)).

Section 161(2) provides that a constable may enter and search any premises for the purpose of exercising the power of arrest if he has reasonable grounds for believing that the person is on the premises.

The power to search conferred by s 161(2) is exercisable only to the extent that is reasonably required for the purpose of exercising the power of arrest (s 161(3)).

However, a constable who has entered premises in exercise of the power conferred by s 161(2) may seize and retain anything which is on the premises if he has reasonable grounds for believing that it has been obtained in consequence of the commission of an offence or it is evidence in relation to an offence, and that it is necessary to seize it in order to prevent it being concealed, lost, damaged, altered, or destroyed (s 161(4)). Here, an 'offence' includes an offence committed outside the UK (s 161(5)).

If the premises contain two or more separate dwellings, the power conferred by s 161(2) is a power to enter and search only any parts of the premises which the occupiers of any dwelling comprised in the premises use in common with the occupiers of any other dwelling comprised in the premises, and any dwelling comprised in the premises in which the constable has reasonable grounds for believing that the person may be.

Section 161 is analogous to s 17 of PACE. In *Riley v DPP* 91 Cr App R 14 the Divisional Court held that where police officers are invited onto premises by an occupier or other person authorized to do so, who had been told by them the reason for their entry, they are lawfully on the premises, and they do not have to comply with s 17, which applies to entry and search in the absence of consent. This reasoning is equally applicable to s 161.

A police officer exercising his power to enter premises by the use of reasonable force, pursuant to ss 17 and 117 of PACE, should, unless the circumstances make it impossible, impracticable, or undesirable, give any occupant present the reason for his exercising that power of entry (*O'Loughlin v Chief Constable of Essex* [1998] 1 WLR 374). Again, similar principles apply in the exercise of the power under s 161.

For guidance on the exercise of the power under s 161, see Code B, para 4.

13.7.2 Entry and Search of Premises on Arrest (Section 162)

Section 162 applies if a person has been arrested under an extradition arrest power at a place other than a police station.

Section 162(2) provides that a constable may enter and search any premises in which the person was at the time of his arrest or immediately before his arrest if he has reasonable grounds for believing:

(a) if the person has not been convicted of the 'relevant offence', that there is on the premises evidence (other than items subject to legal privilege) relating to the relevant offence;

(b) in any case, that there is on the premises evidence (other than items subject to legal privilege) relating to the identity of the person.

By s 162(3) the relevant offence is the offence:

(a) referred to in the Part 1 warrant, if the arrest was under a Part 1 warrant;

(b) in respect of which the constable has reasonable grounds for believing that a Part 1 warrant has been or will be issued, if the arrest was under s 5;

(c) in respect of which extradition is requested, if the arrest was under a warrant issued under s 71;

(d) of which the person is accused, if the arrest was under a provisional warrant.

The power to search conferred by s 162(2), if the person has not been convicted of the relevant offence, is a power to search for evidence (other than items subject to legal privilege) relating to the relevant offence, and in any case, is a power to search for evidence (other than items subject to legal privilege) relating to the identity of the person (s 162(4)).

The power to search conferred by s 162(2) is exercisable only to the extent that it is reasonably required for the purpose of discovering evidence in respect of which the power is available by virtue of s 162(4) (s 162(5)).

By s 162(6), a constable may seize and retain anything for which he may search by virtue of s 162(4) and (5).

A constable who has entered premises in exercise of the power conferred by s 162(2) may seize and retain anything which is on the premises if he has reasonable grounds for believing that it has been obtained in consequence of the commission of an offence or it is evidence in relation to an offence, and that it is necessary to seize it in order to prevent it being concealed, lost, damaged, altered, or destroyed. An offence includes an offence committed outside the UK (s 162(8)).

If the premises contain two or more separate dwellings, the power conferred by s 162(2) is a power to enter and search only any dwelling in which the arrest took place or in which the person was immediately before his arrest, and any parts of the premises which the occupier of any such dwelling uses in common with the occupiers of any other dwelling comprised in the premises (s 162(9)).

The power under s 162 is analogous to the power of entry and search conferred by s 32(2)(b) (cf *R (Hewitson) v Chief Constable of Dorset*, The Times, 6 January 2004).

For guidance on the exercise of the power under s 162, see Code B, para 4.

13.7.3 Search of Person on Arrest (Section 163)

Section 163 applies if a person has been arrested under an extradition arrest power at a place other than a police station.

By s 163(2) a constable may search the person if he has reasonable grounds for believing that the person may present a danger to himself or others.

A constable may search the person under s 163(3) if he has reasonable grounds for believing that the person may have concealed on him anything which he might use to assist him to escape from lawful custody or anything which might be evidence relating to an offence or to the identity of the person.

The power to search conferred by s 163(3) is a power to search for anything falling within paragraph (a) or (b) of s 163(3) and is exercisable only to the extent that is reasonably required for the purpose of discovering such a thing (s 163(4)).

The powers conferred by s 163(2) and (3) do not authorize a constable to require a person to remove any of his clothing in public, other than an outer coat, jacket, or gloves, but they do authorize a search of a person's mouth (s 163(5)).

A constable searching a person in exercise of the power conferred by s 163(2) may seize and retain anything he finds, if he has reasonable grounds for believing that the person searched might use it to cause physical injury to himself or to any other person (s 163(6)).

A constable searching a person in exercise of the power conferred by s 163(3) may seize and retain anything he finds if he has reasonable grounds for believing that the person might use it to assist him to escape from lawful custody or that it is evidence of an offence or of the identity of the person or has been obtained in consequence of the commission of an offence (s 163(7)).

Section 51 of the Criminal Justice and Police Act 2001 allows material to be seized from a person in order to determine whether it is material which may lawfully be seized. Section 165(1) of the EA 2003 extends Sch 1 of the Criminal Justice and Police Act 2001 to include the powers of seizure in s 163(6) and (7) among the powers to which s 51 applies.

By s 163(8), an offence includes an offence committed outside the UK.

Nothing in s 163 affects the power conferred by s 43 of the Terrorism Act 2000 to stop and search persons reasonably suspected of being terrorists.

Section 163 is analogous to the powers of search contained in s 32(1) and (2)(a) of PACE.

For guidance on exercise of the power under s 163, see Code B, paras 4.3–4.11.

13.7.4 Entry and Search of Premises after Arrest (Section 164)

Section 164 applies if a person has been arrested under an extradition arrest power.

By s 164(2), a constable may enter and search any premises occupied or controlled by the person if the constable has reasonable grounds for suspecting, if the person has not been convicted of the relevant offence, that there is on the premises evidence (other than items subject to legal privilege) relating to the relevant offence, and in any case, that there is on the premises evidence (other than items subject to legal privilege) relating to the identity of the person.

The relevant offence is defined by s 164(3) to be the offence:

(a) referred to in the Part 1 warrant, if the arrest was under a Part 1 warrant;

(b) in respect of which the constable has reasonable grounds for believing that a Part 1 warrant has been or will be issued, if the arrest was under s 5;

(c) in respect of which extradition is requested, if the arrest was under a warrant issued under s 71;

(d) of which the person is accused, if the arrest was under a provisional warrant.

The power to search conferred by s 164(2), if the person has not been convicted of the relevant offence, is a power to search for evidence (other than items subject to legal privilege) relating to the relevant offence and, in any case, is a power to search for evidence (other than items subject to legal privilege) relating to the identity of the person.

The power to search conferred by s 164(2) is exercisable only to the extent that it is reasonably required for the purpose of discovering evidence in respect of which the power is available by virtue of s 164(4).

A constable may seize and retain anything for which he may search by virtue of s 164(4) and (5).

A constable who has entered premises in exercise of the power conferred by s 164(2) may seize and retain anything which is on the premises if he has reasonable grounds for believing that it has been obtained in consequence of the commission of an offence or it is evidence in relation to an offence, and that it is necessary to seize it in order to prevent it being concealed, lost, damaged, altered, or destroyed.

An offence includes an offence committed outside the UK (s 164(8)).

The powers conferred by s 164(2) and (6) may be exercised only if a police officer of the rank of inspector or above has given written authorization for their exercise (s 164(9)). But the power conferred by s 164(2) may be exercised without this authorization if it is exercised before the person arrested is taken to a police station, and the presence of the person at a place other than a police station is necessary for the effective exercise of the power to search (s 164(10)).

Section 164(9) and (10) do not apply to Scotland.

Section 164 is analogous to the power to search premises under s 18 of PACE, considered in *R (Rottman) v Commissioner of Police for the Metropolis* [2002] 2 WLR 1315.

For guidance on the exercise of the power under s 164 see Code B, paras 4.12–4.16.

13.8 TREATMENT AFTER ARREST

Code C, para 2.1 provides that an officer arresting a person wanted for extradition under the EA 2003 must caution the person in the following terms:

You do not have to say anything, but anything you do say may be given in evidence.

and must give the person a copy of the warrant as soon as practicable after arrest. The detained person must then be taken to a police station, and treated in accordance with Code C.

Sections 166–168 and s 171 provide statutory authority for the fingerprinting and search of extradition defendants at police stations. Section 169 amends the analogous sections of PACE, namely ss 54A, 61, 63, and 64A, so as to exclude persons arrested under extradition powers.

The terms 'appropriate consent', 'fingerprints', 'intimate search', and 'non-intimate sample' as used in these sections bear the same meaning as in s 65 of PACE (EA 2003, s 174(7)).

13.8.1 Fingerprints and Non-intimate Samples (Section 166)

Section 166 applies if a person has been arrested under an extradition arrest power and is detained at a police station.

Fingerprints may be taken from the person only if they are taken by a constable with the appropriate consent given in writing, or, without that consent, under s 166(4) (s 166(2)).

A non-intimate sample may be taken from the person only if it is taken by a constable with the appropriate consent given in writing, or, without that consent, under s 166(4) (s 166(3)).

Section 166(4) provides that fingerprints or a non-intimate sample may be taken from the person without the appropriate consent only if a police officer of at least the rank of inspector authorizes the fingerprints or sample to be taken.

For guidance on the exercise of these powers, see Code D, para 3.

13.8.2 Searches and Examination for the Purposes of Ascertaining Identity (Section 167)

In extradition cases it is necessary to show that the person who has been arrested is the person whose extradition is sought by the requesting state (see *Re Anthony*, Unreported, 27 June 1995, CO/1657/94). Mistakes do sometimes occur. For example, in 2003 a British man, Derek Bond, was imprisoned in South Africa following a request for extradition by the United States for a different Derek Bond (*The Times*, 27 February 2003).

Section 167 applies if a person has been arrested under an extradition arrest power and is detained at a police station, and empowers the police to take steps to ascertain the identity of the arrested person.

Section 167(2) provides that if a police officer of at least the rank of inspector authorizes it, the person may be searched or examined, or both, for the purpose of facilitating the ascertainment of his identity. In this case, ascertaining a person's identity includes showing that he is not a particular person (s 167(7)).

An identifying mark found on a search or examination under s 167 may be photographed with the appropriate consent, or without the appropriate consent, if that consent is withheld or it is not practicable to obtain it (s 167(3)). 'Taking a photograph' includes using a process by means of which a visual image may be produced (s 167(8)). 'Mark' includes features and injuries, and a mark is an identifying mark if its existence in a person's case facilitates the ascertainment of his identity (s 167(9)).

The only persons entitled to carry out a search or examination, or take a photograph, under s 167 are constables and persons designated for the purposes of s 167 by the appropriate police officer (s 167(4)). In England and Wales the appropriate police officer is the chief officer of police for the police area in which the police station in question is situated (s 167(10)).

Section 167 does not authorize a person either to carry out a search or examination of a person of the opposite sex, or to take a photograph of any part of the body (other than the face) of a person of the opposite sex (s 167(5)). Nor does it permit an intimate search to be carried out (s 167(6)).

Section 169 amends the sections of PACE dealing with evidence of identity.

Guidance of the exercise of the powers under s 167 is contained in Code D, para 4.

13.8.3 Photographing Detainees

Section 168 applies if a person has been arrested under an extradition arrest power and is detained at a police station. The person may be photographed with the appropriate consent, or without the appropriate consent, if that consent is withheld or it is not practicable to obtain it (s 168(2)). 'Taking a photograph' includes using a process by means of which a visual image may be produced (s 168(5)).

A person proposing to take a photograph of a person under s 168 may, for the purpose of doing so, require the removal of any item or substance worn on or over the whole or any part of the head or face of the person to be photographed, and, if the requirement is not complied with, may remove the item or substance himself (s 168(3)).

The only persons entitled to take a photograph under s 168 are constables and persons designated for the purposes of this section by the appropriate police officer (s 168(4)). In England and Wales the appropriate police officer is the chief officer of police for the police area in which the police station in question is situated (s 168(6)).

13.8.4 Other Treatment and Rights of Detained Persons

PACE contains a number of provisions relating to detained persons which have no equivalents in the EA 2003. Section 171 enables subordinate legislation to be made to extend these PACE provisions to such persons.

Section 171 applies in relation to cases where a person:

(a) is arrested under an extradition arrest power at a police station;

(b) is taken to a police station after being arrested elsewhere under an extradition arrest power;

(c) is detained at a police station after being arrested under an extradition arrest power.

In relation to those cases the Secretary of State may by order apply the following provisions of PACE (and the Northern Irish equivalents in s 171(4)) with specified modifications (s 54 (searches of detained persons); s 55 (intimate searches); s 56 (right to have someone informed when arrested); s 58 (access to legal advice)).

The Extradition Act 2003 (Police Powers) Order 2003 (SI 2003/3106) has been made under s 171. It provides that these sections of PACE shall apply in the circumstances described in s 171(1) with the modifications specified in Articles 2(2), 2(3), and 2(4) of the Order.

13.9 DELIVERY OF SEIZED PROPERTY TO THE REQUESTING STATE

As has been seen, many extradition treaties require property seized that is relevant to the extradition offence to be delivered up to the requesting state. The EA 2003 places the mechanism for doing so on a statutory footing for the first time in s 172.

Section 172 applies to:

(a) anything which has been seized or produced under Part 4, or

(b) anything which has been seized under ss 50 or 51 of the Criminal Justice and Police Act 2001 in reliance on a power of seizure conferred by Part 4.

A constable may deliver any such thing to a person who is or is acting on behalf of an authority if the constable has reasonable grounds for believing that the authority is an authority of the 'relevant territory', and that it has functions such that it is appropriate for the thing to be delivered to it (s 172(2)).

'Relevant territory' is defined in s 172(3) and (4). If the relevant seizure power was a warrant issued under Part 4, or the thing was produced under an order made under Part 4, the relevant territory is the Category 1 or Category 2 territory specified in the application for the warrant or order.

If the relevant seizure power was s 161(4), s 162(6) or (7), s 163(6) or (7), or s 164(6) or (7), the relevant territory is:

(a) the territory in which the Part 1 warrant was issued, in a case where the applicable extradition arrest power is a Part 1 warrant in respect of which a certificate under s 2 has been issued;

(b) the territory in which a constable has reasonable grounds for believing that a Part 1 warrant has been or will be issued, in a case where the applicable extradition arrest power is s 5;

(c) the territory to which a person's extradition is requested, in a case where the applicable extradition arrest power is a warrant issued under s 71;

(d) the territory in which a person is accused of the commission of an offence or has been convicted of an offence, in a case where the applicable extradition arrest power is a provisional warrant under s 73.

The applicable extradition arrest power is defined by s 172(5) to be:

(a) the extradition arrest power under which a constable had a power of arrest, if the relevant seizure power was s 161(4);

(b) the extradition arrest power under which a person was arrested, if the relevant seizure power was s 162(6) or (7), s 163(6) or (7), or s 164(6) or (7).

For these purposes, the 'relevant seizure power' is the power under which the thing was seized, or the power in reliance on which the thing was seized under s 50 or s 51 of the Criminal Justice and Police Act 2001 (s 172(6)).

Guidance on retention and delivery of property is contained in Code B, paras 7 and 8.

14

POST-SURRENDER MATTERS

14.1 INTRODUCTION

The UK's involvement in the extradition process does not necessarily end with the defendant's surrender to the requesting territory. As explained in earlier chapters, most extradition treaties incorporate the rule of speciality and the rule against re-extradition. These place restrictions on how an extradited defendant can be dealt with in the requesting state. If the state wishes to try the defendant for an offence other than one for which he was extradited, or if it wishes to extradite him to a third state, then it may be necessary for it to seek the consent of the UK.

This chapter considers how such consent is to be given under the EA 2003. Under the EA 1989 in all cases it was for the Secretary of State to grant or refuse consent. The EA 2003 divides responsibility between the appropriate judge and the Secretary of State depending upon the status of the requesting state under the Act.

As has been seen, it is possible under the EA 2003 for a serving prisoner to be extradited from the UK, dealt with in the requesting territory, and then returned to the UK to complete his UK sentence before serving any sentence imposed abroad (see ss 37 and 119, considered at 10.2.3 and 10.3.3 above). Sections 186–189 and Sch 1 provide for what is to happen in this situation, and they are considered in the last section of this chapter.

14.2 CONSENT TO PROSECUTION FOR FURTHER OFFENCES

14.2.1 Consent following Extradition to a Category 1 Territory

In this section the mechanism for granting consent to the requesting Category 1 territory to try the defendant for additional offences is considered. In essence, it is for the appropriate judge to grant or refuse consent in accordance with the procedure contained in ss 54 and 55.

Section 54 applies if:

(a) a person is extradited to a Category 1 territory in respect of an offence in accordance with Part 1 of the EA 2003;

(b) the appropriate judge receives a request for consent to the person being dealt with in the Category 1 territory for another offence;

(c) the request is certified under s 54 by the Part 1 designated authority.

The designated authority may certify a request for consent if it believes that the authority making the request:

(a) is a judicial authority of the Category 1 territory;

(b) has the function of making requests for the consent referred to in s 54(1)(b) in that territory.

The certificate must contain the information specified in s 54(3).

The judge must serve notice on the person that he has received the request for consent unless he is satisfied that it would not be practicable to do so (s 54(4)).

The consent hearing must begin within 21 days of the request being received unless the period is extended under s 54(6) (s 54(5)).

Section 55 specifies the questions which must be decided at the consent hearing. First, the judge must decide whether consent is, in fact, required (s 55(1)). Consent is not required to the person being dealt with in the territory for the offence if the person has been given an opportunity to leave the territory and he has not done so before the end of the permitted period, or if he did so before the end of the permitted period, he has returned there (s 55(8)). The permitted period is 45 days starting with the day on which the person arrived in the territory following his extradition there in accordance with Part 1 (s 55(9)). If the judge decides that consent is not required then he must inform the requesting state accordingly (s 55(2)).

If consent is required, the judge must then decide whether the offence for which consent is requested is an extradition offence (s 55(3)). If it is not, then he must refuse consent (s 55(4)).

If the offence is an extradition offence, by virtue of s 55(5) the judge must decide whether he would order the person's extradition under ss 11–25 if the person were in the UK and the judge were required to proceed under s 11 in respect of the offence for which consent is requested. In effect, the judge is required to conduct an extradition hearing under Part 1.

If he decides in the affirmative he must grant consent, otherwise he must refuse consent (s 55(6) and (7)).

14.2.2 Consent following Extradition to a Category 2 Territory

Where consent is sought from a Category 2 territory then it is for the Secretary of State to decide under s 129 whether consent should be given for the defendant to be dealt with in the territory for a further offence.

Section 129 applies if:

(a) a person is extradited to a Category 2 territory in accordance with Part 2;

(b) the Secretary of State receives a valid request for his consent to the person being dealt with in the territory for an offence other than the offence in respect of which he was extradited.

A request for consent is valid if it is made by an authority which is an authority of the territory and which the Secretary of State believes has the function of making requests for the consent referred to in s 129(1)(b) in that territory (s 129(2)).

Following receipt of the request the Secretary of State must serve notice on the person that he has received the request for consent, unless he is satisfied that it would not be practicable to do so (s 129(3)).

The Secretary of State must then decide whether the offence is an extradition offence (s 129(4)). If he decides this question negatively he must refuse his consent (s 129(5)).

If, however, he decides that question in the affirmative he must decide whether the appropriate judge would send the case to him (for his decision whether the person was to be extradited) under ss 79–91 if the person were in the UK and the judge were required to proceed under s 79 in respect of the offence for which the Secretary of State's consent is requested (s 129(6)).

If the Secretary of State decides this question negatively he must refuse his consent (s 129(7)). If the Secretary of State decides that question in the affirmative he must decide whether, if the person were in the UK, his extradition in respect of the offence would be prohibited under ss 94, 95, or 96 (s 129(8)).

If the Secretary of State decides the question in s 129(8) in the affirmative he must refuse his consent (s 129(9)). If, however, he decides that question in the negative he may give his consent (s 129(10)).

14.3 CONSENT TO RE-EXTRADITION

14.3.1 Re-extradition to a Category 1 Territory from a Category 1 Territory

The appropriate judge has jurisdiction under ss 56 and 57 to grant consent on behalf of the UK for re-extradition to a Category 1 territory from the Category 1 territory to which the defendant was extradited under Part 1.

Section 56 applies if (s 56(1)):

(a) a person is extradited to a Category 1 territory in accordance with Part 1;

(b) the appropriate judge receives a request for consent to the person's extradition to another Category 1 territory for an offence;

(c) the request is certified under this section by the designated authority.

The designated authority may certify a request for consent under this section if it believes that the authority making the request is a judicial authority of the requesting territory, and has the function of making requests for the consent referred to in s 56(1)(b) in that territory (s 56(2)).

The certificate under s 56(2) must contain the information required by s 56(3).

The judge must serve notice on the person that he has received the request for consent, unless he is satisfied that it would not be practicable to do so (s 56(4)).

Following receipt of the request the judge must hold a consent hearing. This must begin before the end of the required period, which is 21 days starting with the day on which the request for consent is received by the designated authority (s 56(5)). However, the judge may extend the required period if he believes there are exceptional circumstances (s 56(6)).

If the consent hearing does not begin before the end of the required period and the judge does not exercise the power in s 56(6) to extend the period, the judge must refuse consent (s 56(8)).

The questions for decision at the consent hearing are specified in s 57.

First, the judge must decide whether consent is required to the person's extradition to the other Category 1 territory for the offence (s 57(1)). Section 57(10) provides that subject to s 57(8), the judge must decide whether consent is required to the person's extradition to the other territory for the offence by reference to what appears to him to be the arrangements made between the requesting territory and the UK. Section 57(8) provides that consent is not required to the person's extradition to the other territory for the offence if the person has been given an opportunity to leave the requesting territory and he has not done so before the end of the permitted period, or if he did so before the end of the permitted period, he has returned there. The permitted period is 45 days starting with the day on which the person arrived in the requesting territory following his extradition there in accordance with Part 1 (s 57(9)).

If the judge decides that consent is not required he must inform the authority making the request of his decision (s 57(2)).

If the judge decides that consent is required he must decide whether the offence is an extradition offence in relation to the Category 1 territory referred to in s 57(1)(b). If the judge decides that it is not then he must refuse consent.

If the judge decides that the offence is an extradition offence he must decide whether he would order the person's extradition under ss 11–26 if (s 58(5)):

(a) the person were in the UK, and

(b) the judge were required to proceed under s 11 in respect of the offence for which consent is requested.

If the judge decides the question in s 58(5) in the affirmative he must give consent, otherwise he must refuse consent.

14.3.2 Re-extradition to a Category 2 Territory from a Category 1 Territory

Section 58 applies where a person has been extradited to a Category 1 territory and a request for his re-extradition is received by the Secretary of State for consent to his extradition to a Category 2 territory and the request has been certificated by the designated authority under s 58(2).

The designated authority may certify a request for consent under s 58(2) if it believes that the authority making the request:

(a) is a judicial authority of the requesting territory, and

(b) has the function of making requests for the consent referred to in s 59(1)(b) in that territory.

A certificate under s 58(2) must contain the information required by s 58(3).

By s 58(4), the Secretary of State must serve notice on the person that he has received the request for consent, unless he is satisfied that it would not be practicable to do so.

The Secretary of State must then decide whether the offence is an extradition offence within the meaning given by s 137 in relation to the Category 2 territory (s 58(5)). If the Secretary of State decides this question negatively he must refuse consent (s 58(6)).

If the Secretary of State decides that the offence is an extradition offence he must decide whether the appropriate judge would send the case to him for his decision whether the person was to be extradited under ss 79–91 if (s 58(7)):

(a) the person were in the UK, and

(b) the judge were required to proceed under s 80 in respect of the offence for which the Secretary of State's consent is requested.

If the Secretary of State decides this question in the negative he must refuse his consent (s 58(8)).

If decides the question affirmatively he must decide whether, if the person were in the UK, his extradition to the Category 2 territory in respect of the offence would be prohibited under ss 94, 95, or 96 (s 58(9)). If the Secretary of State decides this question negatively he may give consent. If the Secretary of State decides that question in the affirmative he must refuse consent.

14.3.3 Re-extradition to a Category 1 Territory from a Category 2 Territory

It is for the Secretary of State to decide under s 131 whether consent should be given for re-extradition to a Category 1 territory from the Category 2 territory to which the defendant was extradited.

Section 131 applies if the defendant is extradited to a Category 2 territory (the requesting territory) in accordance with Part 2 and the Secretary of State receives a valid request for his consent to his extradition to a Category 1 territory for an offence other than the offence in respect of which he was extradited.

A request for consent is valid if it is made by an authority which is an authority of the requesting territory and which the Secretary of State believes has the function of making requests for the consent referred to in s 131(1)(b) in that territory (s 131(2)).

The Secretary of State must serve notice on the person that he has received the request for consent, unless he is satisfied that it would not be practicable to do so (s 131(3)).

The Secretary of State must decide whether the offence is an extradition offence within the meaning given by s 64 in relation to the Category 1 territory (s 131(4)).

If the Secretary of State decides the question in s 131(4) in the negative he must refuse his consent (s 131(5)).

If the Secretary of State decides that question in the affirmative he must decide whether the appropriate judge would order the person's extradition under ss 11–25 if the person were in the UK and the judge were required to proceed under s 11 in respect of the offence for which the Secretary of State's consent is requested (s 131(6)).

If the Secretary of State decides the question in s 131(6) in the affirmative he must give his consent (s 131(7)). If, however, he decides that question in the negative he must refuse his consent (s 131(8)).

14.3.4 Re-extradition to a Category 2 Territory from a Category 2 Territory

It is for the Secretary of State to decide under s 130 whether consent should be given for re-extradition to a Category 2 territory from a Category 2 territory.

Section 130 applies if the defendant is extradited to a Category 2 territory (the requesting territory) in accordance with Part 2 and the Secretary of State receives a valid request for his consent to the person's extradition to another Category 2 territory for an offence other than the offence in respect of which he was extradited.

A request for consent is valid if it is made by an authority which is an authority of the requesting territory and which the Secretary of State believes has the function of making requests for the consent referred to in s 130(1)(b) in that territory (s 130(2)).

The Secretary of State must serve notice on the person that he has received the request for consent, unless he is satisfied that it would not be practicable to do so (s 130(3)).

The Secretary of State must then decide whether the offence is an extradition offence in relation to the Category 2 territory referred to in s 130(1)(b) (s 130(4)). If the Secretary of State decides this in the negative he must refuse his consent (s 130(5)). If he decides that question in the affirmative he must decide whether the appropriate judge would send the case to him (for his decision whether the person was to be extradited) under ss 79–91 if the person were in the UK and the judge were required to proceed under s 79 in respect of the offence for which the Secretary of State's consent is requested (s 130(6)).

If the Secretary of State decides the question in s 130(6) in the negative he must refuse his consent (s 130(7)). If the Secretary of State decides that question in the affirmative he must decide whether, if the person were in the United Kingdom, his extradition in respect of the offence would be prohibited under ss 94, 95, or 96 (s 130(8)).

If the Secretary of State decides the question in s 130(8) in the affirmative he must refuse his consent. If, however, he decides that question in the negative he may give his consent (s 130(9)).

14.4 RE-EXTRADITION OF SERVING PRISONERS

Sections 186–189 and Sch 1 of the EA 2003 contain elaborate provisions governing how serving UK prisoners who were extradited, sentenced, but then returned to the UK to serve out their UK sentences are to be dealt with at the conclusion of their sentences.

Section 186 provides that s 187 applies in relation to a person if the following conditions in s 186(2)–(6) are satisfied:

(a) The first condition is that the person was extradited to a territory in accordance with Part 1 or Part 2.

(b) The second condition is that the person was serving a sentence of imprisonment or another form of detention in the UK (the UK sentence) before he was extradited.

(c) The third condition is that, if the person was extradited in accordance with Part 1, the Part 1 warrant in pursuance of which he was extradited contained a statement that it was issued with a view to his extradition for the purpose of being prosecuted for an offence; or, if the person was extradited in accordance with Part 2, the request in pursuance of which the person was extradited contained a statement that the person was accused of the commission of an offence.

(d) The fourth condition is that a certificate issued by a judicial authority of the territory shows that:

(i) a sentence of imprisonment or another form of detention for a term of 4 months or a greater punishment (the overseas sentence) was imposed on the person in the territory; and

(ii) the overseas sentence was imposed on him in respect of the offence specified in the warrant or request, or any other offence committed before his extradition in respect of which he was permitted to be dealt with in the territory.

(e) The fifth condition is that before serving the overseas sentence the person was returned to the UK to serve the remainder of the UK sentence.

If s 187 applies in relation to a person, as soon as practicable after the relevant time the person must be brought before the appropriate judge for the judge to decide whether the person is to be extradited again to the territory in which the overseas sentence was imposed (s 187(1)).

The relevant time is the time at which the person would otherwise be released from detention pursuant to the UK sentence (whether or not on licence) (s 187(2)).

If s 187(1) is not complied with and the person applies to the judge to be discharged, the judge must order his discharge.

By s 187(4) the person must be treated as continuing in legal custody until he is brought before the appropriate judge under s 187(1) or he is discharged under s 187(3).

Section 187(5) provides that if the person is brought before the appropriate judge under s 187(1), the judge must decide whether the territory in which the overseas sentence was imposed is a Category 1 territory, a Category 2 territory, or neither a Category 1 territory nor a Category 2 territory.

If the judge decides that the territory is a Category 1 territory, s 188 applies (s 187(6)). If the judge decides that the territory is a Category 2 territory, s 189 applies (s 187(7)). If the judge decides that the territory is neither a Category 1 territory nor a Category 2 territory, he must order the person's discharge (s 187(8)).

A person's discharge as a result of ss 187, 188, or 189 does not affect any conditions on which he is released from detention pursuant to the UK sentence.

Section 139 applies for determining the appropriate judge for the purposes of s 187.

14.4.1 Re-extradition to Category 1 Territories

If s 188 applies, the EA 2003 applies as it would if:

(a) a Part 1 warrant had been issued in respect of the person;

(b) the warrant contained a statement that the person was alleged to be unlawfully at large after conviction of the relevant offence, and the warrant was issued with a view to the person's arrest and extradition to the territory for the purpose of serving a sentence imposed in respect of the relevant offence;

(c) the warrant were issued by the authority of the territory which issued the certificate referred to in s 186(5);

(d) the relevant offence were specified in the warrant;

(e) the judge were the appropriate judge for the purposes of Part 1;

(f) the hearing at which the judge is to make the decision referred to in s 187(1) were the extradition hearing;

(g) the proceedings before the judge were under Part 1.

As applied by s 188(1) the EA 2003 has effect with the modifications set out in Part 1 of Sch 1.

The relevant offence is the offence in respect of which the overseas sentence is imposed.

14.4.2 Re-extradition to Category 2 Territories

If s 189 applies, the Act applies as it would if:

(a) a valid request for the person's extradition to the territory had been made;

(b) the request contained a statement that the person was alleged to be unlawfully at large after conviction of the relevant offence;

(c) the relevant offence were specified in the request;

(d) the hearing at which the appropriate judge is to make the decision referred to in s 187(1) were the extradition hearing;

(e) the proceedings before the judge were under Part 2.

As applied by s 189(1) the EA 2003 has effect with the modifications set out in Part 2 of Sch 1.

The relevant offence is the offence in respect of which the overseas sentence is imposed (s 189(3)).

Appendix 1
An Act to make provision about extradition
[20th November 2003]

Be it enacted by the Queen's most Excellent Majesty, by and with the advice and consent of the Lords Spiritual and Temporal, and Commons, in this present Parliament assembled, and by the authority of the same, as follows:

CONTENTS

PART 1
EXTRADITION TO CATEGORY 1 TERRITORIES

PART 2
EXTRADITION TO CATEGORY 2 TERRITORIES

PART 3
EXTRADITION TO THE UNITED KINGDOM

PART 4

POLICE POWERS

225. Finance
226. Extent
227. Short title

PART 1
EXTRADITION TO CATEGORY 1 TERRITORIES

Introduction

[Note: Cross-references to the text throughout Appendix 1 refer to sections in the main body of this work and appear here in italics.]

1. Extradition to category 1 territories   *Text: 3.1*

(1) This Part deals with extradition from the United Kingdom to the territories designated for the purposes of this Part by order made by the Secretary of State.

(2) In this Act references to category 1 territories are to the territories designated for the purposes of this Part.

(3) A territory may not be designated for the purposes of this Part if a person found guilty in the territory of a criminal offence may be sentenced to death for the offence under the general criminal law of the territory.

2. Part 1 warrant and certificate   *Text: 4.2.2.1*

(1) This section applies if the designated authority receives a Part 1 warrant in respect of a person.

(2) A Part 1 warrant is an arrest warrant which is issued by a judicial authority of a category 1 territory and which contains—

(a) the statement referred to in subsection (3) and the information referred to in subsection (4), or

(b) the statement referred to in subsection (5) and the information referred to in subsection (6).

(3) The statement is one that—

(a) the person in respect of whom the Part 1 warrant is issued is accused in the category 1 territory of the commission of an offence specified in the warrant, and

(b) the Part 1 warrant is issued with a view to his arrest and extradition to the category 1 territory for the purpose of being prosecuted for the offence.

(4) The information is—

(a) particulars of the person's identity;

(b) particulars of any other warrant issued in the category 1 territory for the person's arrest in respect of the offence;

(c) particulars of the circumstances in which the person is alleged to have committed the offence, including the conduct alleged to constitute the offence, the time and place at which he is alleged to have committed the offence and any provision of the law of the category 1 territory under which the conduct is alleged to constitute an offence;

(d) particulars of the sentence which may be imposed under the law of the category 1 territory in respect of the offence if the person is convicted of it.

(5) The statement is one that—

(a) the person in respect of whom the Part 1 warrant is issued is alleged to be unlawfully at large after conviction of an offence specified in the warrant by a court in the category 1 territory, and

(b) the Part 1 warrant is issued with a view to his arrest and extradition to the category 1 territory for the purpose of being sentenced for the offence or of serving a sentence of imprisonment or another form of detention imposed in respect of the offence.

(6) The information is—

(a) particulars of the person's identity;

(b) particulars of the conviction;

(c) particulars of any other warrant issued in the category 1 territory for the person's arrest in respect of the offence;

(d) particulars of the sentence which may be imposed under the law of the category 1 territory in respect of the offence, if the person has not been sentenced for the offence;

(e) particulars of the sentence which has been imposed under the law of the category 1 territory in respect of the offence, if the person has been sentenced for the offence.

(7) The designated authority may issue a certificate under this section if it believes that the authority which issued the Part 1 warrant has the function of issuing arrest warrants in the category 1 territory.

(8) A certificate under this section must certify that the authority which issued the Part 1 warrant has the function of issuing arrest warrants in the category 1 territory.

(9) The designated authority is the authority designated for the purposes of this Part by order made by the Secretary of State.

(10) An order made under subsection (9) may—

(a) designate more than one authority;

(b) designate different authorities for different parts of the United Kingdom.

Arrest

3. Arrest under certified Part 1 warrant   *Text: 4.2.2.1*

(1) This section applies if a certificate is issued under section 2 in respect of a Part 1 warrant issued in respect of a person.

(2) The warrant may be executed by a constable or a customs officer in any part of the United Kingdom.

(3) The warrant may be executed by a service policeman, but only if the service policeman would have power to arrest the person under the appropriate service law if the person had committed an offence under that law.

(4) If a service policeman has power to execute the warrant under subsection (3), he may execute the warrant in any place where he would have power to arrest the person under the appropriate service law if the person had committed an offence under that law.

(5) The warrant may be executed even if neither the warrant nor a copy of it is in the possession of the person executing it at the time of the arrest.

(6) The appropriate service law is—

(a) the Army Act 1955 (3 & 4 Eliz. 2 c. 18), if the person in respect of whom the warrant is issued is subject to military law;

(b) the Air Force Act 1955 (3 & 4 Eliz. 2 c. 19), if that person is subject to air-force law;

(c) the Naval Discipline Act 1957 (c. 53), if that person is subject to that Act.

4. Person arrested under Part 1 warrant *Text: 4.2.2.1*

(1) This section applies if a person is arrested under a Part 1 warrant.

(2) A copy of the warrant must be given to the person as soon as practicable after his arrest.

(3) The person must be brought as soon as practicable before the appropriate judge.

(4) If subsection (2) is not complied with and the person applies to the judge to be discharged, the judge may order his discharge.

(5) If subsection (3) is not complied with and the person applies to the judge to be discharged, the judge must order his discharge.

(6) A person arrested under the warrant must be treated as continuing in legal custody until he is brought before the appropriate judge under subsection (3) or he is discharged under subsection (4) or (5).

5. Provisional arrest *Text: 4.2.2.2*

(1) A constable, a customs officer or a service policeman may arrest a person without a warrant if he has reasonable grounds for believing—

(a) that a Part 1 warrant has been or will be issued in respect of the person by an authority of a category 1 territory, and

(b) that the authority has the function of issuing arrest warrants in the category 1 territory.

(2) A constable or a customs officer may arrest a person under subsection (1) in any part of the United Kingdom.

(3) A service policeman may arrest a person under subsection (1) only if the service policeman would have power to arrest the person under the appropriate service law if the person had committed an offence under that law.

(4) If a service policeman has power to arrest a person under subsection (1), the service policeman may exercise the power in any place where he would have power to arrest the person for an offence under the appropriate service law if the person had committed an offence under that law.

(5) The appropriate service law is—

(a) the Army Act 1955 (3 & 4 Eliz. 2 c. 18), if the person to be arrested is subject to military law;

(b) the Air Force Act 1955 (3 & 4 Eliz. 2 c. 19), if that person is subject to air-force law;

(c) the Naval Discipline Act 1957 (c. 53), if that person is subject to that Act.

6. Person arrested under section 5 *Text: 4.2.2.2*

(1) This section applies if a person is arrested under section 5.

(2) The following must occur within the required period—

(a) the person must be brought before the appropriate judge;

(b) the documents specified in subsection (4) must be produced to the judge.

(3) The required period is 48 hours starting with the time when the person is arrested.

(4) The documents are—

(a) a Part 1 warrant in respect of the person;

(b) a certificate under section 2 in respect of the warrant.

(5) A copy of the warrant must be given to the person as soon as practicable after his arrest.

(6) If subsection (2) is not complied with and the person applies to the judge to be discharged, the judge must order his discharge.

(7) If subsection (5) is not complied with and the person applies to the judge to be discharged, the judge may order his discharge.

(8) The person must be treated as continuing in legal custody until he is brought before the appropriate judge under subsection (2) or he is discharged under subsection (6) or (7).

(9) Subsection (10) applies if—

(a) a person is arrested under section 5 on the basis of a belief that a Part 1 warrant has been or will be issued in respect of him;

(b) the person is discharged under subsection (6) or (7).

(10) The person must not be arrested again under section 5 on the basis of a belief relating to the same Part 1 warrant.

The initial hearing

7. Identity of person arrested   *Text: 4.7.1.1*

(1) This section applies if—

(a) a person arrested under a Part 1 warrant is brought before the appropriate judge under section 4(3), or

(b) a person is arrested under section 5 and section 6(2) is complied with in relation to him.

(2) The judge must decide whether the person brought before him is the person in respect of whom—

(a) the warrant referred to in subsection (1)(a) was issued, or

(b) the warrant referred to in section 6(4) was issued.

(3) The judge must decide the question in subsection (2) on a balance of probabilities.

(4) If the judge decides the question in subsection (2) in the negative he must order the person's discharge.

(5) If the judge decides that question in the affirmative he must proceed under section 8.

(6) In England and Wales, the judge has the same powers (as nearly as may be) as a magistrates' court would have if the proceedings were the summary trial of an information against the person.

(7) In Scotland—

(a) the judge has the same powers (as nearly as may be) as if the proceedings were summary proceedings in respect of an offence alleged to have been committed by the person; but

(b) in his making any decision under subsection (2) evidence from a single source shall be sufficient.

(8) In Northern Ireland, the judge has the same powers (as nearly as may be) as a magistrates' court would have if the proceedings were the hearing and determination of a complaint against the person.

(9) If the judge exercises his power to adjourn the proceedings he must remand the person in custody or on bail.

(10) If the judge remands the person in custody he may later grant bail.

8. Remand etc.   *Text: 4.7.1.3*

(1) If the judge is required to proceed under this section he must—

   (a) fix a date on which the extradition hearing is to begin;

   (b) inform the person of the contents of the Part 1 warrant;

   (c) give the person the required information about consent;

   (d) remand the person in custody or on bail.

(2) If the judge remands the person in custody he may later grant bail.

(3) The required information about consent is—

   (a) that the person may consent to his extradition to the category 1 territory in which the Part 1 warrant was issued;

   (b) an explanation of the effect of consent and the procedure that will apply if he gives consent;

   (c) that consent must be given before the judge and is irrevocable.

(4) The date fixed under subsection (1) must not be later than the end of the permitted period, which is 21 days starting with the date of the arrest referred to in section 7(1)(a) or (b).

(5) If before the date fixed under subsection (1) (or this subsection) a party to the proceedings applies to the judge for a later date to be fixed and the judge believes it to be in the interests of justice to do so, he may fix a later date; and this subsection may apply more than once.

(6) Subsections (7) and (8) apply if the extradition hearing does not begin on or before the date fixed under this section.

(7) If the person applies to the judge to be discharged the judge must order his discharge, unless reasonable cause is shown for the delay.

(8) If no application is made under subsection (7) the judge must order the person's discharge on the first occasion after the date fixed under this section when the person appears or is brought before the judge, unless reasonable cause is shown for the delay.

The extradition hearing

9. Judge's powers at extradition hearing   *Text: 5.3*

(1) In England and Wales, at the extradition hearing the appropriate judge has the same powers (as nearly as may be) as a magistrates' court would have if the proceedings were the summary trial of an information against the person in respect of whom the Part 1 warrant was issued.

(2) In Scotland, at the extradition hearing the appropriate judge has the same powers (as nearly as may be) as if the proceedings were summary proceedings in respect of an

offence alleged to have been committed by the person in respect of whom the Part 1 warrant was issued.

(3) In Northern Ireland, at the extradition hearing the appropriate judge has the same powers (as nearly as may be) as a magistrates' court would have if the proceedings were the hearing and determination of a complaint against the person in respect of whom the Part 1 warrant was issued.

(4) If the judge adjourns the extradition hearing he must remand the person in custody or on bail.

(5) If the judge remands the person in custody he may later grant bail.

10. Initial stage of extradition hearing
Text: 5.7

(1) This section applies if a person in respect of whom a Part 1 warrant is issued appears or is brought before the appropriate judge for the extradition hearing.

(2) The judge must decide whether the offence specified in the Part 1 warrant is an extradition offence.

(3) If the judge decides the question in subsection (2) in the negative he must order the person's discharge.

(4) If the judge decides that question in the affirmative he must proceed under section 11.

11. Bars to extradition
Text: 5.8

(1) If the judge is required to proceed under this section he must decide whether the person's extradition to the category 1 territory is barred by reason of—

(a) the rule against double jeopardy;

(b) extraneous considerations;

(c) the passage of time;

(d) the person's age;

(e) hostage-taking considerations;

(f) speciality;

(g) the person's earlier extradition to the United Kingdom from another category 1 territory;

(h) the person's earlier extradition to the United Kingdom from a non-category 1 territory.

(2) Sections 12 to 19 apply for the interpretation of subsection (1).

(3) If the judge decides any of the questions in subsection (1) in the affirmative he must order the person's discharge.

(4) If the judge decides those questions in the negative and the person is alleged to be unlawfully at large after conviction of the extradition offence, the judge must proceed under section 20.

(5) If the judge decides those questions in the negative and the person is accused of the commission of the extradition offence but is not alleged to be unlawfully at large after conviction of it, the judge must proceed under section 21.

12. Rule against double jeopardy   *Text: 5.8.1*

A person's extradition to a category 1 territory is barred by reason of the rule against double jeopardy if (and only if) it appears that he would be entitled to be discharged under any rule of law relating to previous acquittal or conviction on the assumption—

(a) that the conduct constituting the extradition offence constituted an offence in the part of the United Kingdom where the judge exercises jurisdiction;

(b) that the person were charged with the extradition offence in that part of the United Kingdom.

13. Extraneous considerations   *Text: 5.8.2*

A person's extradition to a category 1 territory is barred by reason of extraneous considerations if (and only if) it appears that—

(a) the Part 1 warrant issued in respect of him (though purporting to be issued on account of the extradition offence) is in fact issued for the purpose of prosecuting or punishing him on account of his race, religion, nationality, gender, sexual orientation or political opinions, or

(b) if extradited he might be prejudiced at his trial or punished, detained or restricted in his personal liberty by reason of his race, religion, nationality, gender, sexual orientation or political opinions.

14. Passage of time   *Text: 5.8.3*

A person's extradition to a category 1 territory is barred by reason of the passage of time if (and only if) it appears that it would be unjust or oppressive to extradite him by reason of the passage of time since he is alleged to have committed the extradition offence or since he is alleged to have become unlawfully at large (as the case may be).

15. Age   *Text: 5.8.4*

A person's extradition to a category 1 territory is barred by reason of his age if (and only if) it would be conclusively presumed because of his age that he could not be guilty of the extradition offence on the assumption—

(a) that the conduct constituting the extradition offence constituted an offence in the part of the United Kingdom where the judge exercises jurisdiction;

(b) that the person carried out the conduct when the extradition offence was committed (or alleged to be committed);

(c) that the person carried out the conduct in the part of the United Kingdom where the judge exercises jurisdiction.

16. Hostage-taking considerations   *Text: 5.8.5*

(1) A person's extradition to a category 1 territory is barred by reason of hostage-taking considerations if (and only if) the territory is a party to the Hostage-taking Convention and it appears that—

(a) if extradited he might be prejudiced at his trial because communication between him and the appropriate authorities would not be possible, and

214

(b) the act or omission constituting the extradition offence also constitutes an offence under section 1 of the Taking of Hostages Act 1982 (c. 28) or an attempt to commit such an offence.

(2) The appropriate authorities are the authorities of the territory which are entitled to exercise rights of protection in relation to him.

(3) A certificate issued by the Secretary of State that a territory is a party to the Hostage-taking Convention is conclusive evidence of that fact for the purposes of subsection (1).

(4) The Hostage-taking Convention is the International Convention against the Taking of Hostages opened for signature at New York on 18 December 1979.

17. Speciality   *Text: 5.8.6*

(1) A person's extradition to a category 1 territory is barred by reason of speciality if (and only if) there are no speciality arrangements with the category 1 territory.

(2) There are speciality arrangements with a category 1 territory if, under the law of that territory or arrangements made between it and the United Kingdom, a person who is extradited to the territory from the United Kingdom may be dealt with in the territory for an offence committed before his extradition only if—

(a) the offence is one falling within subsection (3), or

(b) the condition in subsection (4) is satisfied.

(3) The offences are—

(a) the offence in respect of which the person is extradited;

(b) an extradition offence disclosed by the same facts as that offence;

(c) an extradition offence in respect of which the appropriate judge gives his consent under section 55 to the person being dealt with;

(d) an offence which is not punishable with imprisonment or another form of detention;

(e) an offence in respect of which the person will not be detained in connection with his trial, sentence or appeal;

(f) an offence in respect of which the person waives the right that he would have (but for this paragraph) not to be dealt with for the offence.

(4) The condition is that the person is given an opportunity to leave the category 1 territory and—

(a) he does not do so before the end of the permitted period, or

(b) if he does so before the end of the permitted period, he returns there.

(5) The permitted period is 45 days starting with the day on which the person arrives in the category 1 territory.

(6) Arrangements made with a category 1 territory which is a Commonwealth country or a British overseas territory may be made for a particular case or more generally.

(7) A certificate issued by or under the authority of the Secretary of State confirming the existence of arrangements with a category 1 territory which is a Commonwealth country or a British overseas territory and stating the terms of the arrangements is conclusive evidence of those matters.

18. Earlier extradition to United Kingdom from category 1 territory *Text: 5.8.7*
A person's extradition to a category 1 territory is barred by reason of his earlier extradition to the United Kingdom from another category 1 territory if (and only if)—

(a) the person was extradited to the United Kingdom from another category 1 territory (the extraditing territory);

(b) under arrangements between the United Kingdom and the extraditing territory, that territory's consent is required to the person's extradition from the United Kingdom to the category 1 territory in respect of the extradition offence under consideration;

(c) that consent has not been given on behalf of the extraditing territory.

19. Earlier extradition to United Kingdom from non-category 1 territory *Text: 5.8.7*
A person's extradition to a category 1 territory is barred by reason of his earlier extradition to the United Kingdom from a non-category 1 territory if (and only if)—

(a) the person was extradited to the United Kingdom from a territory that is not a category 1 territory (the extraditing territory);

(b) under arrangements between the United Kingdom and the extraditing territory, that territory's consent is required to the person's being dealt with in the United Kingdom in respect of the extradition offence under consideration;

(c) consent has not been given on behalf of the extraditing territory to the person's extradition from the United Kingdom to the category 1 territory in respect of the extradition offence under consideration.

20. Case where person has been convicted *Text: 5.8.8*
(1) If the judge is required to proceed under this section (by virtue of section 11) he must decide whether the person was convicted in his presence.

(2) If the judge decides the question in subsection (1) in the affirmative he must proceed under section 21.

(3) If the judge decides that question in the negative he must decide whether the person deliberately absented himself from his trial.

(4) If the judge decides the question in subsection (3) in the affirmative he must proceed under section 21.

(5) If the judge decides that question in the negative he must decide whether the person would be entitled to a retrial or (on appeal) to a review amounting to a retrial.

(6) If the judge decides the question in subsection (5) in the affirmative he must proceed under section 21.

(7) If the judge decides that question in the negative he must order the person's discharge.

(8) The judge must not decide the question in subsection (5) in the affirmative unless, in any proceedings that it is alleged would constitute a retrial or a review amounting to a retrial, the person would have these rights—

(a) the right to defend himself in person or through legal assistance of his own choosing or, if he had not sufficient means to pay for legal assistance, to be given it free when the interests of justice so required;

(b) the right to examine or have examined witnesses against him and to obtain the attendance and examination of witnesses on his behalf under the same conditions as witnesses against him.

21. Human rights *Text: 5.8.9; Chapter 7*

(1) If the judge is required to proceed under this section (by virtue of section 11 or 20) he must decide whether the person's extradition would be compatible with the Convention rights within the meaning of the Human Rights Act 1998 (c. 42).

(2) If the judge decides the question in subsection (1) in the negative he must order the person's discharge.

(3) If the judge decides that question in the affirmative he must order the person to be extradited to the category 1 territory in which the warrant was issued.

(4) If the judge makes an order under subsection (3) he must remand the person in custody or on bail to wait for his extradition to the category 1 territory.

(5) If the judge remands the person in custody he may later grant bail.

Matters arising before end of extradition hearing

22. Person charged with offence in United Kingdom *Text: 5.11*

(1) This section applies if at any time in the extradition hearing the judge is informed that the person in respect of whom the Part 1 warrant is issued is charged with an offence in the United Kingdom.

(2) The judge must adjourn the extradition hearing until one of these occurs—

(a) the charge is disposed of;

(b) the charge is withdrawn;

(c) proceedings in respect of the charge are discontinued;

(d) an order is made for the charge to lie on the file, or in relation to Scotland, the diet is deserted *pro loco et tempore.*

(3) If a sentence of imprisonment or another form of detention is imposed in respect of the offence charged, the judge may adjourn the extradition hearing until the sentence has been served.

(4) If before he adjourns the extradition hearing under subsection (2) the judge has decided under section 11 whether the person's extradition is barred by reason of the rule against double jeopardy, the judge must decide that question again after the resumption of the hearing.

23. Person serving sentence in United Kingdom *Text: 5.11*

(1) This section applies if at any time in the extradition hearing the judge is informed that the person in respect of whom the Part 1 warrant is issued is serving a sentence of imprisonment or another form of detention in the United Kingdom.

(2) The judge may adjourn the extradition hearing until the sentence has been served.

24. Extradition request *Text: 8.4.1*

(1) This section applies if at any time in the extradition hearing the judge is informed that—

(a) a certificate has been issued under section 70 in respect of a request for the person's extradition;

(b) the request has not been disposed of;

(c) an order has been made under section 179(2) for further proceedings on the warrant to be deferred until the request has been disposed of.

(2) The judge must remand the person in custody or on bail.

(3) If the judge remands the person in custody he may later grant bail.

25. Physical or mental condition *Text: 5.9.1*

(1) This section applies if at any time in the extradition hearing it appears to the judge that the condition in subsection (2) is satisfied.

(2) The condition is that the physical or mental condition of the person in respect of whom the Part 1 warrant is issued is such that it would be unjust or oppressive to extradite him.

(3) The judge must—

(a) order the person's discharge, or

(b) adjourn the extradition hearing until it appears to him that the condition in subsection (2) is no longer satisfied.

Appeals

26. Appeal against extradition order *Text: 9.2.1*

(1) If the appropriate judge orders a person's extradition under this Part, the person may appeal to the High Court against the order.

(2) But subsection (1) does not apply if the order is made under section 46 or 48.

(3) An appeal under this section may be brought on a question of law or fact.

(4) Notice of an appeal under this section must be given in accordance with rules of court before the end of the permitted period, which is 7 days starting with the day on which the order is made.

27. Court's powers on appeal under section 26 *Text: 9.2.1*

(1) On an appeal under section 26 the High Court may—

(a) allow the appeal;

(b) dismiss the appeal.

(2) The court may allow the appeal only if the conditions in subsection (3) or the conditions in subsection (4) are satisfied.

(3) The conditions are that—

(a) the appropriate judge ought to have decided a question before him at the extradition hearing differently;

(b) if he had decided the question in the way he ought to have done, he would have been required to order the person's discharge.

(4) The conditions are that—

(a) an issue is raised that was not raised at the extradition hearing or evidence is available that was not available at the extradition hearing;

(b) the issue or evidence would have resulted in the appropriate judge deciding a question before him at the extradition hearing differently;

(c) if he had decided the question in that way, he would have been required to order the person's discharge.

(5) If the court allows the appeal it must—

(a) order the person's discharge;

(b) quash the order for his extradition.

28. Appeal against discharge at extradition hearing *Text: 9.2.2*

(1) If the judge orders a person's discharge at the extradition hearing the authority which issued the Part 1 warrant may appeal to the High Court against the relevant decision.

(2) But subsection (1) does not apply if the order for the person's discharge was under section 41.

(3) The relevant decision is the decision which resulted in the order for the person's discharge.

(4) An appeal under this section may be brought on a question of law or fact.

(5) Notice of an appeal under this section must be given in accordance with rules of court before the end of the permitted period, which is 7 days starting with the day on which the order for the person's discharge is made.

29. Court's powers on appeal under section 28 *Text: 9.2.2*

(1) On an appeal under section 28 the High Court may—

(a) allow the appeal;

(b) dismiss the appeal.

(2) The court may allow the appeal only if the conditions in subsection (3) or the conditions in subsection (4) are satisfied.

(3) The conditions are that—

(a) the judge ought to have decided the relevant question differently;

(b) if he had decided the question in the way he ought to have done, he would not have been required to order the person's discharge.

(4) The conditions are that—

(a) an issue is raised that was not raised at the extradition hearing or evidence is available that was not available at the extradition hearing;

(b) the issue or evidence would have resulted in the judge deciding the relevant question differently;

(c) if he had decided the question in that way, he would not have been required to order the person's discharge.

(5) If the court allows the appeal it must—

(a) quash the order discharging the person;

(b) remit the case to the judge;

(c) direct him to proceed as he would have been required to do if he had decided the relevant question differently at the extradition hearing.

(6) A question is the relevant question if the judge's decision on it resulted in the order for the person's discharge.

30. Detention pending conclusion of appeal under section 28 *Text: 9.2.3*

(1) This section applies if immediately after the judge orders the person's discharge the judge is informed by the authority which issued the Part 1 warrant that it intends to appeal under section 28.

(2) The judge must remand the person in custody or on bail while the appeal is pending.

(3) If the judge remands the person in custody he may later grant bail.

(4) An appeal under section 28 ceases to be pending at the earliest of these times—

(a) when the proceedings on the appeal are discontinued;

(b) when the High Court dismisses the appeal, if the authority does not immediately inform the court that it intends to apply for leave to appeal to the House of Lords;

(c) at the end of the permitted period, which is 28 days starting with the day on which leave to appeal to the House of Lords against the decision of the High Court on the appeal is granted;

(d) when there is no further step that can be taken by the authority which issued the Part 1 warrant in relation to the appeal (ignoring any power of a court to grant leave to take a step out of time).

(5) The preceding provisions of this section apply to Scotland with these modifications—

(a) in subsection (4)(b) omit the words from "if" to the end;

(b) omit subsection (4)(c).

31. Appeal to High Court: time limit for start of hearing *Text: 9.2.4*

(1) Rules of court must prescribe the period (the relevant period) within which the High Court must begin to hear an appeal under section 26 or 28.

(2) Rules of court must provide for the relevant period to start with the date on which the person in respect of whom a Part 1 warrant is issued—

(a) was arrested under section 5, if he was arrested under that section;

(b) was arrested under the Part 1 warrant, if he was not arrested under section 5.

(3) The High Court must begin to hear the appeal before the end of the relevant period.

(4) The High Court may extend the relevant period if it believes it to be in the interests of justice to do so; and this subsection may apply more than once.

(5) The power in subsection (4) may be exercised even after the end of the relevant period.

(6) If subsection (3) is not complied with and the appeal is under section 26—

(a) the appeal must be taken to have been allowed by a decision of the High Court;

(b) the person whose extradition has been ordered must be taken to have been discharged by the High Court;

(c) the order for the person's extradition must be taken to have been quashed by the High Court.

(7) If subsection (3) is not complied with and the appeal is under section 28 the appeal must be taken to have been dismissed by a decision of the High Court.

32. Appeal to House of Lords *Text: 9.2.5*

(1) An appeal lies to the House of Lords from a decision of the High Court on an appeal under section 26 or 28.

(2) An appeal under this section lies at the instance of—

(a) the person in respect of whom the Part 1 warrant was issued;

(b) the authority which issued the Part 1 warrant.

(3) An appeal under this section lies only with the leave of the High Court or the House of Lords.

(4) Leave to appeal under this section must not be granted unless—

(a) the High Court has certified that there is a point of law of general public importance involved in the decision, and

(b) it appears to the court granting leave that the point is one which ought to be considered by the House of Lords.

(5) An application to the High Court for leave to appeal under this section must be made before the end of the permitted period, which is 14 days starting with the day on which the court makes its decision on the appeal to it.

(6) An application to the House of Lords for leave to appeal under this section must be made before the end of the permitted period, which is 14 days starting with the day on which the High Court refuses leave to appeal.

(7) If leave to appeal under this section is granted, the appeal must be brought before the end of the permitted period, which is 28 days starting with the day on which leave is granted.

(8) If subsection (7) is not complied with—

(a) the appeal must be taken to have been brought;

(b) the appeal must be taken to have been dismissed by the House of Lords immediately after the end of the period permitted under that subsection.

(9) These must be ignored for the purposes of subsection (8)(b)—

(a) any power of a court to extend the period permitted for bringing the appeal;

(b) any power of a court to grant leave to take a step out of time.

(10) The High Court may grant bail to a person appealing under this section or applying for leave to appeal under this section.

(11) Section 5 of the Appellate Jurisdiction Act 1876 (c. 59) (composition of House of Lords for hearing and determination of appeals) applies in relation to an appeal under this section or an application for leave to appeal under this section as it applies in relation to an appeal under that Act.

(12) An order of the House of Lords which provides for an application for leave to appeal under this section to be determined by a committee constituted in accordance with section 5 of the Appellate Jurisdiction Act 1876 may direct that the decision of the committee is taken on behalf of the House.

(13) The preceding provisions of this section do not apply to Scotland.

33. Powers of House of Lords on appeal under section 32 *Text: 9.2.6*

(1) On an appeal under section 32 the House of Lords may—

(a) allow the appeal;

(b) dismiss the appeal.

(2) Subsection (3) applies if—

(a) the person in respect of whom the Part 1 warrant was issued brings an appeal under section 32, and

(b) the House of Lords allows the appeal.

(3) The House of Lords must—

(a) order the person's discharge;

(b) quash the order for his extradition, if the appeal was against a decision of the High Court to dismiss an appeal under section 26.

(4) Subsection (5) applies if—

(a) the High Court allows an appeal under section 26 by the person in respect of whom the Part 1 warrant was issued,

(b) the authority which issued the warrant brings an appeal under section 32 against the decision of the High Court, and

(c) the House of Lords allows the appeal.

(5) The House of Lords must—

(a) quash the order of the High Court under section 27(5) discharging the person;

(b) order the person to be extradited to the category 1 territory in which the warrant was issued.

(6) Subsections (7) and (8) apply if—

(a) the High Court dismisses an appeal under section 28 against a decision made by the judge at the extradition hearing,

(b) the authority which issued the Part 1 warrant brings an appeal under section 32 against the decision of the High Court, and

(c) the House of Lords allows the appeal.

(7) If the judge would have been required to order the person in respect of whom the warrant was issued to be extradited had he decided the relevant question differently, the House of Lords must—

(a) quash the order of the judge discharging the person;

(b) order the person to be extradited to the category 1 territory in which the warrant was issued.

(8) In any other case, the House of Lords must—

(a) quash the order of the judge discharging the person in respect of whom the warrant was issued;

(b) remit the case to the judge;

(c) direct him to proceed as he would have been required to do if he had decided the relevant question differently at the extradition hearing.

(9) A question is the relevant question if the judge's decision on it resulted in the order for the person's discharge.

34. Appeals: general

A decision of the judge under this Part may be questioned in legal proceedings only by means of an appeal under this Part.

Time for extradition

35. Extradition where no appeal
Text: 10.2.1

(1) This section applies if—

(a) the appropriate judge orders a person's extradition to a category 1 territory under this Part, and

(b) no notice of an appeal under section 26 is given before the end of the period permitted under that section.

(2) But this section does not apply if the order is made under section 46 or 48.

(3) The person must be extradited to the category 1 territory before the end of the required period.

(4) The required period is—

(a) 10 days starting with the day on which the judge makes the order, or

(b) if the judge and the authority which issued the Part 1 warrant agree a later date, 10 days starting with the later date.

(5) If subsection (3) is not complied with and the person applies to the appropriate judge to be discharged the judge must order his discharge, unless reasonable cause is shown for the delay.

(6) These must be ignored for the purposes of subsection (1)(b)—

(a) any power of a court to extend the period permitted for giving notice of appeal;

(b) any power of a court to grant leave to take a step out of time.

36. Extradition following appeal
Text: 10.2.2

(1) This section applies if—

(a) there is an appeal to the High Court under section 26 against an order for a person's extradition to a category 1 territory, and

(b) the effect of the decision of the relevant court on the appeal is that the person is to be extradited there.

(2) The person must be extradited to the category 1 territory before the end of the required period.

(3) The required period is—

(a) 10 days starting with the day on which the decision of the relevant court on the appeal becomes final or proceedings on the appeal are discontinued, or

(b) if the relevant court and the authority which issued the Part 1 warrant agree a later date, 10 days starting with the later date.

(4) The relevant court is—

(a) the High Court, if there is no appeal to the House of Lords against the decision of the High Court on the appeal;

(b) the House of Lords, if there is such an appeal.

(5) The decision of the High Court on the appeal becomes final—

(a) when the period permitted for applying to the High Court for leave to appeal to the House of Lords ends, if there is no such application;

(b) when the period permitted for applying to the House of Lords for leave to appeal to it ends, if the High Court refuses leave to appeal and there is no application to the House of Lords for leave to appeal;

(c) when the House of Lords refuses leave to appeal to it;

(d) at the end of the permitted period, which is 28 days starting with the day on which leave to appeal to the House of Lords is granted, if no such appeal is brought before the end of that period.

(6) These must be ignored for the purposes of subsection (5)—

(a) any power of a court to extend the period permitted for applying for leave to appeal;

(b) any power of a court to grant leave to take a step out of time.

(7) The decision of the House of Lords on the appeal becomes final when it is made.

(8) If subsection (2) is not complied with and the person applies to the appropriate judge to be discharged the judge must order his discharge, unless reasonable cause is shown for the delay.

(9) The preceding provisions of this section apply to Scotland with these modifications—

(a) in subsections (1) and (3) for "relevant court" substitute "High Court";

(b) omit subsections (4) to (7).

37. Undertaking in relation to person serving sentence in United Kingdom   *Text: 10.2.3*

(1) This section applies if—

(a) the appropriate judge orders a person's extradition to a category 1 territory under this Part;

(b) the person is serving a sentence of imprisonment or another form of detention in the United Kingdom.

(2) But this section does not apply if the order is made under section 46 or 48.

(3) The judge may make the order for extradition subject to the condition that extradition is not to take place before he receives an undertaking given on behalf of the category 1 territory in terms specified by him.

(4) The terms which may be specified by the judge in relation to a person accused in a category 1 territory of the commission of an offence include terms—

(a) that the person be kept in custody until the conclusion of the proceedings against him for the offence and any other offence in respect of which he is permitted to be dealt with in the category 1 territory;

(b) that the person be returned to the United Kingdom to serve the remainder of his sentence on the conclusion of those proceedings.

(5) The terms which may be specified by the judge in relation to a person alleged to be unlawfully at large after conviction of an offence by a court in a category 1 territory include terms that the person be returned to the United Kingdom to serve the remainder of his sentence after serving any sentence imposed on him in the category 1 territory for—

(a) the offence, and

(b) any other offence in respect of which he is permitted to be dealt with in the category 1 territory.

(6) Subsections (7) and (8) apply if the judge makes an order for extradition subject to a condition under subsection (3).

(7) If the judge does not receive the undertaking before the end of the period of 21 days starting with the day on which he makes the order and the person applies to the appropriate judge to be discharged, the judge must order his discharge.

(8) If the judge receives the undertaking before the end of that period—

(a) in a case where section 35 applies, the required period for the purposes of section 35(3) is 10 days starting with the day on which the judge receives the undertaking;

(b) in a case where section 36 applies, the required period for the purposes of section 36(2) is 10 days starting with the day on which the decision of the relevant court on the appeal becomes final (within the meaning of that section) or (if later) the day on which the judge receives the undertaking.

38. Extradition following deferral for competing claim   *Text: 10.2.4*

(1) This section applies if—

(a) an order is made under this Part for a person to be extradited to a category 1 territory in pursuance of a Part 1 warrant;

(b) before the person is extradited to the territory an order is made under section 44(4)(b) or 179(2)(b) for the person's extradition in pursuance of the warrant to be deferred;

(c) the appropriate judge makes an order under section 181(2) for the person's extradition in pursuance of the warrant to cease to be deferred.

(2) But this section does not apply if the order for the person's extradition is made under section 46 or 48.

(3) In a case where section 35 applies, the required period for the purposes of section 35(3) is 10 days starting with the day on which the order under section 181(2) is made.

(4) In a case where section 36 applies, the required period for the purposes of section 36(2) is 10 days starting with the day on which the decision of the relevant court on the appeal becomes final (within the meaning of that section) or (if later) the day on which the order under section 181(2) is made.

39. Asylum claim   *Text: 8.5.1*

(1) This section applies if—

(a) a person in respect of whom a Part 1 warrant is issued makes an asylum claim at any time in the relevant period;

(b) an order is made under this Part for the person to be extradited in pursuance of the warrant.

(2) The relevant period is the period—

(a) starting when a certificate is issued under section 2 in respect of the warrant;

(b) ending when the person is extradited in pursuance of the warrant.

(3) The person must not be extradited in pursuance of the warrant before the asylum claim is finally determined; and sections 35, 36, 47 and 49 have effect subject to this.

(4) Subsection (3) is subject to section 40.

(5) If the Secretary of State allows the asylum claim, the claim is finally determined when he makes his decision on the claim.

(6) If the Secretary of State rejects the asylum claim, the claim is finally determined—

(a) when the Secretary of State makes his decision on the claim, if there is no right to appeal against the Secretary of State's decision on the claim;

(b) when the period permitted for appealing against the Secretary of State's decision on the claim ends, if there is such a right but there is no such appeal;

(c) when the appeal against that decision is finally determined or is withdrawn or abandoned, if there is such an appeal.

(7) An appeal against the Secretary of State's decision on an asylum claim is not finally determined for the purposes of subsection (6) at any time when a further appeal or an application for leave to bring a further appeal—

(a) has been instituted and has not been finally determined or withdrawn or abandoned, or

(b) may be brought.

(8) The remittal of an appeal is not a final determination for the purposes of subsection (7).

(9) The possibility of an appeal out of time with leave must be ignored for the purposes of subsections (6) and (7).

40. Certificate in respect of asylum claimant *Text: 8.5.1*

(1) Section 39(3) does not apply in relation to a person if the Secretary of State has certified that the conditions in subsection (2) or the conditions in subsection (3) are satisfied in relation to him.

(2) The conditions are that—

(a) the category 1 territory to which the person's extradition has been ordered has accepted that, under standing arrangements, it is the responsible State in relation to the person's asylum claim;

(b) in the opinion of the Secretary of State, the person is not a national or citizen of the territory.

(3) The conditions are that, in the opinion of the Secretary of State—

(a) the person is not a national or citizen of the category 1 territory to which his extradition has been ordered;

(b) the person's life and liberty would not be threatened in that territory by reason of his race, religion, nationality, political opinion or membership of a particular social group;

(c) the government of the territory would not send the person to another country otherwise than in accordance with the Refugee Convention.

(4) In this section—

"the Refugee Convention" has the meaning given by section 167(1) of the Immigration and Asylum Act 1999 (c. 33);

"standing arrangements" means arrangements in force between the United Kingdom and the category 1 territory for determining which State is responsible for considering applications for asylum.

Withdrawal of Part 1 warrant

41. Withdrawal of warrant before extradition *Text: 11.3.1*

(1) This section applies if at any time in the relevant period the appropriate judge is informed by the designated authority that a Part 1 warrant issued in respect of a person has been withdrawn.

(2) The relevant period is the period—

(a) starting when the person is first brought before the appropriate judge following his arrest under this Part;

(b) ending when the person is extradited in pursuance of the warrant or discharged.

(3) The judge must order the person's discharge.

(4) If the person is not before the judge at the time the judge orders his discharge, the judge must inform him of the order as soon as practicable.

42. Withdrawal of warrant while appeal to High Court pending *Text: 11.3.1*

(1) This section applies if at any time in the relevant period the High Court is informed by the designated authority that a Part 1 warrant issued in respect of a person has been withdrawn.

(2) The relevant period is the period—

(a) starting when notice of an appeal to the court is given by the person or the authority which issued the warrant;

(b) ending when proceedings on the appeal are discontinued or the court makes its decision on the appeal.

(3) The court must—

(a) if the appeal is under section 26, order the person's discharge and quash the order for his extradition;

(b) if the appeal is under section 28, dismiss the appeal.

(4) If the person is not before the court at the time the court orders his discharge, the court must inform him of the order as soon as practicable.

43. Withdrawal of warrant while appeal to House of Lords pending *Text: 11.3.1*

(1) This section applies if at any time in the relevant period the House of Lords is informed by the designated authority that a Part 1 warrant issued in respect of a person has been withdrawn.

(2) The relevant period is the period—

(a) starting when leave to appeal to the House of Lords is granted to the person or the authority which issued the warrant;

(b) ending when proceedings on the appeal are discontinued or the House of Lords makes its decision on the appeal.

(3) If the appeal is brought by the person in respect of whom the warrant was issued the House of Lords must—

(a) order the person's discharge;

(b) quash the order for his extradition, in a case where the appeal was against a decision of the High Court to dismiss an appeal under section 26.

(4) If the appeal is brought by the authority which issued the warrant the House of Lords must dismiss the appeal.

(5) If the person is not before the House of Lords at the time it orders his discharge, the House of Lords must inform him of the order as soon as practicable.

Competing Part 1 warrants

44. Competing Part 1 warrants *Text: 5.10*

(1) This section applies if at any time in the relevant period the conditions in subsection (3) are satisfied in relation to a person in respect of whom a Part 1 warrant has been issued.

(2) The relevant period is the period—

(a) starting when the person is first brought before the appropriate judge following his arrest under this Part;

(b) ending when the person is extradited in pursuance of the warrant or discharged.

(3) The conditions are that—

(a) the judge is informed that another Part 1 warrant has been issued in respect of the person;

(b) the other warrant falls to be dealt with by the judge or by a judge who is the appropriate judge in another part of the United Kingdom;

(c) the other warrant has not been disposed of.

(4) The judge may—

(a) order further proceedings on the warrant under consideration to be deferred until the other warrant has been disposed of, if the warrant under consideration has not been disposed of;

(b) order the person's extradition in pursuance of the warrant under consideration to be deferred until the other warrant has been disposed of, if an order for his extradition in pursuance of the warrant under consideration has been made.

(5) If the judge makes an order under subsection (4) and the person is not already remanded in custody or on bail, the judge must remand the person in custody or on bail.

(6) If the judge remands the person in custody he may later grant bail.

(7) In applying subsection (4) the judge must take account in particular of these matters—

(a) the relative seriousness of the offences concerned;

(b) the place where each offence was committed (or was alleged to have been committed);

(c) the date on which each warrant was issued;

(d) whether, in the case of each offence, the person is accused of its commission (but not alleged to have been convicted) or is alleged to be unlawfully at large after conviction.

Consent to extradition

45. Consent to extradition   *Text: 11.2.1*

(1) A person arrested under a Part 1 warrant may consent to his extradition to the category 1 territory in which the warrant was issued.

(2) A person arrested under section 5 may consent to his extradition to the category 1 territory referred to in subsection (1) of that section.

(3) If a person consents to his extradition under this section he must be taken to have waived any right he would have (apart from the consent) not to be dealt with in the category 1 territory for an offence committed before his extradition.

(4) Consent under this section—

(a) must be given before the appropriate judge;

(b) must be recorded in writing;

(c) is irrevocable.

(5) A person may not give his consent under this section unless—

(a) he is legally represented before the appropriate judge at the time he gives consent, or

(b) he is a person to whom subsection (6) applies.

(6) This subsection applies to a person if—

(a) he has been informed of his right to apply for legal aid and has had the opportunity to apply for legal aid, but he has refused or failed to apply;

(b) he has applied for legal aid but his application has been refused;

(c) he was granted legal aid but the legal aid was withdrawn.

(7) In subsection (6) "legal aid" means—

(a) in England and Wales, a right to representation funded by the Legal Services Commission as part of the Criminal Defence Service;

(b) in Scotland, such legal aid as is available by virtue of section 183(a) of this Act;

(c) in Northern Ireland, such free legal aid as is available by virtue of sections 184 and 185 of this Act.

(8) For the purposes of subsection (5) a person is to be treated as legally represented before the appropriate judge if (and only if) he has the assistance of counsel or a solicitor to represent him in the proceedings before the appropriate judge.

46. Extradition order following consent   *Text: 11.2.1*

(1) This section applies if a person consents to his extradition under section 45.

(2) The judge must remand the person in custody or on bail.

(3) If the judge remands the person in custody he may later grant bail.

(4) If the judge has not fixed a date under section 8 on which the extradition hearing is to begin he is not required to do so.

(5) If the extradition hearing has begun the judge is no longer required to proceed or continue proceeding under sections 10 to 25.

(6) The judge must within the period of 10 days starting with the day on which consent is given order the person's extradition to the category 1 territory.

(7) Subsection (6) has effect subject to sections 48 and 51.

(8) If subsection (6) is not complied with and the person applies to the judge to be discharged the judge must order his discharge.

47. Extradition to category 1 territory following consent   *Text: 11.2.1*

(1) This section applies if the appropriate judge makes an order under section 46(6) for a person's extradition to a category 1 territory.

(2) The person must be extradited to the category 1 territory before the end of the required period.

(3) The required period is—

(a) 10 days starting with the day on which the order is made, or

(b) if the judge and the authority which issued the Part 1 warrant agree a later date, 10 days starting with the later date.

(4) If subsection (2) is not complied with and the person applies to the judge to be discharged the judge must order his discharge, unless reasonable cause is shown for the delay.

(5) If before the person is extradited to the category 1 territory the judge is informed by the designated authority that the Part 1 warrant has been withdrawn—

(a) subsection (2) does not apply, and

(b) the judge must order the person's discharge.

48. Other warrant issued following consent

Text: 11.2.1.1

(1) This section applies if—

(a) a person consents under section 45 to his extradition to a category 1 territory, and

(b) the conditions in subsection (2) are satisfied before the judge orders his extradition under section 46(6).

(2) The conditions are that—

(a) the judge is informed that another Part 1 warrant has been issued in respect of the person;

(b) the warrant falls to be dealt with by the judge or by a judge who is the appropriate judge in another part of the United Kingdom;

(c) the warrant has not been disposed of.

(3) Section 46(6) does not apply but the judge may—

(a) order the person's extradition in pursuance of his consent, or

(b) order further proceedings on the warrant under consideration to be deferred until the other warrant has been disposed of.

(4) Subsection (3) is subject to section 51.

(5) In applying subsection (3) the judge must take account in particular of these matters—

(a) the relative seriousness of the offences concerned;

(b) the place where each offence was committed (or was alleged to have been committed);

(c) the date on which each warrant was issued;

(d) whether, in the case of each offence, the person is accused of its commission (but not alleged to have been convicted) or is alleged to be unlawfully at large after conviction.

49. Other warrant issued: extradition to category 1 territory

Text: 11.2.1.1

(1) This section applies if the appropriate judge makes an order under section 48(3)(a) for a person's extradition to a category 1 territory.

(2) The person must be extradited to the category 1 territory before the end of the required period.

(3) The required period is—

(a) 10 days starting with the day on which the order is made, or

(b) if the judge and the authority which issued the Part 1 warrant agree a later date, 10 days starting with the later date.

(4) If subsection (2) is not complied with and the person applies to the judge to be discharged the judge must order his discharge, unless reasonable cause is shown for the delay.

(5) If before the person is extradited to the category 1 territory the judge is informed by the designated authority that the Part 1 warrant has been withdrawn—

(a) subsection (2) does not apply, and

(b) the judge must order the person's discharge.

50. Other warrant issued: proceedings deferred

Text: 11.2.1.1

(1) This section applies if the appropriate judge makes an order under section 48(3)(b) for further proceedings on a Part 1 warrant to be deferred.

(2) The judge must remand the person in respect of whom the warrant was issued in custody or on bail.

(3) If the judge remands the person in custody he may later grant bail.

(4) If an order is made under section 180 for proceedings on the warrant to be resumed, the period specified in section 46(6) must be taken to be 10 days starting with the day on which the order under section 180 is made.

51. Extradition request following consent

Text: 11.2.1.2

(1) This section applies if—

(a) a person in respect of whom a Part 1 warrant is issued consents under section 45 to his extradition to the category 1 territory in which the warrant was issued, and

(b) the condition in subsection (2) is satisfied before the judge orders his extradition under section 46(6) or 48(3)(a).

(2) The condition is that the judge is informed that—

(a) a certificate has been issued under section 70 in respect of a request for the person's extradition;

(b) the request has not been disposed of.

(3) The judge must not make an order under section 46(6) or 48(3) until he is informed what order has been made under section 179(2).

(4) If the order under section 179(2) is for further proceedings on the warrant to be deferred until the request has been disposed of, the judge must remand the person in custody or on bail.

(5) If the judge remands the person in custody he may later grant bail.

(6) If—

(a) the order under section 179(2) is for further proceedings on the warrant to be deferred until the request has been disposed of, and

(b) an order is made under section 180 for proceedings on the warrant to be resumed,

the period specified in section 46(6) must be taken to be 10 days starting with the day on which the order under section 180 is made.

(7) If the order under section 179(2) is for further proceedings on the request to be deferred until the warrant has been disposed of, the period specified in section 46(6) must be taken to be 10 days starting with the day on which the judge is informed of the order.

52. Undertaking in relation to person serving sentence   *Text: 11.2.1.3*

(1) This section applies if—

   (a) the appropriate judge makes an order under section 46(6) or 48(3)(a) for a person's extradition to a category 1 territory;

   (b) the person is serving a sentence of imprisonment or another form of detention in the United Kingdom.

(2) The judge may make the order for extradition subject to the condition that extradition is not to take place before he receives an undertaking given on behalf of the category 1 territory in terms specified by him.

(3) The terms which may be specified by the judge in relation to a person accused in a category 1 territory of the commission of an offence include terms—

   (a) that the person be kept in custody until the conclusion of the proceedings against him for the offence and any other offence in respect of which he is permitted to be dealt with in the category 1 territory;

   (b) that the person be returned to the United Kingdom to serve the remainder of his sentence on the conclusion of those proceedings.

(4) The terms which may be specified by the judge in relation to a person alleged to be unlawfully at large after conviction of an offence by a court in a category 1 territory include terms that the person be returned to the United Kingdom to serve the remainder of his sentence after serving any sentence imposed on him in the category 1 territory for—

   (a) the offence, and

   (b) any other offence in respect of which he is permitted to be dealt with in the category 1 territory.

(5) If the judge makes an order for extradition subject to a condition under subsection (2) the required period for the purposes of sections 47(2) and 49(2) is 10 days starting with the day on which the judge receives the undertaking.

53. Extradition following deferral for competing claim

(1) This section applies if—

   (a) an order is made under section 46(6) or 48(3)(a) for a person to be extradited to a category 1 territory in pursuance of a Part 1 warrant;

   (b) before the person is extradited to the territory an order is made under section 44(4)(b) or 179(2)(b) for the person's extradition in pursuance of the warrant to be deferred;

   (c) the appropriate judge makes an order under section 181(2) for the person's extradition in pursuance of the warrant to cease to be deferred.

(2) The required period for the purposes of sections 47(2) and 49(2) is 10 days starting with the day on which the order under section 181(2) is made.

Post-extradition matters

54. Request for consent to other offence being dealt with   *Text: 14.2.1*

(1) This section applies if—

   (a) a person is extradited to a category 1 territory in respect of an offence in accordance with this Part;

(b) the appropriate judge receives a request for consent to the person being dealt with in the territory for another offence;

(c) the request is certified under this section by the designated authority.

(2) The designated authority may certify a request for consent under this section if it believes that the authority making the request—

(a) is a judicial authority of the territory, and

(b) has the function of making requests for the consent referred to in subsection (1)(b) in that territory.

(3) A certificate under subsection (2) must certify that the authority making the request falls within paragraphs (a) and (b) of that subsection.

(4) The judge must serve notice on the person that he has received the request for consent, unless he is satisfied that it would not be practicable to do so.

(5) The consent hearing must begin before the end of the required period, which is 21 days starting with the day on which the request for consent is received by the designated authority.

(6) The judge may extend the required period if he believes it to be in the interests of justice to do so; and this subsection may apply more than once.

(7) The power in subsection (6) may be exercised even after the end of the required period.

(8) If the consent hearing does not begin before the end of the required period and the judge does not exercise the power in subsection (6) to extend the period, he must refuse consent.

(9) The judge may at any time adjourn the consent hearing.

(10) The consent hearing is the hearing at which the judge is to consider the request for consent.

55. Questions for decision at consent hearing   *Text: 14.2.1*

(1) At the consent hearing under section 54 the judge must decide whether consent is required to the person being dealt with in the territory for the offence for which consent is requested.

(2) If the judge decides the question in subsection (1) in the negative he must inform the authority making the request of his decision.

(3) If the judge decides that question in the affirmative he must decide whether the offence for which consent is requested is an extradition offence.

(4) If the judge decides the question in subsection (3) in the negative he must refuse consent.

(5) If the judge decides that question in the affirmative he must decide whether he would order the person's extradition under sections 11 to 25 if—

(a) the person were in the United Kingdom, and

(b) the judge were required to proceed under section 11 in respect of the offence for which consent is requested.

(6) If the judge decides the question in subsection (5) in the affirmative he must give consent.

(7) If the judge decides that question in the negative he must refuse consent.

(8) Consent is not required to the person being dealt with in the territory for the offence if the person has been given an opportunity to leave the territory and—

(a) he has not done so before the end of the permitted period, or

(b) if he did so before the end of the permitted period, he has returned there.

(9) The permitted period is 45 days starting with the day on which the person arrived in the territory following his extradition there in accordance with this Part.

(10) Subject to subsection (8), the judge must decide whether consent is required to the person being dealt with in the territory for the offence by reference to what appears to him to be the law of the territory or arrangements made between the territory and the United Kingdom.

56. Request for consent to further extradition to category 1 territory   *Text: 14.3.1*

(1) This section applies if—

(a) a person is extradited to a category 1 territory (the requesting territory) in accordance with this Part;

(b) the appropriate judge receives a request for consent to the person's extradition to another category 1 territory for an offence;

(c) the request is certified under this section by the designated authority.

(2) The designated authority may certify a request for consent under this section if it believes that the authority making the request—

(a) is a judicial authority of the requesting territory, and

(b) has the function of making requests for the consent referred to in subsection (1)(b) in that territory.

(3) A certificate under subsection (2) must certify that the authority making the request falls within paragraphs (a) and (b) of that subsection.

(4) The judge must serve notice on the person that he has received the request for consent, unless he is satisfied that it would not be practicable to do so.

(5) The consent hearing must begin before the end of the required period, which is 21 days starting with the day on which the request for consent is received by the designated authority.

(6) The judge may extend the required period if he believes it to be in the interests of justice to do so; and this subsection may apply more than once.

(7) The power in subsection (6) may be exercised even after the end of the required period.

(8) If the consent hearing does not begin before the end of the required period and the judge does not exercise the power in subsection (6) to extend the period, he must refuse consent.

(9) The judge may at any time adjourn the consent hearing.

(10) The consent hearing is the hearing at which the judge is to consider the request for consent.

57. Questions for decision at consent hearing   *Text: 14.3.1*

(1) At the consent hearing under section 56 the judge must decide whether consent is required to the person's extradition to the other category 1 territory for the offence.

(2) If the judge decides the question in subsection (1) in the negative he must inform the authority making the request of his decision.

(3) If the judge decides that question in the affirmative he must decide whether the offence is an extradition offence in relation to the category 1 territory referred to in section 56(1)(b).

(4) If the judge decides the question in subsection (3) in the negative he must refuse consent.

(5) If the judge decides that question in the affirmative he must decide whether he would order the person's extradition under sections 11 to 25 if—

(a) the person were in the United Kingdom, and

(b) the judge were required to proceed under section 11 in respect of the offence for which consent is requested.

(6) If the judge decides the question in subsection (5) in the affirmative he must give consent.

(7) If the judge decides that question in the negative he must refuse consent.

(8) Consent is not required to the person's extradition to the other territory for the offence if the person has been given an opportunity to leave the requesting territory and—

(a) he has not done so before the end of the permitted period, or

(b) if he did so before the end of the permitted period, he has returned there.

(9) The permitted period is 45 days starting with the day on which the person arrived in the requesting territory following his extradition there in accordance with this Part.

(10) Subject to subsection (8), the judge must decide whether consent is required to the person's extradition to the other territory for the offence by reference to what appears to him to be the arrangements made between the requesting territory and the United Kingdom.

58. Consent to further extradition to category 2 territory   *Text: 14.3.2*

(1) This section applies if—

(a) a person is extradited to a category 1 territory (the requesting territory) in accordance with this Part;

(b) the Secretary of State receives a request for consent to the person's extradition to a category 2 territory for an offence;

(c) the request is certified under this section by the designated authority.

(2) The designated authority may certify a request for consent under this section if it believes that the authority making the request—

(a) is a judicial authority of the requesting territory, and

(b) has the function of making requests for the consent referred to in subsection (1)(b) in that territory.

(3) A certificate under subsection (2) must certify that the authority making the request falls within paragraphs (a) and (b) of that subsection.

(4) The Secretary of State must serve notice on the person that he has received the request for consent, unless he is satisfied that it would not be practicable to do so.

(5) The Secretary of State must decide whether the offence is an extradition offence within the meaning given by section 137 in relation to the category 2 territory.

(6) If the Secretary of State decides the question in subsection (5) in the negative he must refuse consent.

(7) If the Secretary of State decides that question in the affirmative he must decide whether the appropriate judge would send the case to him (for his decision whether the person was to be extradited) under sections 79 to 91 if—

(a) the person were in the United Kingdom, and

(b) the judge were required to proceed under section 79 in respect of the offence for which the Secretary of State's consent is requested.

(8) If the Secretary of State decides the question in subsection (7) in the negative he must refuse his consent.

(9) If the Secretary of State decides that question in the affirmative he must decide whether, if the person were in the United Kingdom, his extradition to the category 2 territory in respect of the offence would be prohibited under section 94, 95 or 96.

(10) If the Secretary of State decides the question in subsection (9) in the negative he may give consent.

(11) If the Secretary of State decides that question in the affirmative he must refuse consent.

(12) This section applies in relation to any function which falls under this section to be exercised in relation to Scotland only as if the references in this section to the Secretary of State were to the Scottish Ministers.

59. Return of person to serve remainder of sentence

(1) This section applies if—

(a) a person who is serving a sentence of imprisonment or another form of detention in the United Kingdom is extradited to a category 1 territory in accordance with this Part;

(b) the person is returned to the United Kingdom to serve the remainder of his sentence.

(2) The person is liable to be detained in pursuance of his sentence.

(3) If he is at large he must be treated as being unlawfully at large.

(4) Time during which the person was not in the United Kingdom as a result of his extradition does not count as time served by him as part of his sentence.

(5) But subsection (4) does not apply if—

(a) the person was extradited for the purpose of being prosecuted for an offence, and

(b) the person has not been convicted of the offence or of any other offence in respect of which he was permitted to be dealt with in the category 1 territory.

(6) In a case falling within subsection (5), time during which the person was not in the United Kingdom as a result of his extradition counts as time served by him as part of his sentence if (and only if) it was spent in custody in connection with the offence or any other offence in respect of which he was permitted to be dealt with in the territory.

Costs

60. Costs where extradition ordered
Text: 5.12

(1) This section applies if any of the following occurs in relation to a person in respect of whom a Part 1 warrant is issued—

(a) an order for the person's extradition is made under this Part;

(b) the High Court dismisses an appeal under section 26;

(c) the High Court or the House of Lords dismisses an application for leave to appeal to the House of Lords under section 32, if the application is made by the person;

(d) the House of Lords dismisses an appeal under section 32, if the appeal is brought by the person.

(2) In a case falling within subsection (1)(a), the appropriate judge may make such order as he considers just and reasonable with regard to the costs to be paid by the person.

(3) In a case falling within subsection (1)(b), (c) or (d), the court by which the application or appeal is dismissed may make such order as it considers just and reasonable with regard to the costs to be paid by the person.

(4) An order for costs under this section—

(a) must specify their amount;

(b) may name the person to whom they are to be paid.

61. Costs where discharge ordered
Text: 5.12

(1) This section applies if any of the following occurs in relation to a person in respect of whom a Part 1 warrant is issued—

(a) an order for the person's discharge is made under this Part;

(b) the person is taken to be discharged under this Part;

(c) the High Court dismisses an appeal under section 28;

(d) the High Court or the House of Lords dismisses an application for leave to appeal to the House of Lords under section 32, if the application is made by the authority which issued the warrant;

(e) the House of Lords dismisses an appeal under section 32, if the appeal is brought by the authority which issued the warrant.

(2) In a case falling within subsection (1)(a), an order under subsection (5) in favour of the person may be made by—

(a) the appropriate judge, if the order for the person's discharge is made by him;

(b) the High Court, if the order for the person's discharge is made by it;

(c) the House of Lords, if the order for the person's discharge is made by it.

(3) In a case falling within subsection (1)(b), the appropriate judge may make an order under subsection (5) in favour of the person.

(4) In a case falling within subsection (1)(c), (d) or (e), the court by which the application or appeal is dismissed may make an order under subsection (5) in favour of the person.

(5) An order under this subsection in favour of a person is an order for a payment of the appropriate amount to be made to the person out of money provided by Parliament.

(6) The appropriate amount is such amount as the judge or court making the order under subsection (5) considers reasonably sufficient to compensate the person in whose favour the order is made for any expenses properly incurred by him in the proceedings under this Part.

(7) But if the judge or court making an order under subsection (5) is of the opinion that there are circumstances which make it inappropriate that the person in whose favour the order is made should recover the full amount mentioned in subsection (6), the judge or court must—

(a) assess what amount would in his or its opinion be just and reasonable;

(b) specify that amount in the order as the appropriate amount.

(8) Unless subsection (7) applies, the appropriate amount—

(a) must be specified in the order, if the court considers it appropriate for it to be so specified and the person in whose favour the order is made agrees the amount;

(b) must be determined in accordance with regulations made by the Lord Chancellor for the purposes of this section, in any other case.

62. Costs where discharge ordered: supplementary

(1) In England and Wales, subsections (1) and (3) of section 20 of the Prosecution of Offences Act 1985 (c. 23) (regulations for carrying Part 2 of that Act into effect) apply in relation to section 61 as those subsections apply in relation to Part 2 of that Act.

(2) As so applied those subsections have effect as if an order under section 61(5) were an order under Part 2 of that Act for a payment to be made out of central funds.

(3) In Northern Ireland, section 7 of the Costs in Criminal Cases Act (Northern Ireland) 1968 (c.10) (rules relating to costs) applies in relation to section 61 as that section applies in relation to sections 2 to 5 of that Act.

Repatriation cases

63. Persons serving sentences outside territory where convicted

(1) This section applies if an arrest warrant is issued in respect of a person by an authority of a category 1 territory and the warrant contains the statement referred to in subsection (2).

(2) The statement is one that—

(a) the person is alleged to be unlawfully at large from a prison in one territory (the imprisoning territory) in which he was serving a sentence after conviction of an offence specified in the warrant by a court in another territory (the convicting territory), and

(b) the person was serving the sentence in pursuance of international arrangements for prisoners sentenced in one territory to be repatriated to another territory in order to serve their sentence, and

(c) the warrant is issued with a view to his arrest and extradition to the category 1 territory for the purpose of serving a sentence or another form of detention imposed in respect of the offence.

(3) If the category 1 territory is either the imprisoning territory or the convicting territory, section 2(2)(b) has effect as if the reference to the statement referred to in subsection (5) of that section were a reference to the statement referred to in subsection (2) of this section.

(4) If the category 1 territory is the imprisoning territory—

(a) section 2(6)(e) has effect as if "the category 1 territory" read "the convicting territory";

(b) section 10(2) has effect as if "an extradition offence" read "an extradition offence in relation to the convicting territory";

(c) section 20(5) has effect as if after "entitled" there were inserted "in the convicting territory";

(d) section 37(5) has effect as if "a category 1 territory" read "the convicting territory" and as if "the category 1 territory" in both places read "the convicting territory";

(e) section 52(4) has effect as if "a category 1 territory" read "the convicting territory" and as if "the category 1 territory" in both places read "the convicting territory";

(f) section 65(1) has effect as if "a category 1 territory" read "the convicting territory";

(g) section 65(2) has effect as if "the category 1 territory" in the opening words and paragraphs (a) and (c) read "the convicting territory" and as if "the category 1 territory" in paragraph (b) read "the imprisoning territory";

(h) in section 65, subsections (3), (4), (5), (6) and (8) have effect as if "the category 1 territory" in each place read "the convicting territory".

Interpretation

64. Extradition offences: person not sentenced for offence   *Text: 2.3.2.1; 2.3.2.2*

(1) This section applies in relation to conduct of a person if—

(a) he is accused in a category 1 territory of the commission of an offence constituted by the conduct, or

(b) he is alleged to be unlawfully at large after conviction by a court in a category 1 territory of an offence constituted by the conduct and he has not been sentenced for the offence.

(2) The conduct constitutes an extradition offence in relation to the category 1 territory if these conditions are satisfied—

(a) the conduct occurs in the category 1 territory and no part of it occurs in the United Kingdom;

(b) a certificate issued by an appropriate authority of the category 1 territory shows that the conduct falls within the European framework list;

(c) the certificate shows that the conduct is punishable under the law of the category 1 territory with imprisonment or another form of detention for a term of 3 years or a greater punishment.

(3) The conduct also constitutes an extradition offence in relation to the category 1 territory if these conditions are satisfied—

(a) the conduct occurs in the category 1 territory;

(b) the conduct would constitute an offence under the law of the relevant part of the United Kingdom if it occurred in that part of the United Kingdom;

(c) the conduct is punishable under the law of the category 1 territory with imprisonment or another form of detention for a term of 12 months or a greater punishment (however it is described in that law).

(4) The conduct also constitutes an extradition offence in relation to the category 1 territory if these conditions are satisfied—

(a) the conduct occurs outside the category 1 territory;

(b) the conduct is punishable under the law of the category 1 territory with imprisonment or another form of detention for a term of 12 months or a greater punishment (however it is described in that law);

(c) in corresponding circumstances equivalent conduct would constitute an extra-territorial offence under the law of the relevant part of the United Kingdom punishable with imprisonment or another form of detention for a term of 12 months or a greater punishment.

(5) The conduct also constitutes an extradition offence in relation to the category 1 territory if these conditions are satisfied—

(a) the conduct occurs outside the category 1 territory and no part of it occurs in the United Kingdom;

(b) the conduct would constitute an offence under the law of the relevant part of the United Kingdom punishable with imprisonment or another form of detention for a term of 12 months or a greater punishment if it occurred in that part of the United Kingdom;

(c) the conduct is so punishable under the law of the category 1 territory (however it is described in that law).

(6) The conduct also constitutes an extradition offence in relation to the category 1 territory if these conditions are satisfied—

(a) the conduct occurs outside the category 1 territory and no part of it occurs in the United Kingdom;

(b) the conduct is punishable under the law of the category 1 territory with imprisonment or another form of detention for a term of 12 months or a greater punishment (however it is described in that law);

(c) the conduct constitutes or if committed in the United Kingdom would constitute an offence mentioned in subsection (7).

(7) The offences are—

(a) an offence under section 51 or 58 of the International Criminal Court Act 2001 (c. 17) (genocide, crimes against humanity and war crimes);

(b) an offence under section 52 or 59 of that Act (conduct ancillary to genocide etc. committed outside the jurisdiction);

(c) an ancillary offence, as defined in section 55 or 62 of that Act, in relation to an offence falling within paragraph (a) or (b);

(d) an offence under section 1 of the International Criminal Court (Scotland) Act 2001 (asp 13) (genocide, crimes against humanity and war crimes);

(e) an offence under section 2 of that Act (conduct ancillary to genocide etc. committed outside the jurisdiction);

(f) an ancillary offence, as defined in section 7 of that Act, in relation to an offence falling within paragraph (d) or (e).

(8) For the purposes of subsections (3)(b), (4)(c) and (5)(b)—

(a) if the conduct relates to a tax or duty, it is immaterial that the law of the relevant part of the United Kingdom does not impose the same kind of tax or duty or does not contain rules of the same kind as those of the law of the category 1 territory;

(b) if the conduct relates to customs or exchange, it is immaterial that the law of the relevant part of the United Kingdom does not contain rules of the same kind as those of the law of the category 1 territory.

(9) This section applies for the purposes of this Part.

65. Extradition offences: person sentenced for offence   *Text: 2.3.2.3*

(1) This section applies in relation to conduct of a person if—

(a) he is alleged to be unlawfully at large after conviction by a court in a category 1 territory of an offence constituted by the conduct, and

(b) he has been sentenced for the offence.

(2) The conduct constitutes an extradition offence in relation to the category 1 territory if these conditions are satisfied—

(a) the conduct occurs in the category 1 territory and no part of it occurs in the United Kingdom;

(b) a certificate issued by an appropriate authority of the category 1 territory shows that the conduct falls within the European framework list;

(c) the certificate shows that a sentence of imprisonment or another form of detention for a term of 12 months or a greater punishment has been imposed in the category 1 territory in respect of the conduct.

(3) The conduct also constitutes an extradition offence in relation to the category 1 territory if these conditions are satisfied—

(a) the conduct occurs in the category 1 territory;

(b) the conduct would constitute an offence under the law of the relevant part of the United Kingdom if it occurred in that part of the United Kingdom;

(c) a sentence of imprisonment or another form of detention for a term of 4 months or a greater punishment has been imposed in the category 1 territory in respect of the conduct.

(4) The conduct also constitutes an extradition offence in relation to the category 1 territory if these conditions are satisfied—

(a) the conduct occurs outside the category 1 territory;

(b) a sentence of imprisonment or another form of detention for a term of 4 months or a greater punishment has been imposed in the category 1 territory in respect of the conduct;

(c) in corresponding circumstances equivalent conduct would constitute an extraterritorial offence under the law of the relevant part of the United Kingdom punishable with imprisonment or another form of detention for a term of 12 months or a greater punishment.

(5) The conduct also constitutes an extradition offence in relation to the category 1 territory if these conditions are satisfied—

(a) the conduct occurs outside the category 1 territory and no part of it occurs in the United Kingdom;

(b) the conduct would constitute an offence under the law of the relevant part of the United Kingdom punishable with imprisonment or another form of detention for a term of 12 months or a greater punishment if it occurred in that part of the United Kingdom;

(c) a sentence of imprisonment or another form of detention for a term of 4 months or a greater punishment has been imposed in the category 1 territory in respect of the conduct.

(6) The conduct also constitutes an extradition offence in relation to the category 1 territory if these conditions are satisfied—

(a) the conduct occurs outside the category 1 territory and no part of it occurs in the United Kingdom;

(b) a sentence of imprisonment or another form of detention for a term of 4 months or a greater punishment has been imposed in the category 1 territory in respect of the conduct;

(c) the conduct constitutes or if committed in the United Kingdom would constitute an offence mentioned in subsection (7).

(7) The offences are—

(a) an offence under section 51 or 58 of the International Criminal Court Act 2001 (c. 17) (genocide, crimes against humanity and war crimes);

(b) an offence under section 52 or 59 of that Act (conduct ancillary to genocide etc. committed outside the jurisdiction);

(c) an ancillary offence, as defined in section 55 or 62 of that Act, in relation to an offence falling within paragraph (a) or (b);

(d) an offence under section 1 of the International Criminal Court (Scotland) Act 2001 (asp 13) (genocide, crimes against humanity and war crimes);

(e) an offence under section 2 of that Act (conduct ancillary to genocide etc. committed outside the jurisdiction);

(f) an ancillary offence, as defined in section 7 of that Act, in relation to an offence falling within paragraph (d) or (e).

(8) For the purposes of subsections (3)(b), (4)(c) and (5)(b)—

(a) if the conduct relates to a tax or duty, it is immaterial that the law of the relevant part of the United Kingdom does not impose the same kind of tax or duty or does not contain rules of the same kind as those of the law of the category 1 territory;

(b) if the conduct relates to customs or exchange, it is immaterial that the law of the relevant part of the United Kingdom does not contain rules of the same kind as those of the law of the category 1 territory.

(9) This section applies for the purposes of this Part.

66. Extradition offences: supplementary

Text: 2.3.2.1

(1) Subsections (2) to (4) apply for the purposes of sections 64 and 65.

(2) An appropriate authority of a category 1 territory is a judicial authority of the territory which the appropriate judge believes has the function of issuing arrest warrants in that territory.

(3) The law of a territory is the general criminal law of the territory.

(4) The relevant part of the United Kingdom is the part of the United Kingdom in which the relevant proceedings are taking place.

(5) The relevant proceedings are the proceedings in which it is necessary to decide whether conduct constitutes an extradition offence.

67. The appropriate judge

(1) The appropriate judge is—

(a) in England and Wales, a District Judge (Magistrates' Courts) designated for the purposes of this Part by the Lord Chancellor;

(b) in Scotland, the sheriff of Lothian and Borders;

(c) in Northern Ireland, such county court judge or resident magistrate as is designated for the purposes of this Part by the Lord Chancellor.

(2) A designation under subsection (1) may be made for all cases or for such cases (or cases of such description) as the designation stipulates.

(3) More than one designation may be made under subsection (1).

(4) This section applies for the purposes of this Part.

68. The extradition hearing

(1) The extradition hearing is the hearing at which the appropriate judge is to decide whether a person in respect of whom a Part 1 warrant was issued is to be extradited to the category 1 territory in which it was issued.

(2) This section applies for the purposes of this Part.

PART 2
EXTRADITION TO CATEGORY 2 TERRITORIES

Introduction

69. Extradition to category 2 territories *Text: 3.1.3*

(1) This Part deals with extradition from the United Kingdom to the territories designated for the purposes of this Part by order made by the Secretary of State.

(2) In this Act references to category 2 territories are to the territories designated for the purposes of this Part.

70. Extradition request and certificate *Text: 4.2.3.1; 6.6.1*

(1) The Secretary of State must issue a certificate under this section if he receives a valid request for the extradition to a category 2 territory of a person who is in the United Kingdom.

(2) But subsection (1) does not apply if the Secretary of State decides under section 126 that the request is not to be proceeded with.

(3) A request for a person's extradition is valid if—

(a) it contains the statement referred to in subsection (4), and

(b) it is made in the approved way.

(4) The statement is one that the person—

(a) is accused in the category 2 territory of the commission of an offence specified in the request, or

(b) is alleged to be unlawfully at large after conviction by a court in the category 2 territory of an offence specified in the request.

(5) A request for extradition to a category 2 territory which is a British overseas territory is made in the approved way if it is made by or on behalf of the person administering the territory.

(6) A request for extradition to a category 2 territory which is the Hong Kong Special Administrative Region of the People's Republic of China is made in the approved way if it is made by or on behalf of the government of the Region.

(7) A request for extradition to any other category 2 territory is made in the approved way if it is made—

(a) by an authority of the territory which the Secretary of State believes has the function of making requests for extradition in that territory, or

(b) by a person recognised by the Secretary of State as a diplomatic or consular representative of the territory.

(8) A certificate under this section must certify that the request is made in the approved way.

(9) If a certificate is issued under this section the Secretary of State must send these documents to the appropriate judge—

(a) the request;

(b) the certificate;

(c) a copy of any relevant Order in Council.

Arrest

71. Arrest warrant following extradition request   *Text: 4.2.3.1*

(1) This section applies if the Secretary of State sends documents to the appropriate judge under section 70.

(2) The judge may issue a warrant for the arrest of the person whose extradition is requested if the judge has reasonable grounds for believing that—

(a) the offence in respect of which extradition is requested is an extradition offence, and

(b) there is evidence falling within subsection (3).

(3) The evidence is—

(a) evidence that would justify the issue of a warrant for the arrest of a person accused of the offence within the judge's jurisdiction, if the person whose extradition is requested is accused of the commission of the offence;

(b) evidence that would justify the issue of a warrant for the arrest of a person unlawfully at large after conviction of the offence within the judge's jurisdiction, if the person whose extradition is requested is alleged to be unlawfully at large after conviction of the offence.

(4) But if the category 2 territory to which extradition is requested is designated for the purposes of this section by order made by the Secretary of State, subsections (2) and (3) have effect as if "evidence" read "information".

(5) A warrant issued under this section may—

(a) be executed by any person to whom it is directed or by any constable or customs officer;

(b) be executed even if neither the warrant nor a copy of it is in the possession of the person executing it at the time of the arrest.

(6) If a warrant issued under this section in respect of a person is directed to a service policeman, it may be executed in any place where the service policeman would have power to arrest the person under the appropriate service law if the person had committed an offence under that law.

(7) In any other case, a warrant issued under this section may be executed in any part of the United Kingdom.

(8) The appropriate service law is—

(a) the Army Act 1955 (3 & 4 Eliz. 2 c. 18), if the person in respect of whom the warrant is issued is subject to military law;

(b) the Air Force Act 1955 (3 & 4 Eliz. 2 c. 19), if that person is subject to air-force law;

(c) the Naval Discipline Act 1957 (c. 53), if that person is subject to that Act.

72. Person arrested under section 71   *Text: 4.2.3.2*

(1) This section applies if a person is arrested under a warrant issued under section 71.

(2) A copy of the warrant must be given to the person as soon as practicable after his arrest.

(3) The person must be brought as soon as practicable before the appropriate judge.

(4) But subsection (3) does not apply if—

(a) the person is granted bail by a constable following his arrest, or

(b) the Secretary of State decides under section 126 that the request for the person's extradition is not to be proceeded with.

(5) If subsection (2) is not complied with and the person applies to the judge to be discharged, the judge may order his discharge.

(6) If subsection (3) is not complied with and the person applies to the judge to be discharged, the judge must order his discharge.

(7) When the person first appears or is brought before the appropriate judge, the judge must—

(a) inform him of the contents of the request for his extradition;

(b) give him the required information about consent;

(c) remand him in custody or on bail.

(8) The required information about consent is—

(a) that the person may consent to his extradition to the category 2 territory to which his extradition is requested;

(b) an explanation of the effect of consent and the procedure that will apply if he gives consent;

(c) that consent must be given in writing and is irrevocable.

(9) If the judge remands the person in custody he may later grant bail.

(10) Subsection (4)(a) applies to Scotland with the omission of the words "by a constable".

73. Provisional warrant

Text: 4.2.3.3

(1) This section applies if a justice of the peace is satisfied on information in writing and on oath that a person within subsection (2)—

(a) is or is believed to be in the United Kingdom, or

(b) is or is believed to be on his way to the United Kingdom.

(2) A person is within this subsection if—

(a) he is accused in a category 2 territory of the commission of an offence, or

(b) he is alleged to be unlawfully at large after conviction of an offence by a court in a category 2 territory.

(3) The justice may issue a warrant for the arrest of the person (a provisional warrant) if he has reasonable grounds for believing that—

(a) the offence of which the person is accused or has been convicted is an extradition offence, and

(b) there is written evidence falling within subsection (4).

(4) The evidence is—

(a) evidence that would justify the issue of a warrant for the arrest of a person accused of the offence within the justice's jurisdiction, if the person in respect of whom the warrant is sought is accused of the commission of the offence;

(b) evidence that would justify the issue of a warrant for the arrest of a person unlawfully at large after conviction of the offence within the justice's jurisdiction, if the person in respect of whom the warrant is sought is alleged to be unlawfully at large after conviction of the offence.

(5) But if the category 2 territory is designated for the purposes of this section by order made by the Secretary of State, subsections (3) and (4) have effect as if "evidence" read "information".

(6) A provisional warrant may—

(a) be executed by any person to whom it is directed or by any constable or customs officer;

(b) be executed even if neither the warrant nor a copy of it is in the possession of the person executing it at the time of the arrest.

(7) If a warrant issued under this section in respect of a person is directed to a service policeman, it may be executed in any place where the service policeman would have power to arrest the person under the appropriate service law if the person had committed an offence under that law.

(8) In any other case, a warrant issued under this section may be executed in any part of the United Kingdom.

(9) The appropriate service law is—

(a) the Army Act 1955 (3 & 4 Eliz. 2 c. 18), if the person in respect of whom the warrant is issued is subject to military law;

(b) the Air Force Act 1955 (3 & 4 Eliz. 2 c. 19), if that person is subject to air-force law;

(c) the Naval Discipline Act 1957 (c. 53), if that person is subject to that Act.

(10) The preceding provisions of this section apply to Scotland with these modifications—

(a) in subsection (1) for "justice of the peace is satisfied on information in writing and on oath" substitute "sheriff is satisfied, on an application by a procurator fiscal,";

(b) in subsection (3) for "justice" substitute "sheriff";

(c) in subsection (4) for "justice's", in paragraphs (a) and (b), substitute "sheriff's".

(11) Subsection (1) applies to Northern Ireland with the substitution of "a complaint" for "information".

74. Person arrested under provisional warrant   *Text: 4.2.3.3; 4.7.2.1*

(1) This section applies if a person is arrested under a provisional warrant.

(2) A copy of the warrant must be given to the person as soon as practicable after his arrest.

(3) The person must be brought as soon as practicable before the appropriate judge.

(4) But subsection (3) does not apply if—

(a) the person is granted bail by a constable following his arrest, or

(b) in a case where the Secretary of State has received a valid request for the person's extradition, the Secretary of State decides under section 126 that the request is not to be proceeded with.

(5) If subsection (2) is not complied with and the person applies to the judge to be discharged, the judge may order his discharge.

(6) If subsection (3) is not complied with and the person applies to the judge to be discharged, the judge must order his discharge.

(7) When the person first appears or is brought before the appropriate judge, the judge must—

(a) inform him that he is accused of the commission of an offence in a category 2 territory or that he is alleged to be unlawfully at large after conviction of an offence by a court in a category 2 territory;

(b) give him the required information about consent;

(c) remand him in custody or on bail.

(8) The required information about consent is—

(a) that the person may consent to his extradition to the category 2 territory in which he is accused of the commission of an offence or is alleged to have been convicted of an offence;

(b) an explanation of the effect of consent and the procedure that will apply if he gives consent;

(c) that consent must be given in writing and is irrevocable.

(9) If the judge remands the person in custody he may later grant bail.

(10) The judge must order the person's discharge if the documents referred to in section 70(9) are not received by the judge within the required period.

(11) The required period is—

(a) 45 days starting with the day on which the person was arrested, or

(b) if the category 2 territory is designated by order made by the Secretary of State for the purposes of this section, any longer period permitted by the order.

(12) Subsection (4)(a) applies to Scotland with the omission of the words "by a constable".

The extradition hearing

75. Date of extradition hearing: arrest under section 71   *Text: 6.2*

(1) When a person arrested under a warrant issued under section 71 first appears or is brought before the appropriate judge, the judge must fix a date on which the extradition hearing is to begin.

(2) The date fixed under subsection (1) must not be later than the end of the permitted period, which is 2 months starting with the date on which the person first appears or is brought before the judge.

(3) If before the date fixed under subsection (1) (or this subsection) a party to the proceedings applies to the judge for a later date to be fixed and the judge believes it to be in the interests of justice to do so, he may fix a later date; and this subsection may apply more than once.

(4) If the extradition hearing does not begin on or before the date fixed under this section and the person applies to the judge to be discharged, the judge must order his discharge.

76. Date of extradition hearing: arrest under provisional warrant   *Text: 6.2*

(1) Subsection (2) applies if—

(a) a person is arrested under a provisional warrant, and

(b) the documents referred to in section 70(9) are received by the appropriate judge within the period required under section 74(10).

(2) The judge must fix a date on which the extradition hearing is to begin.

(3) The date fixed under subsection (2) must not be later than the end of the permitted period, which is 2 months starting with the date on which the judge receives the documents.

(4) If before the date fixed under subsection (2) (or this subsection) a party to the proceedings applies to the judge for a later date to be fixed and the judge believes it to be in the interests of justice to do so, he may fix a later date; and this subsection may apply more than once.

(5) If the extradition hearing does not begin on or before the date fixed under this section and the person applies to the judge to be discharged, the judge must order his discharge.

77. Judge's powers at extradition hearing   *Text: 6.3*

(1) In England and Wales, at the extradition hearing the appropriate judge has the same powers (as nearly as may be) as a magistrates' court would have if the proceedings were the summary trial of an information against the person whose extradition is requested.

(2) In Scotland—

(a) at the extradition hearing the appropriate judge has the same powers (as nearly as may be) as if the proceedings were summary proceedings in respect of an offence alleged to have been committed by the person whose extradition is requested; but

(b) in his making any decision under section 78(4)(a) evidence from a single source shall be sufficient.

(3) In Northern Ireland, at the extradition hearing the appropriate judge has the same powers (as nearly as may be) as a magistrates' court would have if the proceedings were the hearing and determination of a complaint against the person whose extradition is requested.

(4) If the judge adjourns the extradition hearing he must remand the person in custody or on bail.

(5) If the judge remands the person in custody he may later grant bail.

78. Initial stages of extradition hearing   *Text: 6.6; 6.8*

(1) This section applies if a person alleged to be the person whose extradition is requested appears or is brought before the appropriate judge for the extradition hearing.

(2) The judge must decide whether the documents sent to him by the Secretary of State consist of (or include)—

(a) the documents referred to in section 70(9);

(b) particulars of the person whose extradition is requested;

(c) particulars of the offence specified in the request;

(d) in the case of a person accused of an offence, a warrant for his arrest issued in the category 2 territory;

(e) in the case of a person alleged to be unlawfully at large after conviction of an offence, a certificate issued in the category 2 territory of the conviction and (if he has been sentenced) of the sentence.

(3) If the judge decides the question in subsection (2) in the negative he must order the person's discharge.

(4) If the judge decides that question in the affirmative he must decide whether—

(a) the person appearing or brought before him is the person whose extradition is requested;

(b) the offence specified in the request is an extradition offence;

(c) copies of the documents sent to the judge by the Secretary of State have been served on the person.

(5) The judge must decide the question in subsection (4)(a) on a balance of probabilities.

(6) If the judge decides any of the questions in subsection (4) in the negative he must order the person's discharge.

(7) If the judge decides those questions in the affirmative he must proceed under section 79.

(8) The reference in subsection (2)(d) to a warrant for a person's arrest includes a reference to a judicial document authorising his arrest.

79. Bars to extradition
Text: 6.9

(1) If the judge is required to proceed under this section he must decide whether the person's extradition to the category 2 territory is barred by reason of—

(a) the rule against double jeopardy;

(b) extraneous considerations;

(c) the passage of time;

(d) hostage-taking considerations.

(2) Sections 80 to 83 apply for the interpretation of subsection (1).

(3) If the judge decides any of the questions in subsection (1) in the affirmative he must order the person's discharge.

(4) If the judge decides those questions in the negative and the person is accused of the commission of the extradition offence but is not alleged to be unlawfully at large after conviction of it, the judge must proceed under section 84.

(5) If the judge decides those questions in the negative and the person is alleged to be unlawfully at large after conviction of the extradition offence, the judge must proceed under section 85.

80. Rule against double jeopardy
Text: 6.9.1

A person's extradition to a category 2 territory is barred by reason of the rule against double jeopardy if (and only if) it appears that he would be entitled to be discharged under any rule of law relating to previous acquittal or conviction if he were charged with the extradition offence in the part of the United Kingdom where the judge exercises his jurisdiction.

81. Extraneous considerations *Text: 6.9.2*

A person's extradition to a category 2 territory is barred by reason of extraneous considerations if (and only if) it appears that—

(a) the request for his extradition (though purporting to be made on account of the extradition offence) is in fact made for the purpose of prosecuting or punishing him on account of his race, religion, nationality, gender, sexual orientation or political opinions, or

(b) if extradited he might be prejudiced at his trial or punished, detained or restricted in his personal liberty by reason of his race, religion, nationality, gender, sexual orientation or political opinions.

82. Passage of time *Text: 6.9.3*

A person's extradition to a category 2 territory is barred by reason of the passage of time if (and only if) it appears that it would be unjust or oppressive to extradite him by reason of the passage of time since he is alleged to have committed the extradition offence or since he is alleged to have become unlawfully at large (as the case may be).

83. Hostage-taking considerations *Text: 6.9.4*

(1) A person's extradition to a category 2 territory is barred by reason of hostage-taking considerations if (and only if) the territory is a party to the Hostage-taking Convention and it appears that—

(a) if extradited he might be prejudiced at his trial because communication between him and the appropriate authorities would not be possible, and

(b) the act or omission constituting the extradition offence also constitutes an offence under section 1 of the Taking of Hostages Act 1982 (c. 28) or an attempt to commit such an offence.

(2) The appropriate authorities are the authorities of the territory which are entitled to exercise rights of protection in relation to him.

(3) A certificate issued by the Secretary of State that a territory is a party to the Hostage-taking Convention is conclusive evidence of that fact for the purposes of subsection (1).

(4) The Hostage-taking Convention is the International Convention against the Taking of Hostages opened for signature at New York on 18 December 1979.

84. Case where person has not been convicted *Text: 6.10*

(1) If the judge is required to proceed under this section he must decide whether there is evidence which would be sufficient to make a case requiring an answer by the person if the proceedings were the summary trial of an information against him.

(2) In deciding the question in subsection (1) the judge may treat a statement made by a person in a document as admissible evidence of a fact if—

(a) the statement is made by the person to a police officer or another person charged with the duty of investigating offences or charging offenders, and

(b) direct oral evidence by the person of the fact would be admissible.

(3) In deciding whether to treat a statement made by a person in a document as admissible evidence of a fact, the judge must in particular have regard—

(a) to the nature and source of the document;

(b) to whether or not, having regard to the nature and source of the document and to any other circumstances that appear to the judge to be relevant, it is likely that the document is authentic;

(c) to the extent to which the statement appears to supply evidence which would not be readily available if the statement were not treated as being admissible evidence of the fact;

(d) to the relevance of the evidence that the statement appears to supply to any issue likely to have to be determined by the judge in deciding the question in subsection (1);

(e) to any risk that the admission or exclusion of the statement will result in unfairness to the person whose extradition is sought, having regard in particular to whether it is likely to be possible to controvert the statement if the person making it does not attend to give oral evidence in the proceedings.

(4) A summary in a document of a statement made by a person must be treated as a statement made by the person in the document for the purposes of subsection (2).

(5) If the judge decides the question in subsection (1) in the negative he must order the person's discharge.

(6) If the judge decides that question in the affirmative he must proceed under section 87.

(7) If the judge is required to proceed under this section and the category 2 territory to which extradition is requested is designated for the purposes of this section by order made by the Secretary of State—

(a) the judge must not decide under subsection (1), and

(b) he must proceed under section 87.

(8) Subsection (1) applies to Scotland with the substitution of "summary proceedings in respect of an offence alleged to have been committed by the person (except that for this purpose evidence from a single source shall be sufficient)" for "the summary trial of an information against him".

(9) Subsection (1) applies to Northern Ireland with the substitution of "the hearing and determination of a complaint" for "the summary trial of an information".

85. Case where person has been convicted   *Text: 6.11*

(1) If the judge is required to proceed under this section he must decide whether the person was convicted in his presence.

(2) If the judge decides the question in subsection (1) in the affirmative he must proceed under section 87.

(3) If the judge decides that question in the negative he must decide whether the person deliberately absented himself from his trial.

(4) If the judge decides the question in subsection (3) in the affirmative he must proceed under section 87.

(5) If the judge decides that question in the negative he must decide whether the person would be entitled to a retrial or (on appeal) to a review amounting to a retrial.

(6) If the judge decides the question in subsection (5) in the affirmative he must proceed under section 86.

(7) If the judge decides that question in the negative he must order the person's discharge.

(8) The judge must not decide the question in subsection (5) in the affirmative unless, in any proceedings that it is alleged would constitute a retrial or a review amounting to a retrial, the person would have these rights—

(a) the right to defend himself in person or through legal assistance of his own choosing or, if he had not sufficient means to pay for legal assistance, to be given it free when the interests of justice so required;

(b) the right to examine or have examined witnesses against him and to obtain the attendance and examination of witnesses on his behalf under the same conditions as witnesses against him.

86. Conviction in person's absence *Text: 6.10*

(1) If the judge is required to proceed under this section he must decide whether there is evidence which would be sufficient to make a case requiring an answer by the person if the proceedings were the summary trial of an information against him.

(2) In deciding the question in subsection (1) the judge may treat a statement made by a person in a document as admissible evidence of a fact if—

(a) the statement is made by the person to a police officer or another person charged with the duty of investigating offences or charging offenders, and

(b) direct oral evidence by the person of the fact would be admissible.

(3) In deciding whether to treat a statement made by a person in a document as admissible evidence of a fact, the judge must in particular have regard—

(a) to the nature and source of the document;

(b) to whether or not, having regard to the nature and source of the document and to any other circumstances that appear to the judge to be relevant, it is likely that the document is authentic;

(c) to the extent to which the statement appears to supply evidence which would not be readily available if the statement were not treated as being admissible evidence of the fact;

(d) to the relevance of the evidence that the statement appears to supply to any issue likely to have to be determined by the judge in deciding the question in subsection (1);

(e) to any risk that the admission or exclusion of the statement will result in unfairness to the person whose extradition is sought, having regard in particular to whether it is likely to be possible to controvert the statement if the person making it does not attend to give oral evidence in the proceedings.

(4) A summary in a document of a statement made by a person must be treated as a statement made by the person in the document for the purposes of subsection (2).

(5) If the judge decides the question in subsection (1) in the negative he must order the person's discharge.

(6) If the judge decides that question in the affirmative he must proceed under section 87.

(7) If the judge is required to proceed under this section and the category 2 territory to which extradition is requested is designated for the purposes of this section by order made by the Secretary of State—

(a) the judge must not decide under subsection (1), and

(b) he must proceed under section 87.

(8) Subsection (1) applies to Scotland with the substitution of "summary proceedings in respect of an offence alleged to have been committed by the person (except that for this purpose evidence from a single source shall be sufficient)" for "the summary trial of an information against him".

(9) Subsection (1) applies to Northern Ireland with the substitution of "the hearing and determination of a complaint" for "the summary trial of an information".

87. Human rights
Text: 6.12; Chapter 7

(1) If the judge is required to proceed under this section (by virtue of section 84, 85 or 86) he must decide whether the person's extradition would be compatible with the Convention rights within the meaning of the Human Rights Act 1998 (c. 42).

(2) If the judge decides the question in subsection (1) in the negative he must order the person's discharge.

(3) If the judge decides that question in the affirmative he must send the case to the Secretary of State for his decision whether the person is to be extradited.

88. Person charged with offence in United Kingdom
Text: 6.14.1

(1) This section applies if at any time in the extradition hearing the judge is informed that the person is charged with an offence in the United Kingdom.

(2) The judge must adjourn the extradition hearing until one of these occurs—

(a) the charge is disposed of;

(b) the charge is withdrawn;

(c) proceedings in respect of the charge are discontinued;

(d) an order is made for the charge to lie on the file, or in relation to Scotland, the diet is deserted *pro loco et tempore*.

(3) If a sentence of imprisonment or another form of detention is imposed in respect of the offence charged, the judge may adjourn the extradition hearing until the sentence has been served.

(4) If before he adjourns the extradition hearing under subsection (2) the judge has decided under section 79 whether the person's extradition is barred by reason of the rule against double jeopardy, the judge must decide that question again after the resumption of the hearing.

89. Person serving sentence in United Kingdom
Text: 6.14.2

(1) This section applies if at any time in the extradition hearing the judge is informed that the person is serving a sentence of imprisonment or another form of detention in the United Kingdom.

(2) The judge may adjourn the extradition hearing until the sentence has been served.

90. Competing extradition claim *Text: 6.14.3*

(1) This section applies if at any time in the extradition hearing the judge is informed that the conditions in subsection (2) or (3) are met.

(2) The conditions are that—

(a) the Secretary of State has received another valid request for the person's extradition to a category 2 territory;

(b) the other request has not been disposed of;

(c) the Secretary of State has made an order under section 126(2) for further proceedings on the request under consideration to be deferred until the other request has been disposed of.

(3) The conditions are that—

(a) a certificate has been issued under section 2 in respect of a Part 1 warrant issued in respect of the person;

(b) the warrant has not been disposed of;

(c) the Secretary of State has made an order under section 179(2) for further proceedings on the request to be deferred until the warrant has been disposed of.

(4) The judge must remand the person in custody or on bail.

(5) If the judge remands the person in custody he may later grant bail.

91. Physical or mental condition *Text: 16.13.1*

(1) This section applies if at any time in the extradition hearing it appears to the judge that the condition in subsection (2) is satisfied.

(2) The condition is that the physical or mental condition of the person is such that it would be unjust or oppressive to extradite him.

(3) The judge must—

(a) order the person's discharge, or

(b) adjourn the extradition hearing until it appears to him that the condition in subsection (2) is no longer satisfied.

92. Case sent to Secretary of State

(1) This section applies if the appropriate judge sends a case to the Secretary of State under this Part for his decision whether a person is to be extradited.

(2) The judge must inform the person in ordinary language that—

(a) he has a right to appeal to the High Court;

(b) if he exercises the right the appeal will not be heard until the Secretary of State has made his decision.

(3) But subsection (2) does not apply if the person has consented to his extradition under section 127.

(4) The judge must remand the person in custody or on bail—

(a) to wait for the Secretary of State's decision, and

(b) to wait for his extradition to the territory to which extradition is requested (if the Secretary of State orders him to be extradited).

(5) If the judge remands the person in custody he may later grant bail.

Secretary of State's functions

93. Secretary of State's consideration of case *Text: 8.2*

(1) This section applies if the appropriate judge sends a case to the Secretary of State under this Part for his decision whether a person is to be extradited.

(2) The Secretary of State must decide whether he is prohibited from ordering the person's extradition under any of these sections—

(a) section 94 (death penalty);

(b) section 95 (speciality);

(c) section 96 (earlier extradition to United Kingdom from other territory).

(3) If the Secretary of State decides any of the questions in subsection (2) in the affirmative he must order the person's discharge.

(4) If the Secretary of State decides those questions in the negative he must order the person to be extradited to the territory to which his extradition is requested unless—

(a) he is informed that the request has been withdrawn,

(b) he makes an order under section 126(2) or 179(2) for further proceedings on the request to be deferred and the person is discharged under section 180, or

(c) he orders the person's discharge under section 208.

(5) In deciding the questions in subsection (2), the Secretary of State is not required to consider any representations received by him after the end of the permitted period.

(6) The permitted period is the period of 6 weeks starting with the appropriate day.

94. Death penalty *Text: 7.3.7; 8.2.2*

(1) The Secretary of State must not order a person's extradition to a category 2 territory if he could be, will be or has been sentenced to death for the offence concerned in the category 2 territory.

(2) Subsection (1) does not apply if the Secretary of State receives a written assurance which he considers adequate that a sentence of death—

(a) will not be imposed, or

(b) will not be carried out (if imposed).

95. Speciality *Text: 8.2.3*

(1) The Secretary of State must not order a person's extradition to a category 2 territory if there are no speciality arrangements with the category 2 territory.

(2) But subsection (1) does not apply if the person consented to his extradition under section 127 before his case was sent to the Secretary of State.

(3) There are speciality arrangements with a category 2 territory if (and only if) under the law of that territory or arrangements made between it and the United Kingdom a person

who is extradited to the territory from the United Kingdom may be dealt with in the territory for an offence committed before his extradition only if—

(a) the offence is one falling within subsection (4), or

(b) he is first given an opportunity to leave the territory.

(4) The offences are—

(a) the offence in respect of which the person is extradited;

(b) an extradition offence disclosed by the same facts as that offence, other than one in respect of which a sentence of death could be imposed;

(c) an extradition offence in respect of which the Secretary of State consents to the person being dealt with;

(d) an offence in respect of which the person waives the right that he would have (but for this paragraph) not to be dealt with for the offence.

(5) Arrangements made with a category 2 territory which is a Commonwealth country or a British overseas territory may be made for a particular case or more generally.

(6) A certificate issued by or under the authority of the Secretary of State confirming the existence of arrangements with a category 2 territory which is a Commonwealth country or a British overseas territory and stating the terms of the arrangements is conclusive evidence of those matters.

96. Earlier extradition to United Kingdom from other territory   *Text: 8.2.4*

The Secretary of State must not order a person's extradition to a category 2 territory if—

(a) the person was extradited to the United Kingdom from another territory (the extraditing territory);

(b) under arrangements between the United Kingdom and the extraditing territory, that territory's consent is required to the person's extradition from the United Kingdom to the category 2 territory in respect of the extradition offence under consideration;

(c) that consent has not been given on behalf of the extraditing territory.

97. Deferral: person charged with offence in United Kingdom

(1) This section applies if—

(a) the appropriate judge sends a case to the Secretary of State under this Part for his decision whether a person is to be extradited;

(b) the person is charged with an offence in the United Kingdom.

(2) The Secretary of State must not make a decision with regard to the person's extradition until one of these occurs—

(a) the charge is disposed of;

(b) the charge is withdrawn;

(c) proceedings in respect of the charge are discontinued;

(d) an order is made for the charge to lie on the file or, in relation to Scotland, the diet is deserted *pro loco et tempore*.

(3) If a sentence of imprisonment or another form of detention is imposed in respect of the offence charged, the Secretary of State may defer making a decision with regard to the person's extradition until the sentence has been served.

98. Deferral: person serving sentence in United Kingdom

(1) This section applies if—

(a) the appropriate judge sends a case to the Secretary of State under this Part for his decision whether a person is to be extradited;

(b) the person is serving a sentence of imprisonment or another form of detention in the United Kingdom.

(2) The Secretary of State may defer making a decision with regard to the person's extradition until the sentence has been served.

99. Time limit for order for extradition or discharge *Text: 8.3.2*

(1) This section applies if—

(a) the appropriate judge sends a case to the Secretary of State under this Part for his decision whether a person is to be extradited;

(b) within the required period the Secretary of State does not make an order for the person's extradition or discharge.

(2) If the person applies to the High Court to be discharged, the court must order his discharge.

(3) The required period is the period of 2 months starting with the appropriate day.

(4) If before the required period ends the Secretary of State applies to the High Court for it to be extended the High Court may make an order accordingly; and this subsection may apply more than once.

100. Information *Text: 8.3.1*

(1) If the Secretary of State orders a person's extradition under this Part he must—

(a) inform the person of the order;

(b) inform him in ordinary language that he has a right of appeal to the High Court;

(c) inform a person acting on behalf of the category 2 territory of the order.

(2) But subsection (1)(b) does not apply if the person has consented to his extradition under section 127.

(3) If the Secretary of State orders a person's extradition under this Part and he has received an assurance such as is mentioned in section 94(2), he must give the person a copy of the assurance when he informs him under subsection (1) of the order.

(4) If the Secretary of State orders a person's discharge under this Part he must—

(a) inform him of the order;

(b) inform a person acting on behalf of the category 2 territory of the order.

101. Making of order for extradition or discharge *Text: 8.3.1*

(1) An order to which this section applies must be made under the hand of one of these—

(a) the Secretary of State;

(b) a Minister of State;

(c) a Parliamentary Under-Secretary of State;

(d) a senior official.

(2) But, in relation to Scotland, an order to which this section applies must be made under the hand of one of these—

(a) a member of the Scottish Executive or a junior Scottish Minister;

(b) a senior official who is a member of the staff of the Scottish Administration.

(3) This section applies to—

(a) an order under section 93 for a person's extradition;

(b) an order under section 93 or 123 for a person's discharge.

(4) A senior official is—

(a) a member of the Senior Civil Service;

(b) a member of the Senior Management Structure of Her Majesty's Diplomatic Service.

(5) If it appears to the Secretary of State that it is necessary to do so in consequence of any changes to the structure or grading of the home civil service or diplomatic service, he may by order make such amendments to subsection (4) as appear to him appropriate to preserve (so far as practicable) the effect of that subsection.

102. The appropriate day
Text: 8.3.2

(1) This section applies for the purposes of sections 93 and 99 if the appropriate judge sends a case to the Secretary of State under this Part for his decision whether a person is to be extradited.

(2) If the person is charged with an offence in the United Kingdom, the appropriate day is the day on which one of these occurs—

(a) the charge is disposed of;

(b) the charge is withdrawn;

(c) proceedings in respect of the charge are discontinued;

(d) an order is made for the charge to lie on the file, or in relation to Scotland, the diet is deserted *pro loco et tempore*.

(3) If under section 97(3) or 98(2) the Secretary of State defers making a decision until the person has served a sentence, the appropriate day is the day on which the person finishes serving the sentence.

(4) If section 126 applies in relation to the request for the person's extradition (the request concerned) the appropriate day is—

(a) the day on which the Secretary of State makes an order under that section, if the order is for proceedings on the other request to be deferred;

(b) the day on which an order under section 180 is made, if the order under section 126 is for proceedings on the request concerned to be deferred and the order under section 180 is for the proceedings to be resumed.

(5) If section 179 applies in relation to the request for the person's extradition, the appropriate day is—

(a) the day on which the Secretary of State makes an order under that section, if the order is for proceedings on the warrant to be deferred;

(b) the day on which an order under section 180 is made, if the order under section 179 is for proceedings on the request to be deferred and the order under section 180 is for the proceedings to be resumed.

(6) If more than one of subsections (2) to (5) applies, the appropriate day is the latest of the days found under the subsections which apply.

(7) In any other case, the appropriate day is the day on which the judge sends the case to the Secretary of State for his decision whether the person is to be extradited.

Appeals

103. Appeal where case sent to Secretary of State   *Text: 9.3.1*

(1) If the judge sends a case to the Secretary of State under this Part for his decision whether a person is to be extradited, the person may appeal to the High Court against the relevant decision.

(2) But subsection (1) does not apply if the person consented to his extradition under section 127 before his case was sent to the Secretary of State.

(3) The relevant decision is the decision that resulted in the case being sent to the Secretary of State.

(4) An appeal under this section may be brought on a question of law or fact.

(5) If an appeal is brought under this section before the Secretary of State has decided whether the person is to be extradited the appeal must not be heard until after the Secretary of State has made his decision.

(6) If the Secretary of State orders the person's discharge the appeal must not be proceeded with.

(7) No appeal may be brought under this section if the Secretary of State has ordered the person's discharge.

(8) If notice of an appeal under section 110 against the decision which resulted in the order for the person's discharge is given in accordance with subsection (5) of that section—

(a) subsections (6) and (7) do not apply;

(b) no appeal may be brought under this section if the High Court has made its decision on the appeal.

(9) Notice of an appeal under this section must be given in accordance with rules of court before the end of the permitted period, which is 14 days starting with the day on which the Secretary of State informs the person under section 100(1) or (4) of the order he has made in respect of the person.

104. Court's powers on appeal under section 103   *Text: 9.3.1*

(1) On an appeal under section 103 the High Court may—

(a) allow the appeal;

(b) direct the judge to decide again a question (or questions) which he decided at the extradition hearing;

(c) dismiss the appeal.

(2) The court may allow the appeal only if the conditions in subsection (3) or the conditions in subsection (4) are satisfied.

(3) The conditions are that—

(a) the judge ought to have decided a question before him at the extradition hearing differently;

(b) if he had decided the question in the way he ought to have done, he would have been required to order the person's discharge.

(4) The conditions are that—

(a) an issue is raised that was not raised at the extradition hearing or evidence is available that was not available at the extradition hearing;

(b) the issue or evidence would have resulted in the judge deciding a question before him at the extradition hearing differently;

(c) if he had decided the question in that way, he would have been required to order the person's discharge.

(5) If the court allows the appeal it must—

(a) order the person's discharge;

(b) quash the order for his extradition.

(6) If the judge comes to a different decision on any question that is the subject of a direction under subsection (1)(b) he must order the person's discharge.

(7) If the judge comes to the same decision as he did at the extradition hearing on the question that is (or all the questions that are) the subject of a direction under subsection (1)(b) the appeal must be taken to have been dismissed by a decision of the High Court.

105. Appeal against discharge at extradition hearing *Text: 9.3.2*

(1) If at the extradition hearing the judge orders a person's discharge, an appeal to the High Court may be brought on behalf of the category 2 territory against the relevant decision.

(2) But subsection (1) does not apply if the order for the person's discharge was under section 122.

(3) The relevant decision is the decision which resulted in the order for the person's discharge.

(4) An appeal under this section may be brought on a question of law or fact.

(5) Notice of an appeal under this section must be given in accordance with rules of court before the end of the permitted period, which is 14 days starting with the day on which the order for the person's discharge is made.

106. Court's powers on appeal under section 105 *Text: 9.3.2*

(1) On an appeal under section 105 the High Court may—

(a) allow the appeal;

(b) direct the judge to decide the relevant question again;

(c) dismiss the appeal.

(2) A question is the relevant question if the judge's decision on it resulted in the order for the person's discharge.

(3) The court may allow the appeal only if the conditions in subsection (4) or the conditions in subsection (5) are satisfied.

(4) The conditions are that—

(a) the judge ought to have decided the relevant question differently;

(b) if he had decided the question in the way he ought to have done, he would not have been required to order the person's discharge.

(5) The conditions are that—

(a) an issue is raised that was not raised at the extradition hearing or evidence is available that was not available at the extradition hearing;

(b) the issue or evidence would have resulted in the judge deciding the relevant question differently;

(c) if he had decided the question in that way, he would not have been required to order the person's discharge.

(6) If the court allows the appeal it must—

(a) quash the order discharging the person;

(b) remit the case to the judge;

(c) direct him to proceed as he would have been required to do if he had decided the relevant question differently at the extradition hearing.

(7) If the court makes a direction under subsection (1)(b) and the judge decides the relevant question differently he must proceed as he would have been required to do if he had decided that question differently at the extradition hearing.

(8) If the court makes a direction under subsection (1)(b) and the judge does not decide the relevant question differently the appeal must be taken to have been dismissed by a decision of the High Court.

107. Detention pending conclusion of appeal under section 105   *Text: 9.3.3*

(1) This section applies if immediately after the judge orders the person's discharge the judge is informed on behalf of the category 2 territory of an intention to appeal under section 105.

(2) The judge must remand the person in custody or on bail while the appeal is pending.

(3) If the judge remands the person in custody he may later grant bail.

(4) An appeal under section 105 ceases to be pending at the earliest of these times—

(a) when the proceedings on the appeal are discontinued;

(b) when the High Court dismisses the appeal, if the court is not immediately informed on behalf of the category 2 territory of an intention to apply for leave to appeal to the House of Lords;

(c) at the end of the permitted period, which is 28 days starting with the day on which leave to appeal to the House of Lords against the decision of the High Court on the appeal is granted;

(d) when there is no further step that can be taken on behalf of the category 2 territory in relation to the appeal (ignoring any power of a court to grant leave to take a step out of time).

(5) The preceding provisions of this section apply to Scotland with these modifications—

(a) in subsection (4)(b) omit the words from "if" to the end;

(b) omit subsection (4)(c).

108. Appeal against extradition order
Text: 9.3.4

(1) If the Secretary of State orders a person's extradition under this Part, the person may appeal to the High Court against the order.

(2) But subsection (1) does not apply if the person has consented to his extradition under section 127.

(3) An appeal under this section may be brought on a question of law or fact.

(4) Notice of an appeal under this section must be given in accordance with rules of court before the end of the permitted period, which is 14 days starting with the day on which the Secretary of State informs the person of the order under section 100(1).

109. Court's powers on appeal under section 108
Text: 9.3.4

(1) On an appeal under section 108 the High Court may—

(a) allow the appeal;

(b) dismiss the appeal.

(2) The court may allow the appeal only if the conditions in subsection (3) or the conditions in subsection (4) are satisfied.

(3) The conditions are that—

(a) the Secretary of State ought to have decided a question before him differently;

(b) if he had decided the question in the way he ought to have done, he would not have ordered the person's extradition.

(4) The conditions are that—

(a) an issue is raised that was not raised when the case was being considered by the Secretary of State or information is available that was not available at that time;

(b) the issue or information would have resulted in the Secretary of State deciding a question before him differently;

(c) if he had decided the question in that way, he would not have ordered the person's extradition.

(5) If the court allows the appeal it must—

(a) order the person's discharge;

(b) quash the order for his extradition.

110. Appeal against discharge by Secretary of State
Text: 9.3.5

(1) If the Secretary of State makes an order for a person's discharge under this Part, an appeal to the High Court may be brought on behalf of the category 2 territory against the relevant decision.

(2) But subsection (1) does not apply if the order for the person's discharge was under section 123.

(3) The relevant decision is the decision which resulted in the order for the person's discharge.

(4) An appeal under this section may be brought on a question of law or fact.

(5) Notice of an appeal under this section must be given in accordance with rules of court before the end of the permitted period, which is 14 days starting with the day on which (under section 100(4)) the Secretary of State informs a person acting on behalf of the category 2 territory of the order.

111. Court's powers on appeal under section 110   *Text: 9.3.5*

(1) On an appeal under section 110 the High Court may—

(a) allow the appeal;

(b) dismiss the appeal.

(2) The court may allow the appeal only if the conditions in subsection (3) or the conditions in subsection (4) are satisfied.

(3) The conditions are that—

(a) the Secretary of State ought to have decided a question before him differently;

(b) if he had decided the question in the way he ought to have done, he would have ordered the person's extradition.

(4) The conditions are that—

(a) an issue is raised that was not raised when the case was being considered by the Secretary of State or information is available that was not available at that time;

(b) the issue or information would have resulted in the Secretary of State deciding a question before him differently;

(c) if he had decided the question in that way, he would have ordered the person's extradition.

(5) If the court allows the appeal it must—

(a) quash the order discharging the person;

(b) order the person's extradition.

112. Detention pending conclusion of appeal under section 110   *Text: 9.3.6*

(1) This section applies if immediately after the Secretary of State orders the person's discharge under this Part the Secretary of State is informed on behalf of the category 2 territory of an intention to appeal under section 110.

(2) The judge must remand the person in custody or on bail while the appeal is pending.

(3) If the judge remands the person in custody he may later grant bail.

(4) An appeal under section 110 ceases to be pending at the earliest of these times—

(a) when the proceedings on the appeal are discontinued;

(b) when the High Court dismisses the appeal, if the court is not immediately informed on behalf of the category 2 territory of an intention to apply for leave to appeal to the House of Lords;

(c) at the end of the permitted period, which is 28 days starting with the day on which leave to appeal to the House of Lords against the decision of the High Court on the appeal is granted;

(d) when there is no further step that can be taken on behalf of the category 2 territory in relation to the appeal (ignoring any power of a court to grant leave to take a step out of time).

(5) The preceding provisions of this section apply to Scotland with these modifications—

(a) in subsection (4)(b) omit the words from "if" to the end;

(b) omit subsection (4)(c).

113. Appeal to High Court: time limit for start of hearing *Text: 9.3.7*

(1) Rules of court must prescribe the period (the relevant period) within which the High Court must begin to hear an appeal under section 103, 105, 108 or 110.

(2) The High Court must begin to hear the appeal before the end of the relevant period.

(3) The High Court may extend the relevant period if it believes it to be in the interests of justice to do so; and this subsection may apply more than once.

(4) The power in subsection (3) may be exercised even after the end of the relevant period.

(5) If subsection (2) is not complied with and the appeal is under section 103 or 108—

(a) the appeal must be taken to have been allowed by a decision of the High Court;

(b) the person whose extradition has been ordered must be taken to have been discharged by the High Court;

(c) the order for the person's extradition must be taken to have been quashed by the High Court.

(6) If subsection (2) is not complied with and the appeal is under section 105 or 110 the appeal must be taken to have been dismissed by a decision of the High Court.

114. Appeal to House of Lords *Text: 9.3.8*

(1) An appeal lies to the House of Lords from a decision of the High Court on an appeal under section 103, 105, 108 or 110.

(2) An appeal under this section lies at the instance of—

(a) the person whose extradition is requested;

(b) a person acting on behalf of the category 2 territory.

(3) An appeal under this section lies only with the leave of the High Court or the House of Lords.

(4) Leave to appeal under this section must not be granted unless—

(a) the High Court has certified that there is a point of law of general public importance involved in the decision, and

(b) it appears to the court granting leave that the point is one which ought to be considered by the House of Lords.

(5) An application to the High Court for leave to appeal under this section must be made before the end of the permitted period, which is 14 days starting with the day on which the court makes its decision on the appeal to it.

(6) An application to the House of Lords for leave to appeal under this section must be made before the end of the permitted period, which is 14 days starting with the day on which the High Court refuses leave to appeal.

(7) If leave to appeal under this section is granted, the appeal must be brought before the end of the permitted period, which is 28 days starting with the day on which leave is granted.

(8) If subsection (7) is not complied with—

(a) the appeal must be taken to have been brought;

(b) the appeal must be taken to have been dismissed by the House of Lords immediately after the end of the period permitted under that subsection.

(9) These must be ignored for the purposes of subsection (8)(b)—

(a) any power of a court to extend the period permitted for bringing the appeal;

(b) any power of a court to grant leave to take a step out of time.

(10) The High Court may grant bail to a person appealing under this section or applying for leave to appeal under this section.

(11) Section 5 of the Appellate Jurisdiction Act 1876 (c. 59) (composition of House of Lords for hearing and determination of appeals) applies in relation to an appeal under this section or an application for leave to appeal under this section as it applies in relation to an appeal under that Act.

(12) An order of the House of Lords which provides for an application for leave to appeal under this section to be determined by a committee constituted in accordance with section 5 of the Appellate Jurisdiction Act 1876 may direct that the decision of the committee is taken on behalf of the House.

(13) The preceding provisions of this section do not apply to Scotland.

115. Powers of House of Lords on appeal under section 114 *Text: 9.3.8*

(1) On an appeal under section 114 the House of Lords may—

(a) allow the appeal;

(b) dismiss the appeal.

(2) Subsection (3) applies if—

(a) the person whose extradition is requested brings an appeal under section 114, and

(b) the House of Lords allows the appeal.

(3) The House of Lords must—

(a) order the person's discharge;

(b) quash the order for his extradition, if the appeal was against a decision of the High Court to dismiss an appeal under section 103 or 108 or to allow an appeal under section 110.

(4) Subsection (5) applies if—

(a) the High Court allows an appeal under section 103 or 108 by the person whose extradition is requested or dismisses an appeal under section 110 by a person acting on behalf of the category 2 territory,

(b) a person acting on behalf of the category 2 territory brings an appeal under section 114 against the decision of the High Court, and

(c) the House of Lords allows the appeal.

(5) The House of Lords must—

(a) quash the order discharging the person made by the High Court under section 104(5) or 109(5) or by the Secretary of State under this Part;

(b) order the person to be extradited to the category 2 territory.

(6) Subsection (7) applies if—

(a) the High Court dismisses an appeal under section 105 against a decision made by the judge at the extradition hearing,

(b) a person acting on behalf of the category 2 territory brings an appeal under section 114 against the decision of the High Court, and

(c) the House of Lords allows the appeal.

(7) The House of Lords must—

(a) quash the order of the judge discharging the person whose extradition is requested;

(b) remit the case to the judge;

(c) direct him to proceed as he would have been required to do if he had decided the relevant question differently at the extradition hearing.

(8) A question is the relevant question if the judge's decision on it resulted in the order for the person's discharge.

116. Appeals: general
A decision under this Part of the judge or the Secretary of State may be questioned in legal proceedings only by means of an appeal under this Part.

Time for extradition

117. Extradition where no appeal   *Text: 10.3.1*
(1) This section applies if—

(a) the Secretary of State orders a person's extradition to a category 2 territory under this Part, and

(b) no notice of an appeal under section 103 or 108 is given before the end of the permitted period, which is 14 days starting with the day on which the Secretary of State informs the person under section 100(1) that he has ordered his extradition.

(2) The person must be extradited to the category 2 territory before the end of the required period, which is 28 days starting with the day on which the Secretary of State makes the order.

(3) If subsection (2) is not complied with and the person applies to the appropriate judge to be discharged the judge must order his discharge, unless reasonable cause is shown for the delay.

(4) These must be ignored for the purposes of subsection (1)(b)—

(a) any power of a court to extend the period permitted for giving notice of appeal;

(b) any power of a court to grant leave to take a step out of time.

118. Extradition following appeal   *Text: 10.3.2*

(1) This section applies if—

(a) there is an appeal to the High Court under section 103, 108 or 110 against a decision or order relating to a person's extradition to a category 2 territory, and

(b) the effect of the decision of the relevant court on the appeal is that the person is to be extradited there.

(2) The person must be extradited to the category 2 territory before the end of the required period, which is 28 days starting with—

(a) the day on which the decision of the relevant court on the appeal becomes final, or

(b) the day on which proceedings on the appeal are discontinued.

(3) The relevant court is—

(a) the High Court, if there is no appeal to the House of Lords against the decision of the High Court on the appeal;

(b) the House of Lords, if there is such an appeal.

(4) The decision of the High Court on the appeal becomes final—

(a) when the period permitted for applying to the High Court for leave to appeal to the House of Lords ends, if there is no such application;

(b) when the period permitted for applying to the House of Lords for leave to appeal to it ends, if the High Court refuses leave to appeal and there is no application to the House of Lords for leave to appeal;

(c) when the House of Lords refuses leave to appeal to it;

(d) at the end of the permitted period, which is 28 days starting with the day on which leave to appeal to the House of Lords is granted, if no such appeal is brought before the end of that period.

(5) These must be ignored for the purposes of subsection (4)—

(a) any power of a court to extend the period permitted for applying for leave to appeal;

(b) any power of a court to grant leave to take a step out of time.

(6) The decision of the House of Lords on the appeal becomes final when it is made.

(7) If subsection (2) is not complied with and the person applies to the appropriate judge to be discharged the judge must order his discharge, unless reasonable cause is shown for the delay.

(8) The preceding provisions of this section apply to Scotland with these modifications—

(a) in subsections (1) and (2) for "relevant court" substitute "High Court";

(b) omit subsections (3) to (6).

119. Undertaking in relation to person serving sentence in United Kingdom   *Text: 10.3.3*

(1) This section applies if—

(a) the Secretary of State orders a person's extradition to a category 2 territory under this Part;

(b) the person is serving a sentence of imprisonment or another form of detention in the United Kingdom.

(2) The Secretary of State may make the order for extradition subject to the condition that extradition is not to take place before he receives an undertaking given on behalf of the category 2 territory in terms specified by him.

(3) The terms which may be specified by the Secretary of State in relation to a person accused in a category 2 territory of the commission of an offence include terms—

(a) that the person be kept in custody until the conclusion of the proceedings against him for the offence and any other offence in respect of which he is permitted to be dealt with in the category 2 territory;

(b) that the person be returned to the United Kingdom to serve the remainder of his sentence on the conclusion of those proceedings.

(4) The terms which may be specified by the Secretary of State in relation to a person alleged to be unlawfully at large after conviction of an offence by a court in a category 2 territory include terms that the person be returned to the United Kingdom to serve the remainder of his sentence after serving any sentence imposed on him in the category 2 territory for—

(a) the offence, and

(b) any other offence in respect of which he is permitted to be dealt with in the category 2 territory.

(5) Subsections (6) and (7) apply if the Secretary of State makes an order for extradition subject to a condition under subsection (2).

(6) If the Secretary of State does not receive the undertaking before the end of the period of 21 days starting with the day on which he makes the order and the person applies to the High Court to be discharged, the court must order his discharge.

(7) If the Secretary of State receives the undertaking before the end of that period—

(a) in a case where section 117 applies, the required period for the purposes of section 117(2) is 28 days starting with the day on which the Secretary of State receives the undertaking;

(b) in a case where section 118 applies, the required period for the purposes of section 118(2) is 28 days starting with the day on which the decision of the relevant court on the appeal becomes final (within the meaning of that section) or (if later) the day on which the Secretary of State receives the undertaking.

120. Extradition following deferral for competing claim   *Text: 10.3.4*

(1) This section applies if—

(a) an order is made under this Part for a person to be extradited to a category 2 territory in pursuance of a request for his extradition;

(b) before the person is extradited to the territory an order is made under section 126(2) or 179(2) for the person's extradition in pursuance of the request to be deferred;

(c) the appropriate judge makes an order under section 181(2) for the person's extradition in pursuance of the request to cease to be deferred.

(2) In a case where section 117 applies, the required period for the purposes of section 117(2) is 28 days starting with the day on which the order under section 181(2) is made.

(3) In a case where section 118 applies, the required period for the purposes of section 118(2) is 28 days starting with the day on which the decision of the relevant court on the

appeal becomes final (within the meaning of that section) or (if later) the day on which the order under section 181(2) is made.

121. Asylum claim   *Text: 8.5.2*

(1) This section applies if—

(a) a person whose extradition is requested makes an asylum claim at any time in the relevant period;

(b) an order is made under this Part for the person to be extradited in pursuance of the request.

(2) The relevant period is the period—

(a) starting when a certificate is issued under section 70 in respect of the request;

(b) ending when the person is extradited in pursuance of the request.

(3) The person must not be extradited in pursuance of the request before the asylum claim is finally determined; and sections 117 and 118 have effect subject to this.

(4) If the Secretary of State allows the asylum claim, the claim is finally determined when he makes his decision on the claim.

(5) If the Secretary of State rejects the asylum claim, the claim is finally determined—

(a) when the Secretary of State makes his decision on the claim, if there is no right to appeal against the Secretary of State's decision on the claim;

(b) when the period permitted for appealing against the Secretary of State's decision on the claim ends, if there is such a right but there is no such appeal;

(c) when the appeal against that decision is finally determined or is withdrawn or abandoned, if there is such an appeal.

(6) An appeal against the Secretary of State's decision on an asylum claim is not finally determined for the purposes of subsection (5) at any time when a further appeal or an application for leave to bring a further appeal—

(a) has been instituted and has not been finally determined or withdrawn or abandoned, or

(b) may be brought.

(7) The remittal of an appeal is not a final determination for the purposes of subsection (6).

(8) The possibility of an appeal out of time with leave must be ignored for the purposes of subsections (5) and (6).

Withdrawal of extradition request

122. Withdrawal of request before end of extradition hearing   *Text: 11.3.2*

(1) This section applies if at any time in the relevant period the appropriate judge is informed by the Secretary of State that a request for a person's extradition has been withdrawn.

(2) The relevant period is the period—

(a) starting when the person first appears or is brought before the appropriate judge following his arrest under this Part;

(b) ending when the judge orders the person's discharge or sends the case to the Secretary of State for his decision whether the person is to be extradited.

(3) The judge must order the person's discharge.

(4) If the person is not before the judge at the time the judge orders his discharge, the judge must inform him of the order as soon as practicable.

123. Withdrawal of request after case sent to Secretary of State   *Text: 11.3.2*

(1) This section applies if at any time in the relevant period the Secretary of State is informed that a request for a person's extradition has been withdrawn.

(2) The relevant period is the period—

(a) starting when the judge sends the case to the Secretary of State for his decision whether the person is to be extradited;

(b) ending when the person is extradited in pursuance of the request or discharged.

(3) The Secretary of State must order the person's discharge.

124. Withdrawal of request while appeal to High Court pending   *Text: 11.3.2*

(1) This section applies if at any time in the relevant period the High Court is informed by the Secretary of State that a request for a person's extradition has been withdrawn.

(2) The relevant period is the period—

(a) starting when notice of an appeal to the court is given by the person whose extradition is requested or by a person acting on behalf of the category 2 territory to which his extradition is requested;

(b) ending when proceedings on the appeal are discontinued or the court makes its decision on the appeal.

(3) If the appeal is under section 103 or 108, the court must—

(a) order the person's discharge;

(b) quash the order for his extradition, if the Secretary of State has ordered his extradition.

(4) If the appeal is under section 105 or 110, the court must dismiss the appeal.

(5) If the person is not before the court at the time the court orders his discharge, the court must inform him of the order as soon as practicable.

125. Withdrawal of request while appeal to House of Lords pending   *Text: 11.3.2*

(1) This section applies if at any time in the relevant period the House of Lords is informed by the Secretary of State that a request for a person's extradition has been withdrawn.

(2) The relevant period is the period—

(a) starting when leave to appeal to the House of Lords is granted to the person whose extradition is requested or a person acting on behalf of the category 2 territory to which his extradition is requested;

(b) ending when proceedings on the appeal are discontinued or the House of Lords makes its decision on the appeal.

(3) If the appeal is brought by the person whose extradition is requested the House of Lords must—

(a) order the person's discharge;

(b) quash the order for his extradition, in a case where the appeal was against a decision of the High Court to dismiss an appeal under section 103 or 108.

(4) If the appeal is brought by a person acting on behalf of the category 2 territory the House of Lords must dismiss the appeal.

(5) If the person whose extradition is requested is not before the House of Lords at the time it orders his discharge, the House of Lords must inform him of the order as soon as practicable.

Competing extradition requests

126. Competing extradition requests   *Text: 8.4.2*

(1) This section applies if—

(a) the Secretary of State receives a valid request for a person's extradition to a category 2 territory;

(b) the person is in the United Kingdom;

(c) before the person is extradited in pursuance of the request or discharged, the Secretary of State receives another valid request for the person's extradition.

(2) The Secretary of State may—

(a) order proceedings (or further proceedings) on one of the requests to be deferred until the other one has been disposed of, if neither of the requests has been disposed of;

(b) order the person's extradition in pursuance of the request under consideration to be deferred until the other request has been disposed of, if an order for his extradition in pursuance of the request under consideration has been made.

(3) In applying subsection (2) the Secretary of State must take account in particular of these matters—

(a) the relative seriousness of the offences concerned;

(b) the place where each offence was committed (or was alleged to have been committed);

(c) the date when each request was received;

(d) whether, in the case of each offence, the person is accused of its commission (but not alleged to have been convicted) or is alleged to be unlawfully at large after conviction.

Consent to extradition

127. Consent to extradition: general   *Text: 11.2.2*

(1) A person arrested under a warrant issued under section 71 may consent to his extradition to the category 2 territory to which his extradition is requested.

(2) A person arrested under a provisional warrant may consent to his extradition to the category 2 territory in which he is accused of the commission of an offence or is alleged to have been convicted of an offence.

(3) Consent under this section—

(a) must be given in writing;

(b) is irrevocable.

(4) Consent under this section which is given by a person before his case is sent to the Secretary of State for the Secretary of State's decision whether he is to be extradited must be given before the appropriate judge.

(5) Consent under this section which is given in any other case must be given to the Secretary of State.

(6) A person may not give his consent under this section before the appropriate judge unless—

(a) he is legally represented before the appropriate judge at the time he gives consent, or

(b) he is a person to whom subsection (7) applies.

(7) This subsection applies to a person if—

(a) he has been informed of his right to apply for legal aid and has had the opportunity to apply for legal aid, but he has refused or failed to apply;

(b) he has applied for legal aid but his application has been refused;

(c) he was granted legal aid but the legal aid was withdrawn.

(8) In subsection (7) "legal aid" means—

(a) in England and Wales, a right to representation funded by the Legal Services Commission as part of the Criminal Defence Service;

(b) in Scotland, such legal aid as is available by virtue of section 183(a) of this Act;

(c) in Northern Ireland, such free legal aid as is available by virtue of sections 184 and 185 of this Act.

(9) For the purposes of subsection (6) a person is to be treated as legally represented before the appropriate judge if (and only if) he has the assistance of counsel or a solicitor to represent him in the proceedings before the appropriate judge.

128. Consent to extradition before case sent to Secretary of State   *Text: 11.2.2*

(1) This section applies if a person gives his consent under section 127 to the appropriate judge.

(2) If the judge has not fixed a date under section 75 or 76 on which the extradition hearing is to begin he is not required to do so.

(3) If the extradition hearing has begun the judge is no longer required to proceed or continue proceeding under sections 78 to 91.

(4) The judge must send the case to the Secretary of State for his decision whether the person is to be extradited.

(5) The person must be taken to have waived any right he would have (apart from the consent) not to be dealt with in the category 2 territory for an offence committed before his extradition.

Post-extradition matters

129. Consent to other offence being dealt with   *Text: 14.2.2*

(1) This section applies if—

(a) a person is extradited to a category 2 territory in accordance with this Part;

(b) the Secretary of State receives a valid request for his consent to the person being dealt with in the territory for an offence other than the offence in respect of which he was extradited.

(2) A request for consent is valid if it is made by an authority which is an authority of the territory and which the Secretary of State believes has the function of making requests for the consent referred to in subsection (1)(b) in that territory.

(3) The Secretary of State must serve notice on the person that he has received the request for consent, unless he is satisfied that it would not be practicable to do so.

(4) The Secretary of State must decide whether the offence is an extradition offence.

(5) If the Secretary of State decides the question in subsection (4) in the negative he must refuse his consent.

(6) If the Secretary of State decides that question in the affirmative he must decide whether the appropriate judge would send the case to him (for his decision whether the person was to be extradited) under sections 79 to 91 if—

(a) the person were in the United Kingdom, and

(b) the judge were required to proceed under section 79 in respect of the offence for which the Secretary of State's consent is requested.

(7) If the Secretary of State decides the question in subsection (6) in the negative he must refuse his consent.

(8) If the Secretary of State decides that question in the affirmative he must decide whether, if the person were in the United Kingdom, his extradition in respect of the offence would be prohibited under section 94, 95 or 96.

(9) If the Secretary of State decides the question in subsection (8) in the affirmative he must refuse his consent.

(10) If the Secretary of State decides that question in the negative he may give his consent.

130. Consent to further extradition to category 2 territory   *Text: 14.3.4*

(1) This section applies if—

(a) a person is extradited to a category 2 territory (the requesting territory) in accordance with this Part;

(b) the Secretary of State receives a valid request for his consent to the person's extradition to another category 2 territory for an offence other than the offence in respect of which he was extradited.

(2) A request for consent is valid if it is made by an authority which is an authority of the requesting territory and which the Secretary of State believes has the function of making requests for the consent referred to in subsection (1)(b) in that territory.

(3) The Secretary of State must serve notice on the person that he has received the request for consent, unless he is satisfied that it would not be practicable to do so.

(4) The Secretary of State must decide whether the offence is an extradition offence in relation to the category 2 territory referred to in subsection (1)(b).

(5) If the Secretary of State decides the question in subsection (4) in the negative he must refuse his consent.

(6) If the Secretary of State decides that question in the affirmative he must decide whether the appropriate judge would send the case to him (for his decision whether the person was to be extradited) under sections 79 to 91 if—

(a) the person were in the United Kingdom, and

(b) the judge were required to proceed under section 79 in respect of the offence for which the Secretary of State's consent is requested.

(7) If the Secretary of State decides the question in subsection (6) in the negative he must refuse his consent.

(8) If the Secretary of State decides that question in the affirmative he must decide whether, if the person were in the United Kingdom, his extradition in respect of the offence would be prohibited under section 94, 95 or 96.

(9) If the Secretary of State decides the question in subsection (8) in the affirmative he must refuse his consent.

(10) If the Secretary of State decides that question in the negative he may give his consent.

131. Consent to further extradition to category 1 territory   *Text: 14.3.3*

(1) This section applies if—

(a) a person is extradited to a category 2 territory (the requesting territory) in accordance with this Part;

(b) the Secretary of State receives a valid request for his consent to the person's extradition to a category 1 territory for an offence other than the offence in respect of which he was extradited.

(2) A request for consent is valid if it is made by an authority which is an authority of the requesting territory and which the Secretary of State believes has the function of making requests for the consent referred to in subsection (1)(b) in that territory.

(3) The Secretary of State must serve notice on the person that he has received the request for consent, unless he is satisfied that it would not be practicable to do so.

(4) The Secretary of State must decide whether the offence is an extradition offence within the meaning given by section 64 in relation to the category 1 territory.

(5) If the Secretary of State decides the question in subsection (4) in the negative he must refuse his consent.

(6) If the Secretary of State decides that question in the affirmative he must decide whether the appropriate judge would order the person's extradition under sections 11 to 25 if—

(a) the person were in the United Kingdom, and

(b) the judge were required to proceed under section 11 in respect of the offence for which the Secretary of State's consent is requested.

(7) If the Secretary of State decides the question in subsection (6) in the affirmative he must give his consent.

(8) If the Secretary of State decides that question in the negative he must refuse his consent.

132. Return of person to serve remainder of sentence

(1) This section applies if—

(a) a person who is serving a sentence of imprisonment or another form of detention in the United Kingdom is extradited to a category 2 territory in accordance with this Part;

(b) the person is returned to the United Kingdom to serve the remainder of his sentence.

(2) The person is liable to be detained in pursuance of his sentence.

(3) If he is at large he must be treated as being unlawfully at large.

(4) Time during which the person was not in the United Kingdom as a result of his extradition does not count as time served by him as part of his sentence.

(5) But subsection (4) does not apply if—

(a) the person was extradited for the purpose of being prosecuted for an offence, and

(b) the person has not been convicted of the offence or of any other offence in respect of which he was permitted to be dealt with in the category 2 territory.

(6) In a case falling within subsection (5), time during which the person was not in the United Kingdom as a result of his extradition counts as time served by him as part of his sentence if (and only if) it was spent in custody in connection with the offence or any other offence in respect of which he was permitted to be dealt with in the territory.

Costs

133. Costs where extradition ordered   *Text: 6.15*

(1) This section applies if any of the following occurs in relation to a person whose extradition is requested under this Part—

(a) an order for the person's extradition is made under this Part;

(b) the High Court dismisses an appeal under section 103 or 108;

(c) the High Court or the House of Lords dismisses an application for leave to appeal to the House of Lords under section 114, if the application is made by the person;

(d) the House of Lords dismisses an appeal under section 114, if the appeal is brought by the person.

(2) In a case falling within subsection (1)(a), the appropriate judge may make such order as he considers just and reasonable with regard to the costs to be paid by the person.

(3) In a case falling within subsection (1)(b) by virtue of section 104(7), the judge who decides the question that is (or all the questions that are) the subject of a direction under section 104(1)(b) may make such order as he considers just and reasonable with regard to the costs to be paid by the person.

(4) In any other case falling within subsection (1)(b), the High Court may make such order as it considers just and reasonable with regard to the costs to be paid by the person.

(5) In a case falling within subsection (1)(c) or (d), the court by which the application or appeal is dismissed may make such order as it considers just and reasonable with regard to the costs to be paid by the person.

(6) An order for costs under this section—

(a) must specify their amount;

(b) may name the person to whom they are to be paid.

134. Costs where discharge ordered   *Text: 6.15*

(1) This section applies if any of the following occurs in relation to a person whose extradition to a category 2 territory is requested under this Part—

(a) an order for the person's discharge is made under this Part;

(b) the person is taken to be discharged under this Part;

(c) the High Court dismisses an appeal under section 105 or 110;

(d) the High Court or the House of Lords dismisses an application for leave to appeal to the House of Lords under section 114, if the application is made on behalf of the category 2 territory;

(e) the House of Lords dismisses an appeal under section 114, if the appeal is brought on behalf of the category 2 territory.

(2) In a case falling within subsection (1)(a), an order under subsection (5) in favour of the person may be made by—

(a) the appropriate judge, if the order for the person's discharge is made by him or by the Secretary of State;

(b) the High Court, if the order for the person's discharge is made by it;

(c) the House of Lords, if the order for the person's discharge is made by it.

(3) In a case falling within subsection (1)(b), the appropriate judge may make an order under subsection (5) in favour of the person.

(4) In a case falling within subsection (1)(c), (d) or (e), the court by which the application or appeal is dismissed may make an order under subsection (5) in favour of the person.

(5) An order under this subsection in favour of a person is an order for a payment of the appropriate amount to be made to the person out of money provided by Parliament.

(6) The appropriate amount is such amount as the judge or court making the order under subsection (5) considers reasonably sufficient to compensate the person in whose favour the order is made for any expenses properly incurred by him in the proceedings under this Part.

(7) But if the judge or court making an order under subsection (5) is of the opinion that there are circumstances which make it inappropriate that the person in whose favour the order is made should recover the full amount mentioned in subsection (6), the judge or court must—

(a) assess what amount would in his or its opinion be just and reasonable;

(b) specify that amount in the order as the appropriate amount.

(8) Unless subsection (7) applies, the appropriate amount—

(a) must be specified in the order, if the court considers it appropriate for it to be so specified and the person in whose favour the order is made agrees the amount;

(b) must be determined in accordance with regulations made by the Lord Chancellor for the purposes of this section, in any other case.

135. Costs where discharge ordered: supplementary

(1) In England and Wales, subsections (1) and (3) of section 20 of the Prosecution of Offences Act 1985 (c. 23) (regulations for carrying Part 2 of that Act into effect) apply in relation to section 134 as those subsections apply in relation to Part 2 of that Act.

(2) As so applied those subsections have effect as if an order under section 134(5) were an order under Part 2 of that Act for a payment to be made out of central funds.

(3) In Northern Ireland, section 7 of the Costs in Criminal Cases Act (Northern Ireland) 1968 (c.10) (rules relating to costs) applies in relation to section 134 as that section applies in relation to sections 2 to 5 of that Act.

Repatriation cases

136. Persons serving sentences outside territory where convicted

(1) This section applies if—

(a) a request is made for a person's extradition to a category 2 territory and the request contains the statement referred to in subsection (2), or

(b) a provisional warrant for a person's arrest is sought on behalf of a category 2 territory and the information laid before the justice contains the statement referred to in subsection (2).

(2) The statement is one that the person—

(a) is alleged to be unlawfully at large from a prison in one territory (the imprisoning territory) in which he was serving a sentence after conviction of an offence specified in the request by a court in another territory (the convicting territory), and

(b) was serving the sentence in pursuance of international arrangements for prisoners sentenced in one territory to be repatriated to another territory in order to serve their sentence.

(3) If the category 2 territory is either the imprisoning territory or the convicting territory—

(a) section 70(3) has effect as if the reference to the statement referred to in subsection (4) of that section were a reference to the statement referred to in subsection (2) of this section;

(b) section 73(1) has effect as if the reference to a person within subsection (2) of that section were a reference to the person referred to in subsection (1)(b) of this section.

(4) If the category 2 territory is the imprisoning territory—

(a) sections 71(2)(a), 73(3)(a) and 78(4)(b) have effect as if "an extradition offence" read "an extradition offence in relation to the convicting territory";

(b) sections 74(8)(a) and 127(2) have effect as if "the category 2 territory in which he is accused of the commission of an offence or is alleged to have been convicted of an offence" read "the imprisoning territory";

(c) section 74(11)(b) has effect as if "the category 2 territory" read "the imprisoning territory";

(d) section 78(2)(e) has effect as if "the category 2 territory" read "the convicting territory";

(e) section 85(5) has effect as if after "entitled" there were inserted "in the convicting territory";

(f) section 119(4) has effect as if "a category 2 territory" read "the convicting territory" and as if "the category 2 territory" in both places read "the convicting territory";

(g) section 138(1) has effect as if "a category 2 territory" read "the convicting territory";

(h) in section 138, subsections (2), (3), (4), (5) and (7) have effect as if "the category 2 territory" read "the convicting territory".

(5) Subsection (1)(b) applies to Scotland with the substitution of "application by the procurator fiscal sets out the matters referred to in paragraphs (a) and (b) of subsection (2)" for "information laid by the justice contains the statement referred to in subsection (2)".

(6) Subsection (1)(b) applies to Northern Ireland with the substitution of "the complaint made to" for "the information laid before".

Interpretation

137. Extradition offences: person not sentenced for offence

Text: 2.3.3.1

(1) This section applies in relation to conduct of a person if—

(a) he is accused in a category 2 territory of the commission of an offence constituted by the conduct, or

(b) he is alleged to be unlawfully at large after conviction by a court in a category 2 territory of an offence constituted by the conduct and he has not been sentenced for the offence.

(2) The conduct constitutes an extradition offence in relation to the category 2 territory if these conditions are satisfied—

(a) the conduct occurs in the category 2 territory;

(b) the conduct would constitute an offence under the law of the relevant part of the United Kingdom punishable with imprisonment or another form of detention for a term of 12 months or a greater punishment if it occurred in that part of the United Kingdom;

(c) the conduct is so punishable under the law of the category 2 territory (however it is described in that law).

(3) The conduct also constitutes an extradition offence in relation to the category 2 territory if these conditions are satisfied—

(a) the conduct occurs outside the category 2 territory;

(b) the conduct is punishable under the law of the category 2 territory with imprisonment or another form of detention for a term of 12 months or a greater punishment (however it is described in that law);

(c) in corresponding circumstances equivalent conduct would constitute an extra-territorial offence under the law of the relevant part of the United Kingdom punishable with imprisonment or another form of detention for a term of 12 months or a greater punishment.

(4) The conduct also constitutes an extradition offence in relation to the category 2 territory if these conditions are satisfied—

(a) the conduct occurs outside the category 2 territory and no part of it occurs in the United Kingdom;

(b) the conduct would constitute an offence under the law of the relevant part of the United Kingdom punishable with imprisonment or another form of detention for a term of 12 months or a greater punishment if it occurred in that part of the United Kingdom;

(c) the conduct is so punishable under the law of the category 2 territory (however it is described in that law).

(5) The conduct also constitutes an extradition offence in relation to the category 2 territory if these conditions are satisfied—

(a) the conduct occurs outside the category 2 territory and no part of it occurs in the United Kingdom;

(b) the conduct is punishable under the law of the category 2 territory with imprisonment for a term of 12 months or another form of detention or a greater punishment (however it is described in that law);

(c) the conduct constitutes or if committed in the United Kingdom would constitute an offence mentioned in subsection (6).

(6) The offences are—

(a) an offence under section 51 or 58 of the International Criminal Court Act 2001 (c. 17) (genocide, crimes against humanity and war crimes);

(b) an offence under section 52 or 59 of that Act (conduct ancillary to genocide etc. committed outside the jurisdiction);

(c) an ancillary offence, as defined in section 55 or 62 of that Act, in relation to an offence falling within paragraph (a) or (b);

(d) an offence under section 1 of the International Criminal Court (Scotland) Act 2001 (asp 13) (genocide, crimes against humanity and war crimes);

(e) an offence under section 2 of that Act (conduct ancillary to genocide etc. committed outside the jurisdiction);

(f) an ancillary offence, as defined in section 7 of that Act, in relation to an offence falling within paragraph (d) or (e).

(7) If the conduct constitutes an offence under the military law of the category 2 territory but does not constitute an offence under the general criminal law of the relevant part of the United Kingdom it does not constitute an extradition offence; and subsections (1) to (6) have effect subject to this.

(8) The relevant part of the United Kingdom is the part of the United Kingdom in which—

(a) the extradition hearing took place, if the question of whether conduct constitutes an extradition offence is to be decided by the Secretary of State;

(b) proceedings in which it is necessary to decide that question are taking place, in any other case.

(9) Subsections (1) to (7) apply for the purposes of this Part.

138. Extradition offences: person sentenced for offence *Text: 2.3.3.2*

(1) This section applies in relation to conduct of a person if—

(a) he is alleged to be unlawfully at large after conviction by a court in a category 2 territory of an offence constituted by the conduct, and

(b) he has been sentenced for the offence.

(2) The conduct constitutes an extradition offence in relation to the category 2 territory if these conditions are satisfied—

(a) the conduct occurs in the category 2 territory;

(b) the conduct would constitute an offence under the law of the relevant part of the United Kingdom punishable with imprisonment or another form of detention for a term of 12 months or a greater punishment if it occurred in that part of the United Kingdom;

(c) a sentence of imprisonment or another form of detention for a term of 4 months or a greater punishment has been imposed in the category 2 territory in respect of the conduct.

(3) The conduct also constitutes an extradition offence in relation to the category 2 territory if these conditions are satisfied—

(a) the conduct occurs outside the category 2 territory;

(b) a sentence of imprisonment or another form of detention for a term of 4 months or a greater punishment has been imposed in the category 2 territory in respect of the conduct;

(c) in corresponding circumstances equivalent conduct would constitute an extra-territorial offence under the law of the relevant part of the United Kingdom punishable with imprisonment or another form of detention for a term of 12 months or a greater punishment.

(4) The conduct also constitutes an extradition offence in relation to the category 2 territory if these conditions are satisfied—

(a) the conduct occurs outside the category 2 territory and no part of it occurs in the United Kingdom;

(b) the conduct would constitute an offence under the law of the relevant part of the United Kingdom punishable with imprisonment or another form of detention for a term of 12 months or a greater punishment if it occurred in that part of the United Kingdom;

(c) a sentence of imprisonment or another form of detention for a term of 4 months or a greater punishment has been imposed in the category 2 territory in respect of the conduct.

(5) The conduct also constitutes an extradition offence in relation to the category 2 territory if these conditions are satisfied—

(a) the conduct occurs outside the category 2 territory and no part of it occurs in the United Kingdom;

(b) a sentence of imprisonment or another form of detention for a term of 4 months or a greater punishment has been imposed in the category 2 territory in respect of the conduct;

(c) the conduct constitutes or if committed in the United Kingdom would constitute an offence mentioned in subsection (6).

(6) The offences are—

(a) an offence under section 51 or 58 of the International Criminal Court Act 2001 (c. 17) (genocide, crimes against humanity and war crimes);

(b) an offence under section 52 or 59 of that Act (conduct ancillary to genocide etc. committed outside the jurisdiction);

(c) an ancillary offence, as defined in section 55 or 62 of that Act, in relation to an offence falling within paragraph (a) or (b);

(d) an offence under section 1 of the International Criminal Court (Scotland) Act 2001 (asp 13) (genocide, crimes against humanity and war crimes);

(e) an offence under section 2 of that Act (conduct ancillary to genocide etc. committed outside the jurisdiction);

(f) an ancillary offence, as defined in section 7 of that Act, in relation to an offence falling within paragraph (d) or (e).

(7) If the conduct constitutes an offence under the military law of the category 2 territory but does not constitute an offence under the general criminal law of the relevant part of the United Kingdom it does not constitute an extradition offence; and subsections (1) to (6) have effect subject to this.

(8) The relevant part of the United Kingdom is the part of the United Kingdom in which—

(a) the extradition hearing took place, if the question of whether conduct constitutes an extradition offence is to be decided by the Secretary of State;

(b) proceedings in which it is necessary to decide that question are taking place, in any other case.

(9) Subsections (1) to (7) apply for the purposes of this Part.

139. The appropriate judge

(1) The appropriate judge is—

(a) in England and Wales, a District Judge (Magistrates' Courts) designated for the purposes of this Part by the Lord Chancellor;

(b) in Scotland, the sheriff of Lothian and Borders;

(c) in Northern Ireland, such county court judge or resident magistrate as is designated for the purposes of this Part by the Lord Chancellor.

(2) A designation under subsection (1) may be made for all cases or for such cases (or cases of such description) as the designation stipulates.

(3) More than one designation may be made under subsection (1).

(4) This section applies for the purposes of this Part.

140. The extradition hearing   *Text: Chapter 6*

(1) The extradition hearing is the hearing at which the appropriate judge is to deal with a request for extradition to a category 2 territory.

(2) This section applies for the purposes of this Part.

141. Scotland: references to Secretary of State

(1) This Part applies in relation to any function which falls under this Part to be exercised in relation to Scotland only as if references in this Part to the Secretary of State were to the Scottish Ministers.

(2) Subsection (1) does not apply to the references to the Secretary of State in sections 83(3), 101(5) and 121.

PART 3
EXTRADITION TO THE UNITED KINGDOM

Extradition from category 1 territories

142. Issue of Part 3 warrant   *Text: 12.2.2*

(1) The appropriate judge may issue a Part 3 warrant in respect of a person if—

(a) a constable or an appropriate person applies to the judge for a Part 3 warrant, and

(b) the condition in subsection (2) is satisfied.

(2) The condition is that a domestic warrant has been issued in respect of the person and there are reasonable grounds for believing—

(a) that the person has committed an extradition offence, or

(b) that the person is unlawfully at large after conviction of an extradition offence by a court in the United Kingdom.

(3) A Part 3 warrant is an arrest warrant which contains—

(a) the statement referred to in subsection (4) or the statement referred to in subsection (5), and

(b) the certificate referred to in subsection (6).

(4) The statement is one that—

(a) the person in respect of whom the warrant is issued is accused in the United Kingdom of the commission of an extradition offence specified in the warrant, and

(b) the warrant is issued with a view to his arrest and extradition to the United Kingdom for the purpose of being prosecuted for the offence.

(5) The statement is one that—

(a) the person in respect of whom the warrant is issued is alleged to be unlawfully at large after conviction of an extradition offence specified in the warrant by a court in the United Kingdom, and

(b) the warrant is issued with a view to his arrest and extradition to the United Kingdom for the purpose of being sentenced for the offence or of serving a sentence of imprisonment or another form of detention imposed in respect of the offence.

(6) The certificate is one certifying—

(a) whether the conduct constituting the extradition offence specified in the warrant falls within the European framework list;

(b) whether the offence is an extra-territorial offence;

(c) what is the maximum punishment that may be imposed on conviction of the offence or (if the person has been sentenced for the offence) what sentence has been imposed.

(7) The conduct which falls within the European framework list must be taken for the purposes of subsection (6)(a) to include conduct which constitutes—

(a) an attempt, conspiracy or incitement to carry out conduct falling within the list, or

(b) aiding, abetting, counselling or procuring the carrying out of conduct falling within the list.

(8) A domestic warrant is a warrant for the arrest or apprehension of a person which is issued under any of these—

(a) section 72 of the Criminal Justice Act 1967 (c. 80);

(b) section 7 of the Bail Act 1976 (c. 63);

(c) section 51 of the Judicature (Northern Ireland) Act 1978 (c. 23);

(d) section 1 of the Magistrates' Courts Act 1980 (c. 43);

(e) Article 20 or 25 of the Magistrates' Courts (Northern Ireland) Order 1981 (S.I. 1981/1675 (N.I. 26));

(f) the Criminal Procedure (Scotland) Act 1995 (c. 46).

(9) An appropriate person is a person of a description specified in an order made by the Secretary of State for the purposes of this section.

(10) Subsection (1)(a) applies to Scotland with the substitution of "a procurator fiscal" for "a constable or an appropriate person".

143. Undertaking in relation to person serving sentence   *Text: 12.2.4*
(1) This section applies if—

(a) a Part 3 warrant is issued in respect of a person;

(b) the person is serving a sentence of imprisonment or another form of detention in a category 1 territory;

(c) the person's extradition to the United Kingdom from the category 1 territory in pursuance of the warrant is made subject to a condition that an undertaking is given on behalf of the United Kingdom with regard to his treatment in the United Kingdom or his return to the category 1 territory (or both).

(2) The Secretary of State may give an undertaking to a person acting on behalf of the category 1 territory with regard to either or both of these things—

(a) the treatment in the United Kingdom of the person in respect of whom the warrant is issued;

(b) the return of that person to the category 1 territory.

(3) The terms which may be included by the Secretary of State in an undertaking given under subsection (2) in relation to a person accused in the United Kingdom of the commission of an offence include terms—

(a) that the person be kept in custody until the conclusion of the proceedings against him for the offence and any other offence in respect of which he is permitted to be dealt with in the United Kingdom;

(b) that the person be returned to the category 1 territory to serve the remainder of his sentence on the conclusion of those proceedings.

(4) The terms which may be included by the Secretary of State in an undertaking given under subsection (2) in relation to a person alleged to be unlawfully at large after conviction of an offence by a court in the United Kingdom include terms that the person be returned to the category 1 territory to serve the remainder of his sentence after serving any sentence imposed on him in the United Kingdom.

(5) If the Part 3 warrant was issued by a sheriff, the preceding provisions of this section apply as if the references to the Secretary of State were to the Scottish Ministers.

144. Return to extraditing territory to serve sentence *Text: 12.2.5*

(1) This section applies if—

(a) a Part 3 warrant is issued in respect of a person;

(b) the warrant states that it is issued with a view to his extradition to the United Kingdom for the purpose of being prosecuted for an offence;

(c) he is extradited to the United Kingdom from a category 1 territory in pursuance of the warrant;

(d) he is extradited on the condition that, if he is convicted of the offence and a sentence of imprisonment or another form of detention is imposed in respect of it, he must be returned to the category 1 territory to serve the sentence;

(e) he is convicted of the offence and a sentence of imprisonment or another form of detention is imposed in respect of it.

(2) The person must be returned to the category 1 territory to serve the sentence as soon as is reasonably practicable after the sentence is imposed.

(3) If subsection (2) is complied with the punishment for the offence must be treated as remitted but the person's conviction for the offence must be treated as a conviction for all other purposes.

(4) If subsection (2) is not complied with and the person applies to the appropriate judge to be discharged the judge must order his discharge, unless reasonable cause is shown for the delay.

145. Service of sentence in territory executing Part 3 warrant *Text: 12.2.6*

(1) This section applies if—

(a) a Part 3 warrant is issued in respect of a person;

(b) the certificate contained in the warrant certifies that a sentence has been imposed;

(c) an undertaking is given on behalf of a category 1 territory that the person will be required to serve the sentence in the territory;

(d) on the basis of the undertaking the person is not extradited to the United Kingdom from the category 1 territory.

(2) The punishment for the offence must be treated as remitted but the person's conviction for the offence must be treated as a conviction for all other purposes.

146. Dealing with person for other offences *Text: 12.2.3*

(1) This section applies if a person is extradited to the United Kingdom from a category 1 territory in pursuance of a Part 3 warrant.

(2) The person may be dealt with in the United Kingdom for an offence committed before his extradition only if—

(a) the offence is one falling within subsection (3), or

(b) the condition in subsection (4) is satisfied.

(3) The offences are—

(a) the offence in respect of which the person is extradited;

(b) an offence disclosed by the information provided to the category 1 territory in respect of that offence;

(c) an extradition offence in respect of which consent to the person being dealt with is given on behalf of the territory;

(d) an offence which is not punishable with imprisonment or another form of detention;

(e) an offence in respect of which the person will not be detained in connection with his trial, sentence or appeal;

(f) an offence in respect of which the person waives the right that he would have (but for this paragraph) not to be dealt with for the offence.

(4) The condition is that the person has been given an opportunity to leave the United Kingdom and—

(a) he has not done so before the end of the permitted period, or

(b) he has done so before the end of the permitted period and has returned to the United Kingdom.

(5) The permitted period is 45 days starting with the day on which the person arrives in the United Kingdom.

147. Effect of consent to extradition to the United Kingdom *Text: 12.2.3*

(1) This section applies if—

(a) a person is extradited to the United Kingdom from a category 1 territory in pursuance of a Part 3 warrant;

(b) the person consented to his extradition to the United Kingdom in accordance with the law of the category 1 territory.

(2) Section 146(2) does not apply if the conditions in subsection (3) or the conditions in subsection (4) are satisfied.

(3) The conditions are that—

(a) under the law of the category 1 territory, the effect of the person's consent is to waive his right under section 146(2);

(b) the person has not revoked his consent in accordance with that law, if he is permitted to do so under that law.

(4) The conditions are that—

(a) under the law of the category 1 territory, the effect of the person's consent is not to waive his right under section 146(2);

(b) the person has expressly waived his right under section 146(2) in accordance with that law;

(c) the person has not revoked his consent in accordance with that law, if he is permitted to do so under that law;

(d) the person has not revoked the waiver of his right under section 146(2) in accordance with that law, if he is permitted to do so under that law.

148. Extradition offences   *Text: 12.2.1*

(1) Conduct constitutes an extradition offence in relation to the United Kingdom if these conditions are satisfied—

(a) the conduct occurs in the United Kingdom;

(b) the conduct is punishable under the law of the relevant part of the United Kingdom with imprisonment or another form of detention for a term of 12 months or a greater punishment.

(2) Conduct also constitutes an extradition offence in relation to the United Kingdom if these conditions are satisfied—

(a) the conduct occurs outside the United Kingdom;

(b) the conduct constitutes an extra-territorial offence punishable under the law of the relevant part of the United Kingdom with imprisonment or another form of detention for a term of 12 months or a greater punishment.

(3) But subsections (1) and (2) do not apply in relation to conduct of a person if—

(a) he is alleged to be unlawfully at large after conviction by a court in the United Kingdom of the offence constituted by the conduct, and

(b) he has been sentenced for the offence.

(4) Conduct also constitutes an extradition offence in relation to the United Kingdom if these conditions are satisfied—

(a) the conduct occurs in the United Kingdom;

(b) a sentence of imprisonment or another form of detention for a term of 4 months or a greater punishment has been imposed in the United Kingdom in respect of the conduct.

(5) Conduct also constitutes an extradition offence in relation to the United Kingdom if these conditions are satisfied—

(a) the conduct occurs outside the United Kingdom;

(b) the conduct constitutes an extra-territorial offence;

(c) a sentence of imprisonment or another form of detention for a term of 4 months or a greater punishment has been imposed in the United Kingdom in respect of the conduct.

(6) The relevant part of the United Kingdom is the part of the United Kingdom in which the relevant proceedings are taking place.

(7) The relevant proceedings are the proceedings in which it is necessary to decide whether conduct constitutes an extradition offence.

(8) Subsections (1) to (5) apply for the purposes of sections 142 to 147.

149. The appropriate judge   *Text: 12.2.2*

(1) The appropriate judge is—

(a) in England and Wales, a District Judge (Magistrates' Courts), a justice of the peace or a judge entitled to exercise the jurisdiction of the Crown Court;

(b) in Scotland, a sheriff;

(c) in Northern Ireland, a justice of the peace, a resident magistrate or a Crown Court judge.

(2) This section applies for the purposes of sections 142 to 147.

Extradition from category 2 territories

150. Dealing with person for other offences: Commonwealth countries etc.   *Text: 12.3.1*

(1) This section applies if—

(a) a person is extradited to the United Kingdom from a category 2 territory under law of the territory corresponding to Part 2 of this Act, and

(b) the territory is a Commonwealth country, a British overseas territory or the Hong Kong Special Administrative Region of the People's Republic of China.

(2) The person may be dealt with in the United Kingdom for an offence committed before his extradition only if—

(a) the offence is one falling within subsection (3), or

(b) the condition in subsection (6) is satisfied.

(3) The offences are—

(a) the offence in respect of which the person is extradited;

(b) a lesser offence disclosed by the information provided to the category 2 territory in respect of that offence;

(c) an offence in respect of which consent to the person being dealt with is given by or on behalf of the relevant authority.

(4) An offence is a lesser offence in relation to another offence if the maximum punishment for it is less severe than the maximum punishment for the other offence.

(5) The relevant authority is—

(a) if the person has been extradited from a Commonwealth country, the government of the country;

(b) if the person has been extradited from a British overseas territory, the person administering the territory;

(c) if the person has been extradited from the Hong Kong Special Administrative Region of the People's Republic of China, the government of the Region.

(6) The condition is that the protected period has ended.

(7) The protected period is 45 days starting with the first day after his extradition to the United Kingdom on which the person is given an opportunity to leave the United Kingdom.

(8) A person is dealt with in the United Kingdom for an offence if—

(a) he is tried there for it;

(b) he is detained with a view to trial there for it.

151. Dealing with person for other offences: other category 2 territories   *Text: 12.3.2*

(1) This section applies if—

(a) a person is extradited to the United Kingdom from a category 2 territory under law of the territory corresponding to Part 2 of this Act, and

(b) the territory is not one falling within section 150(1)(b).

(2) The person may be dealt with in the United Kingdom for an offence committed before his extradition only if—

(a) the offence is one falling within subsection (3), or

(b) the condition in subsection (4) is satisfied.

(3) The offences are—

(a) the offence in respect of which the person is extradited;

(b) an offence disclosed by the information provided to the category 2 territory in respect of that offence;

(c) an offence in respect of which consent to the person being dealt with is given on behalf of the territory.

(4) The condition is that—

(a) the person has returned to the territory from which he was extradited, or

(b) the person has been given an opportunity to leave the United Kingdom.

(5) A person is dealt with in the United Kingdom for an offence if—

(a) he is tried there for it;

(b) he is detained with a view to trial there for it.

General

152. Remission of punishment for other offences   *Text: 12.5.2*

(1) This section applies if—

(a) a person is extradited to the United Kingdom from—

(i) a category 1 territory under law of the territory corresponding to Part 1 of this Act, or

(ii) a category 2 territory under law of the territory corresponding to Part 2 of this Act;

(b) before his extradition he has been convicted of an offence in the United Kingdom;

(c) he has not been extradited in respect of that offence.

(2) The punishment for the offence must be treated as remitted but the person's conviction for the offence must be treated as a conviction for all other purposes.

153. Return of person acquitted or not tried   *Text: 12.5.3*

(1) This section applies if—

(a) a person is accused in the United Kingdom of the commission of an offence;

(b) the person is extradited to the United Kingdom in respect of the offence from—

(i) a category 1 territory under law of the territory corresponding to Part 1 of this Act, or

(ii) a category 2 territory under law of the territory corresponding to Part 2 of this Act;

(c) the condition in subsection (2) or the condition in subsection (3) is satisfied.

(2) The condition is that—

(a) proceedings against the person for the offence are not begun before the end of the required period, which is 6 months starting with the day on which the person arrives in the United Kingdom on his extradition, and

(b) before the end of the period of 3 months starting immediately after the end of the required period the person asks the Secretary of State to return him to the territory from which he was extradited.

(3) The condition is that—

(a) at his trial for the offence the person is acquitted or is discharged under any of the provisions specified in subsection (4), and

(b) before the end of the period of 3 months starting immediately after the date of his acquittal or discharge the person asks the Secretary of State to return him to the territory from which he was extradited.

(4) The provisions are—

(a) section 12(1) of the Powers of Criminal Courts (Sentencing) Act 2000 (c. 6);

(b) section 246(1), (2) or (3) of the Criminal Procedure (Scotland) Act 1995 (c. 46);

(c) Article 4(1) of the Criminal Justice (Northern Ireland) Order 1996 (S.I. 1996/3160 (N.I. 24)).

(5) The Secretary of State must arrange for him to be sent back, free of charge and with as little delay as possible, to the territory from which he was extradited to the United Kingdom in respect of the offence.

(6) If the accusation in subsection (1)(a) relates to the commission of an offence in Scotland, subsections (2)(b), (3)(b) and (5) apply as if the references to the Secretary of State were references to the Scottish Ministers.

154. Restriction on bail where undertaking given by Secretary of State   *Text: 12.5.1*

(1) This section applies in relation to a person if—

(a) the Secretary of State has given an undertaking in connection with the person's extradition to the United Kingdom, and

(b) the undertaking includes terms that the person be kept in custody until the conclusion of any proceedings against him in the United Kingdom for an offence.

(2) A court, judge or justice of the peace may grant bail to the person in the proceedings only if the court, judge or justice of the peace considers that there are exceptional circumstances which justify it.

155. Service personnel
The Secretary of State may by order provide for the preceding provisions of this Part to have effect with specified modifications in relation to a case where the person whose extradition is sought or ordered is subject to military law, air-force law or the Naval Discipline Act 1957 (c. 53).

PART 4
POLICE POWERS

Warrants and orders

156. Search and seizure warrants   *Text: 13.6.1*

(1) A justice of the peace may, on an application made to him by a constable, issue a search and seizure warrant if he is satisfied that the requirements for the issue of a search and seizure warrant are fulfilled.

(2) The application for a search and seizure warrant must state that—

(a) the extradition of a person specified in the application is sought under Part 1 or Part 2;

(b) the warrant is sought in relation to premises specified in the application;

(c) the warrant is sought in relation to material, or material of a description, specified in the application;

(d) that material, or material of that description, is believed to be on the premises.

(3) If the application states that the extradition of the person is sought under Part 1, the application must also state that the person is accused in a category 1 territory specified in the application of the commission of an offence—

(a) which is specified in the application, and

(b) which is an extradition offence within the meaning given by section 64.

(4) If the application states that the extradition of the person is sought under Part 2, the application must also state that the person is accused in a category 2 territory specified in the application of the commission of an offence—

(a) which is specified in the application, and

(b) which is an extradition offence within the meaning given by section 137.

(5) A search and seizure warrant is a warrant authorising a constable—

(a) to enter and search the premises specified in the application for the warrant, and

(b) to seize and retain any material found there which falls within subsection (6).

(6) Material falls within this subsection if—

(a) it would be likely to be admissible evidence at a trial in the relevant part of the United Kingdom for the offence specified in the application for the warrant (on the assumption that conduct constituting that offence would constitute an offence in that part of the United Kingdom), and

(b) it does not consist of or include items subject to legal privilege, excluded material or special procedure material.

(7) The relevant part of the United Kingdom is the part of the United Kingdom where the justice of the peace exercises jurisdiction.

(8) The requirements for the issue of a search and seizure warrant are that there are reasonable grounds for believing that—

(a) the offence specified in the application has been committed by the person so specified;

(b) the person is in the United Kingdom or is on his way to the United Kingdom;

(c) the offence is an extradition offence within the meaning given by section 64 (if subsection (3) applies) or section 137 (if subsection (4) applies);

(d) there is material on premises specified in the application which falls within subsection (6);

(e) any of the conditions referred to in subsection (9) is satisfied.

(9) The conditions are—

(a) that it is not practicable to communicate with a person entitled to grant entry to the premises;

(b) that it is practicable to communicate with a person entitled to grant entry to the premises but it is not practicable to communicate with a person entitled to grant access to the material referred to in subsection (8)(d);

(c) that entry to the premises will not be granted unless a warrant is produced;

(d) that the purpose of a search may be frustrated or seriously prejudiced unless a constable arriving at the premises can secure immediate entry to them.

(10) The preceding provisions of this section apply to Scotland with these modifications—

(a) in subsections (1) and (7) for "justice of the peace" substitute "sheriff";

(b) in subsection (1) for "constable" substitute "procurator fiscal";

(c) for "search and seizure warrant" substitute "warrant to search";

(d) in subsection (6)(b) omit the words ", excluded material or special procedure material";

(e) subsections (8)(e) and (9) are omitted.

157. Production orders
Text: 13.6.2

(1) A judge may, on an application made to him by a constable, make a production order if he is satisfied that the requirements for the making of a production order are fulfilled.

(2) The application for a production order must state that—

(a) the extradition of a person specified in the application is sought under Part 1 or Part 2;

(b) the order is sought in relation to premises specified in the application;

(c) the order is sought in relation to material, or material of a description, specified in the application;

(d) the material is special procedure material or excluded material;

(e) a person specified in the application appears to be in possession or control of the material.

(3) If the application states that the extradition of the person is sought under Part 1, the application must also state that the person is accused in a category 1 territory specified in the application of the commission of an offence—

(a) which is specified in the application, and

(b) which is an extradition offence within the meaning given by section 64.

(4) If the application states that the extradition of the person is sought under Part 2, the application must also state that the person is accused in a category 2 territory specified in the application of the commission of an offence—

(a) which is specified in the application, and

(b) which is an extradition offence within the meaning given by section 137.

(5) A production order is an order either—

(a) requiring the person the application for the order specifies as appearing to be in possession or control of special procedure material or excluded material to produce it to a constable (within the period stated in the order) for him to take away, or

(b) requiring that person to give a constable access to the special procedure material or excluded material within the period stated in the order.

(6) The period stated in a production order must be a period of 7 days starting with the day on which the order is made, unless it appears to the judge by whom the order is made that a longer period would be appropriate.

(7) Production orders have effect as if they were orders of the court.

(8) In this section "judge"—

(a) in England and Wales, means a circuit judge;

(b) in Northern Ireland, means a Crown Court judge.

158. Requirements for making of production order   *Text: 13.6.2.1*

(1) These are the requirements for the making of a production order.

(2) There must be reasonable grounds for believing that—

(a) the offence specified in the application has been committed by the person so specified;

(b) the person is in the United Kingdom or is on his way to the United Kingdom;

(c) the offence is an extradition offence within the meaning given by section 64 (if section 157(3) applies) or section 137 (if section 157(4) applies);

(d) there is material which consists of or includes special procedure material or excluded material on premises specified in the application;

(e) the material would be likely to be admissible evidence at a trial in the relevant part of the United Kingdom for the offence specified in the application (on the assumption that conduct constituting that offence would constitute an offence in that part of the United Kingdom).

(3) The relevant part of the United Kingdom is the part of the United Kingdom where the judge exercises jurisdiction.

(4) It must appear that other methods of obtaining the material—

(a) have been tried without success, or

(b) have not been tried because they were bound to fail.

(5) It must be in the public interest that the material should be produced or that access to it should be given.

159. Computer information   *Text: 13.6.2.3*

(1) This section applies if any of the special procedure material or excluded material specified in an application for a production order consists of information stored in any electronic form.

(2) If the order is an order requiring a person to produce the material to a constable for him to take away, it has effect as an order to produce the material in a form—

(a) in which it can be taken away by him;

(b) in which it is visible and legible or from which it can readily be produced in a visible and legible form.

(3) If the order is an order requiring a person to give a constable access to the material, it has effect as an order to give him access to the material in a form—

(a) in which it is visible and legible, or

(b) from which it can readily be produced in a visible and legible form.

160. Warrants: special procedure material and excluded material   *Text: 13.6.3*

(1) A judge may, on an application made to him by a constable, issue a warrant under this section if he is satisfied that—

(a) the requirements for the making of a production order are fulfilled, and

(b) the further requirement for the issue of a warrant under this section is fulfilled.

(2) The application for a warrant under this section must state that—

(a) the extradition of a person specified in the application is sought under Part 1 or Part 2;

(b) the warrant is sought in relation to premises specified in the application;

(c) the warrant is sought in relation to material, or material of a description, specified in the application;

(d) the material is special procedure material or excluded material.

(3) If the application states that the extradition of the person is sought under Part 1, the application must also state that the person is accused in a category 1 territory specified in the application of the commission of an offence—

(a) which is specified in the application, and

(b) which is an extradition offence within the meaning given by section 64.

(4) If the application states that the extradition of the person is sought under Part 2, the application must also state that the person is accused in a category 2 territory specified in the application of the commission of an offence—

(a) which is specified in the application, and

(b) which is an extradition offence within the meaning given by section 137.

(5) A warrant under this section authorises a constable to enter and search the premises specified in the application for the warrant and—

(a) to seize and retain any material found there which falls within subsection (6) and which is special procedure material, if the application for the warrant states that the warrant is sought in relation to special procedure material;

(b) to seize and retain any material found there which falls within subsection (6) and which is excluded material, if the application for the warrant states that the warrant is sought in relation to excluded material.

(6) Material falls within this subsection if it would be likely to be admissible evidence at a trial in the relevant part of the United Kingdom for the offence specified in the application for the warrant (on the assumption that conduct constituting that offence would constitute an offence in that part of the United Kingdom).

(7) The relevant part of the United Kingdom is the part of the United Kingdom where the judge exercises jurisdiction.

(8) The further requirement for the issue of a warrant under this section is that any of these conditions is satisfied—

(a) it is not practicable to communicate with a person entitled to grant entry to the premises;

(b) it is practicable to communicate with a person entitled to grant entry to the premises but it is not practicable to communicate with a person entitled to grant access to the material referred to in section 158(2)(d);

(c) the material contains information which is subject to a restriction on disclosure or an obligation of secrecy contained in an enactment (including one passed after this Act) and is likely to be disclosed in breach of the restriction or obligation if a warrant is not issued.

(9) In this section "judge"—

(a) in England and Wales, means a circuit judge;

(b) in Northern Ireland, means a Crown Court judge.

Search and seizure without warrant

161. Entry and search of premises for purposes of arrest   *Text: 13.7.1*

(1) This section applies if a constable has power to arrest a person under an extradition arrest power.

(2) A constable may enter and search any premises for the purpose of exercising the power of arrest if he has reasonable grounds for believing that the person is on the premises.

(3) The power to search conferred by subsection (2) is exercisable only to the extent that is reasonably required for the purpose of exercising the power of arrest.

(4) A constable who has entered premises in exercise of the power conferred by subsection (2) may seize and retain anything which is on the premises if he has reasonable grounds for believing—

(a) that it has been obtained in consequence of the commission of an offence or it is evidence in relation to an offence, and

(b) that it is necessary to seize it in order to prevent it being concealed, lost, damaged, altered or destroyed.

(5) An offence includes an offence committed outside the United Kingdom.

(6) If the premises contain 2 or more separate dwellings, the power conferred by subsection (2) is a power to enter and search only—

(a) any parts of the premises which the occupiers of any dwelling comprised in the premises use in common with the occupiers of any other dwelling comprised in the premises, and

(b) any dwelling comprised in the premises in which the constable has reasonable grounds for believing that the person may be.

162. Entry and search of premises on arrest   *Text: 13.7.2*

(1) This section applies if a person has been arrested under an extradition arrest power at a place other than a police station.

(2) A constable may enter and search any premises in which the person was at the time of his arrest or immediately before his arrest if he has reasonable grounds for believing—

(a) if the person has not been convicted of the relevant offence, that there is on the premises evidence (other than items subject to legal privilege) relating to the relevant offence;

(b) in any case, that there is on the premises evidence (other than items subject to legal privilege) relating to the identity of the person.

(3) The relevant offence is the offence—

(a) referred to in the Part 1 warrant, if the arrest was under a Part 1 warrant;

(b) in respect of which the constable has reasonable grounds for believing that a Part 1 warrant has been or will be issued, if the arrest was under section 5;

(c) in respect of which extradition is requested, if the arrest was under a warrant issued under section 71;

(d) of which the person is accused, if the arrest was under a provisional warrant.

(4) The power to search conferred by subsection (2)—

(a) if the person has not been convicted of the relevant offence, is a power to search for evidence (other than items subject to legal privilege) relating to the relevant offence;

(b) in any case, is a power to search for evidence (other than items subject to legal privilege) relating to the identity of the person.

(5) The power to search conferred by subsection (2) is exercisable only to the extent that it is reasonably required for the purpose of discovering evidence in respect of which the power is available by virtue of subsection (4).

(6) A constable may seize and retain anything for which he may search by virtue of subsections (4) and (5).

(7) A constable who has entered premises in exercise of the power conferred by subsection (2) may seize and retain anything which is on the premises if he has reasonable grounds for believing—

(a) that it has been obtained in consequence of the commission of an offence or it is evidence in relation to an offence, and

(b) that it is necessary to seize it in order to prevent it being concealed, lost, damaged, altered or destroyed.

(8) An offence includes an offence committed outside the United Kingdom.

(9) If the premises contain 2 or more separate dwellings, the power conferred by subsection (2) is a power to enter and search only—

(a) any dwelling in which the arrest took place or in which the person was immediately before his arrest, and

(b) any parts of the premises which the occupier of any such dwelling uses in common with the occupiers of any other dwelling comprised in the premises.

163. Search of person on arrest   *Text: 13.7.3*

(1) This section applies if a person has been arrested under an extradition arrest power at a place other than a police station.

(2) A constable may search the person if he has reasonable grounds for believing that the person may present a danger to himself or others.

(3) A constable may search the person if he has reasonable grounds for believing that the person may have concealed on him anything—

(a) which he might use to assist him to escape from lawful custody;

(b) which might be evidence relating to an offence or to the identity of the person.

(4) The power to search conferred by subsection (3)—

(a) is a power to search for anything falling within paragraph (a) or (b) of that subsection;

(b) is exercisable only to the extent that is reasonably required for the purpose of discovering such a thing.

(5) The powers conferred by subsections (2) and (3)—

(a) do not authorise a constable to require a person to remove any of his clothing in public, other than an outer coat, jacket or gloves;

(b) authorise a search of a person's mouth.

(6) A constable searching a person in exercise of the power conferred by subsection (2) may seize and retain anything he finds, if he has reasonable grounds for believing that the person searched might use it to cause physical injury to himself or to any other person.

(7) A constable searching a person in exercise of the power conferred by subsection (3) may seize and retain anything he finds if he has reasonable grounds for believing—

(a) that the person might use it to assist him to escape from lawful custody;

(b) that it is evidence of an offence or of the identity of the person or has been obtained in consequence of the commission of an offence.

(8) An offence includes an offence committed outside the United Kingdom.

(9) Nothing in this section affects the power conferred by section 43 of the Terrorism Act 2000 (c. 11).

164. Entry and search of premises after arrest   *Text: 13.7.4*

(1) This section applies if a person has been arrested under an extradition arrest power.

(2) A constable may enter and search any premises occupied or controlled by the person if the constable has reasonable grounds for suspecting—

(a) if the person has not been convicted of the relevant offence, that there is on the premises evidence (other than items subject to legal privilege) relating to the relevant offence;

(b) in any case, that there is on the premises evidence (other than items subject to legal privilege) relating to the identity of the person.

(3) The relevant offence is the offence—

(a) referred to in the Part 1 warrant, if the arrest was under a Part 1 warrant;

(b) in respect of which the constable has reasonable grounds for believing that a Part 1 warrant has been or will be issued, if the arrest was under section 5;

(c) in respect of which extradition is requested, if the arrest was under a warrant issued under section 71;

(d) of which the person is accused, if the arrest was under a provisional warrant.

(4) The power to search conferred by subsection (2)—

(a) if the person has not been convicted of the relevant offence, is a power to search for evidence (other than items subject to legal privilege) relating to the relevant offence;

(b) in any case, is a power to search for evidence (other than items subject to legal privilege) relating to the identity of the person.

(5) The power to search conferred by subsection (2) is exercisable only to the extent that it is reasonably required for the purpose of discovering evidence in respect of which the power is available by virtue of subsection (4).

(6) A constable may seize and retain anything for which he may search by virtue of subsections (4) and (5).

(7) A constable who has entered premises in exercise of the power conferred by subsection (2) may seize and retain anything which is on the premises if he has reasonable grounds for believing—

(a) that it has been obtained in consequence of the commission of an offence or it is evidence in relation to an offence, and

(b) that it is necessary to seize it in order to prevent it being concealed, lost, damaged, altered or destroyed.

(8) An offence includes an offence committed outside the United Kingdom.

(9) The powers conferred by subsections (2) and (6) may be exercised only if a police officer of the rank of inspector or above has given written authorisation for their exercise.

(10) But the power conferred by subsection (2) may be exercised without authorisation under subsection (9) if—

(a) it is exercised before the person arrested is taken to a police station, and

(b) the presence of the person at a place other than a police station is necessary for the effective exercise of the power to search.

(11) Subsections (9) and (10) do not apply to Scotland.

165. Additional seizure powers

(1) The Criminal Justice and Police Act 2001 (c. 16) is amended as follows.

(2) In Part 1 of Schedule 1 (powers of seizure to which section 50 of that Act applies) at the end add—

"73D *Extradition Act 2003 (c. 41)*

The powers of seizure conferred by sections 156(5), 160(5), 161(4), 162(6) and (7) and 164(6) and (7) of the Extradition Act 2003 (seizure in connection with extradition)."

(3) In Part 2 of Schedule 1 (powers of seizure to which section 51 of that Act applies) at the end add-

"83A *Extradition Act 2003 (c. 41)*

The powers of seizure conferred by section 163(6) and (7) of the Extradition Act 2003 (seizure in connection with extradition)."

Treatment following arrest

166. Fingerprints and samples
Text: 13.8.1

(1) This section applies if a person has been arrested under an extradition arrest power and is detained at a police station.

(2) Fingerprints may be taken from the person only if they are taken by a constable—

(a) with the appropriate consent given in writing, or

(b) without that consent, under subsection (4).

(3) A non-intimate sample may be taken from the person only if it is taken by a constable—

(a) with the appropriate consent given in writing, or

(b) without that consent, under subsection (4).

(4) Fingerprints or a non-intimate sample may be taken from the person without the appropriate consent only if a police officer of at least the rank of inspector authorises the fingerprints or sample to be taken.

167. Searches and examination
Text: 13.8.2

(1) This section applies if a person has been arrested under an extradition arrest power and is detained at a police station.

(2) If a police officer of at least the rank of inspector authorises it, the person may be searched or examined, or both, for the purpose of facilitating the ascertainment of his identity.

(3) An identifying mark found on a search or examination under this section may be photographed—

(a) with the appropriate consent, or

(b) without the appropriate consent, if that consent is withheld or it is not practicable to obtain it.

(4) The only persons entitled to carry out a search or examination, or take a photograph, under this section are—

(a) constables;

(b) persons designated for the purposes of this section by the appropriate police officer.

(5) A person may not under this section—

(a) carry out a search or examination of a person of the opposite sex;

(b) take a photograph of any part of the body (other than the face) of a person of the opposite sex.

(6) An intimate search may not be carried out under this section.

(7) Ascertaining a person's identity includes showing that he is not a particular person.

(8) Taking a photograph includes using a process by means of which a visual image may be produced; and photographing a person must be construed accordingly.

(9) Mark includes features and injuries and a mark is an identifying mark if its existence in a person's case facilitates the ascertainment of his identity.

(10) The appropriate police officer is—

(a) in England and Wales, the chief officer of police for the police area in which the police station in question is situated;

(b) in Northern Ireland, the Chief Constable of the Police Service of Northern Ireland.

168. Photographs
Text: 13.8.3

(1) This section applies if a person has been arrested under an extradition arrest power and is detained at a police station.

(2) The person may be photographed—

(a) with the appropriate consent, or

(b) without the appropriate consent, if that consent is withheld or it is not practicable to obtain it.

(3) A person proposing to take a photograph of a person under this section—

(a) may for the purpose of doing so require the removal of any item or substance worn on or over the whole or any part of the head or face of the person to be photographed, and

(b) if the requirement is not complied with may remove the item or substance himself.

(4) The only persons entitled to take a photograph under this section are—

(a) constables;

(b) persons designated for the purposes of this section by the appropriate police officer.

(5) Taking a photograph includes using a process by means of which a visual image may be produced; and photographing a person must be construed accordingly.

(6) The appropriate police officer is—

(a) in England and Wales, the chief officer of police for the police area in which the police station in question is situated;

(b) in Northern Ireland, the Chief Constable of the Police Service of Northern Ireland.

169. Evidence of identity: England and Wales

(1) The Police and Criminal Evidence Act 1984 (c. 60) is amended as follows.

(2) In section 54A (searches and examination to ascertain identity) at the end insert—

"(13) Nothing in this section applies to a person arrested under an extradition arrest power."

(3) In section 61 (fingerprinting) at the end insert—

"(10) Nothing in this section applies to a person arrested under an extradition arrest power."

(4) In section 63 (non-intimate samples) at the end insert—

"(11) Nothing in this section applies to a person arrested under an extradition arrest power."

(5) In section 64A (photographing of suspects etc.) at the end insert—

"(7) Nothing in this section applies to a person arrested under an extradition arrest power."

(6) In section 65 (interpretation of Part 5) after the definition of "appropriate consent" insert—

" "extradition arrest power" means any of the following—

(a) a Part 1 warrant (within the meaning given by the Extradition Act 2003) in respect of which a certificate under section 2 of that Act has been issued;

(b) section 5 of that Act;

(c) a warrant issued under section 71 of that Act;

(d) a provisional warrant (within the meaning given by that Act)."

170. Evidence of identity: Northern Ireland

(1) The Police and Criminal Evidence (Northern Ireland) Order 1989 (S.I. 1989/ 1341 (N.I. 12)) is amended as follows.

(2) In Article 55A (searches and examination to ascertain identity) at the end insert—

"(13) Nothing in this Article applies to a person arrested under an extradition arrest power."

(3) In Article 61 (fingerprinting) at the end insert—

"(10) Nothing in this Article applies to a person arrested under an extradition arrest power."

(4) In Article 63 (non-intimate samples) at the end insert—

"(12) Nothing in this Article applies to a person arrested under an extradition arrest power."

(5) In Article 64A (photographing of suspects etc.) at the end insert—

"(7) Nothing in this Article applies to a person arrested under an extradition arrest power."

(6) In Article 53 (interpretation) after the definition of "drug trafficking" and "drug trafficking offence" insert—

" "extradition arrest power" means any of the following—

(a) a Part 1 warrant (within the meaning given by the Extradition Act 2003) in respect of which a certificate under section 2 of that Act has been issued;

(b) section 5 of that Act;

(c) a warrant issued under section 71 of that Act;

(d) a provisional warrant (within the meaning given by that Act)."

171. Other treatment and rights   *Text: 13.8.4*

(1) This section applies in relation to cases where a person—

(a) is arrested under an extradition arrest power at a police station;

(b) is taken to a police station after being arrested elsewhere under an extradition arrest power;

(c) is detained at a police station after being arrested under an extradition arrest power.

(2) In relation to those cases the Secretary of State may by order apply the provisions mentioned in subsections (3) and (4) with specified modifications.

(3) The provisions are these provisions of the Police and Criminal Evidence Act 1984 (c. 60)—

(a) section 54 (searches of detained persons);

(b) section 55 (intimate searches);

(c) section 56 (right to have someone informed when arrested);

(d) section 58 (access to legal advice).

(4) The provisions are these provisions of the Police and Criminal Evidence (Northern Ireland) Order 1989 (S.I. 1989/1341 (N.I. 12))—

(a) Article 55 (searches of detained persons);

(b) Article 56 (intimate searches);

(c) Article 57 (right to have someone informed when arrested);

(d) Article 59 (access to legal advice).

Delivery of seized property

172. Delivery of seized property   *Text: 13.9*

(1) This section applies to—

(a) anything which has been seized or produced under this Part, or

(b) anything which has been seized under section 50 or 51 of the Criminal Justice and Police Act 2001 (c. 16) in reliance on a power of seizure conferred by this Part.

(2) A constable may deliver any such thing to a person who is or is acting on behalf of an authority if the constable has reasonable grounds for believing that the authority—

(a) is an authority of the relevant territory, and

(b) has functions such that it is appropriate for the thing to be delivered to it.

(3) If the relevant seizure power was a warrant issued under this Part, or the thing was produced under an order made under this Part, the relevant territory is the category 1 or category 2 territory specified in the application for the warrant or order.

(4) If the relevant seizure power was section 161(4), 162(6) or (7), 163(6) or (7) or 164(6) or (7), the relevant territory is—

(a) the territory in which the Part 1 warrant was issued, in a case where the applicable extradition arrest power is a Part 1 warrant in respect of which a certificate under section 2 has been issued;

(b) the territory in which a constable has reasonable grounds for believing that a Part 1 warrant has been or will be issued, in a case where the applicable extradition arrest power is section 5;

(c) the territory to which a person's extradition is requested, in a case where the applicable extradition arrest power is a warrant issued under section 71;

(d) the territory in which a person is accused of the commission of an offence or has been convicted of an offence, in a case where the applicable extradition arrest power is a provisional warrant.

(5) The applicable extradition arrest power is—

(a) the extradition arrest power under which a constable had a power of arrest, if the relevant seizure power was section 161(4);

(b) the extradition arrest power under which a person was arrested, if the relevant seizure power was section 162(6) or (7), 163(6) or (7) or 164(6) or (7).

(6) The relevant seizure power is—

(a) the power under which the thing was seized, or

(b) the power in reliance on which the thing was seized under section 50 or 51 of the Criminal Justice and Police Act 2001 (c. 16).

(7) Subsection (1)(a) applies to Scotland with the insertion after "Part" of "(so far as it applies to Scotland) or for the purposes of this Act (as it so applies) by virtue of any enactment or rule of law".

(8) Subsection (2) applies to Scotland with the substitution of "procurator fiscal" for "constable".

(9) In subsection (7) "enactment" includes an enactment comprised in, or in an instrument made under, an Act of the Scottish Parliament.

Codes of practice

173. Codes of practice   *Text: 4.3.1; 13.2*

(1) The Secretary of State must issue codes of practice in connection with—

(a) the exercise of the powers conferred by this Part;

(b) the retention, use and return of anything seized or produced under this Part;

(c) access to and the taking of photographs and copies of anything so seized or produced;

(d) the retention, use, disclosure and destruction of fingerprints, a sample or a photograph taken under this Part.

(2) If the Secretary of State proposes to issue a code of practice under this section he must—

(a) publish a draft of the code;

(b) consider any representations made to him about the draft;

(c) if he thinks it appropriate, modify the draft in the light of any such representations.

(3) The Secretary of State must lay the code before Parliament.

(4) When he has done so he may bring the code into operation by order.

(5) The Secretary of State may revise the whole or any part of a code issued under this section and issue the code as revised; and subsections (2) to (4) apply to such a revised code as they apply to the original code.

(6) A failure by a constable to comply with a provision of a code issued under this section does not of itself make him liable to criminal or civil proceedings.

(7) A code issued under this section is admissible in evidence in proceedings under this Act and must be taken into account by a judge or court in determining any question to which it appears to the judge or the court to be relevant.

(8) If the Secretary of State publishes a draft code of practice in connection with a matter specified in subsection (1) before the date on which this section comes into force—

(a) the draft is as effective as one published under subsection (2) on or after that date;

(b) representations made to the Secretary of State about the draft before that date are as effective as representations made to him about it after that date;

(c) modifications made by the Secretary of State to the draft in the light of any such representations before that date are as effective as any such modifications made by him on or after that date.

General

174. Interpretation

(1) Subsections (2) to (8) apply for the purposes of this Part.

(2) Each of these is an extradition arrest power—

(a) a Part 1 warrant in respect of which a certificate under section 2 has been issued;

(b) section 5;

(c) a warrant issued under section 71;

(d) a provisional warrant.

(3) "Excluded material"—

(a) in England and Wales, has the meaning given by section 11 of the 1984 Act;

(b) in Northern Ireland, has the meaning given by Article 13 of the 1989 Order.

(4) "Items subject to legal privilege"—

(a) in England and Wales, has the meaning given by section 10 of the 1984 Act;

(b) in Scotland, has the meaning given by section 412 of the 2002 Act;

(c) in Northern Ireland, has the meaning given by Article 12 of the 1989 Order.

(5) "Premises"—

(a) in England and Wales, has the meaning given by section 23 of the 1984 Act;

(b) in Scotland, has the meaning given by section 412 of the 2002 Act;

(c) in Northern Ireland, has the meaning given by Article 25 of the 1989 Order.

(6) "Special procedure material"—

(a) in England and Wales, has the meaning given by section 14 of the 1984 Act;

(b) in Northern Ireland, has the meaning given by Article 16 of the 1989 Order.

(7) The expressions in subsection (8) have the meanings given—

(a) in England and Wales, by section 65 of the 1984 Act;

(b) in Northern Ireland, by Article 53 of the 1989 Order.

(8) The expressions are—

(a) appropriate consent;

(b) fingerprints;

(c) intimate search;

(d) non-intimate sample.

(9) The 1984 Act is the Police and Criminal Evidence Act 1984 (c. 60).

(10) The 1989 Order is the Police and Criminal Evidence (Northern Ireland) Order 1989 (S.I. 1989/1341 (N.I. 12)).

(11) The 2002 Act is the Proceeds of Crime Act 2002 (c. 29).

175. Customs officers *Text: 13.4*

The Treasury may by order provide for any provision of this Part which applies in relation to police officers or persons arrested by police officers to apply with specified modifications in relation to customs officers or persons arrested by customs officers.

176. Service policemen

The Secretary of State may by order provide for any provision of this Part which applies in relation to police officers or persons arrested by police officers to apply with specified modifications in relation to service policemen or persons arrested by service policemen.

PART 5
MISCELLANEOUS AND GENERAL

British overseas territories

177. Extradition from British overseas territories *Text: 3.2.4*

(1) This section applies in relation to extradition—

(a) from a British overseas territory to a category 1 territory;

(b) from a British overseas territory to the United Kingdom;

(c) from a British overseas territory to a category 2 territory;

(d) from a British overseas territory to any of the Channel Islands or the Isle of Man.

(2) An Order in Council may provide for any provision of this Act applicable to extradition from the United Kingdom to apply to extradition in a case falling within subsection (1)(a) or (b).

(3) An Order in Council may provide for any provision of this Act applicable to extradition from the United Kingdom to a category 2 territory to apply to extradition in a case falling within subsection (1)(c) or (d).

(4) An Order in Council under this section may provide that the provision applied has effect with specified modifications.

178. Extradition to British overseas territories *Text: 3.2.5*
(1) This section applies in relation to extradition—

(a) to a British overseas territory from a category 1 territory;

(b) to a British overseas territory from the United Kingdom;

(c) to a British overseas territory from a category 2 territory;

(d) to a British overseas territory from any of the Channel Islands or the Isle of Man.

(2) An Order in Council may provide for any provision of this Act applicable to extradition to the United Kingdom to apply to extradition in a case falling within subsection (1)(a) or (b).

(3) An Order in Council may provide for any provision of this Act applicable to extradition to the United Kingdom from a category 2 territory to apply to extradition in a case falling within subsection (1)(c) or (d).

(4) An Order in Council under this section may provide that the provision applied has effect with specified modifications.

Competing extradition claims

179. Competing claims to extradition *Text: 8.4.1*
(1) This section applies if at the same time—

(a) there is a Part 1 warrant in respect of a person, a certificate has been issued under section 2 in respect of the warrant, and the person has not been extradited in pursuance of the warrant or discharged, and

(b) there is a request for the same person's extradition, a certificate has been issued under section 70 in respect of the request, and the person has not been extradited in pursuance of the request or discharged.

(2) The Secretary of State may—

(a) order proceedings (or further proceedings) on one of them (the warrant or the request) to be deferred until the other one has been disposed of, if neither the warrant nor the request has been disposed of;

(b) order the person's extradition in pursuance of the warrant to be deferred until the request has been disposed of, if an order for his extradition in pursuance of the warrant has been made;

(c) order the person's extradition in pursuance of the request to be deferred until the warrant has been disposed of, if an order for his extradition in pursuance of the request has been made.

(3) In applying subsection (2) the Secretary of State must take account in particular of these matters—

(a) the relative seriousness of the offences concerned;

(b) the place where each offence was committed (or was alleged to have been committed);

(c) the date when the warrant was issued and the date when the request was received;

(d) whether, in the case of each offence, the person is accused of its commission (but not alleged to have been convicted) or is alleged to be unlawfully at large after conviction.

(4) If both the certificates referred to in subsection (1) are issued in Scotland, the preceding provisions of this section apply as if the references to the Secretary of State were to the Scottish Ministers.

180. Proceedings on deferred warrant or request   *Text: 8.4.3*

(1) This section applies if—

(a) an order is made under this Act deferring proceedings on an extradition claim in respect of a person (the deferred claim) until another extradition claim in respect of the person has been disposed of, and

(b) the other extradition claim is disposed of.

(2) The judge may make an order for proceedings on the deferred claim to be resumed.

(3) No order under subsection (2) may be made after the end of the required period.

(4) If the person applies to the appropriate judge to be discharged, the judge may order his discharge.

(5) If the person applies to the appropriate judge to be discharged, the judge must order his discharge if—

(a) the required period has ended, and

(b) the judge has not made an order under subsection (2) or ordered the person's discharge.

(6) The required period is 21 days starting with the day on which the other extradition claim is disposed of.

(7) If the proceedings on the deferred claim were under Part 1, section 67 applies for determining the appropriate judge.

(8) If the proceedings on the deferred claim were under Part 2, section 139 applies for determining the appropriate judge.

(9) An extradition claim is made in respect of a person if—

(a) a Part 1 warrant is issued in respect of him;

(b) a request for his extradition is made.

181. Proceedings where extradition deferred   *Text: 8.4.4*

(1) This section applies if—

(a) an order is made under this Act deferring a person's extradition in pursuance of an extradition claim (the deferred claim) until another extradition claim in respect of him has been disposed of;

(b) the other extradition claim is disposed of.

(2) The judge may make an order for the person's extradition in pursuance of the deferred claim to cease to be deferred.

(3) No order under subsection (2) may be made after the end of the required period.

(4) If the person applies to the appropriate judge to be discharged, the judge may order his discharge.

(5) If the person applies to the appropriate judge to be discharged, the judge must order his discharge if—

(a) the required period has ended, and

(b) the judge has not made an order under subsection (2) or ordered the person's discharge.

(6) The required period is 21 days starting with the day on which the other extradition claim is disposed of.

(7) If the person's extradition in pursuance of the deferred claim was ordered under Part 1, section 67 applies for determining the appropriate judge.

(8) If the person's extradition in pursuance of the deferred claim was ordered under Part 2, section 139 applies for determining the appropriate judge.

(9) An extradition claim is made in respect of a person if—

(a) a Part 1 warrant is issued in respect of him;

(b) a request for his extradition is made.

Legal aid

182. Legal advice, assistance and representation: England and Wales   *Text: 4.4*

In section 12(2) of the Access to Justice Act 1999 (c. 22) (meaning of "criminal proceedings") for paragraph (c) substitute—

"(c) proceedings for dealing with an individual under the Extradition Act 2003,".

183. Legal aid: Scotland

The provisions of the Legal Aid (Scotland) Act 1986 (c. 47) apply—

(a) in relation to proceedings in Scotland before the appropriate judge under Part 1, 2 or 5 of this Act as those provisions apply in relation to summary proceedings;

(b) in relation to any proceedings on appeal arising out of such proceedings before the appropriate judge as those provisions apply in relation to appeals in summary proceedings.

184. Grant of free legal aid: Northern Ireland

(1) The appropriate judge may grant free legal aid to a person in connection with proceedings under Part 1 or Part 2 before the judge or the High Court.

(2) A judge of the High Court may grant free legal aid to a person in connection with proceedings under Part 1 or Part 2 before the High Court or the House of Lords.

(3) If the appropriate judge refuses to grant free legal aid under subsection (1) in connection with proceedings before the High Court the person may appeal to the High Court against the judge's decision.

(4) A judge of the High Court may grant free legal aid to a person in connection with proceedings on an appeal under subsection (3).

(5) Free legal aid may be granted to a person under subsection (1), (2) or (4) only if it appears to the judge that—

(a) the person's means are insufficient to enable him to obtain legal aid, and

(b) it is desirable in the interests of justice that the person should be granted free legal aid.

(6) On an appeal under subsection (3) the High Court may—

(a) allow the appeal;

(b) dismiss the appeal.

(7) The High Court may allow an appeal under subsection (3) only if it appears to the High Court that—

(a) the person's means are insufficient to enable him to obtain legal aid, and

(b) it is desirable in the interests of justice that the person should be granted free legal aid.

(8) If the High Court allows an appeal under subsection (3) it must grant free legal aid to the person in connection with the proceedings under Part 1 or Part 2 before it.

(9) If on a question of granting free legal aid under this section or of allowing an appeal under subsection (3) there is a doubt as to whether—

(a) the person's means are insufficient to enable him to obtain legal aid, or

(b) it is desirable in the interests of justice that the person should be granted free legal aid, the doubt must be resolved in favour of granting him free legal aid.

(10) References in this section to granting free legal aid to a person are to assigning to him—

(a) a solicitor and counsel, or

(b) a solicitor only, or

(c) counsel only.

185. Free legal aid: supplementary

(1) The provisions of the Legal Aid, Advice and Assistance (Northern Ireland) Order 1981 (S.I. 1981/228 (N.I. 8)) listed in subsection (2) apply in relation to free legal aid under section 184 in connection with proceedings before the appropriate judge or the High Court as they apply in relation to free legal aid under Part III of the Order.

(2) The provisions are—

(a) Article 32 (statements of means);

(b) Article 36(1) (payment of legal aid);

(c) Article 36(3) and (4) (rules);

(d) Article 36A (solicitors excluded from legal aid work);

(e) Article 37 (remuneration of solicitors and counsel);

(f) Article 40 (stamp duty exemption).

(3) As so applied those Articles have effect as if—

(a) a person granted free legal aid under section 184 had been granted a criminal aid certificate under Part III of the Order;

(b) section 184 were contained in Part III of the Order.

(4) The fees of any counsel, and the expenses and fees of any solicitor, assigned to a person under section 184 in connection with proceedings before the House of Lords must be paid by the Lord Chancellor.

(5) The fees and expenses paid under subsection (4) must not exceed the amount allowed by—

(a) the House of Lords, or

(b) such officer or officers of the House of Lords as may be prescribed by order of the House of Lords.

(6) For the purposes of section 184 and this section the appropriate judge is—

(a) such county court judge or resident magistrate as is designated for the purposes of Part 1 by the Lord Chancellor, if the proceedings are under Part 1;

(b) such county court judge or resident magistrate as is designated for the purposes of Part 2 by the Lord Chancellor, if the proceedings are under Part 2.

Re-extradition

186. Re-extradition: preliminary
Text: 14.4

(1) Section 187 applies in relation to a person if the conditions in subsections (2) to (6) are satisfied.

(2) The first condition is that the person was extradited to a territory in accordance with Part 1 or Part 2.

(3) The second condition is that the person was serving a sentence of imprisonment or another form of detention in the United Kingdom (the UK sentence) before he was extradited.

(4) The third condition is that—

(a) if the person was extradited in accordance with Part 1, the Part 1 warrant in pursuance of which he was extradited contained a statement that it was issued with a view to his extradition for the purpose of being prosecuted for an offence;

(b) if the person was extradited in accordance with Part 2, the request in pursuance of which the person was extradited contained a statement that the person was accused of the commission of an offence.

(5) The fourth condition is that a certificate issued by a judicial authority of the territory shows that—

(a) a sentence of imprisonment or another form of detention for a term of 4 months or a greater punishment (the overseas sentence) was imposed on the person in the territory;

(b) the overseas sentence was imposed on him in respect of—

(i) the offence specified in the warrant or request, or

(ii) any other offence committed before his extradition in respect of which he was permitted to be dealt with in the territory.

(6) The fifth condition is that before serving the overseas sentence the person was returned to the United Kingdom to serve the remainder of the UK sentence.

187. Re-extradition hearing   *Text: 14.4*

(1) If this section applies in relation to a person, as soon as practicable after the relevant time the person must be brought before the appropriate judge for the judge to decide whether the person is to be extradited again to the territory in which the overseas sentence was imposed.

(2) The relevant time is the time at which the person would otherwise be released from detention pursuant to the UK sentence (whether or not on licence).

(3) If subsection (1) is not complied with and the person applies to the judge to be discharged, the judge must order his discharge.

(4) The person must be treated as continuing in legal custody until he is brought before the appropriate judge under subsection (1) or he is discharged under subsection (3).

(5) If the person is brought before the appropriate judge under subsection (1) the judge must decide whether the territory in which the overseas sentence was imposed is—

(a) a category 1 territory;

(b) a category 2 territory;

(c) neither a category 1 territory nor a category 2 territory.

(6) If the judge decides that the territory is a category 1 territory, section 188 applies.

(7) If the judge decides that the territory is a category 2 territory, section 189 applies.

(8) If the judge decides that the territory is neither a category 1 territory nor a category 2 territory, he must order the person's discharge.

(9) A person's discharge as a result of this section or section 188 or 189 does not affect any conditions on which he is released from detention pursuant to the UK sentence.

(10) Section 139 applies for determining the appropriate judge for the purposes of this section.

188. Re-extradition to category 1 territories   *Text: 14.4.1*

(1) If this section applies, this Act applies as it would if—

(a) a Part 1 warrant had been issued in respect of the person;

(b) the warrant contained a statement that—

(i) the person was alleged to be unlawfully at large after conviction of the relevant offence, and

(ii) the warrant was issued with a view to the person's arrest and extradition to the territory for the purpose of serving a sentence imposed in respect of the relevant offence;

(c) the warrant were issued by the authority of the territory which issued the certificate referred to in section 186(5);

(d) the relevant offence were specified in the warrant;

(e) the judge were the appropriate judge for the purposes of Part 1;

(f) the hearing at which the judge is to make the decision referred to in section 187(1) were the extradition hearing;

(g) the proceedings before the judge were under Part 1.

(2) As applied by subsection (1) this Act has effect with the modifications set out in Part 1 of Schedule 1.

(3) The relevant offence is the offence in respect of which the overseas sentence is imposed.

189. Re-extradition to category 2 territories *Text: 14.4.2*

(1) If this section applies, this Act applies as it would if—

(a) a valid request for the person's extradition to the territory had been made;

(b) the request contained a statement that the person was alleged to be unlawfully at large after conviction of the relevant offence;

(c) the relevant offence were specified in the request;

(d) the hearing at which the appropriate judge is to make the decision referred to in section 187(1) were the extradition hearing;

(e) the proceedings before the judge were under Part 2.

(2) As applied by subsection (1) this Act has effect with the modifications set out in Part 2 of Schedule 1.

(3) The relevant offence is the offence in respect of which the overseas sentence is imposed.

Conduct of extradition proceedings

190. Crown Prosecution Service: role in extradition proceedings *Text: 4.6*

(1) The Prosecution of Offences Act 1985 (c. 23) is amended as follows.

(2) In section 3 (functions of the Director) in subsection (2) after paragraph (e) insert—

"(ea) to have the conduct of any extradition proceedings;

(eb) to give, to such extent as he considers appropriate, and to such persons as he considers appropriate, advice on any matters relating to extradition proceedings or proposed extradition proceedings;".

(3) In section 3 after subsection (2) insert—

"(2A) Subsection (2)(ea) above does not require the Director to have the conduct of any extradition proceedings in respect of a person if he has received a request not to do so and—

(a) in a case where the proceedings are under Part 1 of the Extradition Act 2003, the request is made by the authority which issued the Part 1 warrant in respect of the person;

(b) in a case where the proceedings are under Part 2 of that Act, the request is made on behalf of the territory to which the person's extradition has been requested."

(4) In section 5(1) (conduct of prosecutions on behalf of Crown Prosecution Service) after "criminal proceedings" insert "or extradition proceedings".

(5) In section 14 (control of fees and expenses etc paid by the Service) in subsection (1)(a) after "criminal proceedings" insert "or extradition proceedings".

(6) In section 15(1) (interpretation of Part 1) in the appropriate place insert—

" "extradition proceedings" means proceedings under the Extradition Act 2003;".

191. Lord Advocate: role in extradition proceedings

(1) The Lord Advocate must—

(a) conduct any extradition proceedings in Scotland;

(b) give, to such extent as he considers appropriate, and to such persons as he considers appropriate, advice on any matters relating to extradition proceedings or proposed extradition proceedings, in Scotland.

(2) Subsection (1)(a) does not require the Lord Advocate to conduct any extradition proceedings in respect of a person if he has received a request not to do so and—

(a) in a case where the proceedings are under Part 1, the request is made by the authority which issued the Part 1 warrant in respect of the person;

(b) in a case where the proceedings are under Part 2, the request is made on behalf of the territory to which the person's extradition has been requested.

192. Northern Ireland DPP and Crown Solicitor: role in extradition proceedings

(1) The Prosecution of Offences (Northern Ireland) Order 1972 (S.I. 1972/538 (N.I. 1)) is amended as set out in subsections (2) to (4).

(2) In article 2(2) (interpretation) in the appropriate place insert—

" "extradition proceedings" means proceedings under the Extradition Act 2003;".

(3) In article 4(7) (conduct of prosecutions on behalf of DPP) after "prosecution" insert "or extradition proceedings".

(4) In article 5 (functions of DPP) after paragraph (1) insert—

"(1A) The Director may—

(a) have the conduct of any extradition proceedings in Northern Ireland;

(b) give to such persons as appear to him appropriate such advice as appears to him appropriate on matters relating to extradition proceedings, or proposed extradition proceedings, in Northern Ireland."

(5) The Justice (Northern Ireland) Act 2002 (c. 26) is amended as set out in subsections (6) to (8).

(6) After section 31 insert—

"31A Conduct of extradition proceedings

(1) The Director may have the conduct of any extradition proceedings in Northern Ireland.

(2) The Director may give to such persons as appear to him appropriate such advice as appears to him appropriate on matters relating to extradition proceedings, or proposed extradition proceedings, in Northern Ireland."

(7) In section 36(2) (conduct of criminal proceedings on behalf of DPP) after "criminal proceedings" insert "or extradition proceedings".

(8) In section 44 (interpretation) after subsection (6) insert—

"(7) For the purposes of this Part "extradition proceedings" means proceedings under the Extradition Act 2003."

(9) The Crown Solicitor for Northern Ireland may—

(a) have the conduct of any proceedings under this Act in Northern Ireland;

(b) give to such persons as appear to him appropriate such advice as appears to him appropriate on matters relating to proceedings under this Act, or proposed proceedings under this Act, in Northern Ireland.

Parties to international Conventions

193. Parties to international Conventions   *Text: 3.1.4*

(1) A territory may be designated by order made by the Secretary of State if—

(a) it is not a category 1 territory or a category 2 territory, and

(b) it is a party to an international Convention to which the United Kingdom is a party.

(2) This Act applies in relation to a territory designated by order under subsection (1) as if the territory were a category 2 territory.

(3) As applied to a territory by subsection (2), this Act has effect as if—

(a) sections 71(4), 73(5), 74(11)(b), 84(7), 86(7), 137 and 138 were omitted;

(b) the conduct that constituted an extradition offence for the purposes of Part 2 were the conduct specified in relation to the territory in the order under subsection (1) designating the territory.

(4) Conduct may be specified in relation to a territory in an order under subsection (1) designating the territory only if it is conduct to which the relevant Convention applies.

(5) The relevant Convention is the Convention referred to in subsection (1)(b) which is specified in relation to the territory in the order under subsection (1) designating it.

Special extradition arrangements

194. Special extradition arrangements   *Text: 3.1.5*

(1) This section applies if the Secretary of State believes that—

(a) arrangements have been made between the United Kingdom and another territory for the extradition of a person to the territory, and

(b) the territory is not a category 1 territory or a category 2 territory.

(2) The Secretary of State may certify that the conditions in paragraphs (a) and (b) of subsection (1) are satisfied in relation to the extradition of the person.

(3) If the Secretary of State issues a certificate under subsection (2) this Act applies in respect of the person's extradition to the territory as if the territory were a category 2 territory.

(4) As applied by subsection (3), this Act has effect—

(a) as if sections 71(4), 73(5), 74(11)(b), 84(7) and 86(7) were omitted;

(b) with any other modifications specified in the certificate.

(5) A certificate under subsection (2) in relation to a person is conclusive evidence that the conditions in paragraphs (a) and (b) of subsection (1) are satisfied in relation to the person's extradition.

Human rights

195. Human rights: appropriate tribunal

(1) The appropriate judge is the only appropriate tribunal in relation to proceedings under section 7(1)(a) of the Human Rights Act 1998 (c. 42) (proceedings for acts incompatible with Convention rights) if the proceedings relate to extradition under Part 1 or Part 2 of this Act.

(2) If the proceedings relate to extradition under Part 1, section 67 applies for determining the appropriate judge.

(3) If the proceedings relate to extradition under Part 2, section 139 applies for determining the appropriate judge.

Genocide etc

196. Genocide, crimes against humanity and war crimes   *Text: 2.3.4*

(1) This section applies if—

(a) a Part 1 warrant in respect of a person is issued in respect of an offence mentioned in subsection (2), or

(b) a valid request for a person's extradition is made in respect of an offence mentioned in subsection (2).

(2) The offences are—

(a) an offence that if committed in the United Kingdom would be punishable as an offence under section 51 or 58 of the International Criminal Court Act 2001 (c. 17) (genocide, crimes against humanity and war crimes);

(b) an offence that if committed in the United Kingdom would be punishable as an offence under section 52 or 59 of that Act (conduct ancillary to genocide, etc. committed outside the jurisdiction);

(c) an offence that if committed in the United Kingdom would be punishable as an ancillary offence, as defined in section 55 or 62 of that Act, in relation to an offence falling within paragraph (a) or (b);

(d) an offence that if committed in the United Kingdom would be punishable as an offence under section 1 of the International Criminal Court (Scotland) Act 2001 (asp 13) (genocide, crimes against humanity and war crimes);

(e) an offence that if committed in the United Kingdom would be punishable as an offence under section 2 of that Act (conduct ancillary to genocide etc. committed outside the jurisdiction);

(f) an offence that if committed in the United Kingdom would be punishable as an ancillary offence, as defined in section 7 of that Act, in relation to an offence falling within paragraph (d) or (e);

(g) any offence punishable in the United Kingdom under section 1 of the Geneva Conventions Act 1957 (c. 52) (grave breach of scheduled conventions).

(3) It is not an objection to extradition under this Act that the person could not have been punished for the offence under the law in force at the time when and in the place where he is alleged to have committed the act of which he is accused or of which he has been convicted.

Custody and bail

197. Custody

(1) If a judge remands a person in custody under this Act, the person must be committed to the institution to which he would have been committed if charged with an offence before the judge.

(2) If a person in custody following his arrest under Part 1 or Part 2 escapes from custody, he may be retaken in any part of the United Kingdom in the same way as he could have been if he had been in custody following his arrest or apprehension under a relevant domestic warrant.

(3) A relevant domestic warrant is a warrant for his arrest or apprehension issued in the part of the United Kingdom in question in respect of an offence committed there.

(4) Subsection (5) applies if—

(a) a person is in custody in one part of the United Kingdom (whether under this Act or otherwise);

(b) he is required to be removed to another part of the United Kingdom after being remanded in custody under this Act;

(c) he is so removed by sea or air.

(5) The person must be treated as continuing in legal custody until he reaches the place to which he is required to be removed.

(6) An order for a person's extradition under this Act is sufficient authority for an appropriate person—

(a) to receive him;

(b) to keep him in custody until he is extradited under this Act;

(c) to convey him to the territory to which he is to be extradited under this Act.

(7) An appropriate person is—

(a) a person to whom the order is directed;

(b) a constable.

198. Bail: England and Wales

(1) The Bail Act 1976 (c. 63) is amended as follows.

(2) In section 1(1) (meaning of "bail in criminal proceedings") after paragraph (b) insert— ", or

(c) bail grantable in connection with extradition proceedings in respect of an offence."

(3) In section 2(2) (other definitions) omit the definition of "proceedings against a fugitive offender" and in the appropriate places insert—

" "extradition proceedings" means proceedings under the Extradition Act 2003;";

" "prosecutor", in relation to extradition proceedings, means the person acting on behalf of the territory to which extradition is sought;".

(4) In section 4 (general right to bail) in subsection (2) omit the words "or proceedings against a fugitive offender for the offence".

(5) In section 4 after subsection (2) insert—

"(2A) This section also applies to a person whose extradition is sought in respect of an offence, when—

(a) he appears or is brought before a court in the course of or in connection with extradition proceedings in respect of the offence, or

(b) he applies to a court for bail or for a variation of the conditions of bail in connection with the proceedings.

(2B) But subsection (2A) above does not apply if the person is alleged to be unlawfully at large after conviction of the offence."

(6) In section 5B (reconsideration of decisions granting bail) for subsection (1) substitute—

"(A1) This section applies in any of these cases—

(a) a magistrates' court has granted bail in criminal proceedings in connection with an offence to which this section applies or proceedings for such an offence;

(b) a constable has granted bail in criminal proceedings in connection with proceedings for such an offence;

(c) a magistrates' court or a constable has granted bail in connection with extradition proceedings.

(1) The court or the appropriate court in relation to the constable may, on application by the prosecutor for the decision to be reconsidered—

(a) vary the conditions of bail,

(b) impose conditions in respect of bail which has been granted unconditionally, or

(c) withhold bail."

(7) In section 7 (liability to arrest for absconding or breaking conditions of bail) after subsection (1) insert—

"(1A) Subsection (1B) applies if—

(a) a person has been released on bail in connection with extradition proceedings,

(b) the person is under a duty to surrender into the custody of a constable, and

(c) the person fails to surrender to custody at the time appointed for him to do so.

(1B) A magistrates' court may issue a warrant for the person's arrest."

(8) In section 7(4) omit the words from "In reckoning" to "Sunday".

(9) In section 7 after subsection (4) insert—

"(4A) A person who has been released on bail in connection with extradition proceedings and is under a duty to surrender into the custody of a constable may be arrested without warrant by a constable on any of the grounds set out in paragraphs (a) to (c) of subsection (3).

(4B) A person arrested in pursuance of subsection (4A) above shall be brought as soon as practicable and in any event within 24 hours after his arrest before a justice of the peace for the petty sessions area in which he was arrested."

(10) In section 7(5) after "subsection (4)" insert "or (4B)".

(11) In section 7 after subsection (6) insert—

"(7) In reckoning for the purposes of this section any period of 24 hours, no account shall be taken of Christmas Day, Good Friday or any Sunday."

(12) In Part 1 of Schedule 1 (defendants accused or convicted of imprisonable offences) for paragraph 1 substitute—

"1 The following provisions of this Part of this Schedule apply to the defendant if—

(a) the offence or one of the offences of which he is accused or convicted in the proceedings is punishable with imprisonment, or

(b) his extradition is sought in respect of an offence."

(13) In Part 1 of Schedule 1 after paragraph 2A insert—

"2B The defendant need not be granted bail in connection with extradition proceedings if—

(a) the conduct constituting the offence would, if carried out by the defendant in England and Wales, constitute an indictable offence or an offence triable either way; and

(b) it appears to the court that the defendant was on bail on the date of the offence."

(14) In Part 1 of Schedule 1 in paragraph 6 after "the offence" insert "or the extradition proceedings".

199. Bail: Scotland
After section 24 of the Criminal Procedure (Scotland) Act 1995 (c. 46) (bail and bail conditions) insert—

"24A Bail: extradition proceedings
(1) In the application of the provisions of this Part by virtue of section 9(2) or 77(2) of the Extradition Act 2003 (judge's powers at extradition hearing), those provisions apply with the modifications that—

(a) references to the prosecutor are to be read as references to a person acting on behalf of the territory to which extradition is sought;

(b) the right of the Lord Advocate mentioned in section 24(2) of this Act applies to a person subject to extradition proceedings as it applies to a person charged with any crime or offence;

(c) the following do not apply—

(i) paragraph (b) of section 24(3); and

(ii) subsection (3) of section 30; and

(d) sections 28(1) and 33 apply to a person subject to extradition proceedings as they apply to an accused.

(2) Section 32 of this Act applies in relation to a refusal of bail, the amount of bail or a decision to allow bail or ordain appearance in proceedings under this Part as the Part applies by virtue of the sections of that Act of 2003 mentioned in subsection (1) above.

(3) The Scottish Ministers may, by order, for the purposes of section 9(2) or 77(2) of the Extradition Act 2003 make such amendments to this Part as they consider necessary or expedient.

(4) The order making power in subsection (3) above shall be exercisable by statutory instrument subject to annulment in pursuance of a resolution of the Scottish Parliament."

200. Appeal against grant of bail   *Text: 4.5.4*

(1) Section 1 of the Bail (Amendment) Act 1993 (c. 26) (prosecution right of appeal against grant of bail) is amended as follows.

(2) After subsection (1) insert—

"(1A) Where a magistrates' court grants bail to a person in connection with extradition proceedings, the prosecution may appeal to a judge of the Crown Court against the granting of bail."

(3) In subsection (3) for "Such an appeal" substitute "An appeal under subsection (1) or (1A)".

(4) In subsection (4)—

(a) after subsection (1) insert "or (1A)";

(b) for "magistrates' court" substitute "court which has granted bail";

(c) omit "such".

(5) In subsection (5) for "magistrates' court" substitute "court which has granted bail".

(6) In subsection (6) for "magistrates' court" substitute "court which has granted bail".

(7) In subsection (8)—

(a) after "subsection (1)" insert "or (1A)";

(b) omit "magistrates' ".

(8) In subsection (10)(b) for "reference in subsection (5) above to remand in custody is" substitute "references in subsections (6) and (9) above to remand in custody are".

(9) After subsection (11) insert—

"(12) In this section—

"extradition proceedings" means proceedings under the Extradition Act 2003;

"magistrates' court" and "court" in relation to extradition proceedings means a District Judge (Magistrates' Courts) designated for the purposes of Part 1 or Part 2 of the Extradition Act 2003 by the Lord Chancellor;

"prosecution" in relation to extradition proceedings means the person acting on behalf of the territory to which extradition is sought."

201. Remand to local authority accommodation

(1) Section 23 of the Children and Young Persons Act 1969 (c. 54) (remand to local authority accommodation) is amended as set out in subsections (2) to (11).

(2) In subsection (1) after "following provisions of this section" insert "(except subsection (1A))".

(3) After subsection (1) insert—

"(1A) Where a court remands a child or young person in connection with extradition proceedings and he is not released on bail the remand shall be to local authority accommodation."

(4) In subsection (4) after "subsections (5) "insert", (5ZA)".

(5) In subsection (5) after "security requirement" insert "in relation to a person remanded in accordance with subsection (1) above".

(6) After subsection (5) insert—

"(5ZA) A court shall not impose a security requirement in relation to a person remanded in accordance with subsection (1A) above unless—

(a) he has attained the age of twelve and is of a prescribed description;

(b) one or both of the conditions set out in subsection (5ZB) below is satisfied; and

(c) the condition set out in subsection (5AA) below is satisfied.

(5ZB) The conditions mentioned in subsection (5ZA)(b) above are—

(a) that the conduct constituting the offence to which the extradition proceedings relate would if committed in the United Kingdom constitute an offence punishable in the case of an adult with imprisonment for a term of fourteen years or more;

(b) that the person has previously absconded from the extradition proceedings or from proceedings in the United Kingdom or the requesting territory which relate to the conduct constituting the offence to which the extradition proceedings relate.

(5ZC) For the purposes of subsection (5ZB) above a person has absconded from proceedings if in relation to those proceedings—

(a) he has been released subject to a requirement to surrender to custody at a particular time and he has failed to surrender to custody at that time, or

(b) he has surrendered into the custody of a court and he has at any time absented himself from the court without its leave."

(7) In subsection (5AA) for "subsection (5)" substitute "subsections (5) and (5ZA)".

(8) In subsection (12) for the definition of "relevant court" substitute—

" "relevant court"—

(a) in relation to a person remanded to local authority accommodation under subsection (1) above, means the court by which he was so remanded, or any magistrates' court having jurisdiction in the place where he is for the time being;

(b) in relation to a person remanded to local authority accommodation under subsection (1A) above, means the court by which he was so remanded."

(9) In subsection (12) in the appropriate places insert—

" "extradition proceedings" means proceedings under the Extradition Act 2003;";

" "requesting territory" means the territory to which a person's extradition is sought in extradition proceedings;".

(10) In section 98(1) of the Crime and Disorder Act 1998 (c. 37) (modifications of section 23 of the Children and Young Persons Act 1969 (c. 54) in relation to 15 and 16 year old boys) after paragraph (b) insert "; and

(c) is not remanded in connection with proceedings under the Extradition Act 2003."

Evidence

202. Receivable documents   *Text: 5.5*

(1) A Part 1 warrant may be received in evidence in proceedings under this Act.

(2) Any other document issued in a category 1 territory may be received in evidence in proceedings under this Act if it is duly authenticated.

(3) A document issued in a category 2 territory may be received in evidence in proceedings under this Act if it is duly authenticated.

(4) A document issued in a category 1 or category 2 territory is duly authenticated if (and only if) one of these applies—

(a) it purports to be signed by a judge, magistrate or other judicial authority of the territory;

(b) it purports to be authenticated by the oath or affirmation of a witness.

(5) Subsections (2) and (3) do not prevent a document that is not duly authenticated from being received in evidence in proceedings under this Act.

203. Documents sent by facsimile   *Text: 5.5*

(1) This section applies if a document to be sent in connection with proceedings under this Act is sent by facsimile transmission.

(2) This Act has effect as if the document received by facsimile transmission were the document used to make the transmission.

204. Part 1 warrant: transmission by other electronic means   *Text: 5.5*

(1) This section applies if a Part 1 warrant is issued and the information contained in the warrant—

(a) is transmitted to the designated authority by electronic means (other than by facsimile transmission), and

(b) is received by the designated authority in a form in which it is intelligible and which is capable of being used for subsequent reference.

(2) This Act has effect as if the information received by the designated authority were the Part 1 warrant.

(3) A copy of the information received by the designated authority may be received in evidence as if it were the Part 1 warrant.

205. Written statements and admissions *Text: 6.10.2*

(1) The provisions mentioned in subsection (2) apply in relation to proceedings under this Act as they apply in relation to proceedings for an offence.

(2) The provisions are—

(a) section 9 of the Criminal Justice Act 1967 (c. 80) (proof by written statement in criminal proceedings);

(b) section 10 of the Criminal Justice Act 1967 (proof by formal admission in criminal proceedings);

(c) section 1 of the Criminal Justice (Miscellaneous Provisions) Act (Northern Ireland) 1968 (c. 28) (proof by written statement in criminal proceedings);

(d) section 2 of the Criminal Justice (Miscellaneous Provisions) Act (Northern Ireland) 1968 (proof by formal admission in criminal proceedings).

(3) As applied by subsection (1) in relation to proceedings under this Act, section 10 of the Criminal Justice Act 1967 and section 2 of the Criminal Justice (Miscellaneous Provisions) Act (Northern Ireland) 1968 have effect as if—

(a) references to the defendant were to the person whose extradition is sought (or who has been extradited);

(b) references to the prosecutor were to the category 1 or category 2 territory concerned;

(c) references to the trial were to the proceedings under this Act for the purposes of which the admission is made;

(d) references to subsequent criminal proceedings were to subsequent proceedings under this Act.

206. Burden and standard of proof *Text: 5.4; 6.4*

(1) This section applies if, in proceedings under this Act, a question arises as to burden or standard of proof.

(2) The question must be decided by applying any enactment or rule of law that would apply if the proceedings were proceedings for an offence.

(3) Any enactment or rule of law applied under subsection (2) to proceedings under this Act must be applied as if—

(a) the person whose extradition is sought (or who has been extradited) were accused of an offence;

(b) the category 1 or category 2 territory concerned were the prosecution.

(4) Subsections (2) and (3) are subject to any express provision of this Act.

(5) In this section "enactment" includes an enactment comprised in, or in an instrument made under, an Act of the Scottish Parliament.

Other miscellaneous provisions

207. Extradition for more than one offence   *Text: 5.6*

The Secretary of State may by order provide for this Act to have effect with specified modifications in relation to a case where—

(a) a Part 1 warrant is issued in respect of more than one offence;

(b) a request for extradition is made in respect of more than one offence.

208. National security

(1) This section applies if the Secretary of State believes that the conditions in subsections (2) to (4) are satisfied in relation to a person.

(2) The first condition is that the person's extradition is sought or will be sought under Part 1 or Part 2 in respect of an offence.

(3) The second condition is that—

(a) in engaging in the conduct constituting (or alleged to constitute) the offence the person was acting for the purpose of assisting in the exercise of a function conferred or imposed by or under an enactment, or

(b) as a result of an authorisation given by the Secretary of State the person is not liable under the criminal law of any part of the United Kingdom for the conduct constituting (or alleged to constitute) the offence.

(4) The third condition is that the person's extradition in respect of the offence would be against the interests of national security.

(5) The Secretary of State may certify that the conditions in subsections (2) to (4) are satisfied in relation to the person.

(6) If the Secretary of State issues a certificate under subsection (5) he may—

(a) direct that a Part 1 warrant issued in respect of the person and in respect of the offence is not to be proceeded with, or

(b) direct that a request for the person's extradition in respect of the offence is not to be proceeded with.

(7) If the Secretary of State issues a certificate under subsection (5) he may order the person's discharge (instead of or in addition to giving a direction under subsection (6)).

(8) These rules apply if the Secretary of State gives a direction under subsection (6)(a) in respect of a warrant—

(a) if the designated authority has not issued a certificate under section 2 in respect of the warrant it must not do so;

(b) if the person is arrested under the warrant or under section 5 there is no requirement for him to be brought before the appropriate judge and he must be discharged;

(c) if the person is brought before the appropriate judge under section 4 or 6 the judge is no longer required to proceed or continue proceeding under sections 7 and 8;

(d) if the extradition hearing has begun the judge is no longer required to proceed or continue proceeding under sections 10 to 25;

(e) if the person has consented to his extradition, the judge is no longer required to order his extradition;

(f) if an appeal to the High Court or House of Lords has been brought, the court is no longer required to hear or continue hearing the appeal;

(g) if the person's extradition has been ordered there is no requirement for him to be extradited.

(9) These rules apply if the Secretary of State gives a direction under subsection (6)(b) in respect of a request—

(a) if he has not issued a certificate under section 70 in respect of the request he is no longer required to do so;

(b) if the person is arrested under a warrant issued under section 71 or under a provisional warrant there is no requirement for him to appear or be brought before the appropriate judge and he must be discharged;

(c) if the person appears or is brought before the appropriate judge the judge is no longer required to proceed or continue proceeding under sections 72, 74, 75 and 76;

(d) if the extradition hearing has begun the judge is no longer required to proceed or continue proceeding under sections 78 to 91;

(e) if the person has given his consent to his extradition to the appropriate judge, the judge is no longer required to send the case to the Secretary of State for his decision whether the person is to be extradited;

(f) if an appeal to the High Court or House of Lords has been brought, the court is no longer required to hear or continue hearing the appeal;

(g) if the person's extradition has been ordered there is no requirement for him to be extradited.

(10) These must be made under the hand of the Secretary of State—

(a) a certificate under subsection (5);

(b) a direction under subsection (6);

(c) an order under subsection (7).

(11) The preceding provisions of this section apply to Scotland with these modifications—

(a) in subsection (9)(a) for "he has" substitute "the Scottish Ministers have" and for "he is" substitute "they are";

(b) in subsection (9)(e) for "Secretary of State for his" substitute "Scottish Ministers for their".

(12) In subsection (3) the reference to an enactment includes an enactment comprised in, or in an instrument made under, an Act of the Scottish Parliament.

209. Reasonable force   *Text: 13.3*
A person may use reasonable force, if necessary, in the exercise of a power conferred by this Act.

210. Rules of court

(1) Rules of court may make provision as to the practice and procedure to be followed in connection with proceedings under this Act.

(2) In Scotland any rules of court under this Act are to be made by Act of Adjournal.

211. Service of notices

Service of a notice on a person under section 54, 56, 58, 129, 130 or 131 may be effected in any of these ways—

(a) by delivering the notice to the person;

(b) by leaving it for him with another person at his last known or usual place of abode;

(c) by sending it by post in a letter addressed to him at his last known or usual place of abode.

212. Article 95 alerts: transitional provision

(1) This section applies in a case where an article 95 alert is issued before 1 January 2004 by an authority of a category 1 territory.

(2) In such a case, this Act applies as if—

(a) the alert were a Part 1 warrant issued by the authority;

(b) any information sent with the alert relating to the case were included in the warrant.

(3) As applied by subsection (2), this Act has effect with these modifications—

(a) in sections 2(7) and (8), 28(1), 30(1) and (4)(d), 32(2)(b), 33(6)(b), 35(4)(b), 36(3)(b), 47(3)(b), 49(3)(b), 190(3) and 191(2)(a) for "authority which issued the Part 1 warrant" substitute "authority at the request of which the alert was issued";

(b) omit section 5;

(c) in sections 33(4)(b), 42(2)(a), 43(2)(a) and (4) and 61(1)(d) and (e), for "authority which issued the warrant" substitute "authority at the request of which the alert was issued";

(d) in section 66(2), for the words from "believes" to the end substitute "believes is the authority at the request of which the alert was issued".

(4) An article 95 alert is an alert issued pursuant to article 95 of the Convention implementing the Schengen agreement of 14th June 1985.

Interpretation

213. Disposal of Part 1 warrant and extradition request

(1) A Part 1 warrant issued in respect of a person is disposed of—

(a) when an order is made for the person's discharge in respect of the warrant and there is no further possibility of an appeal;

(b) when the person is taken to be discharged in respect of the warrant;

(c) when an order is made for the person's extradition in pursuance of the warrant and there is no further possibility of an appeal.

(2) A request for a person's extradition is disposed of—

(a) when an order is made for the person's discharge in respect of the request and there is no further possibility of an appeal;

(b) when the person is taken to be discharged in respect of the request;

(c) when an order is made for the person's extradition in pursuance of the request and there is no further possibility of an appeal.

(3) There is no further possibility of an appeal against an order for a person's discharge or extradition—

(a) when the period permitted for giving notice of an appeal to the High Court ends, if notice is not given before the end of that period;

(b) when the decision of the High Court on an appeal becomes final, if there is no appeal to the House of Lords against that decision;

(c) when the decision of the House of Lords on an appeal is made, if there is such an appeal.

(4) The decision of the High Court on an appeal becomes final—

(a) when the period permitted for applying to the High Court for leave to appeal to the House of Lords ends, if there is no such application;

(b) when the period permitted for applying to the House of Lords for leave to appeal to it ends, if the High Court refuses leave to appeal and there is no application to the House of Lords for leave to appeal;

(c) when the House of Lords refuses leave to appeal to it;

(d) at the end of the permitted period, which is 28 days starting with the day on which leave to appeal to the House of Lords is granted, if no such appeal is brought before the end of that period.

(5) These must be ignored for the purposes of subsections (3) and (4)—

(a) any power of a court to extend the period permitted for giving notice of appeal or for applying for leave to appeal;

(b) any power of a court to grant leave to take a step out of time.

(6) Subsections (3) to (5) do not apply to Scotland.

214. Disposal of charge

(1) A charge against a person is disposed of—

(a) if the person is acquitted in respect of it, when he is acquitted;

(b) if the person is convicted in respect of it, when there is no further possibility of an appeal against the conviction.

(2) There is no further possibility of an appeal against a conviction—

(a) when the period permitted for giving notice of application for leave to appeal to the Court of Appeal against the conviction ends, if the leave of the Court of Appeal is required and no such notice is given before the end of that period;

(b) when the Court of Appeal refuses leave to appeal against the conviction, if the leave of the Court of Appeal is required and notice of application for leave is given before the end of that period;

(c) when the period permitted for giving notice of appeal to the Court of Appeal against the conviction ends, if notice is not given before the end of that period;

(d) when the decision of the Court of Appeal on an appeal becomes final, if there is no appeal to the House of Lords against that decision;

(e) when the decision of the House of Lords on an appeal is made, if there is such an appeal.

(3) The decision of the Court of Appeal on an appeal becomes final—

(a) when the period permitted for applying to the Court of Appeal for leave to appeal to the House of Lords ends, if there is no such application;

(b) when the period permitted for applying to the House of Lords for leave to appeal to it ends, if the Court of Appeal refuses leave to appeal and there is no application to the House of Lords for leave to appeal;

(c) when the House of Lords refuses leave to appeal to it;

(d) at the end of the permitted period, which is 28 days starting with the day on which leave to appeal to the House of Lords is granted, if no such appeal is brought before the end of that period.

(4) These must be ignored for the purposes of subsections (2) and (3)—

(a) any power of a court to extend the period permitted for giving notice of appeal or of application for leave to appeal or for applying for leave to appeal;

(b) any power of a court to grant leave to take a step out of time.

(5) Subsections (2) to (4) do not apply to Scotland.

215. European framework list   *Text: 2.3.2.2*

(1) The European framework list is the list of conduct set out in Schedule 2.

(2) The Secretary of State may by order amend Schedule 2 for the purpose of ensuring that the list of conduct set out in the Schedule corresponds to the list of conduct set out in article 2.2 of the European framework decision.

(3) The European framework decision is the framework decision of the Council of the European Union made on 13 June 2002 on the European arrest warrant and the surrender procedures between member states (2002/584/JHA).

216. Other interpretative provisions

(1) References to a category 1 territory must be read in accordance with section 1.

(2) References to a category 2 territory must be read in accordance with section 69.

(3) References to the designated authority must be read in accordance with section 2(9).

(4) References to a Part 1 warrant must be read in accordance with section 2.

(5) References to a Part 3 warrant must be read in accordance with section 142.

(6) References to a valid request for a person's extradition must be read in accordance with section 70.

(7) "Asylum claim" has the meaning given by section 113(1) of the Nationality, Immigration and Asylum Act 2002 (c. 41).

(8) A customs officer is a person commissioned by the Commissioners of Customs and Excise under section 6(3) of the Customs and Excise Management Act 1979 (c. 2).

(9) "High Court" in relation to Scotland means the High Court of Justiciary.

(10) In relation to Scotland, references to an appeal being discontinued are to be construed as references to its being abandoned.

(11) "Police officer" in relation to Northern Ireland has the same meaning as in the Police (Northern Ireland) Act 2000 (c. 32).

(12) A provisional warrant is a warrant issued under section 73(3).

(13) A service policeman is a member of the Royal Navy Regulating Branch, the Royal Marines Police, the Royal Military Police or the Royal Air Force Police.

(14) The Provost Marshal of the Royal Air Force and any officer appointed to exercise the functions conferred on provost officers by the Air Force Act 1955 (3 & 4 Eliz. 2 c. 19) are to be taken to be members of the Royal Air Force Police for the purposes of subsection (13).

(15) This section and sections 213 to 215 apply for the purposes of this Act.

General

217. Form of documents
The Secretary of State may by regulations prescribe the form of any document required for the purposes of this Act.

218. Existing legislation on extradition
These Acts shall cease to have effect—

(a) the Backing of Warrants (Republic of Ireland) Act 1965 (c. 45);

(b) the Extradition Act 1989 (c. 33).

219. Amendments
(1) Schedule 3 contains miscellaneous and consequential amendments.

(2) The Secretary of State may by order make—

(a) any supplementary, incidental or consequential provision, and

(b) any transitory, transitional or saving provision,

which he considers necessary or expedient for the purposes of, in consequence of, or for giving full effect to any provision of this Act.

(3) An order under subsection (2) may, in particular—

(a) provide for any provision of this Act which comes into force before another such provision has come into force to have effect, until that other provision has come into force, with such modifications as are specified in the order, and

(b) amend, repeal or revoke any enactment other than one contained in an Act passed in a Session after that in which this Act is passed.

(4) The amendments that may be made under subsection (3)(b) are in addition to those made by or under any other provision of this Act.

220. Repeals

Schedule 4 contains repeals.

221. Commencement *Text: 1.3*

The preceding provisions of this Act come into force in accordance with provision made by the Secretary of State by order.

222. Channel Islands and Isle of Man *Text: 3.2.2*

An Order in Council may provide for this Act to extend to any of the Channel Islands or the Isle of Man with the modifications (if any) specified in the Order.

223. Orders and regulations

(1) References in this section to subordinate legislation are to—

(a) an order of the Secretary of State under this Act (other than an order within subsection (2));

(b) an order of the Treasury under this Act;

(c) regulations under this Act.

(2) The orders referred to in subsection (1)(a) are—

(a) an order for a person's extradition or discharge;

(b) an order deferring proceedings on a warrant or request;

(c) an order deferring a person's extradition in pursuance of a warrant or request.

(3) Subordinate legislation—

(a) may make different provision for different purposes;

(b) may include supplementary, incidental, saving or transitional provisions.

(4) A power to make subordinate legislation is exercisable by statutory instrument.

(5) No order mentioned in subsection (6) may be made unless a draft of the order has been laid before Parliament and approved by a resolution of each House.

(6) The orders are—

(a) an order under any of these provisions—

section 1(1);

section 69(1);

section 71(4);

section 73(5);

section 74(11)(b);

section 84(7);

section 86(7);

section 142(9);

section 173(4);

section 215(2);

(b) an order under section 219(2) which contains any provision (whether alone or with other provisions) amending or repealing any Act or provision of an Act.

(7) A statutory instrument is subject to annulment in pursuance of a resolution of either House of Parliament if it contains subordinate legislation other than an order mentioned in subsection (6) or an order under section 221.

(8) A territory may be designated by being named in an order made by the Secretary of State under this Act or by falling within a description set out in such an order.

(9) An order made by the Secretary of State under section 1(1) or 69(1) may provide that this Act has effect in relation to a territory designated by the order with specified modifications.

224. Orders in Council

(1) An Order in Council under section 177 or 178 is subject to annulment in pursuance of a resolution of either House of Parliament.

(2) An Order in Council under this Act—

(a) may make different provision for different purposes;

(b) may include supplementary, incidental, saving or transitional provisions.

225. Finance

The following are to be paid out of money provided by Parliament—

(a) any expenditure incurred by the Lord Chancellor under this Act;

(b) any increase attributable to this Act in the sums payable out of money provided by Parliament under any other enactment.

226. Extent

(1) Sections 157 to 160, 166 to 168, 171, 173 and 205 do not extend to Scotland.

(2) Sections 154, 198, 200 and 201 extend to England and Wales only.

(3) Sections 183 and 199 extend to Scotland only.

(4) Sections 184 and 185 extend to Northern Ireland only.

227. Short title

This Act may be cited as the Extradition Act 2003.

SCHEDULES

SCHEDULE 1

Section 188 and 189

RE -EXTRADITION: MODIFICATIONS
PART 1
CATEGORY 1 TERRITORIES

1 In section 11(1), omit paragraphs (c), (g) and (h).

2 Omit sections 14, 18 and 19.

3 In section 21(3), for "must" substitute "may".

4 In section 31(2), for paragraphs (a) and (b) substitute "would (apart from section 187(1)) be released from detention pursuant to the UK sentence (whether or not on licence)".

5 In section 39(2)(a), for "a certificate is issued under section 2 in respect of the warrant" substitute "the person would (apart from section 187(1)) be released from detention pursuant to the UK sentence (whether or not on licence)".

6 In section 44(2)(a), for "following his arrest under this Part" substitute "under section 187(1)".

7 In section 45(1), for the words from "arrested" to "issued" substitute "brought before the appropriate judge under section 187(1) may consent to his extradition to the territory in which the overseas sentence was imposed".

PART 2
CATEGORY 2 TERRITORIES

8 In section 78, omit subsections (2), (3), (5) and (8).

9 In section 78, for subsection (4) substitute—

"(4) The judge must decide whether the offence specified in the request is an extradition offence."

10 In section 78(6), for "any of the questions" substitute "the question".

11 In section 78(7), for "those questions" substitute "that question".

12 In section 79(1), omit paragraph (c).

13 Omit section 82.

14 In section 87(3), for the words from "must send the case" to "extradited" substitute "may order the person to be extradited to the category 2 territory".

15 In section 87, after subsection (3) insert—

"(4) If the judge makes an order under subsection (3) he must remand the person in custody or on bail to wait for his extradition to the territory.

(5) If the judge remands the person in custody he may later grant bail."

16 In section 103(1)—

(a) for the words from "sends a case" to "extradited" substitute "orders a person's extradition under this Part"; and

(b) for "the relevant decision" substitute "the order".

17 In section 103(2), for the words from "the person" to "the Secretary of State" substitute "the order is made under section 128".

18 In section 103, omit subsections (3), (5), (6), (7) and (8).

19 In section 103(9), for the words from "the Secretary of State" to "person" substitute "the order is made".

20 In section 104, omit subsections (1)(b), (6) and (7).

21 In section 106, omit subsections (1)(b), (7) and (8).

22 In section 117(1)(a), for "the Secretary of State" substitute "the appropriate judge".

23 In section 117(1)(b), for the words from "permitted period" to "extradition" substitute "period permitted under that section".

24 In section 117, after subsection (1) insert—

"(1A) But this section does not apply if the order is made under section 128."

25 In section 117(2), for "the Secretary of State" substitute "the judge".

26 In section 119(1)(a), for "the Secretary of State" substitute "the appropriate judge".

27 In section 119, in subsections (2) to (6) and in each place in subsection (7), for "the Secretary of State" substitute "the judge".

28 In section 120, after subsection (1) insert—

"(1A) But this section does not apply if the order for the person's extradition is made under section 128."

29 In section 121(2)(a), for "a certificate is issued under section 70 in respect of the request" substitute "the person would (apart from section 187(1)) be released from detention pursuant to the UK sentence (whether or not on licence)".

30 In section 127(1), for the words from "arrested" to "requested" substitute "brought before the appropriate judge under section 187(1) may consent to his extradition to the territory in which the overseas sentence was imposed".

31 In section 127(3), before paragraph (a) insert—

"(aa) must be given before the appropriate judge;".

32 In section 127, omit subsections (4) and (5).

33 In section 128, after subsection (1) insert—

"(1A) The judge must remand the person in custody or on bail.

(1B) If the judge remands the person in custody he may later grant bail."

34 In section 128(4), for the words from "send the case" to "extradited" substitute "within the period of 10 days starting with the day on which consent is given order the person's extradition to the category 2 territory".

35 In section 128, after subsection (5) insert—

"(6) Subsection (4) has effect subject to section 128B.

(7) If subsection (4) is not complied with and the person applies to the judge to be discharged the judge must order his discharge."

36 After section 128 insert—

"128A. Extradition to category 2 territory following consent

(1) This section applies if the appropriate judge makes an order under section 128(4) for a person's extradition to a category 2 territory.

(2) The person must be extradited to the category 2 territory before the end of the required period, which is 28 days starting with the day on which the order is made.

(3) If subsection (2) is not complied with and the person applies to the judge to be discharged the judge must order his discharge, unless reasonable cause is shown for the delay.

128B. Extradition claim following consent

(1) This section applies if—

(a) a person consents under section 127 to his extradition to a category 2 territory, and

(b) before the judge orders his extradition under section 128(4), the judge is informed that the conditions in subsection (2) or (3) are met.

(2) The conditions are that—

(a) the Secretary of State has received another valid request for the person's extradition to a category 2 territory;

(b) the other request has not been disposed of.

(3) The conditions are that—

(a) a certificate has been issued under section 2 in respect of a Part 1 warrant issued in respect of the person;

(b) the warrant has not been disposed of.

(4) The judge must not make an order under section 128(4) until he is informed what order has been made under section 126(2) or 179(2).

(5) If the order under section 126(2) or 179(2) is for further proceedings on the request under consideration to be deferred until the other request, or the warrant, has been disposed of, the judge must remand the person in custody or on bail.

(6) If the judge remands the person in custody he may later grant bail.

(7) If—

(a) the order under section 126(2) or 179(2) is for further proceedings on the request under consideration to be deferred until the other request, or the warrant, has been disposed of, and

(b) an order is made under section 180 for proceedings on the request under consideration to be resumed,

the period specified in section 128(4) must be taken to be 10 days starting with the day on which the order under section 180 is made.

(8) If the order under section 126(2) or 179(2) is for further proceedings on the other request, or the warrant, to be deferred until the request under consideration has been disposed of, the period specified in section 128(4) must be taken to be 10 days starting with the day on which the judge is informed of the order.

128C. Extradition following deferral for competing claim

(1) This section applies if—

(a) an order is made under section 128(4) for a person to be extradited to a category 2 territory in pursuance of a request for his extradition;

(b) before the person is extradited to the territory an order is made under section 126(2) or 179(2) for the person's extradition in pursuance of the request to be deferred;

(c) the appropriate judge makes an order under section 181(2) for the person's extradition in pursuance of the request to cease to be deferred.

(2) The required period for the purposes of section 128A(2) is 28 days starting with the day on which the order under section 181(2) is made."

SCHEDULE 2

EUROPEAN FRAMEWORK LIST

1 Participation in a criminal organisation.

2 Terrorism.

3 Trafficking in human beings.

4 Sexual exploitation of children and child pornography.

5 Illicit trafficking in narcotic drugs and psychotropic substances.

6 Illicit trafficking in weapons, munitions and explosives.

7 Corruption.

8 Fraud, including that affecting the financial interests of the European Communities within the meaning of the Convention of 26 July 1995 on the protection of the European Communities' financial interests.

9 Laundering of the proceeds of crime.

10 Counterfeiting currency, including of the euro.

11 Computer-related crime.

12 Environmental crime, including illicit trafficking in endangered animal species and in endangered plant species and varieties.

13 Facilitation of unauthorised entry and residence.

14 Murder, grievous bodily injury.

15 Illicit trade in human organs and tissue.

16 Kidnapping, illegal restraint and hostage-taking.

17 Racism and xenophobia.

18 Organised or armed robbery.

19 Illicit trafficking in cultural goods, including antiques and works of art.

20 Swindling.

21 Racketeering and extortion.

22 Counterfeiting and piracy of products.

23 Forgery of administrative documents and trafficking therein.

24 Forgery of means of payment.

25 Illicit trafficking in hormonal substances and other growth promoters.

26 Illicit trafficking in nuclear or radioactive materials.

27 Trafficking in stolen vehicles.

28 Rape.

29 Arson.

30 Crimes within the jurisdiction of the International Criminal Court.

31 Unlawful seizure of aircraft/ships.

32 Sabotage.

SCHEDULE 3

Section 219

AMENDMENTS

Introduction

1 The amendments specified in this Schedule shall have effect.

Parliamentary Commissioner Act 1967 (c. 13)

2 In Schedule 3 to the Parliamentary Commissioner Act 1967 (c. 13) (matters not subject to investigation) for paragraph 4 substitute-

"4 Action taken by the Secretary of State under the Extradition Act 2003."

Criminal Justice Act 1967 (c. 80)

3 Section 34 of the Criminal Justice Act 1967 (c. 80) (committal of persons under twenty-one accused of extradition crimes) shall cease to have effect.

Suppression of Terrorism Act 1978 (c. 26)

4 Sections 1 (offences not to be regarded as of a political character) and 2 (restrictions on return of criminal under Extradition Act 1870 or to Republic of Ireland) of the Suppression of Terrorism Act 1978 (c. 26) shall cease to have effect.

5 For section 5 of the Suppression of Terrorism Act 1978 substitute—

"5. Power to apply section 4 to non-convention countries

(1) The Secretary of State may by order direct that section 4 above shall apply in relation to a country falling within subsection (2) below as it applies in relation to a convention country, subject to the exceptions (if any) specified in the order.

(2) A country falls within this subsection if—

(a) it is not a convention country; and

(b) it is a category 1 territory or a category 2 territory within the meaning of the Extradition Act 2003."

Criminal Justice (International Co-operation) Act 1990 (c. 5)

6 Section 22(1) of the Criminal Justice (International Co-operation) Act 1990 (c. 5) (offences to which an Order in Council under the Extradition Act 1870 can apply) shall cease to have effect.

Computer Misuse Act 1990 (c. 18)

7 Section 15 of the Computer Misuse Act 1990 (c. 18) (extradition where Schedule 1 to the Extradition Act 1989 applies) shall cease to have effect.

Aviation and Maritime Security Act 1990 (c. 31)

8 Section 49 of the Aviation and Maritime Security Act 1990 (c. 31) (extradition by virtue of Orders in Council under Extradition Act 1870) shall cease to have effect.

Criminal Justice Act 1991 (c. 53)

9 In section 47 of the Criminal Justice Act 1991 (c. 53) (persons extradited to the United Kingdom) subsection (4) shall cease to have effect.

United Nations Personnel Act 1997 (c. 13)

10 Section 6(1) of the United Nations Personnel Act 1997 (c. 13) (offences to which an Order in Council under section 2 of the Extradition Act 1870 can apply) shall cease to have effect.

Terrorism Act 2000 (c. 11)

11 Section 64(5) of the Terrorism Act 2000 (c. 11) (offences to which an Order in Council under section 2 of the Extradition Act 1870 can apply) shall cease to have effect.

International Criminal Court Act 2001 (c. 17)

12 Section 71 of the International Criminal Court Act 2001 (c. 17) (extradition: Orders in Council under the Extradition Act 1870) shall cease to have effect.

13 (1) Part 2 of Schedule 2 to the International Criminal Court Act 2001 (delivery up to International Criminal Court of persons subject to extradition proceedings) is amended as follows.

(2) For paragraph 7 (meaning of "extradition proceedings") substitute—

"7 In this Part of this Schedule "extradition proceedings" means proceedings before a court or judge in the United Kingdom under the Extradition Act 2003."

(3) In paragraph 8 (extradition proceedings in England and Wales or Northern Ireland) after sub-paragraph (5) add—

"(6) References in this paragraph to a court include references to a judge."

(4) In paragraph 9 (extradition proceedings in Scotland) after sub-paragraph (3) add—

"(4) References in this paragraph to a court include references to a judge."

(5) In paragraph 10 (power to suspend or revoke warrant or order) for sub-paragraph (1) substitute—

"(1) Where a court makes a delivery order in respect of a person whose extradition has been ordered under the Extradition Act 2003, it may make any such order as is necessary to enable the delivery order to be executed."

(6) In paragraph 10(2) omit the words "by a court or judicial officer".

Enterprise Act 2002 (c. 40)

14 Section 191 of the Enterprise Act 2002 (c. 40) (offences to which an Order in Council under the Extradition Act 1870 can apply) shall cease to have effect.

SCHEDULE 4

Section 220

REPEALS

Short title and chapter	Extent of repeal
Backing of Warrants (Republic of Ireland) Act 1965 (c. 45)	The whole Act.
Criminal Justice Act 1967 (c. 80)	Section 34.
Criminal Jurisdiction Act 1975 (c. 59)	In Schedule 3, paragraph 1.

Short title and chapter	_Extent of repeal_
Bail Act 1976 (c. 63)	In section 2(2) the definition of "proceedings against a fugitive offender". In section 4(2) the words "or proceedings against a fugitive offender for the offence". In section 7(4) the words from "In reckoning" to "Sunday". In Schedule 2, paragraph 33.
Criminal Law Act 1977 (c. 45)	In Schedule 12, in the entry for the Bail Act 1976, paragraph 4.
Suppression of Terrorism Act 1978 (c. 26)	Sections 1 and 2. In section 8— (a) subsection (5)(a); (b) in subsection (6) the words from "an order made under section 1(4)" to "or".
Extradition Act 1989 (c. 33)	The whole Act.
Criminal Justice (International Co-operation) Act 1990 (c. 5)	Section 22.
Computer Misuse Act 1990 (c. 18)	Section 15.
Aviation and Maritime Security Act 1990 (c. 31)	Section 49.
Criminal Justice Act 1991 (c. 53)	Section 47(4).
Bail (Amendment) Act 1993 (c. 26)	In section 1— (a) in subsection (4), the word "such"; (b) in subsection (8), the word "magistrates' ".
Criminal Justice Act 1993 (c. 36)	Section 72. Section 79(7).
Criminal Justice and Public Order Act 1994 (c. 33)	Sections 158 and 159.
United Nations Personnel Act 1997 (c. 13)	Section 6.
Justices of the Peace Act 1997 (c. 25)	In Schedule 5, paragraph 9.
Access to Justice Act 1999 (c. 22)	In Schedule 11, paragraphs 18 and 31 to 36.
Powers of Criminal Courts (Sentencing) Act 2000 (c. 6)	In Schedule 9, paragraph 124.
Terrorism Act 2000 (c. 11)	Section 64.
International Criminal Court Act 2001 (c. 17)	Sections 71 to 73. In paragraph 10(2) of Schedule 2, the words "by a court or judicial officer".
Proceeds of Crime Act 2002 (c. 29)	In Schedule 11, paragraph 18.
Enterprise Act 2002 (c. 40)	Section 191.

Appendix 2
European Framework Decision

COUNCIL OF
THE EUROPEAN UNION

Brussels, 7 June 2002
(OR. fr)

7253/02

Interinstitutional File:
2001/0215 (CNS)

COPEN 23
CATS 9

LEGISLATIVE ACTS AND OTHER INSTRUMENTS

Subject: Council Framework Decision on the European arrest warrant and the surrender procedures between Member States

COUNCIL FRAMEWORK DECISION 2002/ /JHA
of

on the European arrest warrant and the surrender procedures between Member States

THE COUNCIL OF THE EUROPEAN UNION,

Having regard to the Treaty on European Union, and in particular Article 31(a) and (b) and Article 34(2)(b) thereof,

Having regard to the proposal from the Commission[1],

Having regard to the Opinion of the European Parliament[2],

Whereas:

(1) According to the Conclusions of the Tampere European Council of 15 and 16 October 1999, and in particular point 35 thereof, the formal extradition procedure should be abolished among the Member States in respect of persons who are fleeing from justice after having been finally sentenced and extradition procedures should be speeded up in respect of persons suspected of having committed an offence.

(2) The programme of measures to implement the principle of mutual recognition of criminal decisions envisaged in point 37 of the Tampere European Council Conclusions and adopted by the Council on 30 November 2000[3] addresses the matter of mutual enforcement of arrest warrants.

(3) All or some Member States are parties to a number of conventions in the field of extradition, including the European Convention on extradition of 13 December 1957 and the European Convention on the suppression of terrorism of 27 January 1977. The Nordic States have extradition laws with identical wording.

(4) In addition, the following three Conventions dealing in whole or in part with extradition have been agreed upon among Member States and form part of the Union acquis: the Convention of 19 June 1990 implementing the Schengen Agreement of 14 June 1985 on the gradual abolition of checks at their common borders[4] (regarding relations between the Member States :which are parties to that Convention), the Convention of 10 March 1995 on simplified extradition procedure between the Member States of the European Union[5] and the Convention of 27 September 1996 relating to extradition between the Member States of the European Union[6].

(5) The objective set for the Union to become an area of freedom, security and justice leads to abolishing extradition between Member States and replacing it by a system of surrender between judicial authorities. Further, the introduction of a new simplified system of surrender of sentenced or suspected persons for the purposes of execution or prosecution of criminal sentences makes it possible to remove the complexity and potential for delay inherent in the present extradition procedures. Traditional cooperation relations which have prevailed up till now between Member States should be replaced by a system of free movement of judicial decisions in criminal matters, covering both pre-sentence and final decisions, within an area of freedom, security and justice.

[1] OJ ...   [2] OJ ...   [3] OJ C E 12, 15.1.2001, p. 10.   [4] OJ L 239, 22.9.2000, p. 19.
[5] OJ C 78, 30.3.1995, p. 2.   [6] OJ C 313, 13.10.1996, p. 12.

(6) The European arrest warrant provided for in this Framework Decision is the first concrete measure in the field of criminal law implementing the principle of mutual recognition which the European Council referred to as the "cornerstone" of judicial cooperation.

(7) Since the aim of replacing the system of multilateral extradition built upon the European Convention on Extradition of 13 December 1957 cannot be sufficiently achieved by the Member States acting unilaterally and can therefore, by reason of its scale and effects, be better achieved at Union level, the Council may adopt measures in accordance with the principle of subsidiarity as referred to in Article 2 of the Treaty on European Union and Article 5 of the Treaty establishing the European Community. In accordance with the principle of proportionality, as set out in the latter Article, this Framework Decision does not go beyond what is necessary in order to achieve that objective.

(8) Decisions on the execution of the European arrest warrant must be subject to sufficient controls, which means that a judicial authority of the Member State where the requested person has been arrested will have to take the decision on his or her surrender.

(9) The role of central authorities in the execution of a European arrest warrant must be limited to practical and administrative assistance.

(10) The mechanism of the European arrest warrant is based on a high level of confidence between Member States. Its implementation may be suspended only in the event of a serious and persistent breach by one of the Member States of the principles set out in Article 6(1) of the Treaty on European Union, determined by the Council pursuant to Article 7(1) of the said Treaty with the consequences set out in Article 7(2) thereof.

(11) In relations between Member States, the European arrest warrant should replace all the previous instruments concerning extradition, including the provisions of Title III of the Convention implementing the Schengen Agreement which concern extradition.

(12) This Framework Decision respects fundamental rights and observes the principles recognised by Article 6 of the Treaty on European Union and reflected in the Charter of Fundamental Rights of the European Union[7], in particular Chapter VI thereof. Nothing in this Framework Decision may be interpreted as prohibiting refusal to surrender a person for whom a European arrest warrant has been issued when there are reasons to believe, on the basis of objective elements, that the said arrest warrant has been issued for the purpose of prosecuting or punishing a person on the grounds of his or her sex, race, religion, ethnic origin, nationality, language, political opinions or sexual orientation, or that that person's position may be prejudiced for any of these reasons.

This Framework Decision does not prevent a Member State from applying its constitutional rules relating to due process, freedom of association, freedom of the press and freedom of expression in other media.

(13) No person should be removed, expelled or extradited to a State where there is a serious risk that he or she would be subjected to the death penalty, torture or other inhuman or degrading treatment or punishment.

(14) Since all Member States have ratified the Council of Europe Convention of 28 January 1981 for the protection of individuals with regard to automatic processing of personal data, the personal data processed in the context of the implementation of this Framework Decision should be protected in accordance with the principles of the said Convention,

[7] OJ C 364, 18.12.2000, p. 1.

HAS ADOPTED THIS FRAMEWORK DECISION:

CHAPTER 1
General principles

Article 1
Definition of the European arrest warrant and obligation to execute it

1. The European arrest warrant is a judicial decision issued by a Member State with a view to the arrest and surrender by another Member State of a requested person, for the purposes of conducting a criminal prosecution or executing a custodial sentence or detention order.

2. Member States shall execute any European arrest warrant on the basis of the principle of mutual recognition and in accordance with the provisions of this Framework Decision.

3. This Framework Decision shall not have the effect of modifying the obligation to respect fundamental rights and fundamental legal principles as enshrined in Article 6 of the Treaty on European Union.

Article 2
Scope of the European arrest warrant

1. A European arrest warrant may be issued for acts punishable by the law of the issuing Member State by a custodial sentence or a detention order for a maximum period of at least twelve months or, where a sentence has been passed or a detention order has been made, for sentences of at least four months.

2. The following offences, if they are punishable in the issuing Member State by a custodial sentence or a detention order for a maximum period of at least 3 years and as they are defined by the law of the issuing Member State, shall, under the terms of this Framework Decision and without verification of the double criminality of the act, give rise to surrender pursuant to a European arrest warrant:

—participation in a criminal organisation,

—terrorism,

—trafficking in human beings,

—sexual exploitation of children and child pornography,

—illicit trafficking in narcotic drugs and psychotropic substances,

—illicit trafficking in weapons, munitions and explosives,

—corruption,

—fraud, including that affecting the financial interests of the European Communities within the meaning of the Convention of 26 July 1995 on the protection of the European Communities' financial interests,

—laundering of the proceeds of crime,

—counterfeiting currency, including of the euro,

—computer-related crime,

—environmental crime, including illicit trafficking in endangered animal species and in endangered plant species and varieties,

—facilitation of unauthorised entry and residence,

—murder, grievous bodily injury,

—illicit trade in human organs and tissue,

—kidnapping, illegal restraint and hostage-taking,

—racism and xenophobia,

—organised or armed robbery,

—illicit trafficking in cultural goods, including antiques and works of art,

—swindling,

—racketeering and extortion,

—counterfeiting and piracy of products,

—forgery of administrative documents and trafficking therein,

—forgery of means of payment,

—illicit trafficking in hormonal substances and other growth promoters,

—illicit trafficking in nuclear or radioactive materials,

—trafficking in stolen vehicles,

—rape,

—arson,

—crimes within the jurisdiction of the International Criminal Court,

—unlawful seizure of aircraft/ships,

—sabotage.

3. The Council may decide at any time, acting unanimously after consultation of the European Parliament under the conditions laid down in Article 39(1) of the Treaty on European Union (TEU), to add other categories of offence to the list contained in paragraph 2. The Council shall examine, in the light of the report submitted by the Commission pursuant to Article 34(3), whether the list should be extended or amended.

4. For offences other than those covered by paragraph 2, surrender may be subject to the condition that the acts for which the European arrest warrant has been issued constitute an offence under the law of the executing Member State, whatever the constituent elements or however it is described.

Article 3
Grounds for mandatory non-execution of the European arrest warrant

The executing judicial authority of the Member State of execution (hereinafter "executing judicial authority") shall refuse to execute the European arrest warrant in the following cases:

1) if the offence on which the arrest warrant is based is covered by amnesty in the executing Member State, where that State had jurisdiction to prosecute the offence under its own criminal law;

343

2) if the executing judicial authority is informed that the requested person has been finally judged by a Member State in respect of the same acts provided that, where there has been sentence, the sentence has been served or is currently being served or may no longer be executed under the law of the sentencing Member State;

3) if the person who is the subject of the European arrest warrant may not, owing to his age, be held criminally responsible for the acts on which the arrest warrant is based under the law of the executing State.

Article 4
Grounds for optional non-execution of the European arrest warrant

The executing judicial authority may refuse to execute the European arrest warrant:

1) if, in one of the cases referred to in Article 2(4), the act on which the European arrest warrant is based does not constitute an offence under the law of the executing Member State; however, in relation to taxes or duties, customs and exchange, execution of the European arrest warrant shall not be refused on the ground that the law of the executing Member State does not impose the same kind of tax or duty or does not contain the same type of rules as regards taxes, duties and customs and exchange regulations as the law of the issuing Member State;

2) where the person who is the subject of the European arrest warrant is being prosecuted in the executing Member State for the same act as that on which the European arrest warrant is based;

3) where the judicial authorities of the executing Member State have decided either not to prosecute for the offence on which the European arrest warrant is based or to halt proceedings, or where a final judgment has been passed upon the requested person in a Member State, in respect of the same acts, which prevents further proceedings;

4) where the criminal prosecution or punishment of the requested person is statute-barred according to the law of the executing Member State and the acts fall within the jurisdiction of that Member State under its own criminal law;

5) if the executing judicial authority is informed that the requested person has been finally judged by a third State in respect of the same acts provided that, where there has been sentence, the sentence has been served or is currently being served or may no longer be executed under the law of the sentencing country;

6) if the European arrest warrant has been issued for the purposes of execution of a custodial sentence or detention order, where the requested person is staying in, or is a national or a resident of the executing Member State and that State undertakes to execute the sentence or detention order in accordance with its domestic law;

7) where the European arrest warrant relates to offences which:

(a) are regarded by the law of the executing Member State as having been committed in whole or in part in the territory of the executing Member State or in a place treated as such; or

(b) have been committed outside the territory of the issuing Member State and the law of the executing Member State does not allow prosecution for the same offences when committed outside its territory.

Article 5
Guarantees to be given by the issuing Member State in particular cases

The execution of the European arrest warrant by the executing judicial authority may, by the law of the executing Member State, be subject to the following conditions:

1) where the European arrest warrant has been issued for the purposes of executing a [...] sentence or a detention order imposed by a decision rendered in absentia [...] and if the person concerned has not been summoned in person or otherwise informed of the date and place of the hearing which led to the decision rendered in absentia, surrender may be subject to the condition that the issuing judicial authority gives an assurance deemed adequate to guarantee the person who is the subject of the European arrest warrant that he or she will have an opportunity to apply for a retrial of the case in the issuing Member State and to be present at the judgment;

2) if the offence on the basis of which the European arrest warrant has been issued is punishable by custodial life sentence or life-time detention order, the execution of the said arrest warrant may be subject to the condition that the issuing Member State has provisions in its legal system for a review of the penalty or measure imposed – on request or at the latest after 20 years – or for the application of measures of clemency to which the person is entitled to apply for under the law or practice of the issuing Member State, aiming at a non-execution of such penalty or measure;

3) where a person who is the subject of a European arrest warrant for the purposes of prosecution is a national or resident of the executing Member State, surrender may be subject to the condition that the person, after being heard, is returned to the executing Member State in order to serve there the custodial sentence or detention order passed against him in the issuing Member State.

Article 6
Determination of the competent judicial authorities

1. The issuing judicial authority shall be the judicial authority of the issuing Member State which is competent to issue a European arrest warrant by virtue of the law of that State.

2. The executing judicial authority shall be the judicial authority of the executing Member State which is competent to execute the European arrest warrant by virtue of the law of that State.

3. Each Member State shall inform the General Secretariat of the Council of the competent judicial authority under its law.

Article 7
Recourse to the central authority

1. Each Member State may designate a central authority or, when its legal system so provides, more than one central authority to assist the competent judicial authorities.

2. A Member State may, if it is necessary as a result of the organisation of its internal judicial system, make its central authority(ies) responsible for the administrative transmission and reception of European arrest warrants as well as for all other official correspondence relating thereto.

A Member State wishing to make use of the possibilities referred to in this Article shall communicate to the General Secretariat of the Council information relating to the designated central authority or central authorities. These indications shall be binding upon all the authorities of the issuing Member State.

Article 8
Content and form of the European arrest warrant

1. The European arrest warrant shall contain the following information set out in accordance with the form contained in the Annex:

(a) the identity and nationality of the requested person;

(b) the name, address, telephone and fax numbers and e-mail address of the issuing judicial authority;

(c) evidence of an enforceable judgment, an arrest warrant or any other enforceable judicial decision having the same effect, coming within the scope of Articles 1 and 2;

(d) the nature and legal classification of the offence, particularly in respect of Article 2;

(e) a description of the circumstances in which the offence was committed, including the time, place and degree of participation in the offence by the requested person;

(f) the penalty imposed, if there is a final judgment, or the prescribed scale of penalties for the offence under the law of the issuing Member State;

(g) if possible, other consequences of the offence.

2. The European arrest warrant must be translated into the official language or one of the official languages of the executing Member State. Any Member State may, when this Framework Decision is adopted or at a later date, state in a declaration deposited with the General Secretariat of the Council that it will accept a translation in one or more other official languages of the Institutions of the European Communities.

CHAPTER 2
Surrender procedure

Article 9
Transmission of a European arrest warrant

1. When the location of the requested person is known, the issuing judicial authority may transmit the European arrest warrant directly to the executing judicial authority.

2. The issuing judicial authority may, in any event, decide to issue an alert for the requested person in the Schengen Information System (SIS).

3. Such an alert shall be effected in accordance with the provisions of Article 95 of the Convention of 19 June 1990 implementing the Schengen Agreement of 14 June 1985 on the gradual abolition of controls at common borders. An alert in the Schengen Information System shall be equivalent to a European arrest warrant accompanied by the information set out in Article 8(1).

For a transitional period, until the SIS is capable of transmitting all the information described in Article 8, the alert shall be equivalent to a European arrest warrant pending the receipt of the original in due and proper form by the executing judicial authority.

Article 10
Detailed procedures for transmitting a European arrest warrant

1. If the issuing judicial authority does not know the competent executing judicial authority, it shall make the requisite enquiries, including through the contact points of the European Judicial Network[8], in order to obtain that information from the executing Member State.

2. If the issuing judicial authority so wishes, transmission may be effected via the secure telecommunications system of the European Judicial Network.

3. If it is not possible to call on the services of the SIS, the issuing judicial authority may call on Interpol to transmit a European arrest warrant.

4. The issuing judicial authority may forward the European arrest warrant by any secure means capable of producing written records under conditions allowing the executing Member State to establish its authenticity.

5. All difficulties concerning the transmission or the authenticity of any document needed for the execution of the European arrest warrant shall be dealt with by direct contacts between the judicial authorities involved, or, where appropriate, with the involvement of the central authorities of the Member States.

6. If the authority which receives a European arrest warrant is not competent to act upon it, it shall automatically forward the European arrest warrant to the competent authority in its Member State and shall inform the issuing judicial authority accordingly.

Article 11
Rights of a requested person

1. When a requested person is arrested, the executing competent judicial authority shall, in accordance with its national law, inform that person of the European arrest warrant and of its contents, and also of the possibility of consenting to surrender to the issuing judicial authority.

2. A requested person who is arrested for the purpose of the execution of a European arrest warrant shall have a right to be assisted by a legal counsel and by an interpreter in accordance with the national law of the executing Member State.

Article 12
Keeping the person in detention

When a person is arrested on the basis of a European arrest warrant, the executing judicial authority shall take a decision on whether the requested person should remain in

---

[8] Council Joint Action 98/428/JHA of 29 June 1998 on the creation of a European Judicial Network (OJ L 191, 7.7.1998, p. 4).

detention, in accordance with the law of the executing Member State. The person may be released provisionally at any time in conformity with the domestic law of the executing Member State, provided that the competent authority of the said Member State takes all the measures it deems necessary to prevent the person absconding.

Article 13
Consent to surrender

1. If the arrested person indicates that he or she consents to surrender, that consent and, if appropriate, express renunciation of entitlement to the "speciality rule", referred to in Article 27(2), shall be given before the executing judicial authority, in accordance with the domestic law of the executing Member State.

2. Each Member State shall adopt the measures necessary to ensure that consent and, where appropriate, renunciation, as referred to in paragraph 1, are established in such a way as to show that the person concerned has expressed them voluntarily and in full awareness of the consequences. To that end, the requested person shall have the right to legal counsel.

3. The consent and, where appropriate, renunciation, as referred to in paragraph 1, shall be formally recorded in accordance with the procedure laid down by the domestic law of the executing Member State.

4. In principle, consent may not be revoked. Each Member State may provide that consent and, if appropriate, renunciation may be revoked, in accordance with the rules applicable under its domestic law. In this case, the period between the date of consent and that of its revocation shall not be taken into consideration in establishing the time limits laid down in Article 17. A Member State which wishes to have recourse to this possibility shall inform the General Secretariat of the Council accordingly when this Framework Decision is adopted and shall specify the procedures whereby revocation of consent shall be possible and any amendment to them.

Article 14
Hearing of the requested person

Where the arrested person does not consent to his or her surrender as referred to in Article 13, he or she shall be entitled to be heard by the executing judicial authority, in accordance with the law of the executing Member State.

Article 15
Surrender decision

1. The executing judicial authority shall decide, within the time-limits and under the conditions defined in this Framework Decision, whether the person is to be surrendered.

2. If the executing judicial authority finds the information communicated by the issuing Member State to be insufficient to allow it to decide on surrender, it shall request that the necessary supplementary information, in particular with respect to Articles 3 to 5 and Article 8, be furnished as a matter of urgency and may fix a time limit for the receipt thereof, taking into account the need to observe the time limits set in Article 17.

3. The issuing judicial authority may at any time forward any additional useful information to the executing judicial authority.

Article 16
Decision in the event of multiple requests

1. If two or more Member States have issued European arrest warrants for the same person, the decision on which of the European arrest warrants shall be executed shall be taken by the executing judicial authority with due consideration of all the circumstances and especially the relative seriousness and place of the offences, the respective dates of the European arrest warrants and whether the warrant has been issued for the purposes of prosecution or for execution of a custodial sentence or detention order.

2. The executing judicial authority may seek the advice of Eurojust[9] when making the choice referred to in paragraph 1.

3. In the event of a conflict between a European arrest warrant and a request for extradition presented by a third country, the decision on whether the European arrest warrant or the extradition request takes precedence shall be taken by the competent authority of the executing Member State with due consideration of all the circumstances, in particular those referred to in paragraph 1 and those mentioned in the applicable convention.

4. This Article shall be without prejudice to Member States' obligations under the Statute of the International Criminal Court.

Article 17
Time limits and procedures for the decision to execute the
European arrest warrant

1. A European arrest warrant shall be dealt with and executed as a matter of urgency.

2. In cases where the requested person consents to his surrender, the final decision on the execution of the European arrest warrant should be taken within a period of 10 days after consent has been given.

3. In other cases, the final decision on the execution of the European arrest warrant should be taken within a period of 60 days after the arrest of the requested person.

4. Where in specific cases the European arrest warrant cannot be executed within the time limits laid down in paragraphs 2 or 3, the executing judicial authority shall immediately inform the issuing judicial authority thereof, giving the reasons for the delay. In such case, the time limits may be extended by a further 30 days.

5. As long as the executing judicial authority has not taken a final decision on the European arrest warrant, it shall ensure that the material conditions necessary for effective surrender of the person remain fulfilled.

6. Reasons must be given for any refusal to execute a European arrest warrant.

7. Where in exceptional circumstances a Member State cannot observe the time limits provided for in this Article, it shall inform Eurojust, giving the reasons for the delay. In addition, a Member State which has experienced repeated delays on the part of another Member State in the execution of European arrest warrants shall inform the Council with a view to evaluating the implementation of this Framework Decision at Member State level.

[9] Council Decision 2002/187/JHA of 28 February 2002 setting up Eurojust with a view to reinforcing the fight against serious crime (OJ L 63, 6.3.2002, p. 1).

Article 18
Situation pending the decision

1. Where the European arrest warrant has been issued for the purpose of conducting a criminal prosecution, the executing judicial authority must:

(a) either agree that the requested person should be heard according to Article 19;

(b) or agree to the temporary transfer of the requested person.

2. The conditions and the duration of the temporary transfer shall be determined by mutual agreement between the issuing and executing judicial authorities.

3. In the case of temporary transfer, the person must be able to return to the executing Member State to attend hearings concerning him or her as part of the surrender procedure.

[*Article 19*
Hearing the person pending the decision

1. The requested person shall be heard by a judicial authority, assisted by another person designated in accordance with the law of the Member State of the requesting court.

2. The requested person shall be heard in accordance with the law of the executing Member State and with the conditions determined by mutual agreement between the issuing and executing judicial authorities.

3. The competent executing judicial authority may assign another judicial authority of its Member State to take part in the hearing of the requested person in order to ensure the proper application of this Article and of the conditions laid down.]

Article 20
Privileges and immunities

1. Where the requested person enjoys a privilege or immunity regarding jurisdiction or execution in the executing Member State, the time limits referred to in Article 17 shall not start running unless, and counting from the day when, the executing judicial authority is informed of the fact that the privilege or immunity has been waived.

The executing Member State shall ensure that the material conditions necessary for effective surrender are fulfilled when the person no longer enjoys such privilege or immunity.

2. Where power to waive the privilege or immunity lies with an authority of the executing Member State, the executing judicial authority shall request it to exercise that power forthwith. Where power to waive the privilege or immunity lies with an authority of another State or international organisation, it shall be for the issuing judicial authority to request it to exercise that power.

Article 21
Competing international obligations

This Framework Decision shall not prejudice the obligations of the executing Member State where the requested person has been extradited to that Member State from a third State and where that person is protected by provisions of the arrangement under which he or she was extradited concerning speciality. The executing Member State shall take all necessary measures for requesting forthwith the consent of the State from which the requested person was extradited so that he or she can be surrendered to the Member State which issued the European arrest warrant. The time limits referred to in Article 17 shall not start running until the day on which these speciality rules cease to apply. Pending the decision of the State from which the requested person was extradited, the executing Member State will ensure that the material conditions necessary for effective surrender remain fulfilled.

Article 22
Notification of the decision

The executing judicial authority shall notify the issuing judicial authority immediately of the decision on the action to be taken on the European arrest warrant.

Article 23
Time limits for surrender of the person

1. The person requested shall be surrendered as soon as possible on a date agreed between the authorities concerned.

2. He or she shall be surrendered no later than ten days after the final decision on the execution of the European arrest warrant.

3. If the surrender of the requested person within the period laid down in paragraph 2 is prevented by circumstances beyond the control of any of the Member States, the executing and issuing judicial authorities shall immediately contact each other and agree on a new surrender date. In that event, the surrender shall take place within ten days of the new date thus agreed.

4. The surrender may exceptionally be temporarily postponed for serious humanitarian reasons, for example if there are substantial grounds for believing that it would manifestly endanger the requested person's life or health. The execution of the European arrest warrant shall take place as soon as these grounds have ceased to exist. The executing judicial authority shall immediately inform the issuing judicial authority and agree on a new surrender date. In that event, the surrender shall take place within ten days of the new date thus agreed.

5. Upon expiry of the time limits referred to in paragraphs 2 to 4, if the person is still being held in custody he shall be released.

Article 24
Postponed or conditional surrender

1. The executing judicial authority may, after deciding to execute the European arrest warrant, postpone the surrender of the requested person so that he or she may be prosecuted in the executing Member State or, if he or she has already been sentenced, so that he or she may serve, in its territory, a sentence passed for an act other than that referred to in the European arrest warrant.

2. Instead of postponing the surrender, the executing judicial authority may temporarily surrender the requested person to the issuing Member State under conditions to be determined by mutual agreement between the executing and the issuing judicial authorities. The

agreement shall be made in writing and the conditions shall be binding on all the authorities in the issuing Member State.

Article 25
Transit

1. Each Member State shall, except when it avails itself of the possibility of refusal when the transit of a national or a resident is requested for the purpose of the execution of a custodial sentence or detention order, permit the transit through its territory of a requested person who is being surrendered provided that it has been given information on:

(a) the identity and nationality of the person subject to the European arrest warrant;

(b) the existence of a European arrest warrant;

(c) the nature and legal classification of the offence;

(d) the description of the circumstances of the offence, including the date and place.

Where a person who is the subject of a European arrest warrant for the purposes of prosecution is a national or resident of the Member State of transit, transit may be subject to the condition that the person, after being heard, is returned to the transit Member State to serve the custodial sentence or detention order passed against him in the issuing Member State.

2. Each Member State shall designate an authority responsible for receiving transit requests and the necessary documents, as well as any other official correspondence relating to transit requests. Member States shall communicate this designation to the General Secretariat of the Council.

3. The transit request and the information set out in paragraph 1 may be addressed to the authority designated pursuant to paragraph 2 by any means capable of producing a written record. The Member State of transit shall notify its decision by the same procedure.

4. This Framework Decision does not apply in the case of transport by air without a scheduled stopover. However, if an unscheduled landing occurs, the issuing Member State shall provide the authority designated pursuant to paragraph 2 with the information provided for in paragraph 1.

5. Where a transit concerns a person who is to be extradited from a third State to a Member State this Article will apply mutatis mutandis. In particular the expression "European arrest warrant" shall be deemed to be replaced by "extradition request".

CHAPTER 3
Effects of the surrender

Article 26
Deduction of the period of detention served in the executing Member State

1. The issuing Member State shall deduct all periods of detention arising from the execution of a European arrest warrant from the total period of detention to be served in the issuing Member State as a result of a custodial sentence or detention order being passed.

2. To that end, all information concerning the duration of the detention of the requested person on the basis of the European arrest warrant shall be transmitted by the executing judicial authority or the central authority designated under Article 7 to the issuing judicial authority at the time of the surrender.

Article 27
Possible prosecution for other offences

1. Each Member State may notify the General Secretariat of the Council that, in its relations with other Member States that have given the same notification, consent is presumed to have been given for the prosecution, sentencing or detention with a view to the carrying out of a custodial sentence or detention order for an offence committed prior to his or her surrender, other than that for which he or she was surrendered, unless in a particular case the executing judicial authority states otherwise in its decision on surrender.

2. Except in the cases referred to in paragraphs 1 and 3, a person surrendered may not be prosecuted, sentenced or otherwise deprived of his or her liberty for an offence committed prior to his or her surrender other than that for which he or she was surrendered.

3. Paragraph 2 does not apply in the following cases:

(a) when the person having had an opportunity to leave the territory of the Member State to which he or she has been surrendered has not done so within 45 days of his or her final discharge, or has returned to that territory after leaving it;

(b) the offence is not punishable by a custodial sentence or detention order;

(c) the criminal proceedings do not give rise to the application of a measure restricting personal liberty;

(d) when the person could be liable to a penalty or a measure not involving the deprivation of liberty, in particular a financial penalty or a measure in lieu thereof, even if the penalty or measure may give rise to a restriction of his or her personal liberty;

(e) when the person consented to be surrendered, where appropriate at the same time as he or she renounced the speciality rule, in accordance with Article 13;

(f) when the person, after his/her surrender, has expressly renounced entitlement to the speciality rule with regard to specific offences preceding his/her surrender. Renunciation shall be given before the competent judicial authorities of the issuing Member State and shall be recorded in accordance with that State's domestic law. The renunciation shall be drawn up in such a way as to make clear that the person has given it voluntarily and in full awareness of the consequences. To that end, the person shall have the right to legal counsel;

(g) where the executing judicial authority which surrendered the person gives its consent in accordance with paragraph 4.

4. A request for consent shall be submitted to the executing judicial authority, accompanied by the information mentioned in Article 8(1) and a translation. Consent shall be given when the offence for which it is requested is itself subject to surrender in accordance with the provisions of this Framework Decision. Consent shall be refused on the grounds referred to in Article 3 and otherwise may be refused only on the grounds referred to in Article 4. The decision shall be taken no later than 30 days after receipt of the request.

For the situations mentioned in Article 5 the issuing Member State must give the guarantees provided for therein.

Article 28
Surrender or subsequent extradition

1. Each Member State may notify the General Secretariat of the Council that, in its relations with other Member States which have given the same notification, the consent for the surrender of a person to a Member State other than the executing Member State pursuant to a European arrest warrant issued for an offence committed prior to his or her surrender is presumed to have been given, unless in a particular case the executing judicial authority states otherwise in its decision on surrender.

2. In any case, a person who has been surrendered to the issuing Member State pursuant to a European arrest warrant may, without the consent of the executing Member State, be surrendered to a Member State other than the executing Member State pursuant to a European arrest warrant issued for any offence committed prior to his or her surrender in the following cases:

(a) where the requested person, having had an opportunity to leave the territory of the Member State to which he or she has been surrendered, has not done so within 45 days of his final discharge, or has returned to that territory after leaving it;

(b) where the requested person consents to be surrendered to a Member State other than the executing Member State pursuant to a European arrest warrant. Consent shall be given before the competent judicial authorities of the issuing Member State and shall be recorded in accordance with that State's national law. It shall be drawn up in such a way as to make clear that the person concerned has given it voluntarily and in full awareness of the consequences. To that end, the requested person shall have the right to legal counsel;

(c) where the requested person is not subject to the speciality rule, in accordance with Article 27(3)(a), (e), (f) and (g).

3. The executing judicial authority consents to the surrender to another Member State according to the following rules:

(a) the request for consent shall be submitted in accordance with Article 9, accompanied by the information mentioned in Article 8(1) and a translation as stated in Article 8(2);

(b) consent shall be given when the offence for which it is requested is itself subject to surrender in accordance with the provisions of this Framework Decision;

(c) the decision shall be taken no later than 30 days after receipt of the request;

(d) consent shall be refused on the grounds referred to in Article 3 and otherwise may be refused only on the grounds referred to in Article 4.

For the situations referred to in Article 5, the issuing Member State must give the guarantees provided for therein.

Notwithstanding paragraph 1, a person who has been surrendered pursuant to a European arrest warrant shall not be extradited to a third State without the consent of the competent authority of the Member State which surrendered the person. Such consent shall be given in accordance with the Conventions by which that Member State is bound, as well as with its domestic law.

Article 29
Handing over of property

1. At the request of the issuing judicial authority or on its own initiative, the executing judicial authority shall, in accordance with its national law, seize and hand over property which:

(a) may be required as evidence, or

(b) has been acquired by the requested person as a result of the offence.

2. The property referred to in paragraph 1 shall be handed over even if the European arrest warrant cannot be carried out owing to the death or escape of the requested person.

3. If the property referred to in paragraph 1 is liable to seizure or confiscation in the territory of the executing Member State, the latter may, if the property is needed in connection with pending criminal proceedings, temporarily retain it or hand it over to the issuing Member State, on condition that it is returned.

4. Any rights which the executing Member State or third parties may have acquired in the property referred to in paragraph 1 shall be preserved. Where such rights exist, the issuing Member State shall return the property without charge to the executing Member State as soon as the criminal proceedings have been terminated.

Article 30
Expenses

1. Expenses incurred in the territory of the executing Member State for the execution of a European arrest warrant shall be borne by that Member State.

2. All other expenses shall be borne by the issuing Member State.

CHAPTER 4
General and final provisions

Article 31
Relation to other legal instruments

1. Without prejudice to their application in relations between Member States and third States, this Framework Decision shall, from 1 January 2004, replace the corresponding provisions of the following conventions applicable in the field of extradition in relations between the Member States:

(a) the European Convention on Extradition of 13 December 1957, its additional protocol of 15 October 1975, its second additional protocol of 17 March 1978, and the European Convention on the suppression of terrorism of 27 January 1977 as far as extradition is concerned;

(b) the Agreement between the twelve Member States of the European Communities on the simplification and modernisation of methods of transmitting extradition requests of 26 May 1989;

(c) the Convention of 10 March 1995 on simplified extradition procedure between the Member States of the European Union;

(d) the Convention of 27 September 1996 relating to extradition between the Member States of the European Union;

(e) Title III, Chapter 4 of the Convention of 19 June 1990 implementing the Schengen Agreement of 14 June 1985 on the gradual abolition of checks at common borders.

2. Member States may continue to apply bilateral or multilateral agreements or arrangements in force when this Framework Decision is adopted insofar as such agreements or arrangements allow the objectives of this Framework Decision to be extended or enlarged and help to simplify or facilitate further the procedures for surrender of persons who are the subject of European arrest warrants.

Member States may conclude bilateral or multilateral agreements or arrangements after this Framework Decision has come into force insofar as such agreements or arrangements allow the prescriptions of this Framework Decision to be extended or enlarged and help to simplify or facilitate further the procedures for surrender of persons who are the subject of European arrest warrants, in particular by fixing time limits shorter than those fixed in Article 17, by extending the list of offences laid down in Article 2(2), by further limiting the grounds for refusal set out in Articles 3 and 4, or by lowering the threshold provided for in Article 2(1) or (2).

The agreements and arrangements referred to in the second subparagraph may in no case affect relations with Member States which are not parties to them.

Member States shall, within three months from the entry into force of this Framework Decision, notify the Council and the Commission of the existing agreements and arrangements referred to in the first subparagraph which they wish to continue applying.

Member States shall also notify the Council and the Commission of any new agreement or arrangement as referred to in the second subparagraph, within three months of signing it.

3. Where the conventions or agreements referred to in paragraph 1 apply to the territories of Member States or to territories for whose external relations a Member State is responsible to which this Framework Decision does not apply, these instruments shall continue to govern the relations existing between those territories and the other Members States.

Article 32

Transitional provision

Extradition requests received before 1 January 2004 will continue to be governed by existing instruments relating to extradition. Requests received after that date will be governed by the rules adopted by Member States pursuant to this Framework Decision. However, any Member State may, at the time of the adoption of this Framework Decision by the Council, make a statement indicating that as executing Member State it will continue to deal with requests relating to acts committed before a date which it specifies in accordance with the extradition system applicable before 1 January 2004. The date in question may not be later than . . .*. The said statement will be published in the Official Journal of the European Communities. It may be withdrawn at any time.

* The date of entry into force of this Framework Decision.

Article 33
Provisions concerning Austria and Gibraltar

1. As long as Austria has not modified Article 12(1) of the "Auslieferungs- und Rechtshilfegesetz" and, at the latest, until 31 December 2008, it may allow its executing judicial authorities to refuse the enforcement of a European arrest warrant if the requested person is an Austrian citizen and if the act for which the European arrest warrant has been issued is not punishable under Austrian law.

2. This Framework Decision shall apply to Gibraltar.

Article 34
Implementation

1. Member States shall take the necessary measures to comply with the provisions of this Framework Decision by 31 December 2003.

2. Member States shall transmit to the General Secretariat of the Council and to the Commission the text of the provisions transposing into their national law the obligations imposed on them under this Framework Decision. When doing so, each Member State may indicate that it will apply immediately this Framework Decision in its relations with those Member States which have given the same notification.

The General Secretariat of the Council shall communicate to the Member States and to the Commission the information received pursuant to Article 7(2), Article 8(2), Article 13(4) and Article 25(2). It shall also have the information published in the Official Journal of the European Communities.

3. On the basis of the information communicated by the General Secretariat of the Council, the Commission shall, by 31 December 2004 at the latest, submit a report to the European Parliament and to the Council on the operation of this Framework Decision, accompanied, where necessary, by legislative proposals.

4. The Council shall in the second half of 2003 conduct a review, in particular of the practical application, of the provisions of this Framework Decision by the Member States as well as the functioning of the Schengen Information System.

Article 35
Entry into force

This Framework Decision shall enter into force on the twentieth day following that of its publication in the Official Journal of the European Communities.

Done at Brussels,

For the Council
The President

EUROPEAN ARREST WARRANT[10]

(a) Information regarding the identity of the requested person:

Name: . . . .

Forename(s): . . . .

Maiden name, where applicable: . . . .

Aliases, where applicable: . . . .

Sex: . . . .

Nationality: . . . .

Date of birth: . . . .

Place of birth: . . . .

Residence and/or known address: . . . .

Language(s) which the requested person understands (if known):

. . . .

Distinctive marks/description of the requested person: . . . .

. . . .

. . . .

Photo and fingerprints of the requested person, if they are available and can be transmitted, or contact details of the person to be contacted in order to obtain such information or a DNA profile (where this evidence can be supplied but has not been included)

(b) Decision on which the warrant is based:

1. Arrest warrant or judicial decision having the same effect: . . . .

Type: . . . .

2. Enforceable judgement: . . . .

. . . .

Reference: . . . .

(c) Indications on the length of the sentence:

   1. Maximum length of the custodial sentence or detention order which may be imposed for the offence(s):

   ....

   ....

   2. Length of the custodial sentence or detention order imposed:

   ....

   Remaining sentence to be served: ....

   ....

   ....

   ....

[(d) Decision rendered in absentia and [....]:

   — The person concerned has been summoned in person or otherwise informed of the date and place of the hearing which led to the decision rendered in absentia

   or

   — The person concerned has not been summoned in person or otherwise informed of the date and place of the hearing which led to the decision rendered in absentia but has the following legal guarantees after surrender (such guarantees can be given in advance) . . . Specify the legal guarantees ....

   ....

   ....]

(e) Offences:

This warrant relates to in total: . . . offences.

Description of the circumstances in which the offence(s) was (were) committed, including the time, place and degree of participation in the offence(s) by the requested person

. . . .

. . . .

. . . .

Nature and legal classification of the offence(s) and the applicable statutory provision/code:

. . . .

. . . .

. . . .

. . . .

. . . .

I. If applicable, tick one or more of the following offences punishable in the issuing Member State by a custodial sentence or detention order of a maximum of at least 3 years as defined by the laws of the issuing Member State:
- ☐ participation in a criminal organisation;
- ☐ terrorism;
- ☐ trafficking in human beings;
- ☐ sexual exploitation of children and child pornography;
- ☐ illicit trafficking in narcotic drugs and psychotropic substances;
- ☐ illicit trafficking in weapons, munitions and explosives;
- ☐ corruption;
- ☐ fraud, including that affecting the financial interests of the European Communities within the meaning of the Convention of 26 July 1995 on the protection of European Communities' financial interests;
- ☐ laundering of the proceeds of crime;
- ☐ counterfeiting of currency, including the euro;
- ☐ computer-related crime;
- ☐ environmental crime, including illicit trafficking in endangered animal species and in endangered plant species and varieties;
- ☐ facilitation of unauthorised entry and residence;
- ☐ murder, grievous bodily injury;
- ☐ illicit trade in human organs and tissue;
- ☐ kidnapping, illegal restraint and hostage-taking;
- ☐ racism and xenophobia;
- ☐ organised or armed robbery;
- ☐ illicit trafficking in cultural goods, including antiques and works of art;

☐ swindling;
☐ racketeering and extortion;
☐ counterfeiting and piracy of products;
☐ forgery of administrative documents and trafficking therein;
☐ forgery of means of payment;
☐ illicit trafficking in hormonal substances and other growth promoters;
☐ illicit trafficking in nuclear or radioactive materials;
☐ trafficking in stolen vehicles;
☐ rape;
☐ arson;
☐ crimes within the jurisdiction of the International Criminal Court;
☐ unlawful seizure of aircraft/ships;
☐ sabotage.

II. Full descriptions of offence(s) not covered by section I above:

....

(f) Other circumstances relevant to the case (optional information):
(NB: This could cover remarks on extraterritoriality, interruption of periods of time limitation and other consequences of the offence)

....
....

(g) This warrant pertains also to the seizure and handing over of property which may be required as evidence:

This warrant pertains also to the seizure and handing over of property acquired by the requested person as a result of the offence:

Description of the property (and location) (if known):

....
....
....

(h) The offence(s) on the basis of which this warrant has been issued is(are) punishable by/has(have) led to a custodial life sentence or lifetime detention order:

the legal system of the issuing Member State allows for a review of the penalty or measure imposed – on request or at least after 20 years – aiming at a non-execution of such penalty or measure,

and/or

– the legal system of the issuing Member State allows for the application of measures of clemency to which the person is entitled under the law or practice of the issuing Member State, aiming at non-execution of such penalty or measure.

(i) The judicial authority which issued the warrant:

Official name: ....

Name of its representative[11]: ....

Post held (title/grade): ....

File reference: ....

Address: ....

Tel. No.: (country code) (area/city code) (...) ....

....

Fax No. (country code) (area/city code) ( ) ....

E-mail ....

Contact details of the person to contact to make necessary practical arrangements for the surrender: ....

....

---

[11] In the different language versions a reference to the "holder" of the judicial authority will be included.

Where a central authority has been made responsible for the transmission and administrative reception of European arrest warrants:

Name of the central authority: ....

....

Contact person, if applicable (title/grade and name): ....

....

Address: ....

....

Tel. No.: (country code) (area/city code) (...) ....

Fax No.: (country code) (area/city code) (...) ....

E- mail: ....

Signature of the issuing judicial authority and/or its representative:

....

Name: ....

Post held (title/grade): ....

Date: ....

Official stamp (if available)

Appendix 3
The Extradition Act 2003 (Multiple Offences) Order 2003

STATUTORY INSTRUMENT 2003 No. 3150

THE EXTRADITION ACT 2003 (MULTIPLE OFFENCES) ORDER 2003

The text of this Internet version of the Statutory Instrument which is published by the Queen's Printer of Acts of Parliament has been prepared to reflect the text as it was Made. A print version is also available and is published by The Stationery Office Limited as the **The Extradition Act 2003 (Multiple Offences) Order 2003**, ISBN 0110483480. The print version may be purchased by clicking *here*. Braille copies of this Statutory Instrument can also be purchased at the same price as the print edition by contacting TSO Customer Services on 0870 600 5522 or e-mail: customer.services@tso.co.uk.

Further information about the publication of legislation on this website can be found by referring to the *Frequently Asked Questions*.

To ensure fast access over slow connections, large documents have been segmented into "chunks". Where you see a "continue" button at the bottom of the page of text, this indicates that there is another chunk of text available.

STATUTORY INSTRUMENTS

2003 No. 3150

EXTRADITION

The Extradition Act 2003 (Multiple Offences) Order 2003

Made	*4th December 2003*
Laid before Parliament	*11th December 2003*
Coming into force	*1st January 2004*

The Secretary of State, in exercise of the powers conferred on him by sections 207 and 223(3) of the Extradition Act 2003[1], hereby makes the following Order:

1. This Order may be cited as the Extradition Act 2003 (Multiple Offences) Order 2003 and shall come into force on 1st January 2004.

2. — (1) In this Order "the Act" means the Extradition Act 2003.

(2) The Act is to have effect with the modifications specified in the Schedule to this Order in relation to a case where—

(a) a Part 1 warrant is issued for more than one offence;

(b) a request for extradition is made in respect of more than one offence.

Caroline Flint
Parliamentary Under-Secretary of State

Home Office
4th December 2003

SCHEDULE

Article 2(2)

MODIFICATIONS TO THE ACT

General modification

1. — (1) Unless the context otherwise requires, any reference in the Act to an offence (including a reference to an extradition offence) is to be construed as a reference to offences (or extradition offences).

(2) Sub-paragraph (1) does not apply to any reference to an offence—

(a) in a modification made by this Schedule; or

(b) in a provision of the Act which is relevant to such a modification.

Initial stage of extradition hearing

2. — (1) Section 10 is modified as follows.

(2) In subsection (2) for "the offence" substitute "any of the offences".

(3) For subsection (3) substitute—

" (3) If the judge decides the question in subsection (2) in the negative in relation to an offence, he must order the person's discharge in relation to that offence only.".

(4) For subsection (4) substitute —

" (4) If the judge decides that question in the affirmative in relation to one or more offences he must proceed under section 11.".

Bars to extradition

3. — (1) Section 11 is modified as follows.

(2) For subsection (3) substitute —

" (3) If the judge decides any of the questions in subsection (1) in the affirmative in relation to an offence, he must order the person's discharge in relation to that offence only.".

(3) For subsection (4) substitute —

" (4) If the judge decides those questions in the negative in relation to an offence and the person is alleged to be unlawfully at large after conviction of the extradition offence, the judge must proceed under section 20."

(4) For subsection (5) substitute —

" (5) If the judge decides those questions in the negative in relation to an offence and the person is accused of the commission of the extradition offence but is not alleged to be unlawfully at large after conviction of it, the judge must proceed under section 21.".

Case where person has been convicted

4. — (1) Section 20 is modified as follows.

(2) In subsection (1) after "decide" insert "in relation to each offence".

(3) In subsection (2) after "section 21" insert "in relation to the offence in question".

(4) In subsection (3) after "decide" insert "in relation to each offence".

(5) In subsection (4) after "section 21" insert "in relation to the offence in question".

Human rights

5. — (1) Section 21 is modified as follows.

(2) In subsection (1) after "decide" insert "in relation to each offence".

(3) In subsection (2) after "discharge" insert "in relation to the offence in question".

(4) In subsection (3) after "extradited" insert "for the offence in question".

Appeal against extradition order

6. — (1) Section 26 is modified as follows.

(2) In subsection (1) after "extradition" insert "in relation to an offence".

Court's powers on appeal under section 26

7. — (1) Section 27 is modified as follows.

(2) In subsection (5) after "it must" insert "in relation to the relevant offence only".

Appeal against discharge at extradition hearing

8. — (1) Section 28 is modified as follows.

(2) In subsection (1) after "discharge" insert "in relation to an offence".

Court's powers on appeal under section 28

9. — (1) Section 29 is modified as follows.

(2) In subsection (5) after "it must" insert "in relation to the relevant offence only".

Detention pending conclusion of appeal under section 28

10. — (1) Section 30 is modified as follows.

(2) In subsection (1) after "discharge" insert "in relation to an offence".

Appeal to House of Lords

11. — (1) Section 32 is modified as follows.

(2) In subsection (1) after "appeal" insert "in relation to each offence".

Powers of House of Lords on appeal under section 32

12. — (1) Section 33 is modified as follows.

(2) In subsection (3) after "must" insert "in relation to the relevant offence only".

(3) In subsection (5) after "must" insert "in relation to the relevant offence only".

(4) In subsection (7) after "must" insert "in relation to the relevant offence only".

(5) In subsection (8) after "must" insert "in relation to the relevant offence only".

Extradition where no appeal

13. — (1) Section 35 is modified as follows.

(2) In subsection (1)(a) after "extradition" insert "in relation to an offence".

(3) In subsection (4)(b) after the second "date" insert

" , or

(c) if proceedings are continuing in relation to other offences contained in the same Part 1 warrant, 10 days starting with the day on which the judge, the High Court or the House of Lords make the final order in relation to the last of the offences in respect of which the same Part 1 warrant was issued.".

Extradition following an appeal

14. — (1) Section 36 is modified as follows.

(2) In subsection (1)(a) after "territory" insert "in relation to an offence".

(3) In subsection (1)(b) after "there" insert "in relation to that offence".

(4) In subsection (3)(a)—

(a) for "the decision of the relevant court on the appeal becomes" substitute "all decisions of the relevant court on any appeal in relation to any offence in respect of which the same Part 1 warrant was issued become";

(b) for "the appeal are discontinued" insert "any appeal in relation to any offence in respect of which the same Part 1 warrant was issued are discontinued".

Withdrawal of warrant before extradition

15. — (1) Section 41 is modified as follows.

(2) In subsection (1) for the words from "a Part 1 warrant" to the end substitute "they do not wish to proceed with their request for extradition in relation to an offence in respect of which the Part 1 warrant was issued".

(3) In subsection (3) after "discharge" insert "in relation to that offence".

Withdrawal of warrant while appeal to High Court pending

16. — (1) Section 42 is modified as follows.

(2) In subsection (1) for the words from "a Part 1 warrant" to the end substitute "they do not wish to proceed with their request for extradition in relation to an offence in respect of which the Part 1 warrant was issued".

(3) In subsection (3)(a) after "extradition" insert "in relation to that offence".

(4) In subsection (3)(b) after "appeal" insert "in relation to that offence".

Withdrawal of warrant while appeal to House of Lords pending

17. — (1) Section 43 is modified as follows.

(2) In subsection (1) for the words from "a Part 1 warrant" to the end substitute "they do not wish to proceed with their request for extradition in relation to an offence in respect of which the Part 1 warrant was issued".

(3) In subsection (3)(a) after "discharge" insert "in relation to that offence".

(4) In subsection (3)(b) after "extradition" insert "in relation to that offence".

(5) In subsection (4) after "appeal" insert "in relation to that offence".

Consent to extradition

18. — (1) Section 45 is modified as follows.

(2) In subsection (1) after "issued" insert "in relation to any offence contained in the Part 1 warrant".

(3) In subsection (2) after the second "section" insert "in relation to any offence contained in the Part 1 warrant".

(4) In subsection (3) after "section" insert "to every offence contained in the Part 1 warrant".

Extradition to category 1 territory following consent

19. — (1) Section 47 is modified as follows.

(2) In subsection (3)(b) after the second "date" insert

" , or

(c) if proceedings are continuing in relation to other offences contained in the same Part 1 warrant, 10 days starting with the day on which the judge, the High Court or the House of Lords make the final order in relation to the last of the offences in respect of which the same Part 1 warrant was issued.".

(3) In subsection (5) for the words from "the Part 1 warrant" to the end substitute "they do not wish to proceed with their request for extradition in relation to an offence in respect of which the Part 1 warrant was issued".

(4) In subsection (5)(b) after "discharge" insert "in relation to that offence".

Other warrant issued: extradition to category 1 territory

20. — (1) Section 49 is modified as follows.

(2) In subsection (3)(b) after "date" insert

" , or

(c) if proceedings are continuing in relation to other offences contained in the same Part 1 warrant, 10 days starting with the day on which the judge, the High Court or the House of Lords make the final order in relation to the last of the offences in respect of which the same Part 1 warrant was issued.".

(3) In subsection (5) for the words from "the Part 1 warrant" to the end substitute "they do not wish to proceed with their request for extradition in relation to an offence in respect of which the Part 1 warrant was issued".

(4) In subsection (5)(b) after "discharge" insert "in relation to that offence".

Arrest warrant following extradition request

21. — (1) Section 71 is modified as follows.

(2) For subsection (2)(a) substitute "any of the offences in respect of which extradition is requested are extradition offences".

(3) In subsection (2)(b) after "evidence" insert "in relation to that offence".

Provisional warrant

22. — (1) Section 73 is modified as follows.

(2) For subsection (3)(a) substitute—

" (a) any of the offences in respect of which extradition is requested are extradition offences.".

(3) In subsection (3)(b) after "evidence" insert "in relation to that offence".

Initial stages of extradition hearing

23. — (1) Section 78 is modified as follows.

(2) In subsection (2) after "(or include)" insert "in relation to each offence".

(3) In subsection (3) after "discharge" insert "in relation to the relevant offence only".

(4) In subsection (4)(b) for "the offence" substitute "each offence".

(5) In subsection (6) after "discharge" insert "in relation to that offence".

(6) For subsection (7) substitute—

" (7) If the judge decides those questions in the affirmative in relation to one or more offences he must proceed under section 79.".

Bars to extradition

24. — (1) Section 79 is modified as follows.

(2) For subsection (3) substitute—

" (3) If the judge decides any of the questions in subsection (1) in the affirmative in relation to any offence, he must order the person's discharge in relation to that offence only.".

(3) For subsection (4) substitute—

" (4) If the judge decides those questions in the negative in relation to any offence and the person is accused of the commission of the extradition offences but is not alleged to be unlawfully at large after conviction of it, the judge must proceed under section 84 in relation to that offence.".

(4) For subsection (5) substitute—

" (5) If the judge decides any of those questions in the negative in relation to any offence and the person is alleged to be unlawfully at large after conviction of it, the judge must proceed under section 85 in relation to that offence.".

Case where person has not been convicted
25. — (1) Section 84 is modified as follows.

(2) In subsection (1) after "evidence" insert "in relation to each offence".

(3) In subsection (5) after "discharge" insert "in relation to that offence".

(4) In subsections (6) and (7) after "section 87" insert "in relation to that offence".

Case where person has been convicted
26. — (1) Section 85 is modified as follows.

(2) In subsection (1) after "decide" insert "in relation to each offence".

(3) In subsection (2) after "section 87" insert "in relation to the offence".

(4) In subsection (4) after "section 87" insert "in relation to the offence".

(5) In subsection (6) after "section 86" insert "in relation to the offence".

(6) In subsection (7) after "discharge" insert "in relation to the offence".

Conviction in person's absence
27. — (1) Section 86 is modified as follows.

(2) In subsection (1) after "decide" insert "in relation to each offence".

(3) In subsection (5) after "discharge" insert "in relation to the offence".

(4) In subsection (6) after "section 87" insert "in relation to the offence".

(5) In subsection (7)(b) after "section 87" insert "in relation to the offence".

Human rights
28. — (1) Section 87 is modified as follows.

(2) In subsection (1) after "decide" insert "in relation to each offence".

(3) In subsection (2) after "discharge" insert "in relation to the offence".

(4) In subsection (3) after "extradited" insert "for the offence in question".

Case sent to the Secretary of State
29. — (1) Section 92 is modified as follows.

(2) In subsection (2)(a) after "High Court" insert "in relation to each relevant offence".

Secretary of State's consideration of case

30. — (1) Section 93 is modified as follows.

(2) In subsection (2) after "decide" insert "in relation to each offence".

(3) In subsection (3) after "discharge" insert "in relation to the offence".

(4) In subsection (4)—

(a) after "negative" insert "in relation to the offence in question" and

(b) after "requested" insert "for that offence".

Death penalty

31. — (1) Section 94 is modified as follows.

(2) In subsection (1) after the first "territory" insert "in relation to an offence".

(3) In subsection (2) after "assurance" insert "in relation to the relevant offence".

Speciality

32. — (1) Section 95 is modified as follows.

(2) In subsection (2) after "section 127" insert "in relation to all offences contained in the extradition request".

Information

33. — (1) Section 100 is modified as follows.

(2) In subsection (1)(b) after "High Court" insert "in relation to each relevant offence".

(3) In subsection (2) after "extradition" insert "in relation to the offence".

(4) In subsection (4) after "discharge" insert "in relation to an offence".

Appeal where case sent to Secretary of State

34. — (1) Section 103 is modified as follows.

(2) In subsection (1) after "relevant decision" insert "in relation to each offence.

(3) In subsection (2) after "section 127" insert "in relation to the offence".

(4) In subsection (6) after "discharge" insert "in relation to the offence".

(5) In subsection (7) after "discharge" insert "in relation to the offence".

Court's powers on appeal under section 103

35. — (1) Section 104 is modified as follows.

(2) In subsection (5) after "it must" insert "in relation to the relevant offence only".

Appeal against discharge at extradition hearing

36. — (1) Section 105 is modified as follows.

(2) In subsection (1) after "discharge" insert "in relation to an offence".

Court's powers on appeal under section 105

37. — (1) Section 106 is modified as follows.

(2) In subsection (6) after "it must" insert "in relation to the relevant offence only".

Detention pending conclusion of appeal under section 105

38. — (1) Section 107 is modified as follows.

(2) In subsection (1) after "section 105" insert "in relation to at least one offence".

(3) In subsection (4) after "times" insert "taking all offences contained in the extradition request together".

Appeal against extradition order

39. — (1) Section 108 is modified as follows.

(2) In subsection (1) after "extradition" insert "in relation to an offence".

(3) In subsection (2) after "extradition" insert "in relation to the offence".

Court's powers on appeal under section 108

40. — (1) Section 109 is modified as follows.

(2) In subsection (5) after "it must" insert "in relation to the relevant offence only".

Appeal against discharge by Secretary of State

41. — (1) Section 110 is modified as follows.

(2) In subsection (1) after "discharge" insert "in relation to an offence".

Court's powers on appeal under section 110

42. — (1) Section 111 is modified as follows.

(2) In subsection (5) after "it must" insert "in relation to the relevant offence only".

Detention pending conclusion of appeal under section 110

43. — (1) Section 112 is modified as follows.

(2) In subsection (2) for "the appeal" substitute "any appeal".

Appeal to House of Lords

44. — (1) Section 114 is modified as follows.

(2) In subsection (1) after "High Court" insert "in relation to each offence".

Powers of House of Lords on appeal under section 114

45. — (1) Section 115 is modified as follows.

(2) In subsection (3) after "must" insert "in relation to the relevant offence only".

(3) In subsection (5) after "must" insert "in relation to the relevant offence only".

(4) In subsection (7) after "must" insert "in relation to the relevant offence only".

Extradition where no appeal

46. — (1) Section 117 is modified as follows.

(2) In subsection (1)(a) after "extradition" insert "in relation to an offence".

(3) In subsection (2) after "order" insert "or if proceedings are continuing in relation to other offences contained in the extradition request, 10 days starting with the day on which the Secretary of State makes the final order in relation to the last of the offences in respect of which the same extradition request was made".

Extradition following appeal

47. — (1) Section 118 is modified as follows.

(2) In subsection (2)(b) after "discontinued" insert

" ,or

(c) if there is more than one appeal outstanding in relation to offences contained in the same extradition request, the day on which the last decision of the relevant court becomes final or on which the last proceedings on the appeal are discontinued.".

Withdrawal of request before end of extradition hearing

48. — (1) Section 122 is modified as follows.

(2) In subsection (1) after "extradition" insert "in relation to an offence".

(3) In subsection (3) after "discharge" insert "in relation to the offence".

Withdrawal of request after case sent to Secretary of State

49. — (1) Section 123 is modified as follows.

(2) In subsection (1) after "extradition" insert "in relation to an offence".

(3) In subsection (3) after "discharge" insert "in relation to the offence".

Withdrawal of request while appeal to High Court pending

50. — (1) Section 124 is modified as follows.

(2) In subsection (1) after "extradition" insert "in relation to an offence".

(3) In subsection (3) after "must" insert "in relation to the offence".

(4) In subsection (4) after "appeal" insert "in relation to the offence".

Withdrawal of request while appeal to House of Lords pending

51. — (1) Section 125 is modified as follows.

(2) In subsection (1) after "extradition" insert "in relation to an offence".

(3) In subsection (3) after "must" insert "in relation to the offence".

(4) In subsection (4) after "appeal" insert "in relation to the offence".

Consent to extradition: general

52. — (1) Section 127 is modified as follows.

(2) In subsection (1) after "requested" insert "in relation to one or more offences contained within the extradition request".

(3) In subsection (2) after "extradition" insert "in relation to one or more offences contained within the extradition request".

Consent to extradition before case sent to Secretary of State

53. — (1) Section 128 is modified as follows.

(2) In subsection (2) after "so" insert "unless there are other offences contained within the extradition request in relation to which the person has not consented to his extradition".

(3) In subsection (3) after "91" insert "unless there are other offences contained within the extradition request in relation to which the person has not consented to his extradition".

(4) In subsection (5) after "extradition" insert "if he has consented to his extradition in relation to every offence contained within the extradition request".

National security

54. — (1) Section 208 is modified as follows.

(2) In subsection (2) for "an offence" substitute "more than one offence".

(3) In subsection (3)(a) for "the offence" substitute "any of the offences".

(4) In subsection (3)(b) for "the offence" substitute "the offence in question".

(5) In subsection (4) after "the offence" insert "in question".

(6) For subsection (6)(a) substitute—

" (a) direct that proceedings in relation to an offence contained in the Part 1 warrant are not to be proceeded with".

(7) In subsection (6)(b) after "the offence" insert "in question only".

(8) In subsection (7) after "discharge" insert "in relation to the offence".

EXPLANATORY NOTE

(This note is not part of the Order)

This Order provides for the Extradition Act 2003 to have effect with the modifications specified in the Schedule to the Order in relation to the following cases. Those cases are where a Part 1 warrant is issued in respect of more than one offence or where a request for extradition is made in respect of more than one offence.

In particular, the modifications are such as to allow for the partial execution of the Part 1 warrant or the request for extradition in cases where the judge and or the Secretary of State must consider more than one offence for which extradition is sought. It is possible that extradition will be refused in relation to some offences but not all, allowing for extradition to take place in relation to some offences only.

Notes:

[1] 2003 c. 41.

Appendix 4
Category 1 and Category 2 Territories. Territories Designated under the EA 2003

This Appendix lists Category 1 and Category 2 territories and those territories which have been designated by order for various purposes under the Act.

The list is up to date as at 6 January 2004, however because the relevant orders are likely to be amended frequently the most recent version of the order should be always be consulted.

A. Category 1 territories
The following have been designated as Category 1 territories for the purposes of Part 1 of the Act by Article 2(2) of the Extradition Act 2003 (Designation of Part 1 Territories) Order 2003 (SI 2003/3333):

Belgium

Denmark

Finland

Ireland

Portugal

Spain

Sweden

B. Category 2 territories
The following have been designated as Category 2 territories for the purposes of Part 2 of the Act by the Extradition Act 2003 (Designation of Part 2 Territories) Order 2003 (SI 2003/3334), Article 2:

Albania	Bangladesh	Canada
Andorra	Barbados	Chile
Antigua and Barbuda	Belize	Colombia
Argentina	Bolivia	Cook Islands
Armenia	Bosnia and Herzegovina	Croatia
Australia	Botswana	Cuba
Austria	Brazil	Cyprus
Azerbaijan	Brunei	Czech Republic
The Bahamas	Bulgaria	Dominica

Ecuador	Lithuania	San Marino
El Salvador	Luxembourg	Serbia and Montenegro
Estonia	Macedonia FYR	Seychelles
Fiji	Malawi	Sierra Leone
France	Malaysia	Singapore
The Gambia	Maldives	Slovakia
Georgia	Malta	Slovenia
Germany	Mauritius	Solomon Islands
Ghana	Mexico	South Africa
Greece	Moldova	Sri Lanka
Grenada	Monaco	Swaziland
Guatemala	Nauru	Switzerland
Guyana	The Netherlands,	Tanzania
Hong Kong SAR	New Zealand	Thailand
Haiti	Nicaragua	Tonga
Hungary	Nigeria	Trinidad and
Iceland	Norway	Tobago
India	Panama	Turkey
Iraq	Papua New Guinea	Tuvalu
Israel	Paraguay	Uganda
Italy	Peru	Ukraine
Jamaica	Poland	Uruguay
Kenya	Romania	The United States
Kiribati	Russian Federation	of America
Latvia	Saint Christopher and Nevis	Vanuatu
Lesotho	Saint Lucia	Western Samoa
Liberia	Saint Vincent and the	Zambia
Liechtenstein	Grenadines	Zimbabwe

C. Category 2 territories designated for the purposes of sections 71(4), 73(5), 84(7), and 86(7)

The following Category 2 territories have been designated for the purposes of ss 71(4), 73(5), 84(7), and 86(7) by the Extradition Act 2003 (Designation of Part 2 Territories) Order 2003 (SI 2003/3334), Article 3, and they are therefore entitled to supply information rather than evidence in support of an application for an arrest warrant, and they are not required to supply evidence sufficient to prove a *prima facie* case at the extradition hearing:

Albania	Germany	New Zealand
Andorra	Greece	Norway
Armenia	Hungary	Poland
Australia	Iceland	Romania
Austria	Israel	Russian Federation
Azerbaijan	Italy	Serbia and Montenegro
Bulgaria	Latvia	Slovakia
Canada	Liechtenstein	Slovenia
Croatia	Lithuania	South Africa
Cyprus	Luxembourg	Switzerland
Czech Republic	Macedonia FYR	Turkey
Estonia	Malta	Ukraine
France	Moldova	The United States
Georgia	The Netherlands	of America

D. Time limits for receipt of documents following provisional arrest (section 74(11)(b))
The following Category 2 territories have been designated for the purposes of s 74(11)(b) by the Extradition Act 2003 (Designation of Part 2 Territories) Order 2003 (SI 2003/3334), Article 4, and the documents referred to in s 70(9) (request etc) must be received by the appropriate judge within the period specified, starting with the day on which the defendant was arrested:

Bolivia (65 days)	Iraq (65 days)	Peru (95 days)
Bosnia and Herzegovina (65 days)	Liberia (95 days)	San Marino (65 days)
	Monaco (65 days)	
Chile (90 days)	Nicaragua (65 days)	Thailand (65 days)
Cuba (65 days)	Panama (65 days)	The United States of
Haiti (65 days)	Paraguay (65 days)	America (65 days)

In respect of all other territories the documents must be received within 45 days starting with the day on which the defendant was arrested (s 74(11)(a)).

Appendix 5
Useful Web References

Australasian Legal Information Institute
www.austlii.edu.au—access to Australian and Commonwealth legal materials

Supreme Court of Canada
www.scc-csc.gc.ca

Council of Europe
www.coe.int

Crown Prosecution Service
www.cps.gov.uk

European Court of Human Rights
www.echr.coe.int

Federal Bureau of Investigation
www.fbi.gov

Her Majesty's Stationery Office—legislation
www.hmso.gov.uk/legis.htm—allows access to the full text of UK legislation from 1988 onwards. Also allows access to draft legislation.

Home Office Judicial Co-operation Unit
www.homeoffice.gov.uk/inside/org/dob/direct/jcu.html—the extradition section of the Unit is responsible for casework and policy in respect of extradition requests to and from the UK.

Interpol
www.interpol.int

National Criminal Intelligence Service
www.ncis.co.uk—website of NCIS, the designated authority under Part 1 of the EA 2003.

Serious Fraud Office
www.sfo.gov.uk

United States Department of Justice
www.usdoj.gov

United States Supreme Court
www.supremecourtus.gov

University of Minnesota Human Rights Library
www.umn.edu/humanrts—provides access to more than 7,200 human rights related documents, including a detailed search facility and links to more than 3,600 related websites.

Index